CHANGING PATTERNS OF INTERNATIONAL RIVALRY

CHANGING

The International Conference on Business History 17

PATTERNS OF

Proceedings of the Fuji Conference

INTERNATIONAL

edited by ETSUO ABE   YOSHITAKA SUZUKI

RIVALRY

SOME LESSONS FROM
THE STEEL INDUSTRY

UNIVERSITY OF TOKYO PRESS

This volume is the proceedings of the Third Session of the Fourth Series of the International Conference on Business History, which took place from January 5 to 8, 1990. We would like to express our deepest gratitude to the Taniguchi Foundation for its continuing sponsorship of the Conference.

ISBN 4–13–047050–7
ISBN 0–86008–475–2

Contents

Introduction

Etsuo Abe

The 17th International Conference on Business History (The Fuji Conference) was held on January 5–8, 1990 at the foot of Mt. Fuji. The Fuji Conference, which was first convened in 1974, has taken up a wide range of topics over the years and is renowned among scholars worldwide. The topic of the 17th conference was "Changing Patterns of International Rivalry: Some Lessons from the Steel Industry."

The iron and steel industry is, like textiles, one of the typical "old industries." It is said that the industry held a pivotal role in every advanced economy. As the phrase "iron is the state" signifies, the iron and steel industry was the key industry in every industrialized country, even though the ratio of the industry to GNP was lower than one might expect. In retrospect, the supremacy over the industry changed hands from one country to another. From the outset of the Industrial Revolution, Britain's industry was the most competitive in the world and became the largest producer of iron. As a result, Britain became "the ironworks of the world," holding a share of 50% of world production. Yet in the late 19th century, Britain lost its supremacy in the international market and was surpassed by the United States and Germany. By the 1950s, the United States, in turn, was producing 50% of world steel output. Indeed, the U.S. steel industry dominated world markets for the first half of the 20th century. Japan, however, which was defeated in World War II, recovered from the damage wrought by the war, and its steel industry commenced an unbelievably rapid growth that went beyond all expectations. In the 1980s, Japan became the largest producer in the world apart from the U.S.S.R. and was surpassed by none in competitiveness. Why, then, did such shifts occur? Perhaps a brief review of the iron and steel industry since 18th-century Britain will shed light on the question.

Between the 18th century and the mid-19th century, Britain changed from an iron importer to an iron exporter by developing its iron industry. Basically, there were three reasons for this. (1) Britain had an ample supply of raw materials, such as coal and iron ore. (2) The domestic demand for iron products was huge, a consequence of the development of railways, iron bridges, and other ironwork. (3) The entrepreneurs of the time were vigorous and technologically innovative. As inventions such as the coking blast furnace, the puddling and rolling processes, and the hot blast furnace show, the technological level in Britain was higher than in any other country. It exported such technology and engineers to France and Germany because technology flows from more advanced countries to less advanced countries. Due to its international competitiveness, Britain became the largest iron exporter in the world in the mid-19th century. But afterward the iron and steel industry declined in Britain.

In the second half of the 19th century, the United States was the pre-eminent iron and steel producer, partly because it had abundant iron ore and coal in the Midwest on the supply side, and partly because it enjoyed a huge and growing domestic demand from a construction boom of railways and urbanization. In addition, entrepreneurs such as Andrew Carnegie displayed a remarkable boldness in their management policies. The colossal scale that they worked on is best exemplified by the scrap and build policy, hard driving of blast furnaces, forward and backward integration, drastic improvement of transportation, etc. Their objective was to increase output even though it shortened the life of furnaces. In other words, they were *growth oriented*, so their perspective was not short run but long run. It is also said that the rapid growth of U.S. steel companies was financed internally. This was probably true if one considers the immature state of capital markets at that time. These factors combined made the United States the largest iron and steel producer around 1900. Its exports grew after 1900 to some degree, but most of the demand came from within the United States.

On the other hand, Britain faced a host of difficulties. Although it was still able to obtain good coking coal, the production of iron ore dropped and Britain had to import ore from Spain and Sweden. In regard to the demand, the domestic market's growth was slow and the overseas market was partly blocked by foreign tariffs. In the end, British entrepreneurs seemed to have lost their innovative flair. The technological level of Britain certainly lagged behind the United States and Germany. The flow of technology reversed and moved from the United States to Britain, as the fact that many American engineers went to Britain to improve blast-furnace equipment and operations illustrates.

Also, British steelmasters followed a policy of keeping furnaces as long as possible, in contrast with the United States. Hard driving, colossal furnaces and the drastic scrap and build policy were beyond their imaginations. In their steelmaking and rolling processes as well, the two countries were quite different. Regarding the steelmaking process, Britain was very late to adopt basic open-hearth furnaces. Though the material problem must be considered in more detail, if Britain had imported iron ore from Sweden on a larger scale, as the Germans did, it would have been possible to produce more basic open-hearth steel.

Furthermore, there was structural rigidity in Britain, like stringent demarcation of jobs, strong trade unions, and so on. In the United States, labor was surely militant but, as the words, "non-union era" suggest, after the 1892 Homestead Strike the American labor force did not resist new technology. In contrast, British trade unions had real power in deciding workshop labor practices, and fearing the loss of jobs often took a very negative attitude toward new technology. Britain lost its international competitiveness in neutral markets such as South America, and to make matters worse, it was obliged to become the largest importer of iron and steel in the world just before World War I.

Germany's iron and steel production as well as that of the United States grew rapidly in the late 19th century and surpassed that of Britain. On the supply side, minette iron ore was crucial for the German iron and steel industry, but Swedish ore also played a role. The demand was mainly domestic, but, as Germany's notorious overseas dumping suggests, the export market was of great importance. Generally, the technological level of the German iron and steel industry seems to have been higher than Britain. As a result, not only German but also French and Belgian steel products, especially semifinished products, flowed into Britain. Belgium and France had the same iron-ore supplies as Germany and had some international competitiveness.

After the turbulent interwar period, the U.S. steel industry was dominant in the 1950s. At the time, the Japanese steel industry was virtually negligible because of the damage done by the war. However, as early as the 1950s the Japanese steel industry set out on a path of growth. Japan had no raw materials available for iron- and steelmaking, so it had to import all materials. On the demand side, Japan exported, roughly speaking, a third of its steel products in the post–World War II period; accordingly, two-thirds were consumed domestically. This was made possible due to the rapid growth of the Japanese economy in the 1950s and 1960s. The demand for structural materials, ships, and later automobiles skyrocketed. The policy adopted by Japanese steel manufacturers was, as it were, the "build and build" policy. Japan established many greenfield steelworks and enlarged its output. In the 1980s, it became the largest steel producer in the world second to the U.S.S.R. and well before the 1980s, the largest exporter. Along with its aggressive investment policy, the choice of technology such as the LD converter and continuous casting was timely and correct. Also, the size of blast furnaces was on the largest scale possible, as most blast furnaces among the ten largest companies throughout the world are owned by Japanese firms. Also, regarding computerization in the steel industry, Japan leads the world. In comparison with the industry in the United States in its developing stage, it is interesting that Japanese steel firms financed these innovations and expansions mainly through borrowing from banks.

In contrast, after the 1950s, the United States steel industry came to a standstill and lagged in technology far behind the world level. For the supply of its raw materials, conditions deteriorated, especially for iron ore. A plan to build off-shore works was frustrated on the whole. Though the size of the market was quite large, the demand was not growing so fast, influenced by the slow growth of the U.S. economy itself. Imports, moreover, from Japan, Europe, etc. were increasing and in the 1970s the United States became the biggest importer of steel in the world. This situation was quite similar to the situation which Britain faced before World War I. Moreover, U.S. steel manufacturers lagged behind or made mistakes in adopting new technology like the LD converter and continuous casting, and their blast-furnace size was now small by world standards. A symbolic incident is that the technical staffs of Japanese companies assisted in the modernization of the U.S. steel industry recently. Evidently, the U.S. technical level is far behind that of Japan. This indicates another similarity to the situation several decades earlier in Britain, where technical staff came from the United States to modernize the British steel industry.

In regard to finance, U.S. steel firms gave relatively high dividends to their stockholders and invested reserved profits in diversification, not in the modernization of their plants. After profitability declined, it was almost impossible to obtain funds from the capital market because of the high interest rate in the U.S. capital market. Along with the tightness of the capital market, industrial disputes hampered innovation, especially since the entrenchment of powerful unions during the New Deal era. The institutional constraints in the capital market and deteriorating industrial relations made modernization difficult. Finally, the relationship between the government and industry did not facilitate the modernization of the steel industry because the anti-trust policy at times impeded the steel firms from merging or building new works. But, above all, the loss of entrepreneurship and innovative energy seems the major reason for the decline.

Finally, the newest comer to the steel world is Korea. Although Korea has to import its raw materials like Japan, the Korean steel industry has state-of-the-art technology and very low wages. So, it has the strongest international competitiveness in the field of relatively low-quality products. It is said that the Korean steel industry has the firm backing of the government, as the fact that POSCO is a state-owned company shows. Recently, imports from Korea to Japan have been gradually increasing. Will Japan follow the same course as Britain and the United States?

Why and how did the supremacy over the industry change from one country to another? In consideration of this problem, four points were focused on in this conference. First, we needed to discuss the matter in the long term, for instance over a time-span of 100 years, since our aim was to ascertain the reason why the supremacy over the industry moved from one country to another successively. Accordingly, we looked back to the late 19th century and also considered the period after World War II. For convenience, 18th-century Britain is excluded. Second, for the purpose of comparison, it was necessary to study rising countries on one side, and declining countries on the other. First of all, late 19th-century Britain was taken as a declining country, and the United States and Germany as countries in the ascendant. Also, we considered Belgium and France, which played an essential role in the export market at that time and during the interwar period. During the period after World War II, the U.S. industry had been on the decline, while Japan and Korea dominated the world markets.

The third aspect is international competitiveness. Although international competitiveness consists of many elements, ultimately the advantages and disadvantages each country enjoys are reflected in it. Raw material supplies, the demand situation, good or bad management, institutional constraints such as the capital market and industrial relations, all these factors make up the strength or weakness of competitive power. To evaluate one industry's performance, international competition is a good measure. The last aspect under which to examine these problems is the structure of the firm, in other words, the business history approach. An analysis of the industry is not sufficient; an analysis of the firms themselves would be useful in judging the sources of competitiveness.

In the conference, nine papers altogether were contributed from Britain, the United States, Germany, France, Korea, and Japan. The paper by Suzuki Yoshitaka comprehensively surveyed all previous studies as well as discussed methodology. One of the interesting points he raised was the "beyond the steel industry" strategy, whereby firms transferred their managerial resources to other areas. For the first period examined, the late 19th century, the paper by Steven Tolliday looked back to historians who had studied the decline of the British steel industry, and he stressed that institutional constraints played a major role in this decline. Paul Paskoff analyzed the U.S. steel industry in the second half of the 19th century. He focused on several ideas, e.g., technological choice, operation methods like hard driving, and investment policy. In the second part of his paper, he discussed the role of tariffs and their implications, specifically the intention of U.S. Steel Corporation. Being conscious of the anti-trust acts and the regulation authority, U.S. Steel advanced the policy of cooperative competition with small firms.

Rainer Fremdling read a paper about the German iron and steel industry in the 19th century, when the German iron and steel industry started its rapid growth. As the characteristic of the German steel industry, he stressed an increasing propensity toward cartels and vertically integrated firms. Eric Bussière made a presentation about the steel industry of France, Belgium, and Luxemburg, stretching the period to the interwar period. These countries were influenced by Germany and, at one time, the United States. For instance, in Belgium in 1918, the idea to americanize the steel industry completely gained ground.

The second period is the period after World War II. But before this, the Japanese iron and steel industry's history was described by Tetsuji Okazaki, focusing on the policy to replace imports by domestic iron and steel products. Such import substitution also took place in late 18th-century Britain and 19th-century America, but in Japan, which started to produce modern iron products very late, import substitution was a particularly imperative task partly because of nationalism. Okazaki also noted that prewar development prepared the ground for postwar growth. Seiichiro Yonekura reported on the postwar development of the Japanese steel industry, stressing the importance of the entrepreneurship of private steel companies such as Kawasaki Steel. He denies the momentous role of the government as represented by MITI. The United States as a declining country was reported by Paul Tiffany. He emphasized external factors such as the timing in introducing LD converters, the negative effect of anti-trust acts on mergers, the pollution problem, etc., rather than the technological and internal deficiencies of the U.S. steel manufacturers. Sung-il Juhn read a paper about the Korean steel industry, which has probably the most modernized plants in the world. He pointed out that although the role of the government was important, the entrepreneurship of the chairman of POSCO was crucial in developing the Korean steel industry.

A summary of the the concluding discussion will be found in the last chapter of this volume.

The Rise and Decline of Steel Industries: A Business Historical Introduction

Yoshitaka Suzuki

I. A Business History of Steel Industries

Steel, more than any other industry, has been the subject of a wide debate over its international rivalry and the rise and fall of its leading nations. Two major reasons are conceivable for this. Firstly, the steel industry has been, not only economically but also politically, one of the most important industries in the world for the past one hundred years. It has been an indispensable industry for every nation, and therefore its international position was liable to have drawn public attention. Secondly, the steel industry is characterized as an industry with a relatively low level of technological and product differentiation, in which competition occurs internationally and within the industry. The technology and products of the steel industry are relatively homogeneous. Therefore, competition tends to arise over production factor costs, which are determined by individual countries.

This subject has attracted the interest of others several times in the past, not only for academic but also for national-economic or policy-making reasons. Perhaps it is more appropriate to say that it has always been the subject of discussion, which was extensively held in countries whose steel industry capabilities were caught up with or overtaken by overseas latecomers. However, in countries which intended to protect and nurture their infant steel industries, such debates were also observable.

In this conference, we would like to focus on two periods of time in the history of the modern steel industry, and clarify the mechanism of competition from a business historical viewpoint. One of the periods extends from the end of the 19th to the beginning of the present century. The other is the present day. By looking at two periods simultaneously, we may possibly find factors which have been neglected in the discussion, and increase our understanding of each of the two periods. Studying the present-day steel industry may give a new perspective on the rise and fall of the major steel countries at the beginning of the 20th century. Historical studies may contribute to an understanding of present-day international competition.

There is another aim in this conference, or at least in this introductory chapter. A business historical approach might make a new contribution to the understanding of this subject. The meaning of "business historical approach" may vary from person to person. As has been popular among existing studies, a business historical approach may be described as a method which focuses on entrepreneurship and its appropriateness—often leaving institutional conditions as given. We are not content with such an explanation. For other people, business historical approach means the efficiency of the internal organization. Although this may be an important aspect, we would like to deal with a company more radically, that is, taking into consideration the logic of a firm's development.

We would like to set the individual firms that constitute a country's steel industry at the core of the examination of international competition. For these individual firms, the steel industry and the country are important institutional constraints, but these firms are able to allocate their resources outside such constraints if they decide it more appropriate to do so. The steel industry of the succeeding period in a particular country will be determined by the activities of those firms able to make their own decisions. However, many studies in the steel industry have fixed the framework of the industry and the country, and have dealt with the efficiencies of the firms' activities and entrepreneurs within such a framework. These approaches assume that it is important to maintain the international competitive power of the steel industry of a country, and that it is the failure of entrepreneurs when effective measures to maintain competitive power within the industry are not adopted. However, this is not the logic of the resource allocation of firms which actually constitute the economy, though this may be the logic of the political economy. As technology has a tendency to transfer, seeking the most favorable location, so firms allocate their resources to the most effective place. This introductory chapter overviews previous research and analyzes whether a business historical approach can provide new explanations for these phenomena.

II. Hypotheses on the Decline of the British Steel Industry

For the period between the late 19th to the beginning of the present century, the operation of the British steel industry, which was overtaken and outstripped by the American and German steel industries, has been examined in many studies. The relative decline of the British steel industry aroused public interest and provoked controversy from the contemporaries in those earlier periods. The Tariff Commission (1904) recognized the setbacks of the British steel industry and attributed the causes to Britain's free trade policy, coupled with the protective and other policies of foreign countries. Alfred Marshall, on the other hand, regarded the decline as an inevitable result of industrialization abroad and the loss of Britain's comparative advantages in natural resources.[1] By the end of the First World War, it became widely recognized that the decline of the British steel industry was due to an inefficient industrial structure and entrepreneurial failures.[2]

These contemporary indications were compiled in the studies of D. L. Burn,[3] and those of Burnham and Hoskins.[4] After the Second World War, such discussions were extended to the whole of British industry, although iron and steel occupied the main position, as in D.S. Landes's work.[5] Burn argues that the extreme division of production brought about the technological delay and the expansion of scales in the British steel industry after 1880. The British steel industry fell behind America's and Germany's in the development of large-scale firms, new steel plants and their locations, vertical integration, the size of horizontal amalgamation, commercial organization, and associations to control price and output. It should be admitted that the development of the British home market was not rapid. This left a highly developed division of labor which restricted an increase in the size of plants, while the market was differentiated into various products fitted to open-hearths. Besides these institutional factors, however, Burn emphasizes the lack of initiatives among British industrialists toward sales policies, fuel economies, the efficient reallocation of plants, and the reorganization of factories after mergers.[6] Burnham and Hoskins admitted that the stagnation of the British steel industry, symbolized by the decline of steel exports and the increase in imports, was mainly due to the limit an advanced economy can attain both domestically and internationally. However, they regarded the stagnation as not only attributable to these unavoidable factors. For instance, the British industrialists imported Bessemer steel instead of utilizing their abundant phosphorous ores. They also lacked an understanding of technological efficiency, such as the scale of blast furnaces and coke ovens, or the terms of depreciation. These are regarded as the failures of the British industrialists of that time. The fact that these attitudes were not altered was detrimental to the competitive power of the British steel industry, and the British industrialists were responsible for not pursuing technological efficiency in spite of the low cost of raw materials, capital, and labor in their home country.[7]

Many previous studies have pointed out the loss of British leadership by various accounts. That is, (1) the decline in its share or amount in the world export market, (2) the total physical volume, particularly in comparison with the United States and Germany, (3) labor productivity or production costs, and (4) the price of steel products. It is pointed out that such accounts are not appropriate in comparing countries situated in various stages of growth, and in concluding to what extent the decline of competitive power was inevitable and to what extent entrepreneurs were responsible for it.[8] The new subject is how to compare the industry of advanced economies with that of developing economies. Even though such factors are taken into account, conclusions diverge among studies. T. J. Orsagh examined the loss of British leadership, and concluded that the British steel industry was outpaced by its American and German counterparts, which had been more or less similarly developed in 1870. Orsagh argued that the main cause of the British decline was entrepreneurial failure. On the contrary, P. Temin concluded that the relative decline of the British steel industry was caused by inevitable factors. One of these factors was the rapid growth of the demand for steel in the markets of Germany and the United States, from which the British steel industry was barred by protective tariffs. Another was the equalization of resource costs in these three countries as a result of the exploitation of newly found ore deposits. Even if these factors were admitted, it may be asserted that the British industrialists were not producing as efficiently as possible. On that point, Temin concluded that any possible change would not have altered the fortune of the British steel industry.[9]

Likewise, D.N. McCloskey argued that the British steel industry remained equally efficient as its American counterparts before the First World War, and its competitive power did not decline so rapidly. According to his analysis, the relative decline of the British steel industry in the international market was a natural process, and the British entrepreneurs adapted themselves to the circumstances as much as they could through rational decisions.[10] R.C. Allen, on the other hand, calculated that the Americans and the Germans were 15% more efficient than the British through a similar comparison of the costs of input prices. According to Allen, if the British steel producers had utilized Cleveland ironstone with basic open-hearth technology, they could have overcome the cost advantage that the Germans derived from lower labor, scrap, and fuel costs. Actually, several British firms built new integrated basic steelworks and made use of these advantages.[11]

The aforementioned debates concentrated on several points. First, was the British steel industry "caught up with" by the others, as is generally observed in developed countries—or did it in fact lag behind the others? Second, when was the British steel industry "caught up with" by the others, was it by 1870 or not until 1920? Third, was this due to inevitable causes for the early starters, or to institutional causes also inevitable for individual firms but particular to British industries, or to entrepreneurial failure? The third point formed the central issue of prior debates, and many studies actually regarded multiple factors as responsible for the relative British decline.

Recent studies tend to emphasize institutional factors. C.K. Harley insists that, as the choice of technology in the iron and steel industry is not necessarily determined uniformly but depends on the skill of the industrial work force and its cost, every economy chooses a different set of technological systems. In Britain, where the skilled work force was abundant, investment was geared to open-hearths when the overseas markets for rails were invaded by latecomers and the Bessemer technology ended. The same condition impacted the specialization of each of the steelmaking stages in Britain, while its competitors integrated the whole process. In doing so, British industrialists behaved quite rationally in the sense that they utilized an affluent, skilled work force. Harley proposes to discuss the efficiency of a firm in light of a particular set of institutional constraints, rather than the overall technical efficiencies such as the adoption of large-scale and integrated production methods, or an increase in the amount of production.[12] Such a proposal leads us to a more general consideration of other production factors. Where the capital cost is relatively low, the rational choice would be a capital-intensive technology, and where the markets for raw materials and products are developed, the rational choice would be found in non-integrated technologies. There may be more than one choice in every production factor, and as each is not independent, the combination of factors is important. The criterion of rationality should be whether a technology based on a particular set of production factors is affinitive to the institutional conditions of the firm. This method can be called "institutional hypothesis" because each production factor is determined by the markets where the steel industry is situated.

A different evaluation of the British steel industry may arise from the same institutional approach. B. Elbaum pointed out the rigidity of the British labor market, which became one of the main causes of the loss of international competitive power. Elbaum also insists that the industrial structure of Britain was not suitable for large-scale investment. These institutional factors worked toward the relative decline of the British steel industry, which was only rebuilt under the protection of the government and by restructuring.[13]

Most of the discussion tried to make clear why the British steel industry was overtaken. The discussion tended to focus on whether a more efficient method could have been adopted under the limited circumstances. However, it is necessary to ask whether such a proposition is realistic in view of the development of the individual firms. These studies do not necessarily analyze all the alternatives for the British firms: rather, they tend to evaluate the British firms according to the criteria of those in other countries which were catching up with Britain.

III. Aspects of Competition: Earlier Periods

If we turn to the countries which were catching up with the British, the discussion is more simple. The Americans, at the beginning of the present century, did not seriously consider why they were able to outstrip their British counterparts.

Early studies which referred to the American and German steel industries pointed out factors lacking in Britain, and regarded them as the other countries' competitive power. Burn pointed out that the internal growth of firms was prominent in America after 1890. The scale of American blast furnaces was three times as large as that of British firms and converters were two times larger. From early times in Germany, and since 1900 in the United States, firms tended to be located near ore or coal deposits. The integration of iron- and steel-making, and secondary- and final-processing, was prominent in America and Germany, where sales activities were more aggressive. In addition, Burn pointed to the fact that horizontal combination and the production and price control mechanisms were developed in America and Germany.[14] However, this cannot explain why America and Germany were able to attain such superior positions.

Studies on the American steel industry often mention a series of technological changes which took place in the end of the 19th century.[15] These include fast-driving, independent blowing, new blowing-engines, mechanical charging, mechanical casting, and direct delivery of molten iron to steelworks. As a result, the average production capacity of American blast furnaces became one-and-a-half times as large as that of their British counterparts by the early 1880s, and three times as large by the beginning of the present century. In the steelmaking process, large-scale converters were introduced in rail production.

Although these converters were replaced by open-hearths in the beginning of the present century, the organization of production and the technology developed under converters were succeeded by large open-hearths.

P. Berck found that in choosing these technologies, the American industrialists were more rational than the British, though these technologies did not bring about an apparent superiority of the American steel industry. Berck argues that new production technologies reduced labor, fuel, and capital costs, and realized lower cost production. However, such a difference was marginal, and it is not evident whether this marginal difference influenced the declining competitive power of the British steel industry. The choice of new production methods was not fatal to entrepreneurial success or failure. Rather, the development of the domestic market promoted American industrialists to adopt new production methods which resulted in additional profits through increased production.[16]

Allen demonstrated that the Americans caught up with the British in the amount of production, and then by the beginning of the present century, in price. The main cause of the American competitive power was found in the supply of low-cost Lake Superior ores, and then in the introduction of hard-driving technology. On the other hand, wages were higher and labor productivity was initially lower in America than in Europe. However, by the beginning of the present century, the rising labor productivity in the American steel industry more than made up for the high wages.[17]

Feldenkirchen explained that by the 1860s the German steel industry had introduced more excellent technology than Britain, and developed rapidly along with the expansion of the domestic rail markets. The excess capacity after the railway construction boom prompted a modernization of equipment. This opens a discussion as to the competitive level of the German steel industry in the 1870s and 1880s. The cost of steel production in Germany seemed higher than in Britain, because pig iron and iron ores were more expensive while wages were lower, and in total the cost of German steel products was much higher than those of Britain.[18] However, other studies argued that the German steel industry attained the same level as the British steel industry. After the 1890s, the German steel industry increased its competitive power by adopting the basic Bessemer process which enabled it to utilize cheap ores. The scale of plants was then enlarged, vertical integration was promoted, and finally the continuous rolling process was introduced. The efficiencies attained by these technological changes were the main cause of Germany's having caught up. Growth in scale yielded efficiency and mechanization, and the latter in turn yielded growth in size.

It has been asserted that tariffs and cartels played important roles in the development of the German steel industry. Tariffs and cartels had a combined effect, particularly on the integrated steel firms. They also enabled the export of German steel products to the European markets at the beginning of the present century, when the rapid development of the German domestic market was over.[19] By the beginning of the First World War, German steel exports reached the same level as those of the British, which were traditionally heavily dependent on the export market. The remaining question is why such protection resulted in a high competitive power.

For the British steel industry in the international market, the French, Belgian, and Luxemburgian steel industries were more important than the American. The Belgians, particularly, were highly dependent on the export market from its early phase of development, while the other two countries' industries grew large after the First World War and gradually increased their dependence on export markets. The Belgian steel industry bore a strong resemblance to the British industry in terms of weakness of cartels and tariffs, and high dependence on exports, though it differed in plant size and degree of vertical integration.

IV. Aspects of Competition: Contemporary Steel Industries

If we turn to the second period, namely from the 1970s and after, there are many studies on the steel industry from various fields. It is useful to refer to these various studies when we examine the causes of the changing international competitive power historically. We would like to focus on the main trend of the international competition, and the shift in industry leadership from America to Japan, and Japan to the Newly Industrialized Economies. Discussions have been concentrated on the relative decline of the American steel industry. Such a trend is noticeable from the fact that production decreased by 20% while imports increased sixfold during the 20 years following 1965, when domestic steel consumption increased by 25%. A series of discussions reminds us of the example of Britain versus America and Germany at the beginning of the present century. As in the past, debates began by the accusation of dumping exports—but this time, centering around Japan and the European Community countries—then spread to the technological and organizational retardation of American steel firms.

Such changes in international position were triggered by the slump of the 1970s, which reduced domestic steel consumption in advanced nations. The market contraction continued after the slump, when the structure of steel consumption seemed to change, and the construction of large plants decreased. The latecomers, such as Japan, also had to confront the reduction of demand which came mainly from the developing countries. Their production went into the American or the European markets and threatened the steel industries there. In advanced countries, the adoption of import regulations and the protection of domestic steel industries, as well as the control of steel prices and governmental aid, were discussed. In many of the EC nations the steel industries were reconstructed by governmental aid, while in the United States, private firms took initiatives. In the former case, such aid was intended to keep the steel industry going and continue existing business and products. It is noteworthy that the reconstruction was promoted within the steel industry. Particularly, the direction of the reconstruction of state-owned or state-controlled firms was restricted by government policies, which keep the steel industry going. In the United States and Japan, the steel industry was reconstructed along with the decision-making process of individual firms, evidencing the difference between firms. The latter cases are more interesting for us.

The causes of the relative decline of the steel industry in advanced countries are examined by various studies.[20] For the United States many studies point to the inherent weaknesses which have been formed under a long-standing domination over the world market. The basing-point system under an oligopolistic structure (in the past, the basis of U.S. competitive strength), the administered price system, and high wages raised above the level of productivity increase have been regarded as the main causes of U.S. decline. The list of inherent weaknesses is not confined to these: The increasing obsolescence of blast furnaces and converters, the inability to accommodate new types of steel products, the difficulty of reconstructing steel supplying areas in accordance with the changes in industrial structures, and the trigger price system (which was intended to protect the domestic steel industry) injured U.S. competitive power. Paul Tiffany is critical of such an explanation, which emphasizes the decline of competition under an oligopolistic structure. Rather, government free trade and anti-trust policies nurtured U.S. rivals.[21] Behind these discussions, there are divergences of ideas as to the causes of the declining status of the American steel industry: i.e., if it was inevitable, or resulted from entrepreneurial failure, or further, if it was not a mere failure, whether it resulted from some institutional factors such as the labor market or government policies.

For the competing countries, the logic of development is clearer. For Japan, the steel industry between 1950 and 1970 symbolized its high rate of economic growth. During this period, the production of blister steel increased 18 times, and Yawata Steel and Fuji Steel, both of which were less than one-thirteenth the size of U.S. Steel, merged and became Nippon Steel, which became as large as the latter. Except for the former Nippon Steel and Nihon Kōkan, there were no integrated steel companies before 1950. Other companies such as Sumitomo Metal Industries, Kawasaki Heavy Industries, and Kobe Steel Works were open-hearth or heavy engineering firms with no blast furnaces. Although there were some ironmaking firms with blast furnaces, they were small and were not integrated steel companies. Such a balance was broken by the upward integration of open-hearth firms to large-scale blast furnaces. Instead of constructing small-scale furnaces and open-hearths, these firms began to build large-scale furnaces of 500 tons, converters, and rolling mills of the most advanced technology. Their initiators recognized the necessity of turning from the European to the American style of steelmaking. These new integrated steelworks were situated on the seaside for the convenience of transporting raw materials. One of the causes of the rapid advance of the postwar Japanese steel industry was found in the recognition of the necessity of innovation on the part of entrepreneurs.

The largest problem for these integrating firms to solve was how to assimilate necessary technology.[22] Kawasaki Steel staffed their new plants with technicians of the former Shōwa Seikōjo (Shōwa Steelworks, Manchuria) and made use of their technical skills. Sumitomo Metal Industries absorbed a small blast furnace firm to acquire technical skills, then made inroads into the construction of large-scale furnaces. Kobe Steel Works followed the Sumitomo line. There was a system of skill accumulation and diffusion within the Japanese steel industry.

The upward integration of blast furnaces by these open-hearth firms had an effect on the existing integrated firms, and led them into the construction of large-scale integrated mills with converters and rolling mills, which was quite different from their former activities. The beginning of competition among firms, caused by such strategies, was another condition for the postwar development of the Japanese steel industry.

The technological gap to be bridged by the newly developing countries was constantly widening, and becoming less and less easy to span from native resources. Furthermore, this effort required much larger initial investments in capital, unlikely to be found by individual firms. Therefore, such investments were necessarily drawn by banks, by the aid of the governments, or from the advanced countries. The postwar Japanese government set up three five-year plans, first to rationalize equipment, then to develop the domestic steel industry. The latter included the preferential allotment of foreign currency for the introduction of technology and for the import of coal. The domestic steel market was protected from foreign competition until the mid-1960s, while domestic steel production outpaced government plans. The question remains as to why Japanese steel firms attained high international competitive power in such a protected market.

The postwar Japanese government concerned itself with the steel industry by forming cartels during slumps and by approving investments in new plants. Such interventions were criticized as damaging an efficient resource allocation through free competition. New investments for steel firms were approved on the basis of their market shares. Such a mechanism turned the competition into one in which the firms aimed at higher market shares. Despite such cooperation among firms and government regulations, competition continued. In one or two critical cases, individual firms opposed such regulations and acted independently of them. The question is whether such government regulations and cooperative behavior was related to high efficiency or not.

The Japanese steel industry—which had grown rapidly with the growth of the domestic market during the 1950s and 1960s—continued to grow after responding to the increasing demand from automobile and oil industries, and attained the world's lowest production costs between the 1970s and the mid-1980s. However, after the mid-1980s, exports reached the ceiling as the rate of the yen rose, and cheap foreign steel began to flow into the domestic market. The Japanese steel industry used to depend on the export market for 30% of its total output; therefore as exports stagnated, production declined. It was estimated that production would decrease by 10% to 20% from 100 million metric tons in the early 1980s. It was also estimated that this trend would not be temporary, and that the Japanese steel industry would not be able to keep international competitive power by keeping low prices in bulky products.

Steel firms perceived that the market was changing, and began seeking new directions of development, the first being the reduction of production and its cost. Due to the prospect that bulky products would continue to share an increasing part of the demand, the introduction of direct iron ore reduction systems (to enable the utilization of low-grade materials such as powdered ores and ordinary coal) and the distribution control of interposition to reduce energy were attempted. In high-quality steel products, too, resources and energy were reduced in the secondary refining process. In some cases the hot rolling process was reduced and rolling was simplified. The second direction was the development of new steel products, such as new alloys and fine, high-quality steel, that would meet rising demands. These products had to be fitted to the requirements of steel users, and were unable to be produced on a mass-production basis. The third direction was in making inroads into new businesses. Steel companies diversified by making use of related technology and businesses. New products such as ceramics, silicon wafers, carbon fibers, and new business developments such as measuring, control, computers, environment, and by-products are listed. These new areas were developed by applying technical skills accumulated at the plant level, and by-products which were not previously fully utilized. Thus Japanese steel firms had to meet increasing international competition. They tried to reduce cost in bulky products on the one hand, and diversify into new products by making use of market channels or technical skills on the other hand, while further supplementing the reduced share of bulky products. The question remains as to what extent the technical skills and market channels which were developed by steel firms were applicable, and in what areas they were feasible.

While the advanced European, American, and Japanese steel industries stagnated, the governments of the newly developing countries such as Korea, Brazil, Singapore, Taiwan, and Indonesia, endeavored to improve their home steel industries. Some of them succeeded in establishing an international standard, while others failed. They introduced similar technologies, foreign capital by similar conditions, and produced different results. The Korean steel industry, in particular, developed remarkably.

POSCO was set up in the late 1960s when the rapid development of the Japanese steel industry came to an end. Until the mid-1980s, POSCO developed steadily, by attaining the world's lowest production cost in mass-produced goods. At the outset, POSCO was regarded in the same league as Kawasaki Steel, which attempted to construct fully integrated plants on a large scale. It was said that in Korea, the implementation of large-scale integrated works was impossible both for technological and market reasons, and electric furnaces were more appropriate. However, POSCO was successful in establishing large-scale integrated works by introducing plants through international auction when the price of plants was low and foreign capital was cheap. It also secured highly qualified employees by training technical staff within the firm. Furthermore, it purchased ores and coals on a stable basis by long-term contract or through the development of overseas mines, and above all experienced a rapid increase of domestic steel consumption.[23] Some of these factors are found in other countries, but without parallel development.

V. The Decline of Steel Branches and the Growth of Firms

These discussions, though ranging over different periods of time and in different countries, presuppose two sets of frameworks, i.e., the national economy and the industry. This has some meaning, but not enough for our subject. The steel industry is an industry with a low degree of product differentiation, particularly in mass-production goods, and in such an industry, competition normally occurs with regard to price. Price, in turn, is determined by the costs of raw materials, wages, and capital. The steel industry in developing countries could catch up with and outrun advanced countries in productivity levels by introducing the newest equipment, or by having the advantage of low-cost labor and capital. In other words, the steel industry of the leading countries is inevitably outrun by others. If so, it is not enough to examine the steel industry of advanced countries only in terms of new investments or the introduction of new technology, because such measures are more or less temporary in the long run.

Problems which cannot be explained by traditional methods are accelerated by such industry characteristics. Whether the competition is carried out internationally or within the steel industry in one country, it is the firm that actually plays the dominant role. A firm grows by allocating its resources in a manner thought to be the most efficient. For a steel firm, it is not always most efficient to allocate resources continuously to steel. If it is perceived more appropriate to withdraw from steel, a firm will choose to withdraw. In such a case, the steel industry of a country will fail in international competition, but the underlying logic of the firm's growth is perpetuated. It is this latter aspect that we should clarify.

For steel companies in advanced countries, the reconstruction and rationalization of the steel interest is but one available option. If we are to examine the steel firms of advanced countries, it is necessary to examine others as well. The American steel industry is waning. To meet declining conditions for international competition, American steel firms responded differently according to firm and circumstance. Bethlehem Steel and Inland Steel kept the steel industry as their dominant business, though part of each plant was closed. The latter still maintains its competitive position, while the former has continuously shown a loss. On the other hand, USX, LTV, Armco, and National Steel reduced their steel interests and promoted diversification. Each experienced a reduction of steel sales by 25% to 35%. They diversified in new materials, energy, and other unrelated areas. Others can no longer be called steel firms. Here again, some maintain continuous success, while in others, diversification yields losses. Armco, for instance, failed in diversification and returned to steel and experienced a profit gain.[24]

Such varied strategies and their results indicate that the solution to a decline in power is not uniform. However, most of the companies allocated resources other than steel on the assumption that other fields were more profitable. More generally, it is important to examine what kind of resources steel firms have and which areas are effective.

Firms which manufacture traditional bulk products such as plate and bar steel lost competitive advantages, but those which manufacture materials for consumer goods such as steel tube, sheet metal, and special wire rod kept their relative strength. The latter group of companies made use of technical skills which they accumulated by making steel, and later applied to new fields. The demand continues to increase in these markets, and if production is rationalized, they will be able to compete with foreign steel firms.

On the other hand, many of the fully diversified firms utilized managerial or financial resources acquired through steelmaking toward new activities. For financial resources, early Armco acquired unrelated businesses by making use of internal capital, but USX and LTV bought new businesses using borrowed capital. It is not always the case that unrelated diversification is carried out by internal financial resources. For managerial resources, there were cases in which management was supplied externally, and again, these firms did not always develop their internal resources.

These cases suggest that both the technology and the market of the steel industry are difficult to apply to other industry branches. In other words, the degree of fusion with other industries is low in the steel industry. However, the characteristics of the steel industry market and technology and their relationship to other industries change from period to period. Recent Japanese steel firms are adapting themselves progressively to these changes: They not only develop new steel products, such as new alloys and fine steel, but also produce ceramics and fibers by making use of related businesses, and further turning to computers, controlling systems, and measuring machines. These technologies and by-products were developed by the operating units of their steel plants. The modern steel industry acquires a great deal of advanced technology, and some of it can be applied to other fields of activity.

Whether American or Japanese, and whether successful or not, such changes naturally reduce the amount of domestic steel production, and promote transfer from domestic production to import for bulky goods. This is the nature of the changing rivalry of international competition in the steel industry. For steel firms in advanced countries, an effective response to such international competition may be to avoid the introduction of advanced technologies or large-scale investments which their successors often adopt.

To what extent is such a discussion applicable to the earlier period? Vickers, for instance, manufactured railway and other high-grade steel products from the mid-19th century, but changed its product lines into munitions when it faced the depression of the late 1880s. It was evident to Vickers that the future of the steel industry did not look bright, and that the firm expected a more promising business within the munition industry.[25] John Brown made inroads into shipbuilding from armor plate production, while it closed its blast furnaces.[26] Charles Cammell attempted to keep blast furnaces in the northwest to maintain its competitive power but eventually abandoned them, and acquired a shipyard for the outlet of its high-grade steel.[27] These firms did not keep their own blast furnaces, but depended on the outside supply of materials, and advanced into machinery, munitions, rolling stock, ships, and other downward steel products. Other firms in Sheffield, such as Hadfields, maintained an international position in special steel,[28] and in South Wales, firms produced galvanized steel and tin plates which required special technical skills.[29] This symbolized withdrawal of the top firms in the steel industry, and in effect might have spurred the decline of the British steel industry. However, these firms' strategies proved more effective than remaining in steel.

VI. Problems for Further Studies

Many studies focused on the decline of international competitive power in the steel industry of a particular country, and examined its causes. Whether in a discussion which attributed the cause to entrepreneurial failure in the choice of technology, or in a discussion which regarded the decline as inevitable, the focus tended toward what the steel firms were or were not able to do within the steel industry itself. Such a discussion is effective when examining the countries which were able to catch up with the others, but it has not been undertaken in such a manner. When such a discussion is applied to the advancing countries, which can be examined on a national basis for the single-mindedness of their goal, questions remain as to why firms in certain countries were successful and why other similar candidates were not, and in what cases new technologies were transferred and accepted.

If the firms which were overtaken suffered an inevitable decline, the rational response of entrepreneurs would be to transfer their resources to other growing branches or to places with low production factor costs. Entrepreneurial failure must also be re-examined from the standpoint of the effective allocation of resources. It is necessary to reconstruct the logic of the firm from those who were overtaken by firms from other countries.

NOTES

1.   A. Marshall, *Industry and Trade* (London, 1923).
2.   Board of Trade, *Report of Departmental Committee on the Position of the Iron and Steel Industry After the War* (London, 1929).
3.   D.L. Burn, *Economic History of Steel Making 1867–1939. A Study in Competition* (Cambridge, 1940).
4.   T.H. Burnham and G.O Hoskins, *Iron and Steel in Britain 1870–1930* (London, 1943).
5.   D.S. Landes, "Technological Change and Development in Western Europe, 1750–1914," in H.J. Habakkuk and M. Postan (eds.), *The Cambridge Economic History of Europe*, vol. VI (Cambridge, 1966).
6.   Burn, op. cit., pp. 233–305.
7.   Burnham and Hoskins, op. cit., pp. 268–71.
8.   T.J. Orsagh, "Progress in Iron and Steel: 1870–1913," *Comparative Studies in Society and History*, vol. 3, 1960–61.
9.   P. Temin, "The Relative Decline of the British Steel Industry 1880–1913," in H. Rosovsky (ed.), *Industrialization in Two Systems: Essays in Honor of Alexander Gerschenkron* (New York, 1966).
10.   D.N. McCloskey, *Economic Maturity and Entrepreneurial Decline: British Iron and Steel 1870–1913* (Cambridge, Mass., 1973).
11.   R.C. Allen, "International Competition in Iron and Steel 1850–1913," *Journal of Economic History*, vol. 39 (1979); idem, "Entrepreneurship and

Technical Progress in the Northeast Coast Pig Iron Industry: 1850–1913," *Research in Economic History,* vol. 6 (1981).

12. C.K. Harley, "Skilled Labour and the Choice of Technique in Edwardian Industry," *Explorations in Economic History* (Oxford, 1986).

13. B. Elbaum, "The Steel Industry before World War I," in B. Elbaum and W. Lazonick (eds.), *The Decline of the British Economy* (Oxford, 1986).

14. Burn, op. cit., pp. 219–33.

15. P. Temin, *Iron and Steel in Nineteenth Century America* (Cambridge, Mass., 1964), pp. 157–63.

16. P. Berck, "Hard Driving and Efficiency: Iron Production in 1890," *Journal of Economic History,* vol. 38 (1978).

17. R.C. Allen, "The Peculiar Productivity History of American Blast Furnaces, 1840–1913," *Journal of Economic History,* vol. 37 (1977).

18. W. Feldenkirchen, "The Banks and the Steel Industry in the Ruhr. Developments in Relations from 1873 to 1914," in W. Engels and H. Pohl (eds.), *German Yearbook on Business History* (Berlin, 1981).

19. S.B. Webb, "Tariffs, Cartels, Technology and Growth in the German Steel Industry, 1879–1914," *Journal of Economic History,* vol. 40 (1980).

20. Among many works, only the following are consulted in this paper: L. W. Weiss, *Economics and American Industry,* (New York, 1961); D.F. Barnett and L. Schorsch, *Steel: Upheaval in a Basic Industry* (Cambridge, Mass., 1983); R.W. Crandall, *The U.S. Steel Industry in Recurrent Crisis* (Washington, D.C., 1981).

21. P. Tiffany, *The Decline of American Steel* (New York, 1988).

22. S. Yonekura, "Sengo Nihon Tekkōgyō ni okeru Kawasaki Seitetsu no Kakushin Sei" (Entrepreneurship and Innovative Behavior of Kawasaki Steel: The Post-World-War-II Period), *Hitotsubashi Ronsō,* vol. 90 (1983).

23. H. Toda, *Tekkōgyō* (The Steel Industry) (Tokyo, 1987); idem, *Gendai Sekai Tekkōgyō Ron* (The Steel Industry of the Contemporary World) (Tokyo, 1984).

24. J. Strohmeyer, *Crisis in Bethlehem* (New York, 1986).

25. J.D. Scott, *Vickers: A History* (London, 1962) pp. 42–44; C. Trebilcock, *The Vickers Brothers: Armaments and Enterprise, 1854–1914* (London, 1977), pp. 26–37.

26. Sir A. Grant, *Steel and Ships: The History of John Brown's* (London, 1950); Firth & Brown, *100 Years in Steel* (London, 1937).

27. Cammell Laird & Co., *Our First 150 Years* (1978); idem, *Builders of Great Ships* (London, 1959).

28. G. Tweedale, "Sheffield Steel and America: Aspects of the Atlantic Migration of Special Steelmaking Technology, 1850–1930," *Business History,* vol. 25 (1983).

29. W.E. Minchinton, *The British Tinplate Industry: A History* (Oxford, 1957).

Comment

Akitake Taniguchi

Firstly, Professor Suzuki brings up two aims in this conference. One is to find factors which have thus far been neglected in the discussion, by looking at the two historical periods simultaneously. Another is to bring a new contribution to the understanding of this subject through a business historical approach or "by taking into consideration the logic of a firm's development." Then, he excellently reviews and criticizes existing studies on this issue. Because there is nothing I have to add to his review, I would like to expand on his arguments or set forth other points of view to pursue the two aims he proposes.

He surveys existing studies from two points of view, that is, why and how one country caught up with another, and why and how one country was caught up with by others. I would like to propose a third point of view. Why did (and will) one country outdistance others, and how? For instance, why and how did the United States, rather than Germany, lead the others? Being number one is absolutely different from being number two or three.

I think the process of shifts in competitive power in the steel industry can be divided into three phases from the viewpoint of the country which "catches up with" another. At the first phase, the latecomer begins to try to overtake the forerunner by introducing the latest and most efficient technology—which brings about severe competition especially in the domestic market.

This leads to the second phase, where the competition forces firms to improve their technology or change their strategy, at which point the resulting competition among fewer players gets heated. At this phase the latecomer overtakes and begins to outstrip the leading country. At the third phase the competition causes changes in the industrial organization and in the function, structure, and even "culture" of firms. If, at this phase, one country can create a sort of new paradigm of firm and industry which the others try to follow, it will be able to outdistance them. So, according to my hypothesis, the reason why the

United States became number one is that it created a new paradigm called the American System which others had to follow.

The second problem I would like to bring up is one of understanding the two periods comparatively. Needless to say, these two periods are very similar in terms of the shift in leading countries. However, the situation in which the steel industry found itself in each of the two periods differed. Technology, products, the market, the structure of firms, managerial style, and so forth, changed tremendously. Though the current process of catching up is similar to that of the late 19th century, can we think about the process of being caught up with in the same way? Suzuki tries to apply an argument derived from current facts in the United States to the earlier period. However, the argument on moving resources out of the steel industry might be above the argument on the rivalry in the steel industry. We have to focus on the possibility of dematuration within the steel industry first. By turning to the production of higher quality or new steel products, the possibility of the firm's dematuration is now greater than it had been previously. This is due to the fact that mass production of a small number of items was still in the mainstream then.

Moreover, efforts for survival sometimes lead to cooperation, including the formation of joint-stock ventures between firms internationally. Such cooperation and M&A in some cases will possibly change the international industrial organization. At the turn of century the change in industrial organization was domestic rather than international.

Finally, I suppose that we are now in the late stage of the second phase, or the early stage of the third phase in my hypothesis. Japan has caught up with and is outstripping the United States. However, no country has outdistanced the others as of yet. A country which creates a new paradigm would be able to do so, as might firms acting without borders.

Competition and Maturity in the British Steel Industry, 1870–1914

Steven Tolliday

The decline of the British steel industry before the First World War is one of the classic debates of economic history. The broad dimensions of the changes in the industry are not in doubt. Between 1870 and 1914 the British steel industry lost its world pre-eminence. Britain's share of world output in pig iron fell from 50% to 10% and its share of steel output from 43% to 10% (see Table 1). In 1870 Britain was responsible for over three-quarters of world iron and steel exports; by 1914 it accounted for less than a third. At the same time, the British market, which had been almost impervious to exports in the 1870s, became the word's largest iron and steel importer with imports accounting for 29% of domestic consumption.

What is in doubt, and what has been analyzed and re-analyzed by successive generations of historians each with their own distinctive perspectives and methodologies, is the significance and causes of these changes. The genealogy of the historical work is itself long and complex. On the eve of the Second World War, Sir John Clapham and Duncan Burn suggested that Britain's loss of industrial leadership, epitomized by steel, had been due to lags in technical change and innovation and missed opportunities for structural change in the industry. Burn stressed, in particular, weaknesses in technical education and the failure to take advantage of the most modern techniques and the cheapest available raw materials—the so-called neglect of the basic process. During the war itself, T.H. Burnham and G.O. Hoskins developed the lines of this critique and pointed the finger of responsibility at British entrepreneurs.[1]

As the British economy slowed after the postwar boom in the 1960s, the critique of entrepreneurial failure was taken up with renewed vigor by David Landes, Derek Aldcroft, and others.[2] In the 1970s, however, the industry became the focus for the historical revisionism of the new cliometric history. In particular the work of Donald McCloskey and

Robert Allen criticized older uses of the notion of failure, and McCloskey in particular suggested that "by any cogent measure of performance" British entrepreneurs in iron and steel "did very well indeed."[3] Technical innovations were adopted as and when it became rational to do so, the basic process was not unduly neglected, and overall productivity matched that of the United States and Germany very closely. Subsequently, Bernard Elbaum restated the case for failure from a different perspective: entrepreneurs were indeed constrained actors, but possibilities existed to change the constraints. "British steel declined in competitiveness because its firms lagged behind foreign rivals in the adoption of new mass production methods," yet this was not the result of poor entrepreneurship but of the structural fragmentation of the industry, which impeded the achievement of vertical integration and economies of scale. The main problem was the pattern of atomistic competition, which resulted from historical growth patterns including market segmentation and industry wage structure, in conjunction with slow market expansion and problems of rising raw material costs. Consequently, British decline was "less the result of entrepreneurial failure . . . than of the constraints on individual entrepreneurial action posed by market conditions and a rigid institutional environment." These were not overcome because of a series of institutional rigidities in firms and industrial structure.[4]

Despite so much historical research, much remains unknown, obscure, or controversial. Was there structural failure? Was there entrepreneurial failure? Was there failure at all? This essay argues that British firms and managers were much more constrained by markets, raw materials, and the results of industrial maturity than many historians have allowed; in particular it suggests some new insights on the conundrum of the basic process. From this starting point, it goes on to suggest that a long-term comparative perspective may cast a rather different light on the causes and course of decline.

I. Britain and World Trade in Steel

In the early literature the existence of a decline to be explained seemed so obvious as to need no precise measurement. Britain had fallen from its position as world leader: market share had been lost and the advanced technology seen in other countries was used much less widely in Britain. The decline was not in doubt: the task was to explain it. Yet Britain could not reasonably expect indefinitely to sustain world dominance in a primary industry like steel once other nations began to industrialize. The relevant criteria for success or failure need to be established. Could the industry have done better? What constraints were insurmountable barriers and what constraints could be changed?

In an important article, Peter Temin showed that slowly growing markets at home and limited access to the most rapidly growing markets abroad made slower growth of the British iron and steel industry inevitable, and subsequent writers have largely accepted his conclusion.[5] Between 1895 and 1913, British steel consumption as a percentage of world output fell from 16.5% to 8.9%, while the German share increased from 11% to 14%.[6] A high level of competitiveness in Britain might have prevented substantial import penetration of this slowly growing domestic market, but high German and American tariffs effectively segmented the world market and cut Britain off from the world's most expansive markets. Temin showed that even if Britain had imported at only one-third of the 1913 level and had seized Germany's 1913 share of neutral markets, aggregate British output in 1913 would have increased by 2.4 million tons or 31%. The British average annual growth rate between 1890 and 1913 would have risen from 3.4% to 4.6% and the German rate would have fallen from 9.6% to 9.0%.

Britain was therefore bound to grow more slowly than its rivals and could not have sustained world leadership. But a level of output one-third higher in 1913 would clearly have had a major impact. Could Britain have approached this outer bound to possible performance more closely? The main constraints were the dynamics of the world trade system and the structure of the steel product market.

The role of tariffs in the world steel market has been little studied and is still not well understood. While acknowledging the existence of high tariffs, it is often argued that since the efficiency of German and U.S. producers was relatively high the significant impact of the "natural protection" of transport costs would have prevented Britain from supplying large quantities to these markets even without tariffs.[7] This may be broadly true, but it ignores a further important effect of tariffs, the ability of protected producers to use price discrimination in foreign markets. Germany was both a high growth *and* a high price market, which provided a basis for high levels of export success. Tariffs *both* protected the home market *and* subsidized exports. Except in the depression of 1903–4, there is little evidence that the United States used this strategy, even under the cartelized regime of U.S. Steel after 1901. But Germany employed it systematically to penetrate foreign markets. The fullest exploration of the available data on delivered home and export prices remains that by Burn, who showed a continuous two-price policy in rails from 1879 to 1913. The gap was at its widest between 1879 and 1896 (domestic prices 30–40% above export), fell in the late 1890s to 15–20%, rose during depressed trade in 1903–4 to over 20%, and between 1906 and 1913 hovered between 10% and 15%.[8] The decrease in discrimination was due more to reductions in home prices than to increases in export prices. It is likely that Germany dumped below total cost and even variable costs on occasions before 1895 and during 1901–3, though unlikely that they sold "below cost" after that; U.S. dumping was acute only for a few years after 1898.

Differential pricing could provide a powerful weapon for market penetration.[9] Erich Maschke has described how the cartels used the "cartel surcharge" strategically,[10] and Wilfried Feldenkirchen notes that much of the German industry's success was due to a "combination of protective tariffs, cartelization and export dumping,"[11] though he also observes that the cartels were less monolithic and more unstable than is often thought. The Stahlwerksverband (Steel Works Association), shielded by the tariff, set domestic prices high. It could then profitably set export prices below average total costs as long as these prices exceeded marginal variable costs. The consumer industries strongly resented the steel cartels' high-price policies, late deliveries, and exploitative contract provisions before the First World War.[12] At the same time, the cartel structure also created a powerful incentive to produce and sell more and more, especially to export markets, in order to increase quota rights at successive triennial reallocations. One result was a massive rapid overexpansion, particularly in merchant bars and finished products, as part of a scramble for quotas during 1910–12.[13] The evidence suggests that cartelization and price discrimination were used to penetrate markets and that they could also stimulate overexpansion.

Closer attention to the decline of Britain's export position and a disaggregated picture of its exports and imports suggests the possible significance of such actions. British exports peaked in 1882 (4.3 million tons), slumped to 57% of their peak in 1886, and then recovered to levels comparable to the early 1880s by 1890; from then until 1895 they plunged again to 2.7 million tons before rising steadily to reach a new peak in 1907 (5.1 million tons) and to remain close to that level till 1913. In 1906, both Britain and Germany exported about 3 million tons of iron and steel products, but by 1913 Germany exported 5.5 million against Britain's 3.8 million tons. British imports were very limited until 1894 (less than 350,000 tons), before moving upward in spurts in the depressions of the mid-1890s and 1901–4 (to 1.3 million tons) and subsequently slipping back, though not to their previous levels. The most notable feature was the appearance of large quantities of cheap semi-finished steel from Germany and the United States in 1901–4 and the remarkable upward surge of imports in 1910–13, when they almost doubled from 1.25 to 2.25 million tons in the space of four years.

The greatest success of British exports was in pig iron, which, unlike in Germany and the United States, accounted for a high proportion of total British exports for a long time; as late as 1907 they accounted for 38% of all British iron and steel exports (and 75% of world pig-iron exports) before declining absolutely to constitute only 22% in 1913. This reflected Britain's continuing advantage as the world's low-cost supplier of forge and foundry irons. Apart from this, Britain lacked a really dynamic export sector. Rails performed consistently, partly as a result of the high uniform prices and allocated market shares of the international rail cartel, but Britain's dominance of the world ship-building market meant that export opportunities for British shipplates were slight. Britain built 59% of world tonnage in 1913 and the United States and Germany together accounted for a further 37%; there were no other significant shipbuilders to export to.[14] Apart from this, Britain was highly successful in the export of highly finished products (notably tinplate and galvanized sheet), but performed poorly in exports of semi-finished steel. In contrast, German exports of semi-finished steel constituted well over half of the increase in German exports in the spurt before 1913, yet German exports included negligible quantities of highly finished products other than wire.

These contrasting strengths and weaknesses were interconnected. Nearly two-thirds of the British increase in exports between 1906 and 1913 was accounted for by exports of galvanized sheet, tinplate, and wire (which together accounted for 38% of British steel exports in 1913). Galvanized sheet exports grew from 467 to 761 thousand tons per annum and became the biggest steel export product (second only to pig iron). These exports were heavily based on finishing and re-exporting German and Belgian semi-finished steel, and the imported semis for these trades accounted for 25% of the increase in imports between 1906 and 1913. Wire exports were almost wholly based on re-rolled German rods and perhaps two-thirds of galvanized sheet and one-third of tinplate exports were based on re-exported bar.[15]

C. Knick Harley has argued that cheap and abundant skilled labor gave Britain a relative advantage in the fabrication of these high-quality finished products that others could not match.[16] Why could Britain not dominate the steel supplies for its own finishing industries? The answer is that it could in certain segments of the market but not in others. The sheet and tinplate industries catered for a spectrum of quality demands ranging from buckets and corrugated iron roofing to tin cans and boxes for preserved foods, cakes, and biscuits. The high-quality end of the market required a rigorous quality of steel which could only be achieved in the open-hearth process, in which, as we shall, see Britain was the leading producer, while cheaper basic Bessemer steel, in which Germany specialized, was only acceptable as a substitute for the lowest grades.[17] Generally, open-hearth bar was more costly but more reliable in quality and could attract a premium price that more than compensated for the extra cost.[18] The variability in weight and dimensions, poor quality, and limited range of grades of foreign steel limited its application where quality was important. Even at the peak of dumping in 1903–4, Baldwins had to stop using imported bars because of their poor quality.[19] But there was a significantly large sector of the market where quality was less crucial and in which imported semis could establish themselves. It was here in particular that British steelmakers were unable to meet German and Belgian competition.

But the parallel question remains to be asked: If Germany was so strong in the provision of semis, why was it unable to dominate the export markets for finished steel? In one sector, wire, where basic Bessemer was both the cheapest *and,* because of its ductility, the qualitatively superior material, Germany did dominate both semi- and finished exports. In tinplate, however, the trade fear frequently voiced from the late 1880s that Germany would emerge as a major competitor using its cheap basic Bessemer steel never materialized. In fact, the German finishers were major losers from the German cartel system: They had to pay high prices for their semis on the home market and consequently found it very hard to export. In selling their finished steel abroad they faced competition from the U.K. and other re-rollers using cheap German semis delivered abroad at less than domestic market prices. This was a highly controversial issue at the time of negotiations for the renewal of the Stahlwerksverband in 1912.[20]

The balance sheet of this trade is hard to draw. In a sense the German steelmakers discriminated in favor of their foreign competitors, and British exporters of finished goods were able to take advantage of German price discrimination to expand their exports. The development of German finished products was correspondingly delayed. On the other hand, German steelmakers gained an outlet for substantial quantities of steel which, given the underdeveloped nature of the domestic finishing trades and the high degree of product-specific skills involved in developing them, they were unlikely to find among domestic fabricators in the short term. The balance of advantage before the war remained somewhat ambiguous, depending significantly on the future role of quality, skills, and raw materials in the finishing trades.

II. Quality and Demand

Thus by the end of the 19th century, Britain had lost its leadership to Germany and the United States in cheaper, lower grades of steel, even to the extent of relying on imports for many of the grades of steel required by its most important finished steel exports. Part of the explanation for this lies in the differing paths to bulk steelmaking followed in each country. For all of them, bulk steelmaking began with the Bessemer process in the 1850s. The Bessemer converter was initially suitable only for low-phosphorus iron in the so-called acid process. But in 1879 the invention of the basic Bessemer or Thomas-Gilchrist process permitted the use of high-phosphorus iron. The basic Bessemer process was of limited importance in Britain and in the 1880s Britain quickly moved to the open-hearth process. But basic Bessemer dominated the late 19th century surge of European steelmaking. The United States possessed non-phosphoric ores in abundance and therefore never used the basic Bessemer process, concentrating from the first on acid Bessemer.

The Bessemer converter is relatively small physically, but it can produce in bulk because of its very short process time. A corollary, however, is that close quality control is difficult, while the high nitrogen content of the metal, derived from the air blown through the molten burden, made it brittle and less adequate as steel specifications became tighter. The open-hearth furnace held big volumes over a much longer process time (8–12 hours against 15–20 minutes in the Bessemer converter). This long period facilitated quality control, and permitted the use of a wider range of ores and the production of higher and more varied qualities of steel. As with the Bessemer converter, refractory linings of either acid or basic material could be used according to the phosphorus content of the iron. As demand broadened away from the 19th century concentration on simple products like rails, and as a greater variety of better steels were required, the open-hearth furnace proved superior to the converter. The United States moved rapidly from Bessemer to open-hearth practice in the decade preceding the First World War. By 1950, open-hearth was the overwhelmingly dominant technology in the world. In Germany, however, where phosphoric "minette" ores were plentiful, the basic Bessemer process was tenacious. As late as 1964, 33% of German steel still came from the basic Bessemer process.[21]

Temin has shown how the adoption of the Bessemer process, which both required and permitted rapid rates of throughput, formed the basis for the rapid rise of large-scale production in the United States in the 1880s. In the U.K., however, Bessemer demand peaked in the 1880s and thereafter open-hearth steel predominated because of its better suitability for shipplates and high-quality sheets. Elbaum argued that unlike the Bessemer process, the open-hearth process had few economies of scale in its early days. Production costs were higher, but the steel was better and a wider range of ores could potentially be utilized. The slower growth of U.K. demand, its product composition, and its regionally segmented markets resulted in a relatively decentralized industry in the U.K. In contrast, the U.S. firms developed large-scale centralized Bessemer operations at an early stage. When they shifted to open-hearth manufacture under pressure of rising costs of Bessemer ores in 1905–14, they were able to quickly modify open-hearth practice to run at high volumes and to draw on their hard-driven blast furnaces to feed their giant rolling mills.[22]

Why did Britain shift to open-hearth steelmaking first, the United States later, and Germany still later and more partially? The main reason was different demand patterns. The demand for Bessemer steel was dominated by railway demand in all three countries. But by 1880 76% of the U.K. rail network was already in place, compared with only 53% in Germany and 36% in the United States.[23] These giant markets for rails, however, were being closed behind tariff barriers. There was a lack of alternative uses for Bessemer steel. In 1900 approximately 50% of British Bessemer steel went into rails—the remainder was used for simple products such as blooms, billets, bars, plates, angles, girders, and sleepers. Within Britain no single producer could dominate a very regionalized market. The regional rail companies had a strong preference for local firms who used their routes to assemble their materials and freight their products. The other main demand for Bessemer steel was in construction, and some potential may have existed here, but British builders remained loath to use steel in high buildings, even while U.S. skyscrapers proliferated.[24] Thus while Bessemer output continued to expand rapidly in the United States until 1906, it peaked in the U.K. in 1889 at 2.1 million tons. Thereafter, its next best year was 1.97 million tons in 1905 and it stagnated to 1.6 million in 1913 (Table 1). Given the sluggish market and overcapacity there was little obvious scope for new Bessemer plants, and British Bessemer productivity stagnated after 1890.

From the 1880s, shipbuilding was the most dynamic sector of U.K. demand. By 1910–12 shipbuilding absorbed 30% of Britain's total steel output and 42% of its open-hearth steel. Two-thirds of Scottish steel went to shipbuilding.[25] In the 1880s Britain built 85% of European tonnage, and its industry was quite different in scale from that of the United States or Germany. Open-hearth steel costs were always somewhat above those for Bessemer steelmaking. Fuel, labor, and capital costs were all persistently higher and U.S. surveys in 1902–6 and again at the end of the First World War showed that production costs of open-hearth steel were 10–12% higher across a range of plants than basic Bessemer costs.[26] Nevertheless, its quality advantages made it uniquely suitable for shipbuilding. Bessemer was good for rails and well suited to welding, but it lost strength in punching and riveting and, unsuited to large structures, it was never accepted by British shipbuilders (though U.S. shipbuilders did use it on occasion). After 1877 the Admiralty refused to accept Bessemer steel for any of the more important parts of a ship's structure subject to severe tensile pressures. Acid open-hearth remained the preferred shipbuilding material, though basic open-hearth won slow acceptance in the 1890s. Despite improvements in the quality of Bessemer steel in the 1880s and 1890s, distrust of its quality by shipbuilders remained profound: "The very name of it was like a red rag shown to a bull."[27] This bad reputation damaged its acceptability even among pipe and metal manufacturers, whose requirements it better fitted.

Even in Germany, where basic Bessemer was the overwhelmingly dominant product, it was never widely accepted in the shipyards. In the 1890s German shipyards were very reluctant to accept domestic steel until forced to do so by government subsidies and contractual procedures, which continued to exert substantial influence up to 1910. At the same time, Germany created new insurance registers to escape the stringent quality requirements of the Lloyds Register and facilitate the use of poorer domestic open-hearth steel in its shipyards. By 1905 Germany could make open-hearth steel comparable to the British, but they lacked the tradition of high quality and the reputation on which British shipbuilders traded so effectively. German shipyards built excellent ships, but they were largely confined to the home market and received few export orders before 1914.[28]

The other main demand sectors were for high-quality finished products such as sheet and tinplate. British tinplate enjoyed a virtual world monopoly and a continuously growing market until the U.S. market was closed by the McKinley tariffs in 1891. After this, world export demand grew only slowly and the 1891 level of exports was not reached again until 1910. Home demand was low until after 1900. British tin-plate totally dominated both home and export markets, but even so, output grew only 50% during 1891–1912, making it difficult to contemplate new large-scale plants. Nevertheless, Britain dominated the open-hearth end of this trade, but imported German Bessemer steel made substantial headway at the lower end of the market, where it was an adequate substitute.

The stagnant domestic demand for Bessemer steel could not support the construction of modern plants. On the other hand, Britain appeared to perform well in open-hearth steel, where domestic demand was strongest. Between 1900 and 1913 British open-hearth output increased from 3.1 million to 6 million tons, an annual increase of 224,000 tons (compared with 1.4 million tons per year in the United States and 420,000 tons per year in Germany in the same period). (See Table 1.) This demand was sufficient to justify building large new plants like Dalzell (300,000 t) and Normanby Park (100,000 t).

Domestically, Britain faced sluggish demand for Bessemer steel and buoyant demand for open-hearth steel. Internationally, however, the picture was quite different. Demand was high for cheap simple steel and limited for higher-quality steels. It was hard to find big international markets willing to pay a premium price for more costly open-hearth steel: Open-hearth steel's advantages were only powerful once consumers were demanding about steel quality or required more sophisticated products. At home, British steel fed consumer industries more demanding than elsewhere in the world, notably in heavy engineering, shipbuilding, and heavy armaments. But it was on the basis of low-cost Bessemer steel that Germany advanced, using not only its powerful home market, but also a growing world market, including a substantial import demand for semi-finished steel in the U.K. Britain competed effectively in open-hearth steel, but failed to meet German competition in Bessemer. The slow growth of British demand for Bessemer steel does not in itself explain this failure, since growing world demand provided potential alternative outlets. Why was Britain unable to restore its position as a low-cost steel supplier for world markets?

III. The Problem of Rising Costs

As contemporary observers and subsequent historians have been aware, there were two potential paths that Britain could have pursued to tap into more rapidly growing markets. One was the development of cheaper Bessemer steel; the other was to cheapen the manufacture of open-hearth steel to enable it to compete with basic Bessemer in lower grades. Either step would require a switch to lower-cost materials and, in particular, to the basic process. Britain was not only committed to open-hearth steelmaking, but also, in both open-hearth and its remaining Bessemer steel sector, to the acid (non-phosphoric) ore process. By the 1890s Britain's commitment to acid steelmaking was entering a crisis because of the rising costs of the ores on which it was based. The cost of raw materials overwhelmingly dominates steelmaking costs and between the 1880s and 1913 the relative costs of these materials moved sharply against the processes and materials to which British steelmakers were predominantly committed and in favor of the processes and materials to which German and American steelmakers were committed.

Steel containing more than 0.1% phosphorus is too brittle to be of any use.[29] Accordingly, unless the phosphorus is removed during steelmaking only ores with less than 0.5% phosphorus are suitable for steelmaking. Before 1914, the only sources in the world of such "non-phosphoric" ores (usually referred to as hematite ores) were in Cumberland, northern Spain, and Lake Superior. Until 1879, existing metallurgical technology only permitted the production of steel from a limited range of raw materials. Thereafter, however, the invention of the Thomas-Gilchrist or "basic" process enabled the removal of phosphorus during steelmaking through the use of limestone additions to the furnace charge and the converter lining to draw it off into a phosphoric slag. The result was revolutionary in that it permitted the use of a far wider range of ores for the production of steel in either the basic Bessemer or basic open-hearth process.

The enormous ore resources of the Luxemburg-Lorraine (minette) and Westphalian orefields were thereby made available for steelmaking by the basic process and Germany at once specialized in basic steelmaking—initially almost wholly by the basic Bessemer process. From the 1890s Germany began also to make some basic open-hearth steel, and this reached 37% of German output by 1913. The United States focused on Lake Superior hematite ores and made only acid Bessemer steel until the 1890s; it never made basic Bessemer commercially. After 1900, the dominance of Bessemer steel was eroded by the rise of basic open-hearth, which had reached 65% of United States output by 1913 (Table 1).

Thus German steelmaking was basic from the outset and the United

States shifted rapidly toward basic steel from the 1890s. Britain, however, remained predominantly acid (hematite) before the First World War. During the 1890s over 85% of British steel output was acid; after 1900 basic steelmaking expanded rapidly, but the proportion of acid steel was still 72% in 1906 and 57% in 1913 (Table 1). British acid steelmaking was necessarily based on the use of imported ore. By 1900 the available domestic hematite ores in Cumberland were waning and Spanish hematite ores became fundamental to the industry.

The pattern of raw material cost advantages shifted dramatically between 1890 and 1913 (Table 2). In 1896 the combined delivered cost of coke and hematite ore required per ton of *acid* iron on the northeast coast averaged 38 shillings, closely matching Westphalia's cost of 35s per ton of *basic* iron. Both Britain and Germany enjoyed a substantial raw material cost advantage over U.S. producers in Pittsburgh in the early 1890s. By 1906–13, however, British hematite costs on the Northeast coast had soared to an average 58s per ton of iron. But Westphalian basic costs had risen only to 46s and Pittsburgh's had come down to 50s.

What caused these shifts? Coke costs were relatively unimportant. The Northeast coast and the Ruhr had roughly similar coke prices after 1890, while Pittsburgh coke was always substantially cheaper. It was movements in ore prices that were decisive. British acid steel production depended on Cumberland and imported Spanish ores. After 1895 both prices, and especially those of Spanish ores, rose sharply and Britain suffered accordingly. At the same time, the prices of Germany's ore supplies from Lorraine and Westphalia remained fairly stable and Germany also began to import cheap Swedish ores on a large scale. The result was a dramatic divergence in raw material prices. Meanwhile, U.S. ore costs fell sharply after the discovery of the low-cost, rich Mesabi ores. Efficient mining and cheap shipping made these ores potentially even cheaper, but after the formation of U.S. Steel in 1901 the ore trade was effectively cartelized and all other producers had to buy above market prices. Even so, however, U.S. average ore costs were well below British costs. Britain's commitment to acid steel appeared to lock it into increasingly high-cost raw materials and to jeopardize the future of the industry.

IV. The Neglect of the Basic Process?

1. Basic Bessemer from Domestic Ores

Why then did Britain not reorient rapidly to either basic Bessemer or basic open-hearth steelmaking? Basic Bessemer was not in fact revived

TABLE 1 Production of Steel Ingots by Process: U.K., United States, and Germany, 1880–1913 (thousand tons)

Year	Bessemer process			Open-hearth process			
	Acid	Basic	Subtotal	Acid	Basic	Subtotal	Total
Great Britain							
1880			1,042			251	1,293
1886			1,570			694	2,264
1890			2,015			1,564	3,579
1896	1,358	457	1,815	2,145	172	2,317	4,131
1900	1,254	491	1,745	2,863	293	3,156	4,900
1906	1,307	600	1,907	3,379	1,176	4,555	6,462
1913	1,049	552	1,601	3,811	2,252	6,063	7,664
Germany							
1880	679	18	697			36	733
1886	341	784	1,125			211	1,336
1890	351	1,493	1,844			388	2,232
1896	351	3,004	3,355			1,478	4,833
1900	223	4,142	4,365	148	1,997	2,145	6,510
1906	408	6,773	7,181	231	3,534	3,765	10,946
1913	155	10,630	10,785	284	7,330	7,614	18,399

United States

1880	1,074			101	1,175
1886	2,269			219	2,488
1890	3,689			513	4,202
1896	3,920			1,299	5,219
1900	6,685	853	2,545	3,398	10,083
1906	12,275	1,322	9,659	10,981	23,256
1913	9,546	1,255	20,345	21,600	31,146

Sources: NFISM, *Statistical Yearbooks*, various years; James Cecil Carr and Walter Taplin, *History of the British Steel Industry* (Cambridge, Mass., 1962), passim.

TABLE 2 Combined Cost of Ore and Coke for One Ton of Pig Iron (shillings)

	Northeast coast hematite	Cleveland #3	German basic	U.S. Bessemer	U.S. basic
1886	35.4	27.1	37.2	56.7	55.8
1890	51.3	33.3	50.8	63.6	48.0
1896	38.8	27.9	35.3	47.7	42.2
1897	43.2	28.8	37.2	35.6	37.1
1898	43.1	29.4	38.7	35.6	33.2
1899	50.8	37.1	40.0	38.2	37.0
1900	69.4	48.7	43.4	58.3	55.7
1901	46.4	31.3	46.4	44.6	40.8
1902	47.3	33.0	39.9	54.6	53.0
1903	47.4	32.9	39.7	55.4	53.0
1904	44.5	30.6	40.1	39.6	39.4
1905	46.4	32.3	40.0	47.0	46.3
1906	58.4	36.3	41.7	52.3	51.9
1907	68.9	43.3	43.5	58.4	56.8
1908	48.1	36.1	43.8	50.2	47.9
1909	47.5	34.4	41.8	51.5	49.3
1910	55.6	36.2	41.9	54.3	52.3
1911	56.1	34.0	43.7	49.5	47.1
1912	61.6	38.3	45.7	48.8	47.1
1913	66.6	45.6	46.6	52.6	50.6

Note: The cost of ore is the cost of one ton of ore delivered to the furnace divided by its metallic iron content. The cost of coke is the cost per ton delivered to the furnace multiplied by the number of tons consumed per ton of pig iron. Thus, for example, the cost of Northeast coast hematite is the price of a ton of Spanish rubio ore delivered to the furnace, divided by 50% (the guaranteed metallic iron content of the ore), plus the cost of one ton of coke (the average needed to smelt it). The iron content and coke consumption of the other irons are as follows: Cleveland #3, 33% iron content, 1.1 tons coke; German basic (before 1892) 33% iron content, 1.1 tons coke; German basic (1892–1913)=a mixed burden of one-third minette 33% iron content, and two-thirds Swedish ores 66% iron content, plus 1 ton coke; U.S. Bessemer 57% iron content, 1 ton coke; U.S. basic 53% iron content, 1.1 tons coke.

Source: Robert C. Allen, "International Competition and the Growth of the British Iron and Steel Industy, 1830–1913," Ph.D. diss., Harvard University, 1975, Tables 9–1 (pp. 274–75), 9–11 (pp. 301–13), 9–12 (pp. 305–6).

until the 1930s, and although there were important moves into basic open-hearth after 1900, they seemed to many to be delayed and excessively regionalized on the Northeast coast. These observations were the starting point for Duncan Burn's indictment of the British steel industry. Burn argued that the source of German success in Europe before the First World War was its effective use of the basic Bessemer process drawing on cheap raw materials. These consisted of Germany's lean domestic ores and the rich and highly phosphoric imported Swedish ores (suitable for basic Bessemer but impossible to use for open-hearth because of their phosphorus content), which made possible continuously falling costs before the First World War.

In contrast, British costs were rising after 1900 mainly because the prices of ores for acid steel on which they relied were rising sharply. Britain had opportunities to escape from this constraint and imitate the German model by shifting to the use of similar cheap domestic ores located in the East Midlands, notably in Lincolnshire and Northamptonshire. He argued that these ores both could and should have been used to make basic Bessemer steel after the 1890s as cheaply as it was made in the minette areas of Luxemburg and Lorraine. Burn finds the British steelmakers' failure to attempt this incomprehensible: "Since the weakness of the basic steel industry in Britain was not, fundamentally, a reflection of ore resources, it must be regarded as the most notable single instance of the slow adoption of new methods."[30] Burn's technical judgments have been regarded as authoritative and his analysis has played a central role in the debate on entrepreneurial failure; he was closely followed by Burnham and Hoskins, Landes, Aldcroft, and others. His profuse but rather disorganized detail, informed asides, and the nuggets of unique company-level detail in his footnotes all convey conviction. But in fact the basis for his far-reaching judgments was slender and does not bear re-examination.

Burn's estimate that Lincolnshire basic pig iron could have been made and sold profitably at 30s per ton in the 1890s against typical pig-iron prices at the time of 40–50s per ton has been widely quoted. However, since almost no basic pig iron was made in the area at the time, the basis for his cost estimates is very sketchy.[31] Burn attempted to compare the costs of acid Bessemer steel in its existing coastal locations with the potential cost of basic Bessemer at a possible works in Lincolnshire. The basis of his comparison is a claim that the North East Steel Co. (NESCO) was able to make basic Bessemer steel in Cleveland profitably through the 1890s and that its failure after 1900 was due not to problems inherent to the basic Bessemer process but to external forces (German dumping and rising coal prices after 1900). If a Cleveland firm could produce basic Bessemer competitively against acid Bessemer and open-hearth producers, it could be done *a fortiori* by a firm located on the Midlands ores.[32]

In his famous exercise in revisionism, McCloskey accepted Burn's contention about the suitability of Midlands ores, but took up a reservation voiced by Burn that "what they gained on the ores they might lose on the trains"[33] through additional freight costs because of the distance of the Midlands orefields from the coast and manufacturing centers. McCloskey concluded that the price difference in favor of Lincolnshire iron was less than the transport costs to Cleveland and that the higher costs of Cleveland ores were partly offset by lower costs of transport for coke. He concluded, "The costs were virtually equal. . . . Nothing would have been gained by an increase in the relative output of Lincolnshire pig iron. . . . The relative neglect of the Lincolnshire ores, in short, appears to have been a rational adjustment to the balance of locational advantage."[34]

McCloskey's analysis is technically impressive but largely irrelevant. First, he misformulates the nature of Burn's claim. Burn did not envisage freighting East Midlands ore or pig iron to Cleveland, but integrating production of iron and steel at a new location on the orefields (i.e., a precursor of the Corby project of the 1930s, which Burn clearly had in mind).[35] The calculation of intraregional freights in this form is therefore irrelevant to Burn's hypothesis. Secondly, and more fundamental, McCloskey (like Burn and the rest of the literature) overlooked fundamental metallurgical obstacles to the development of a low-cost basic steel industry (either basic Bessemer or basic open-hearth) based on the East Midlands ores. Historians have tended to assume that since these ores were the basis of Stewarts and Lloyds successful revival of the basic Bessemer process at Corby in the 1930s, they could equally well have been utilized for the same purpose before the First World War. This was not the case.

Attempts to use Midlands ores for basic pig iron enjoyed little sucess before the First World War because of severe technical problems that arose from the heavy slags generated in the blast furnace. The high-alumina/high-silicon ores generated slags with high melting points. Unlike normal slags, these were not fully reduced by the hot gases as they descended through the upper parts of the furnace and often arrived in the combustion zone still in solid form, impeding the reaction, slowing the melting, and producing poor-quality iron. In order to melt these slags, blast furnaces could be superheated and run slowly, using high ratios of coke to ore. But the high temperatures needed to melt the slag also reduced large amounts of silicon from the ores which combined with the iron in the furnace to produce a high-silicon pig iron, useful for foundry iron, where a higher silicon content was a virtue, but useless for basic steelmaking. If, on the other hand, blast furnaces were run nearer to normal temperatures to avoid reducing the silicon, the slag became highly viscous, "scaffolds" formed on the inside walls of the furnace, the burden began to hang and stick, pressures rose, and only off-grade iron was produced. Consequently, it was commonly accepted in the industry that the Midlands ores were unsuitable for the manufacture of basic iron, except mixed in limited proportion with other ores.[36] Until the 1930s, therefore, Northamptonshire ores were either mixed with other ores or, when used alone, made only foundry iron at low rates of production and with high fuel consumption.

These ores could produce only a high-silicon iron economically. Nevertheless, steelmakers made numerous attempts to devise ways of using such high-silicon iron for steelmaking before 1914. All of them failed, mainly because the high-silicon iron in the steelmaking furnace resulted in the rapid destruction of converter linings, excessive slags, high fuel costs, and a lack of uniformity in the finished steel.

In particular, there were four sustained efforts to adapt basic Bessemer technology to the requirements of domestic ores before 1914. Peter Payne has described the technologically ambitious attempt made by Glengarnock Iron and Steel Co. in the 1890s, under the direction of the leading Czech-trained metallurgist Maximilian Mannaberg, to use domestic ores with additions of blast-furnace cinder to produce basic Bessemer steel. An inability to deal with the high levels of phosphorus and silicon forced them to abandon the attempt in 1894 and turn to the acid open-hearth process using imported ores.[37] Even more determined experimentation was carried out by two firms on the Northeast coast after 1900. Basic pig iron from Cleveland ores had two major chemical disadvantages for the basic Bessemer process: Not only was it too high in silicon, it was also too low in phosphorus for effective reduction in the Bessemer converter and required additions of high-phosphorus materials. The latter problem was initially overcome cheaply when the process was introduced in the 1880s by the addition of locally available "puddler's tap," a phosphoric waste product of the old iron industry. But once this was exhausted, further additions had to be purchased elsewhere at high cost.[38] This difficulty combined with the silicon problem to create costly and difficult problems for the steelmakers. NESCO used the basic Bessemer process from 1884 until just before the First World War, but they were only able to do so by mixing local ores with high-manganese/low-alumina ores imported from abroad and the resulting high materials and transport costs meant that, contrary to the assertion by Burn noted earlier, they were never really a low-cost producer.[39] Between 1905 and 1911 Bolckow Vaughan tried to escape the need to use such costly manganese or phosphoric additions by pioneering a two-slag process at its Eston works. NESCO followed their lead. However, neither could achieve an acceptable quality and after several years of striving both abandoned the basic Bessemer process before the First World War.[40] The one other firm that used domestic ores for basic Bessemer—the South Staffordshire Steel and Iron Co.—has been cited as a success by Burn, but this is very misleading. They in fact used Northamptonshire ores only in small proportions, mainly mixed with 80% puddled iron scrap. When they did attempt to use higher proportions of local ores, they too were foiled by the high silicon content of the iron.[41]

Burn was aware of some of these problems, but he argued that they could have been resolved by "intelligent groping in the dark."[42] Most of the subsequent historiography has simply accepted this view. In fact the problems of the ores involved fundamental theoretical issues in chemistry and metallurgy that were not solved until the early 1930s.[43] The solution depended on first understanding the chemistry of the furnace reactions and secondly on techniques to predict systematically the behavior of liquid slags. The first step was achieved through the theoretical work of Rankin and Wright in the United States shortly after the outbreak of the First World War. These two chemists demonstrated that a blast-furnace slag in a fluid state did not consist, as previously believed, of a mixture of simple oxides, but that the oxides at high temperatures formed mixtures of specific minerals. Predictions of the behavior of slags had therefore to be based on the observed behavior of these minerals rather than of the oxides.[44] This theoretical work was taken up in the field of applied metallurgy by McCaffery and others working at the Bureau of Mines, the U.S. Geophysics Laboratory, and the University of Wisconsin in the 1920s. Working over a decade, McCaffery et al. defined the melting points of different slag mixtures, their viscosity, and the temperatures at which melting was completed. The results formed the basis for a series of iso-viscosity curves published between 1927 and 1931.[45] These tables provided a basis for the systematic prediction of the properties and behavior of slags of varying composition in the blast furnace. Crucially, this work revealed that, at different temperatures, very slight changes in the composition of a slag could result in a change in its mineral constituents. As a result, the properties of the new slag, determined by the mixture of these new minerals, could be in marked contrast with those of the original material charged into the furnace, accounting for hitherto unexplained sudden and marked changes in the furnace. Relatively small changes of slag composition could produce disproportionate and unexpected changes in furnace behavior or even entirely change the character and behavior of a slag.

Without this knowledge blast-furnace managers had been powerless to predict the widely varying and irregular behavior of such slags, but these findings provided the possibility of fine-tuning furnace slags and using precise temperature control to avoid rapid increases in slag viscosity. From 1930, T. P. Colclough applied what he called "these entirely new principles" in extended experimental tests on Northamptonshire ores and demonstrated that, using these control techniques, it was possible to reduce such ores fully at low temperatures for the first time and thereby produce a low-silicon iron suitable for basic Bessemer steelmaking.[46] Consequently, Midland ores with their high ratio of alumina to silica content became viable for the first time for the manufacture of basic iron by themselves and not only in admixture with other ores. The reintroduction of the basic Bessemer process to Britain in the mid-1930s by Stewarts and Lloyds at Corby was based on these developments. Even at this time further metallurgical problems remained in the use of Midlands ores, and other steelmakers were initially sceptical of Corby's ability to produce a saleable basic pig iron. The new process restricted the scope for desulphurization in the blast furnace and other steelmakers felt that Corby "sails very close to the wind" in the sulphur content of its iron.[47]

Thus, contrary to Burn's supposition, the solution to the metallurgical problems was not a simple matter of trial and error, of which there had been plenty before the First World War. Rather, it depended on prolonged basic scientific research in U.S., German, and British laboratories over almost two decades. According to the British metallurgist F. W. Harbord, this was "one of the best instances he had seen where an almost academic research had been applied to the practical operation of the blast furnace."[48] German metallurgists in the 1920s had also tried to solve the same problems (notably through pioneering ore-dressing techniques at Krupp and basic duplexing at Mannesmann) since a solution would open up extensive reserves of German domestic oolitic ores—but they too had failed.[49]

Burn was writing shortly after the successful launch of the Corby project and a failure to evaluate the metallurgical problems involved seems to have drawn him into an unduly optimistic assessment of the prospects of earlier innovation. In fact, any attempt to produce steel at an East Midlands location using the existing metallurgical techniques and knowledge would have involved costly mixing with imported manganiferous and other ores as well as the high transport charges on coke that McCloskey described.[50] This would eliminate any chance of fundamentally lowering the costs of the British steel industry even if other difficult issues of technique and quality of output could have been effectively resolved.[51]

2. The Basic Open-hearth Process

Thus the Midlands ores necessarily remained a dormant asset for a further 30 years after 1900. The data in Table 2 show that while Britain was suffering from the highest raw material costs of any country in its acid steel, it could also assemble the raw materials for foundry iron in Cleveland more cheaply than anywhere else in the world. These materials were the basis of the rapid transition to basic open-hearth practice that took place in Britain after 1900. Could they have been used more and earlier?

Closer examination shows that, as with the East Midlands ores, the utilization of these resources depended on the prior solution to important metallurgical and technological problems. Before 1900, Cleveland ores could *not* be used to make basic steel. The core of the problem was, in this case, their phosphorus content. Basic Bessemer requires relatively high-phosphorus iron (above 2%), which generates extra heat in the converter as the phosphorus is oxidized. The minette and Swedish ores, which the Germans used for their basic Bessemer steel, both had more than 2% phosphorus. The open-hearth, on the other hand, requires low phosphorus. Even using high proportions of scrap in the steelmaking furnace, the maximum permissible phosphorus level of the iron charged is 0.5%. But the Cleveland ores were awkwardly intermediate at 1.5% and, although to a much lesser extent than in the Midlands, also had a troubling silicon content which created heavy slags, impeded the steel reduction, and resulted in irregular metal.[52] If they were to be effectively used for steelmaking, further processes would be necessary either to raise their phosphorus content into the basic Bessemer bracket or to reduce their phosphorus content into the open-hearth range. Both were tried, but the record was poor and successful results delayed.

During the late 1880s and early 1890s, when substantial amounts of basic Bessemer steel were made on the Northeast coast, only very limited amounts of Cleveland ore were used in the process. It had to be mixed with other, more phosphoric ores to raise it above the 2% phophorus line. In the 1880s and 1890s this was a viable strategy. The Northeast firms were able to add locally available "puddler's tap" to increase the phosphorus levels. While this was plentiful and cheap, it was effective, even though it raised the sulphur content of the iron and necessitated further additions of expensive imported manganiferous ores. The necessary additions to the burden cost 4–6s per ton in the 1890s, and the additional processes also raised operating costs by several shillings per ton and therefore eliminated the potential cost advantage of basic Bessemer over the acid Bessemer process in the region. By 1900 the stocks of "tap" or "cinder" were being exhausted and although converter-slag provided an adequate substitute, it further increased costs.[53]

Another alternative was to mix Cleveland ore with other ores in order to lower the phosphorus content of the resultant iron. Basic open-hearth steelmaking needs *low*-phosphorus iron. If they were to be used for open-hearth steelmaking, the phosphorus content of the Cleveland ores had to be reduced from its natural 1.5% to below 0.5%. Reducing the phosphorus content necessitated mixing with imported ores, specifically the low-phosphorus Spanish hematite (0.1% phosphorus), which was readily available. However, doing this raised costs prohibitively. To achieve a burden with an average phosphorus content of 0.5% phosphorus would require a burden of 72% hematite to 28% Cleveland ore, which would represent only a small saving compared with using hematite alone.[54] Even this saving would be offset by the necessary use of more coke and limestone in the blast furnace. Moreover, the ultimate quality of the steel remained an uncertain proposition.

The third alternative, and the way that ultimately proved successful, was to produce intermediately phosphoric iron in the blast furnace and then deal with the phosphorus in the steelmaking process. Several possible routes were ruled out by their costs. Adding acid steel scrap to the charge incurred the same mathematical difficulties as adding hematite ores to the blast-furnace burden; while specialized methods like duplexing (a partial preliminary reduction of the iron in a basic Bessemer converter) or the Thiel dual open-hearth furnace, incurred very high operating costs and could not deal adequately with the heavy slags generated by the silicon in the Cleveland ores.[55]

The beginning of a solution came in the 1890s with the development of "mixers," intermediate ladles of molten metal between the blast furnace and the steel converter in which further refining could be carried out before the open-hearth. But the innovation which fully opened up the Cleveland ores to basic open-hearth steelmaking was the Talbot tilting furnace, introduced in 1900. Like the earlier mixers, the Talbot furnace facilitated the use of hot metal in the open-hearth furnace. But it did more. The Talbot furnace could be tilted intermittently and partially emptied and recharged. The heavy slags arising from the siliceous ores could be removed as they developed, reducing serious furnace corrosion, and periodic small taps and recharges could keep the average phosphorus level of the charge within the necessary bounds. This process lowered fuel consumption and the cost of handling the slags and made it possible to use intermediately phosphoric ores.

As a result of this innovation, Cleveland ores, even after the increased expense of the process, could be used to make steel much more cheaply than the acid process using hematite ores. The price of inputs was reduced close to the level enjoyed in Westphalia. The results were dramatic: most of the increase in British steel output after 1900 was in basic open-hearth and the iron and steel industry of the Northeast grew dramatically. Nevertheless, the development remained a regional one and not large enough to change the overall pattern of comparative advantage vis-à-vis Germany.

On the basis of these conditions, the Northeast coast established world technical leadership in open-hearth practice, particularly in the introduction of very large furnaces of 100 tons and over. In 1910 Britain had 10.5% of its open-hearth capacity in this category, against only 0.8% in the United States. The United States was only just catching up in the installation of big open-hearth furnaces in 1914.[56] Before the First World War there were only two Talbot furnaces in Germany, even though Germany made more open-hearth steel than Britain. However, German basic open-hearth practice was fundamentally different. Their enormous basic Bessemer industry provided them with abundant basic Bessemer scrap which they used in high proportions in their open-hearth industry. Before the war, German firms commonly used 80% scrap in the open-hearth furnace against a typical 20% in Britain. In many respects their basic open-hearth industry was based on remelting and therefore avoided the phosphorus and slag problems of an industry based on the conversion of iron.[57]

McCloskey saw the Talbot furnace as a simple cost-reducing advantage and did not perceive its importance in opening up the use of Cleveland ores;[58] Allen understood the latter, but he nevertheless remained critical of British entrepreneurs for not making greater use of it: It was too little too late. He argued that the new techniques provided the basis for a radical relocation and development of the British steel industry. What Allen failed to see, however, was that the new techniques only opened a very narrow window of opportunity for Cleveland entrepreneurs. Allen argued that Cleveland steelmakers "had access to the cheapest raw materials in the world"[59] and was puzzled by the steelmakers' failure to restructure fundamentally the industry on the basis of these resources. In fact there were serious problems with the long-run viability of these ores. When Cargo Fleet made a major attempt to establish best-practice iron- and steelmaking on the Cleveland ores between 1903 and 1907, its project was vitiated by the declining and problematic quality of the ores. The increasing proportions of more expensive imported ores that they were forced to use undercut the profitability of the venture.[60] These problems were not untypical. The technical problems of using low-grade ores were considerable and success required significant feats of close process control.[61] Cleveland ironstone was of diminishing iron content and increasingly uneconomical to mine; it was in fact, as Elbaum notes, "within measurable distance of exhaustion." Cleveland ore output peaked in 1880 and the proportion of Cleveland pig iron made from local ore fell from 90% to 47% between 1875 and 1913.[62] In the 1920s the output of local ores dwindled and suffered diminishing returns.

Nevertheless, using the available opportunities, Britain developed its basic open-hearth production rapidly before the First World War. By 1913, 37% of open-hearth output was basic. Between 1900 and 1913 basic open-hearth output grew at 15.6% per year compared with 3.2% for all steel.[63] In 1900, 64% of British, 33% of American, and 32% of German production was open-hearth. By 1913 this had become 79%, 69%, and 40%, representing 6 million, 21.6 million, and 7.6 million tons, respectively (see Table 1).

3. Imported ores
The regional advance in the Northeast was based on technical adaptations that made possible the use of cheap, intermediately phosphoric local ores. As we have seen, these ores were too low in phosphorus for use in the basic Bessemer process. On the other hand, the Midlands ores which had sufficiently high phosphorus faced other metallurgical barriers that prevented their use. It was still impossible to use imported

high-phosphorus ores for the basic open-hearth process except mixed with more costly ores, or (as in Germany) with large proportions of scrap. Hence there was no readily available path to further expansion of cheap, basic open-hearth production in other British regions. The only other feasible production strategies involved the manufacture of basic Bessemer on the basis of imported ores.

Imported Swedish ores played an important role in German success in basic Bessemer production in this period. Could Britain have followed this example? In terms of transport costs there was little to choose between Middlesborough (1,680 miles from Lulea, the main Swedish port) and a works in the Ruhr (1,690 miles). Moreover, it was British entrepreneurs who pioneered the opening of Swedish orefields in the 1860s, often overcoming considerable physical and climatic hazards in the search for raw materials for the iron industry. Interest waned when the rise of steel made these phosphoric ores unattractive, but the discovery of the basic Bessemer process in 1878 created new possibilities for use of the rich ores of Lapland and central and Arctic Sweden, notably those of Gellivara.

A British company, the Swedish and Norwegian Railway Co., took the initiative in the 1880s to commence a £2 million project for the construction of a transpeninsular railway from the port of Lulea on the Baltic to Ofoten (Narvik) on the Norwegian coast to liberate the Gellivara ores. At the same time the Magnetic Iron Smelting Co. was formed in Cleveland, renting two blast furnaces from Bell Bros. to smelt the ore. By 1888 the first 130-mile stage of the railway from Gellivara to Lulea was completed and the new enterprise exported over 70,000 tons of ore, almost all to Britain. The rest, according to Michael Flinn, "should have been plain sailing," but by 1891 the struggling company had sold its railway to the Swedish government and two years later went into liquidation.[64] Thus Britain surrendered the key to the whole Scandinavian ore trade and after 1891 British capital ceased to play any part in the development of the industry. Why?

Some contemporary experts blamed the ineptitude of the managers of the project. The Gellivara orefields contained significant deposits of both highly phosphoric *and* nonphosphoric ores. But, instead of grading and selecting the ores, the exporters shipped consignments of ore mixed from different quarries. As a result, early trials found them to be too high in phosphorus for acid steel and too low in phosphorus for basic.[65] A trade report in 1890 concluded: "The percentage of phosphorus is so extremely variable that it cannot be relied on as a definite source of ore either for the acid or the basic steel process."[66] Gellivara ores were discredited and by 1891 demand had totally collapsed.

The new owner of the railway, the Swedish government, quickly identified the grading problem and by 1894 was already able to export 594,000 tons of ore, mainly to Germany. In the years that followed the trade grew by leaps and bounds. By 1900 Germany imported 1.3 million tons of Swedish ore, mainly to the Ruhr, by 1905 2.5 million tons, and by 1912 Germany was taking over 70% of Sweden's 6.6 million tons of ore exports.[67] Germany seems to have reaped most of the benefits of British entrepreneurs' earlier efforts. But if it was an entrepreneurial error that cost Britain its dominant position in Swedish ores in 1890, it is less obvious why Britain did not re-enter the arena subsequently. Despite German interest in securing exclusive control through direct ownership of Swedish ore mines they had only limited success in this respect. German companies developed comprehensive long-term delivery contracts, but they by no means succeeded in closing off the Swedish ore market.[68]

Part of the explanation for subsequent British neglect of Swedish ores is probably to be found in the timing of shifts in relative costs. In the early 1890s, Swedish ore was still more expensive than imported Spanish hematite per ton of iron content, though it compared well with minette ores used in the Ruhr. In the course of the 1890s the positions of Spanish and Swedish ores were reversed, but it was only in the late 1890s that the trend began to become clearer. In 1894 Bell, Samuelson, and other steelmakers were sceptical that large volumes of Swedish ores could be an economical proposition in the Ruhr. Most dismissed arguments by the metallurgist Jeremiah Head that low-cost transport from the Arctic Circle was bringing about epoch-making changes in raw material costs. According to Bell, "Bringing ore from Sweden on account of its phosphorus to the works on the Rhine was, as a permanent trade, not to be dreamt of."[69] Adverse price movements and doubts about the long-term future of Spanish ores stimulated further close attention to Sweden from 1898 and, in particular, the completion of the rail link to Narvik in 1903 and the consequent opening up of the Kirunavaara ores and lowering of transport costs, attracted increased interest.[70] Thereafter, British imports of Swedish ores rose significantly from negligible amounts in 1902 to 854,000 tons (11.5% of total ore imports) in 1913. However, these imports remained almost exclusively non-phosphoric ores for the acid process; imports of Swedish phosphoric ores remained tiny.

Germany's basic Bessemer industry found it easy to move from local ores to Swedish ores as cost advantages shifted. By the 1890s Germany was the undisputed leader in basic Bessemer techniques. Any British entrepreneur contemplating entry into this trade on the basis of

Swedish ores would have had to penetrate export markets in the face of German competition without the support of an expansive domestic market for this type of steel. As Alfred Chandler put it, "Only a courageous and somewhat irrational set of British steelmakers and financiers would have made the investment required to compete in price with those of Pittsburgh and the Ruhr in order to regain these distant markets."[71] Further work on the costs and problems of Swedish ores will be necessary to quantify this judgment more fully, but it is clear that British steelmakers preferred to seek to build on their existing strengths in open-hearth steel. Thus, even while neglecting the Swedish phosphoric ores, Bolckow Vaughan and Consett, for example, were prepared to make big (and rather speculative) investments in Scandinavia in the quest for further sources of low-cost non-phosphoric ores for the acid process.[72]

II. Productivity and Technical Progress

1. Problems of Evaluation

The preceding discussion suggests that British steelmakers did not fail to take advantage of major opportunities to change fundamentally the cost structure of its iron and steel industry in the 1890s and 1900s. The proposed routes to achieve this were either not open, or else opened only late and briefly, and British entrepreneurs made impressive use of at least one of these windows of opportunity. Other productivity improvements might have had significant impacts on competitiveness, but no others offered the prospects of the sort of major shift in cost structure or an opening to new product markets that either the use of the basic process or the revival of basic Bessemer production could offer.

Nevertheless, alongside criticisms of failure to achieve structural adjustment stands a long tradition of criticism of the level of technical progress and productivity in the industry. International productivity comparisons are notoriously hazardous. The data is often poor and there are great difficulties in establishing suitable measures and weighting them. Nevertheless, research by McCloskey and Allen has raised important comparative questions. McCloskey used input price measures to compare British and U.S. productivity and argued that Britain and the United States were equally efficient by 1913. Allen questioned the validity of price measures and substituted input/output measures based on physical quantities. He differed from McCloskey and argued that by 1913 American and German steel production was

15% "more efficient" than British. Subsequently, Elbaum showed that correcting for hours worked in Allen's labor productivity calculation significantly reduced this efficiency gap.[73]

Perhaps more importantly, all of these studies of productivity treat Bessemer and open-hearth steel as homogeneous and assume the legitimacy of comparing costs in each to measure efficiency. Yet as we have stressed, the steels have very different properties and open-hearth steel is a higher quality and more expensive product, while basic Bessemer is simpler and cheaper.[74] They are substitutable in a certain range of products, but they are not substitutable in many others. This fact, as we have noted, crucially shaped the pattern of British trade and production. Their cost ranges might at times approach each other, but this should not obscure the difference between the processes. McCloskey and Allen are, therefore, comparing the price and factor inputs of different products and starting from incorrect assumptions.

2. Pig Iron
Productivity comparisons are, therefore, most robust at the level of the most homogeneous and least fabricated products. The comparative study of pig-iron productivity carries most conviction, and McCloskey and Allen have substantially reversed the picture drawn by Burn, Landes, Burnham and Hoskins, and others of the relative efficiency of British and American pig-iron manufacture. The earlier writers were very impressed by U.S. technical progress in blast furnaces before 1914. The combination of giant furnaces, hard driving, mechanical handling, and fast throughput appeared to embody a productivity revolution that Europeans failed to match and provided the basis for the United States' high reputation as the technical leader in the industry. They tended to dismiss statements from British blast-furnace managers about the inapplicability of these developments to British conditions as a sign of their intractable conservatism. Certain older historians like Carr and Taplin, however, have long had their doubts about this,[75] and recent research has substantiated their suspicions. McCloskey argues that by the First World War the United States had not yet surpassed British blast-furnace productivity;[76] Allen believes the United States may have been "slightly more efficient;"[77] and Berck that the United States was "barely superior."[78] Whatever the truth in this complex battle of detailed calculations, it is evident that any productivity superiority achieved by the United States by 1914 was slight.

To understand the difference between the old and the new pictures, it is important to analyze the trajectory of comparative blast-furnace productivity development over time. In Britain and Germany, blast-furnace productivity growth was substantial from the 1840s to the 1880s but meager between then and 1914. In contrast, U.S. productivity was low and stagnant from the 1840s to the 1870s and fell far behind European levels. This gap was then eliminated by a spectacular burst of efficiency growth between 1870 and 1890. After that, however, productivity growth in the U.S., as in Europe, stagnated. In all three countries, Britain, Germany, and the United States, fuel productivity converged on a point around one ton of coke per ton of pig iron and did not advance much beyond this plateau until a series of innovations in the 1950s. The issue was one of different routes to the same point rather than different finishing lines.

Until the 1870s, dependence on Pennsylvania's siliceous ores and anthracite fuels provided a strict limit to attainable fuel efficiency in the United States. Once Lake ores and cheap coke became available, an opportunity arose to close the fuel productivity gap rapidly to match Europe. Over half the dramatic increase in fuel productivity in the next two decades was due simply to the substitution of less siliceous, self-fluxing ores with lighter slags and lower fuel requirements. Hard-driving, new blast-furnace designs and mechanical handling played a minor role in the increase in U.S. productivity.[79] Rather, they formed related adaptations of the configuration of plants to take advantage of two distinctive features of the U.S. industry. First, they were well adapted to deal with a high throughput of relatively rich and uniform ores. Secondly, since the U.S. iron and steel industry continuously underestimated the growth of demand, while tariffs hindered the inflow of imports, hard driving permitted the maximization of short-run output to take advantage of supernormal profits at periods of peak demand.[80] By the turn of the century, moreover, there were already dissenting voices within the United States. Some experts argued that high stacks and hard driving were becoming more related to rivalry and prestige than economy, and in the years that followed there was an abandonment of some of the biggest "giants" and a modification of designs in closer accord with British patterns.[81]

The application of similar practices to industries with different raw materials and different prevailing factor prices would not have been rewarding. Sir Lowthian Bell, for example, denounced the "reckless rapid rate" of hard driving at Carnegie's blast furnaces, which wrecked the interior of each furnace and required replacement every three years. Carnegie's blast-furnace superintendent responded: "What do we care about the lining? We think a lining is good for so much iron and the sooner it makes it the better."[82] Other U.S. ironmasters like M. R. Potter opined: "It has been said of our U.S. furnaces that they lead 'a short life but a merry one.' That is literally true, and up to a certain point I regard it as the truest economy."[83] But the British ironmaster's case was based, at least in part, on sound comparative plant analysis.[84] Blast-furnace relining was extremely expensive in Britain, and attempting to achieve high throughput with the lower iron content ores used in Britain created immense problems with the enormous volume of materials that had to pass through the furnace.[85] U.S. practitioners also acknowledged that U.S. practice could not produce high-quality irons like those required by many British steelworks.[86] Within these limits, the new blast furnaces that came on stream after 1900, especially in the Northeast, generally used blast pressures of 12–20 lbs, higher than the U.S. average in the 1890s, though still below the U.S. "giants," which used 20–30 lbs.[87]

The great leap forward in the United States was real and thrilling, but it owed less to changes in American practice than its apostles believed. Berck concluded that American hard-driving techniques offered only small advantages to British manufacturers at prevailing prices with the different raw materials available. Alex Field showed that even this calculation is very sensitive to different estimates of the cost of capital in the two countries, and his recalculation suggests that American techniques would not have been superior at British prices.[88]

A more disaggregated picture of the British industry casts further light on international productivity comparisons. Overall figures appear to show a massive U.S. lead. In 1913 U.S. weekly output averaged 1,739 tons per furnace against 1,108 in Germany and 584 in Britain. But these contrasts must be analyzed with caution. Firstly, part of the U.S. advantage is based on the fact that they smelted richer ores than any European producer. In the 1890s, Carnegie typically used ores with 64% iron content.[89] Plants like the Dowlais-Cardiff works in South Wales which used solely Spanish hematite of 50% iron content, could average 1,200 tons per week in 1896.[90] But most British blast furnaces after 1900 had to use leaner ores. Cleveland ores were typically 30–35% iron, and Germany typically used ores in the 40–45% range.[91] In Alabama, the only region in the United States which used comparable ores, outputs per furnace were probably somewhat below those on the Northeast coast.[92]

Moreover, while United States and German blast furnaces produced a limited range of uniform products, the U.K. comprised a number of pig-iron subindustries producing for a variety of markets, each of which had different implications for output levels. Thus while in Germany average blast-furnace output was regionally very uniform, ranging from some 900 tons per week in Lorraine/Luxemburg, through 1,000 in the Saar to 1,300 in the Rhineland,[93] in Britain the greater complexity of metallurgical conditions and variety of finished products produced much more regional differentiation. While South Wales matched or exceeded German levels, largely because of its specialization in hematite ores, Cleveland averaged 800 tons per week (but 1,100 in its basic iron sector alone), Scotland 300, Lincolnshire 650, and Staffordshire and the Black Country probably less than 250 tons per week.[94] These different output levels did not represent different levels of efficiency so much as different products and product markets. For example, many small blast furnaces countinued to serve the demand for manufactured iron in the Black Country and South Yorkshire, notably for iron agricultural goods.[95] More broadly, in 1913, 37% of U.K. pig-iron output was for forge and foundry iron compared to less than 20% in Germany and the United States; foundry iron was a relatively specialized product produced in small quantities.[96]

National comparisons based on an average of the output of all British blast furnaces (337 in 1913) are therefore inappropriate. To compare like with like it would be necessary to remove from this number at least 150 petty producers in the Black Country and North Midlands, to take account of the peculiarities of the 80-furnace strong coal-iron sector in Scotland,[97] and in addition to account for some 20 further small specialized furnaces in the Sheffield region. It would also be necessary to adjust the German figures, since Germany also had a sector of petty producers, though it was of little significance compared to that in Britain.[98] The net result would be to show a modern sector in basic iron that compared well with Germany, a stagnant hematite sector that was performing rather poorly and subject to disinvestment, and a large sector of petty producers essentially engaged in an autonomous specialist (and declining) ironmaking sector.

Between 1895 and 1914 the United States clearly moved to the forefront of technical innovation in blast furnaces. But the extent to which it was economically justifiable for other countries to imitate their practice was questionable. U.S. practice achieved high productivity by methods appropriate to its factor inputs. Since 1914 blast-furnace practice has increasingly escaped dependence on marginal or poorer quality ores through the assembly of the best raw materials on a global basis. As a result, where U.S. technical innovations led, others have since followed. The world industry has moved from "lean" to "rich" practice. But at the time of the First world War there was no certainty that future methods outside the United States would revolve around "rich" practice. European practice was based on the intensive use of poor raw materials or relatively expensive, high-quality materials like the hematite ores. In this light, other practices achieved results comparable to the United States by sophisticated adaptation. Differences in technique did not necessarily imply lesser technical sophistication or capabilities.

3. Special Steels
Thus British productivity matched that of the United States and Germany in the manufacture of pig iron despite its relatively adverse raw material position, greater product differentiation, and greater complexity in the production process. In highly finished products, from shipplates to finished sheets to special steels, Britain's competitive advantage remained considerable. Geoffrey Tweedale has recently shown that the widespread view "that the United States was virtually self-sufficient in steel production by 1900 and had largely completed the absorption of European technology" is erroneous.[99] The United States and Germany continued to depend heavily on British production and innovation in special steels before the First World War.

Special steels made up less than 2% of total U.K. tonnage before the First World War, but their importance in technical development within the industry was immense and their impact on the broader economy through their crucial applications in cutting and critical machine parts was enormous. As the most highly mechanized economy in the world, the United States depended on these special steels more heavily than any other country; yet it continued to depend on Sheffield special steel technology at least until the First World War.[100] From the 1860s, the United States gradually managed to displace Sheffield imports in ordinary-grade special steels and many processes were invented to produce ordinary grades in more repetitive controlled methods with less reliance on skilled labor. Yet they remained unable to match Sheffield in higher qualities.

Sheffield has been criticized for the conservatism of its practice.[101] However, most of the U.S. innovations which it appeared to neglect depended on larger-scale production of more common grades. Notably, the use of gas furnaces from the 1880s and the development of electric steelmaking after 1908 only had clear-cut advantages for those grades.[102] But Sheffield had no ready access to large markets for common grades and therefore understandably concentrated on its advantage in high grades.

Sheffield made successive breakthroughs in the technology of special steels, notably in the invention of tungsten tool steel (1868), manganese steel (1882), silicon steel (1883), vanadium steel (1900), and stainless steel (1914). But the possibilities for commercial application of these developments in Britain was limited. Electric transformers, for instance, formed the key outlet for high-silicon steel. By 1908 there were a quarter of a million of these in the United States but only a handful in Britain.[103] Similarly, vanadium steel was invented by Arnold at Sheffield University in 1904. In Britain it found few uses. But in the United States it critically facilitated the design innovations in Henry Ford's Model T.[104]

Sheffield's ability to penetrate the big markets for more common grades in the United States was limited by prohibitive tariffs (up to $50 per ton after 1900) and by the need for specialty steelmakers to liaise closely with their customers for products that were usually demand specific. Consequently, once a new technology or a new alloy had been developed, local U.S. producers were generally able to "peel the onion" of Sheffield's position, picking off successive layers of "less special" special steels. Sheffield's only weapons against this were either the maintenance of a technological lead or direct investment in production in the United States.

Before the First World War, Sheffield maintained a clear-cut technical advantage in high-speed and self-hardening tool steels, manganese steel castings, and armor-piercing steel. In high-speed steel, Sheffield exerted a remarkable dominance in the U.S. market. In Britain, sales potential was limited: Few firms used such tools other than as a specialized adjunct for particularly difficult tasks. But in the 1880s and 1890s, American engineers (notably F.W. Taylor) responded to the urgent demands of American fast-paced machine shops and pioneered wider applications of high-speed steel in metal-cutting, essentially by reverse engineering the Sheffield processes and exploring the effects of heat treatment on advanced steels. Nevertheless, such was the comparative backwardness of the U.S. special steelmakers that Sheffield was able to dominate the period of diffusion and application of Taylor's processes. As late as 1907 Sheffield firms supplied the United States with 50% of its annual consumption of high-speed steel.[105]

The leading Sheffield firms realized that here as in other products their innovatory lead could not last indefinitely, and in a remarkable episode in the 1890s and 1900s they established themselves as major foreign manufacturers in the United States. Firth entered the U.S. market through a joint venture with a local company and, as Firth-Sterling, became the leading U.S. producer of high-speed steel in the decade before the First World War. Jessop, Sanderson, and Edgar Allen also opened major subsidiary plants which thrived before the war. The strategy, however, did not prove durable. In 1900 the U.S. Crucible Steel Combine bought out Sanderson, and the war and postwar depression disrupted the other ventures. Even without these exogenous changes, several other factors made direct foreign investment difficult in this industry. The sophistication and novelty of the technology made it difficult to transfer; skilled workers and technicians were in short supply; local partners often proved unreliable or weak; there were co-ordination problems; and, despite the new investments, the U.S. government continued to discriminate against foreign-owned firms in its contracts.[106] Nevertheless, it is hard to see anything other than the multinational route which might have allowed Sheffield steelmakers to escape from market constraints.[107]

4. Mechanization and Standardization

Alongside its big hard-driven blast furnaces, giant rolling mills and the oft-noted profusion of mechanical equipment in the plants symbolized American technical leadership before 1914. Yet it is unwise to accept that the most "advanced" practice was the best and most appropriate regardless of demand patterns and resource endowments. Three-country comparisons reveal complex patterns of technical change responding to different local conditions that belie any notion of a single technical leader in the industry.

American rolling-mill practice from the 1870s focused on the use of three-high mills, well suited to U.S. demand for low-quality products of relatively few sizes and types. High levels of specialization and standardization meant that they could have separate roughing trains for each specialized finishing mill (billet, plate, rail, etc.) instead of a single cogging mill serving all finishing rolls as was customary in Britain. A specialization such as that at Gary, where a single giant mill did nothing but roll 300 tons per hour of 4-inch billets, was inconceivable in Europe. British makers, on the other hand, needed a diversified range for small and specialized orders. The U.S. rail market was very price sensitive, but British railways in the late 19th century usually bought under a guarantee of seven years' life, for which they paid a substantial premium, and enforced conformance with their own precise engineering specifications. American railroads used only flange rails of 66–75 lbs., which came in standard sizes and did not have to conform to the demands of sectional templates for exact and uniform cross-sections which were demanded in Britain. While U.S. rails were secured to sleepers by dog-spikes, in Britain the flange of the rail had to fit exactly into a cast-iron chair.[108]

The British market was a demanding and difficult one. A burdensome variety of sections, shapes, and sizes were demanded by consumers. In part this responded to real needs. Recent work on British engineering shows that it depended heavily on flexibility, specialization, and quality. This resulted in frequent demands for small tonnages to individual specifications involving much roll-changing.[109] Boyce has shown how such rigorous and individuated consumer specifications inhibited economical working at Cargo Fleet before the war.[110] In these conditions, the economic advantages of large three-high mills over more flexible reversing mills was probably narrow.[111]

However, it is not so clear why British engineers were so resistant to the development of common technical standards for rails and other products.While giant consumers in the United States were often powerful enough to dominate and shape demand, this was rare in Britain. Carnegie, for example, forced the pace on standardization by announcing and enforcing higher prices for special sizes. By 1900 70% of all American rails were manufactured to American Society of Civil Engineers standards. But in 1900 there were 122 channel and angle sections in general use in the U.K. compared with 34 in the United States and 32 in Germany.[112] Nevertheless, there were some impressive developments in Britain before the war. Between 1900 and 1909 there was rapid progress in standardization, spearheaded by the British Iron Trades Association and strongly supported by the Admiralty, which led to a reduction in the number of specifications to levels comparable with the United States and Germany. Even so, the underlying diversity of consumer demand remained. A third-country comparison highlights the importance of demand patterns. German steelmakers, despite their greater commitment to standardized output, were unable to match U.S. practices of long runs and large specialized mills. German practice was closer to the British, and there was a large gap between European and American practice.[113]

Similar three-country comparisons illuminate other areas where there was an alleged failure to adopt "best practice." For example, British ironmasters have been criticized for "stubborn prejudice" which delayed the adoption of by-product coke ovens.[114] The standard comparison is with Germany. There, the problems of variable quality coals meant that by-product oven improvements were a prominent feature. In 1901 there were 12,000 by-product ovens in Germany, but only 1,000 in Britain. British ironmasters preferred older beehive furnaces to coke their more uniform coals, arguing that any increased coke yield was offset by higher costs of processing.[115] The usefulness of the innovation depended on the raw materials employed. Hence the United States, which, like Britain, had more uniform coal, also preferred the "backward" beehive. In 1900, the United States had even fewer by-product ovens than Britain. In 1914 Britain made 62% of its coke in by-product ovens, compared with the United States's 17% in 1910.[116]

It has also been suggested that the use of electric motors spread slowly in British steelworks.[117] Yet the balance of costs between steam and electricity was a narrow one, and until 1907 problems with electric reversing motors, as opposed to continuous motors, made it hard to apply them to British reversing mills.[118] When electric reversing mills became feasible in 1907, they spread rapidly in Britain. Germany pioneered the design of electric mill drives; yet, because of the cost advantages of steam, application of electricity was limited and there was actually a shift back toward steam power after 1907. Britain had more electrically powered mills than Germany before the war. Even in the United States, electric driving of rolling mills was rare before 1906, though it spread rapidly after that date.[119]

These issues and others such as mechanical handling, the cleaning of waste gases, and the use of more powerful blowing engines were all widely debated at the Iron and Steel Institute with coherent points of view being put forward both for and against. In mechanical handling, cheaper British labor meant that it was rational to mechanize less, and there were few advantages to the use of Wellman charging machines for open-hearth furnaces. The United States was prolific in inventing mechanical auxiliary and handling appliances to replace heavy manual labor, but these appliances were very costly and only justified by large throughputs. Blowing-engines were the subject of much discussion at the Iron and Steel Institute on several occasions between 1906 and 1912. Consultants were frequently employed by firms to evaluate the relative costs of fuel, the feasibility of adding them to existing plants, and the problems and costs of cleaning waste gases, but seldom found the adoption of gas engines to be an economic proposition.[120]

VI. Education and Research

In each of these cases the balance of advantages was debatable and any

possible profit or output foregone small. But the cumulative neglect of
small developments could have been significant if there had been a
consistent bias toward technical conservatism or a weakness in the
technical capabilities of plant-level managers. This case has been
argued, and Charlotte Erickson has shown that few leading steelmakers
before 1914 had received any technical education.[121] But much of the
evidence for a lag in British technical education is anecdotal and, in
particular, much derives from the "national efficiency" debates of the
1900s. Musgrave, in particular, has drawn on such contemporary criticisms of technique and education and endorsed them.[122] Yet the
matter is far from clear cut and more favorable views of British technical education can easily be culled from the literature of the time.[123]

Until the 1890s it is misleading to measure technical education in
the steel industry by measuring the role of formally trained students.
The level of fundamental metallurgical knowledge in iron and steel in
all countries was slight; the science of the practitioners ran ahead of
the theorists. Scientists had little idea of *how* key processes worked. For
example, the critical process of evaluating the carbon content of steel
could only be done slowly and inadequately by laboratories in the
1890s. The most effective *and* the most accurate method was for an
experienced worker to fracture a bar and gaze at the crystalline structure. This method could give a reading accurate to 0.01%, which
chemical analyses could not match.[124] Scientific insights often ran from
the works to the academy rather than vice versa, and "rule of thumb"
methods were often superior to "science." John Oliver Arnold, one of
the pioneer metallurgical scientists of his day who became professor of
Metallurgy at Sheffield University in 1889, learned his science in practical settings: as a works and naval chemist he acquired "the experience
of steelmaking he reported later in lecture form to his beglamored students."[125] Similarly, Robert Hadfield, the inventor of silicon steel in the
1880s and other important alloys at the turn of the century, refused a
chance to go to Oxbridge, preferring an apprenticeship and opportunities for experimentation in the works that universities could not
match.[126]

A focus on formal educational training also ignores other important
sources of scientific knowledge. The industry could draw on much fundamental metallurgical research undertaken on its fringes by the navy
(especially in stress and micrographic analysis) and on behalf of Lloyds
of London. Michael Sanderson has also recently shown that much fundamental research proceeded "invisibly." The Sheffield steel industry
helped found and remained closely linked to the universities of

Birmingham and Sheffield. Leading academics like Arnold were retained as permanent consultants by a secret combine of Sheffield steelmakers who used his work even while imposing secrecy restrictions on its publication. Industrial consultancy, naval research, and the role of independent companies like Cambridge Scientific Instruments, who pioneered the development of recalescence equipment after 1900, spread the net of scientific resources much wider than the firms themselves.[127]

In the 1880s scarcely any firms had college-trained students. But the works practitioners themselves were in the frontline of metallurgical advance. William Menelaus, Lowthian Bell, and others were the leading research scientists in their field as well as practical plant managers and their students went on to become innovative plant managers and engineers. At Dowlais, Menelaus taught inter alia Edward Williams and E. Windsor Richards of Bolckow Vaughan, William Jenkins of Consett, E.P. Martin of Blaenavon, and G.J. Snelus of West Cumberland, all of whom, in turn, ran plants *and* made important theoretical contributions to the subject.[128]

Based on such practitioners, a sophisticated tradition of technical literature developed. The Iron and Steel Institute (founded in 1869) and regional institutions of engineers had broad memberships of practitioners and a "habit of frank and vigorous discussion of technical problems." An impressive trade press developed, centered on the *Iron and Coal Trades Review* (founded 1866) and the British Iron Trade Association Annual Reports, edited by J.S. Jeans from 1878, which gave comprehensive coverage of the industry. These periodicals provided a remarkable amount of technical and trade information and practical discussion and international comparisons of practice were strong. The depth and complexity of papers delivered to the Iron and Steel Institute were impressive and often embodied technological leaps.[129]

After 1890 it is generally accepted that there was a rapid advance in the application of formal science to the steel industry.[130] At Sheffield University, Arnold presided over the most advanced steel research facilities in the world and the Sheffield colleges provided a steady stream of recruits as chief chemists and there were closer links with metallurgical investigations in the new universities. By the First World War, most of the major Sheffield firms had their own research laboratories, notably the Brown-Firth Research Laboratories opened in 1908. According to Tweedale, these institutions provided a seedbed for the development of pyrometry, metallography, and dynamic mechanical testing and epitomized an increasingly science- and research-based approach that kept

Sheffield in the forefront of special steel technology after 1900. The wider British steel industry also benefited from these researches, though elsewhere works laboratories which conducted primary research as well as testing and analysis remained rare in comparison to Germany.[131] Nevertheless, there appears to be inceasing evidence that casts doubt on a hypothesis of systematic technical conservatism or backwardness in training.

VII. Wage Structure and Collective Bargaining

Recent work has drawn attention to possible links between the collective bargaining and wage structure of the industry and the distinctive structure of the British industry with its large tail of smaller plants. Industrial relations in the steel industry was a paragon of "responsible bargaining" and industrial peace through most of this period: Procedures were rigorously followed and agreements invariably honored. The contrast with embattled industrial relations in other industries was notable; yet commentators suggest that this very harmony may have contributed to industrial decline.[132]

Collective bargaining and wage structures in the industry exhibited remarkable continuity from the iron to the steel era. The structure of collective bargaining remained a two-tier structure of joint wage determination with joint union-employer determination of regional (or, in open-hearth steelmaking, national) base rates and plant-level determination of incentive payments, capped by binding arbitration. In both eras there was a fundamental and stable commitment by both sides to accept wage levels fluctuating automatically with prices through sliding scales. The wage system was directly linked to the ability of the industry and of the firm to pay. At the national level, earnings were linked to movements of product prices. At the plant level, earnings were linked to the individual plant's ability to pay via local determination of incentive tonnage bonus rates, whereby earnings rose or fell with productivity as measured by output per worker. On a daily basis earnings fluctuated with output, and relative earnings could differ widely between plants of different productivity.

Workers at efficient plants made disproportionate gains through productivity improvements arising from learning by doing or piecemeal technical improvements which increased output faster than work loads, an upward ratchet effect that is typical in piecework systems in a context of incremental technical change. Employers were loath to disturb incentive effects by calling for renegotiation of bonus rates at each slight change of process, and bonus earnings therefore drifted upward.[133] Rates were only revised downwards after *major* changes in practice such as the introduction of mechanical charging, hot-metal practice, or tilting furnaces where coordinated central employer control was relatively effective.[134] Hence wide earnings differentials developed between plants of varying efficiency. They also developed *within* plants and between workers of the same grade according to the different productivity of different furnaces or mills in the same plant.

Such arrangements offered significant advantages to employers. The greatest advantage was the downward flexibility of wages in the business cycle, something which employers in other industries have historically found very hard to obtain. In a highly cyclical industry they could reduce their losses in recessions and then recoup them in booms. Relatively high wages were not a great burden to more efficient plants, and the large employers were reluctant to disrupt the incentive effects and peace and harmony of the system for the limited gains of lowering peak wages.[135] If the largest employers had slim incentives for change, the smaller, less efficient firms had nothing at all to gain from revising a tonnage rate system that helped them to stay in business. Any change was likely to push up their wage rates and therefore increase the competitiveness of the biggest firms. Since these smaller firms were also the numerical majority in the national employers' association, there was little likelihood of a strong movement toward wage equalization.

The union perspective was complex and shaped by the occupational structure of the industry and the locus of power within the Smelters' Union. From the 1890s, job structures were dominated by plant-level seniority systems. Horizontal mobility of workers between firms was virtually excluded. Instead, plant-based job ladders only allowed entry at unskilled levels followed by promotion up a hierarchical ladder within a single plant. This system divided the labor market into restricted vertical channels and firmly tied the fortunes of each process worker to a particular plant. The sort of wide differentials between workers within the same plant which we have noted were acceptable to the unions because promotion by seniority led to access by turn to the highest paying machines.

The relative strengths of employers and unions and their strategic roles in creating and perpetuating this structure remain controversial.[136] But whatever the chain of causation, Elbaum and Wilkinson have demonstrated that the wage structure, by relating earnings to plant productivity, could have adversely affected technical progress. Price- and productivity-based earnings eliminated part of the discipline of the market from the tail of smaller producers and inhibited radical restructuring. The direct link between plant productivity and earnings deterred scrapping and new investment because wages rose with technical improvements but stayed low in "obsolete" plants. Wilkinson argues that the system kept wage levels at old plants 20–40% below what they would have been in an industry with leveled earnings. The wage structure increased the possibility for a tail of small producers to cling on, making life difficult for those more efficient producers who wanted to invest in more capital-intensive processes which required a larger market share. It raised the profits of old plants and depressed the profits of new ones and therefore lowered the rate of scrapping and re-equipment and contributed to structural rigidity in the industry. No precise attempts have been made to measure the impact of this phenomenon. Nevertheless, it was clearly a significant factor in the finishing trades, where small producers were prone to enter and leave the industry at different points in the business cycle, utilizing local pools of labor, old plants with low overheads, and imported semifinished steel. The combination of a skilled labor-intensive production process and a wage structure that shielded low-productivity plants may have reinforced the structure of the import/re-export structure of this part of the trade that we noted earlier as a crucial strategic weakness of the British industry on the eve of the First World War.

VIII. Comparative Perspectives

By 1913 Britain had lost its comparative advantage in iron and steel but still retained important competitive strengths. Adverse demand conditions and raw material constraints made it almost impossible for Britain to retain its position as the world's low-cost producer; indeed the adverse movements in the 1890s might well have suggested a grim future for British steel. The British steelmakers' response was twofold: They moved toward the higher-quality end of the market where their reserves of technical skill and ability to produce superior products gave them a residual strength. At the same time, constrained by limited demand they generally took advantage of new technology insofar as it was appropriate and innovated vigorously to overcome resource constraints where necessary. The Northeast coast witnessed highly sophisticated adaptation to changing raw material opportunities, and in shipplates, special steels, and high-quality finished products Britain retained a product and technical superiority. Nevertheless, the picture was a checkered one and there were many question marks over the future, particularly since the fundamental issue of a long-term, viable, low-cost steelmaking base remained in doubt.

This perspective casts doubts on interpretations which locate the roots of later decline in this period. Elbaum, for example, argued that: "the British steel industry had surrendered world leadership and entered a spiral of competitive decline from which it has never fully recovered. The U.S. and German industries, on the other hand, had grown from infancy to an international prominence that they maintained, to a lesser degree, a half-century later."[137] In fact the pattern of decline was not decisively set by World War I. Although the roots of structural fragmentation and institutional rigidities that became increasingly important in the history of the industry can clearly be traced back to the prewar period, they were not yet as powerful as they were to become later;[138] the forces of market and raw material constraints were more central. In this context, the U.K. retained much competitive power, and a great deal of the German advance before the war was proably not sustainable. It was heavily based on (over)production of crude products and was vulnerable to demand shifts away from basic Bessemer toward higher-quality steels. Germany's success owed something to technical superiority and innovation, but more to market organization backed by the state through tariffs and legal and institutional support for cartels. Broader political constraints ruled out any possibility that British competition might be bolstered by state intervention or the strategic use of tariff protection.[139] In the absence of more fundamental changes of this sort, British firms framed strategies within the existing constraints that they faced.

Later developments cast an interesting light on this period. Ingvar Svennilson has shown that, controlling for changes in territorial boundaries, between 1913 and 1936–37, British iron and steel grew more rapidly than German (2.1% per annum compared with Germany's 1.3%.).[140] German steel's sluggish performance occurred despite opportunities for reorganization and modernization after the First World War that were unmatched in Britain. At the end of the war, Stinnes and others were able to take advantage of cash windfalls, resulting from the compulsory sale of German properties in Lorraine to France, to undertake massive re-equipment. Opportunistically using what amounted to government subsidies, German steelmakers were able quickly to replace the plants outside its borders with new plants on an enlarged scale. By the mid-1920s German steel capacity, within reduced boundaries, was 40% above 1913,[141] and the American consultants, H.A. Brassert and Co., concluded in 1925 that the loss of the Lorraine connections was a blessing in disguise, facilitating a more rapid transition toward open-hearth steelmaking and modernization.[142]

At the same time, the German steel industry, according to Feldman, "stood at the forefront of German industry's use of the inflationary pressures and incentives to rebuild its plant and recapture its markets." Most German iron and steel concerns came through the postwar inflation without debts and with modernized plants thanks to "the miracle of the paper mark," which enabled them to undertake massive self-financed reconstructions and ignore the unparalleled squeeze on domestic consumption which made it possible. Inflation proved a greater blessing for the steel industry than the deflation of the victors.[143] These events, followed by the collapse of Stinnes' overblown amalgamation schemes, paved the way for an unencumbered giant merger (the Vereinigte Stahlwerk—"Vestag") to emerge from the debris of financial groupings.

Modernization and rationalization were also facilitated by the receipt of huge sums of money from U.S. bankers in the mid-1920s. According to Alfred Chandler, because the managers' plans made sense to foreign investors in terms of increasing productivity per worker and per unit of capital, and because they were drawn up to be carried out by experienced steelmakers, the Germans had little difficulty in finding funds, primarily in the United States, to pay for these changes. Thus "where Vestag was able to raise more than $100 m . . . British steel firms had problems in raising $5 m to rationalize and update facilities."[144] Clearly the U.S. banks were great admirers of German management, but far more important was the broader political and economic context of the flood of U.S. loans to Germany under the Dawes Plan after 1925. Between 1925 and 1930, U.S. private bankers lent $3 billion to German borrowers, compared with the $1.3 billion Germany received under the Marshall Plan after the Second World War.[145] Foreign lending played a key political role for the U.S. government and bankers since it enabled foreign countries to pay their debts while maintaining high tariffs and low taxes at home.[146] U.S. businessmen were afraid of lending to potentially competitive industries like chemicals, but Dillon Read had little difficulty in raising massive funds for a "noncompeting" industry like steel. The form of the giant trust that Vogler and others created undoubtedly owed much to an eye to American finance. The aim was to create a creditor which would be viewed with confidence in the United States. Outright merger was perceived to be a precondition for American finance,[147] and, according to Feldenkirchen, the Vestag merger might well have stalled on internal doubts and conflicts of interest but for the powerful incentive of available U.S. finance.[148]

Thus the exogeneous conditions for modernization and reorganization were remarkably favorable. Vestag emerged with a wonderfully modern plant, but its technically admirable installations were often economically unviable. It suffered from what Harold James has called "technical hubris," an irrational pursuit of bigness without adequate attention to the question of markets which exacerbated the effects of the Depression.[149] Vestag suffered from an immense burden of fixed costs and grew more slowly than its smaller rivals like Mannesmann and Hösch, who rationalized, specialized, and diversified.[150] Most of its technical improvements came during the war and inflation; thereafter there was rationalization but little modernization. Most of Vestag's rationalization involved massive closure of plants, contraction, the reallocation of work, plant specialization, and administrative reorganization. Between 1925 and 1933 Vestag closed 14 of its 23 blast-furnace plants and 12 out of 20 of its steel plants.[151] Nevertheless, it was not able to overcome the problems of overcapacity and stagnation. It therefore, as Feldman described it: "faced an extremely abrupt reckoning with the structural problems that had been veiled by prewar prosperity and the inflationary reconstruction."[152]

Once the inflation was over, Germany generally had a low rate of technical change, and overcapacity led to desperate dependence on exports in the absence of new market outlets at home. High fixed costs in the 1920s forced up domestic prices and necessitated the restoration of tariffs and international cartels in 1925. Only the "AVI agreement," which established rebates on German iron and steel used in exports, persuaded the machine-building industry to accept being cut off from cheaper imported steel by the tariffs. Severe overcapacity between 1927 and 1934 and desperate attempts to cut costs precipitated serious confrontations with labor. In the 1930s German steel stagnated and there was little modernization. Of 418 rolling mills that existed in 1938, 300 had been built before the First World War, 100 in 1918–29, and only 18 after 1929. In 1950 the average German rolling mill was 42 years old. The contrast with the U.K.'s catch-up and partial modernization in the 1930s is striking, and Germany, for instance, now lagged far behind Britain in the introduction of the continuous strip mill.[153]

Germany also remained excessively dependent on basic Bessemer steel, which could not provide the modern high-quality steel increasingly required. In the 1930s German basic Bessemer steelmakers focused on the quest for "Siemens-Martin parity," the attempt to produce steel of similar quality to the open-hearth using the basic Bessemer process. The postwar reconstruction facilitated the rapid advance of the open-hearth process in Germany, and after 1900 it was only in the areas of minette ores (which could *only* be used for basic Bessemer) that basic Bessemer capacity was expanded. Nevertheless, the legacy of basic Bessemer expansion was weighty. In the Second World War, Germany suffered acutely from this. The imported ores for its open-hearth steel were interrupted, pushing it back into reliance on its basic Bessemer sector, which used ores found within the Reich. But basic Bessemer was not of adequate quality for the most important requirements of the war economy, resulting in critical production bottlenecks.[154]

British steel companies in contrast had no similar opportunity for "clean slate" re-equipment. They were impeded by debt and lacked ready sources of outside finance. Their scattered industrial structure increasingly became an obstacle to coordinated reorganization. Nevertheless, it was a contingent and not predetermined matter that a major tidewater relocation of Scottish industry did not occur in the late 1920s. Instead many very good second-best projects were completed (notably at Corby, Ebbw Vale, Shotton, and Clydebridge). In interwar conditions it is not at all clear that the British industry was not more prudently managed and better run than the German.[155]

Even after the Second World War, the legacy of the British steel industry was still sufficiently dynamic and vigorous to contain the potential for success in the postwar boom. Vigorous modernization after the war was feasible, and the strengths of the industry were still great. Effective re-organization by nationalization, or restructuring and investment to take advantage of new opportunities, could have produced a very different outcome. The factors that explain the postwar decline may have had long historical roots, but that decline was not predetermined even by 1945. Nor was Germany's success. The war, postwar reconstruction, and Marshall Plan aid, however, gave German steel a second major chance for industrial reconstruction. This time Germany took better advantage of its opportunities.

NOTES

I would like to acknowledge the helpful comments of Takamoto Sugisaki, Etsuo Abe, Alfred Chandler, Bernard Elbaum, and Carol Heim.

1.   Sir John Clapham, *An Economic History of Modern Britain, Vol. III: Machines and National Rivalries, 1887–1914* (Cambridge, 1938, pp. 68–72); Duncan L. Burn, *The Economic History of Steelmaking, 1867–1939: A Study in Competition* (Cambridge, 1940); T.H. Burnham and G.O. Hoskins, *Iron and Steel*

in Britain, 1870–1930: A Comparative Study of the Causes which Limited the Economic Development of the British Iron and Steel Industry (London, 1943).

2.   David S. Landes, *The Unbound Prometheus: Technological Change and Industrial Development in Western Europe from 1750 to the Present* (Cambridge, 1969); Derek H. Aldcroft, "The Entrepreneur and the British Economy, 1870–1914," *Economic History Review,* vol. 17 (April 1964): 113–34.

3.   Donald N. McCloskey, *Economic Maturity and Entrepreneurial Decline: British Iron and Steel, 1870–1913* (Cambridge, 1974). The quotation is from p. 125; Robert C. Allen, "International Competition in Iron and Steel, 1850–1913," *Journal of Economic History,* vol. 39 (December 1979): 911-37. Allen developed a similar picture of constrained entrepreneurship but argued that vigorous entrepreneurship could have overcome British disadvantages.

4.   Bernard Elbaum, "The Steel Industry before World War I," in Bernard Elbaum and William Lazonick (eds.), *The Decline of the British Economy* (Oxford, 1986), pp. 51–81 esp. pp. 53 and 54.

5.   Peter Temin, "The Relative Decline of the British Steel Industry, 1880–1913," in Henry Rosovsky (ed.), *Industrialization in Two Systems: Essays in Honor of Alexander Gerschenkron* (New York, 1966), pp. 140–59; McCloskey, op. cit., pp. 40–41; Elbaum, op. cit., pp. 58–59; Allen, op. cit., p. 935.

6.   Robert C. Allen, "International Competition and the Growth of the British Iron and Steel Industry, 1830–1913," Ph.D. diss., Harvard University, 1975, pp. 177–80.

7.   According to Steven Webb, "Tariffs, Cartels, Technology and Growth in the German Steel Industry, 1879–1914," *Journal of Economic History,* vol. 40, no. 2 (June 1980): 310, German tariffs "were redundant in many cases . . . because Germany produced steel cheaply enough to export." German steel tariffs averaged 20% ad valorem after 1879 and the U.S. average was 30% after 1861.

8.   Burn, op. cit., pp. 101–15; similar gaps existed for other products, see Allen, op. cit. (1975), pp. 393–98; James Cecil Carr and Walter Taplin, *History of the British Steel Industry* (Cambridge, Mass., 1962), pp. 199, 242; Gerald D. Feldman, *Iron and Steel in the German Inflation, 1916–23* (Princeton, 1977), p. 30.

9.   Allen, op. cit. (1975), pp. 393–98.

10.   Erich Maschke, "Outline of the History of German Cartels from 1873 to 1914," in F. Crouzet, W. Chaloner, and W. Stern (eds.), *Essays in European Economic History, 1789–1914* (London, 1969), p. 255.

11.   Wilfried Feldenkirchen, "Concentration in German Industry, 1870–1939," in Hans Pohl (ed.), *The Concentration Process in the Entrepreneurial Economy since the Late 19th Century* (Stuttgart, 1988), p. 125.

12.   The machine-building industry and firms like Siemens and AEG found that unless they were vertically integrated with the steel producers they could not secure raw materials at reasonable prices. (Gerald D. Feldman and Ulrich Nocken, "Trade Associations and Economic Power: Interest Group Development in the German Iron and Steel and Machine-Building Industries, 1900–1933," *Business History Review,* vol. 49, no. 4 (Winter 1975): 420–23, 428.

13.   Feldman, op. cit., pp. 30–32; Gerald D. Feldman, "The Collapse of the Steel Works Association, 1912–1919. A Case Study in the Operation of German 'Collective Capitalism'" in Hans-Ulrich Wehler (ed.), *Sozialgeschichte Heute: Festchrift fur Hans Rosenburg zum 70sten Geburtag* (Gottingen, 1974), pp. 576–78.

14. Sidney Pollard and Paul Robertson, *The British Shipbuilding Industry, 1870–1914* (Cambridge, Mass., 1979), pp. 44–45.

15. For continuing British success in highly finished wire products, see J.R. Fisher and A. Smith, "International Competition in the Australian Wire Market, 1880–1914," *Business History*, vol. 22, no. 1 (January 1980).

16. C. Knick Harley, "Skilled Labour and the Choice of Technique in Edwardian England," *Explorations in Economic History*, vol. 11 (Summer 1974): 397–402.

17. The proportion of the trade producing different qualities is hard to ascertain: in 1896 in South Wales the tinplate industry used 25% Bessemer steel at the low end and 64% open-hearth and 10% wrought iron at the high end (Carr and Taplin, op. cit., p. 115). The quality divide in tinplate ran back to the iron era with its high-quality "charcoal bars" and cheaper "coke bars." Open-hearth steel substituted for the former and basic Bessemer for the latter.

18. Walter E. Minchinton, *The British Tinplate Industry: A History* (Oxford, 1957), pp. 36–38; open hearth's principal advantages over Bessemer were smaller losses in conversion, fewer imperfections, and a smoother surface that required a smaller quantity of coating material.

19. Kenneth Warren, *The British Iron and Steel Sheet Industry Since 1840: An Economic Geography* (London, 1970), p. 107.

20. Feldman, op. cit. (1974).

21. United Nations Economic Commission for Europe, *Comparison of Steel-Making Processes* (New York, 1964), pp. 2–3.

22. Elbaum, op. cit., pp. 54–55. As late as 1905 the U.K. made 64% of its steel in the open-hearth and the U.S. only 38%. By 1913 the figures were 78% and 68% respectively.

23. Alexander J. Field, "The Relative Stability of German and American Industrial Growth, 1880–1913," in Reinhard Spree and Wilhelm Schroder (eds.), *Historische-Konjunkturforschung* (Stuttgart, 1987), pp. 222–25.

24. B.H. Thwaite, "The Use of Steel in American Lofty-Building Construction," *Journal of the Iron and Steel Institute*, vol. 65, no. 1 (1904): 391–412.

25. Pollard and Robertson, op. cit., p. 47.

26. Peter Temin, *Iron and Steel in 19th Century America: An Economic Inquiry* (Cambridge, 1964), pp. 140–45; Burnham and Hoskins, op. cit., p. 184.

27. Carr and Taplin, op. cit., p. 156.

28. Wilhelm Treue, "Innovation, Know-How, Rationalization and Investment in the German Shipbuilding Industry, 1860–1930," in Hans Pohl (ed.), *Innovation, Know-How, Rationalization and Investment in the German and Japanese Economies, 1868/71 to 1930–80* (Wiesbaden, 1982), pp. 109–12; Pollard and Robertson, op. cit., pp. 39, 47, 285.

29. H.H. Campbell, *The Manufacture and Properties of Iron and Steel* (New York, 1907), p. 2.

30. Burn, op. cit., pp. 182 and 167–82.

31. Ibid., p. 168, esp. footnotes 3 and 4. His figures are pulled out from a couple of passing references in trade literature.

32. Ibid., p. 169–72.

33. Ibid., p. 181.

34. McCloskey, op. cit., pp. 63–67.

35. Burn, op. cit., p. 172, stresses that it is not appropriate to compare exist-ing price relations between Lincolnshire and Cleveland pig for this reason.

36. T.P. Colclough, "The Constitution of Blast-Furnace Slags in Relation to the Manufacture of Pig Iron," *Journal of the Iron and Steel Institute*, vol. CXXXIV (1936): 547–86.

37. Peter L. Payne, *Colvilles and the Scottish Steel Industry* (Oxford, 1979), pp. 70–71.

38. Carr and Taplin, op. cit., p. 101.

39. Colclough refers to NESCO anonymously, op. cit., p. 560.

40. A. Windsor Richards, "Manufacture of Steel from High-Silicon Phosphorus," *Journal of the Iron and Steel Institute* (1907), Part 1, esp. pp. 104–8 and the discussion on his paper pp. 106-12; Carr and Taplin, op. cit., p. 215.

41. Burn, op. cit., pp. 169, 172; F.W. Harbord, "The Thomas-Gilchrist Basic Process, 1879–1937," *Journal of the Iron and Steel Institute*, vol. 136, no. 2 (1937): 85–86.

42. Burn, op. cit., p. 169.

43. The authoritative American consultants H.A. Brassert & Co. concluded in a 1929 survey that the disadvantages of Midlands ores, notably their irregu-larity and heavy slags, made production of good quality steel "impossible by ordinary means." H.A. Brassert & Co., *Report to Lord Weir of Eastwood on the Manufacture of Iron and Steel in Scotland* (Unpublished report, Chicago, 16 May 1929), pp. 53–55.

44. J. Rankin and J. Wright, "The Ternary System $CaO\text{-}Al_2O_3\text{-}SiO_2$," *American Journal of Science*, vol. 39 (1915): 58.

45. W. McCaffery et al., "Composition of Blast Furnace Slags," *American Institute of Mining and Metallurgical Engineers, Technical Publication No. 19* (1927); W. McCaffery et al., "Viscosity of Blast Furnace Slags," *American Institute of Mining Engineers, Technical Publication*, no. 383 (1931).

46. Colclough, op. cit., pp. 547–86.

47. See the discussion on Colclough's paper, ibid., pp. 574–86.

48. Ibid., p. 576.

49. Ibid., p. 583. The German Mannesmann Co. was developing an effective, though more costly, method of dealing with these ores through basic duplexing. In 1931, Brassert reported that "its wider adoption in [Germany] is more than probable." H.A. Brassert & Co., "Proposals of Stewarts and Lloyds for Steel Manufacture in Northamptonshire as Basis for Re-organisation of British Tube Industry" (Unpublished report, Stewarts and Lloyds Ltd., June 1931). In the end, however, Colclough's work was the basis for the two major basic Bessemer plants of the 1930s at Corby and subsequently at the Hermann Göring steelworks in Germany. For further details on the Corby project, see Steven Tolliday, *Business, Banking and Politics: The Case of British Steeel, 1918–39* (Cambridge Mass., 1987), pp. 221–31.

50. McCloskey's transport cost calculations are sound, but as we have seen, his use of prices of Lincolnshire Foundry pig iron No. 3 as a proxy for the price of basic pig iron produced from Midlands ores is invalid. It was unusable for the manufacture of basic steel because of its high silicon content, and its price bears no determinate relationship to that of basic pig iron.

51. East Midlands ores were also relatively low in phosphorus for basic Bessemer production. This could be solved through the use of phosphoric

additives, but these were expensive and would have seriously compromised the prospects of low-cost steelmaking.

52. I. Lowthian Bell, *Principles of Manufacture of Iron and Steel* (London, 1884), p. 338; Campbell, op. cit., p. 120, 508.

53. Allen, op. cit. (1975), p. 360; Allen, op. cit. (1979), p. 925–26.

54. The saving would be approximately 5s per ton at 1906–13 average prices.

55. E. Bertrand, "The Practice of the Combined Open Hearth Process of Messers Bertrand and Thiel," *Journal of the Iron and Steel Institute*, vol. 51, no. 1 (1897): 137–39; Paul Kupelweiser, "On the Manufacture of Basic Steel at Witkowitz," *Journal of the Iron and Steel Institute*, vol. 44, no. 2 (1893): 7–8, 11–13.

56. Bernard Elbaum, "Industrial Relations and Uneven Development: Wage Structure and Industrial Organization in the British and U.S. Iron and Steel Industries, 1870–1970," Ph.D. diss., Harvard University, 1982, p. 301, Table 8.

57. McCloskey, op. cit., pp. 71–72; Carr and Taplin, op. cit., pp. 216–17.

58. McCloskey, op. cit., p. 71.

59. Allen, op. cit. (1979), pp. 936–37; Robert C. Allen, "Entrepreneurship and Technical Progress in the Northeast Coast Pig Iron Industry, 1850–1913," *Research in Economic History*, vol. 6 (1981): 50.

60. Gordon Boyce, "The Development of the Cargo Fleet Iron Co. 1900–1914: A Study of Entreprencurship, Planning and Production Costs," *Business History Review*, vol. 63, no. 4 (Winter 1989).

61. On the impressive achievements of Lysaght's Normanby Park works in this respect, see Warren, op. cit., p. 111.

62. Elbaum, op. cit. (1986), pp. 72–73.

63. McCloskey, op. cit., p. 70.

64. Michael Flinn, "Scandinavian Ore Mining and the British Steel Industry, 1870–1914," *Scandinavian Economic History Review*, vol. 2 (1954): 38–40.

65. Jeremiah Head, "Scandinavia as a Source of Iron Ore Supply," *Journal of the Iron and Steel Institute*, vol. 45, no. 1 (1894): 51.

66. "Iron Ores," *Journal of the Iron and Steel Institute*, vol. 1 (1890): 189.

67. W. Brugmann, "Progress and Manufacture of Pig Iron in Germany since 1880," *Journal of the Iron and Steel Institute*, vol. 62, no. 2 (1902); R. Karlbom, "Sweden's Iron Ore Exports to Germany, 1933–34," *Scandinavian Economic History Review*, vol. 13, no. 1 (1965): 67–69; Martin Fritz, *German Steel and Swedish Iron Ore, 1939–45* (Gothenburg, 1974).

68. Harm Schröter, "Risk and Control in Multinational Enterprise: German Businesses in Scandinavia, 1918–39," *Business History Review*, vol. 62, no. 3 (Autumn 1988): 425–27; only three German firms secured direct ownership links (Dortmund Union, Bochum, and Hösch), see Burn, op. cit., p. 157.

69. Head, op. cit., pp. 47–77, quote from Bell in discussion on p. 69.

70. Hjalmar Lundbohm, "On the Iron Ore Deposits of Kirnavaara and Luossavaara," *Journal of the Iron and Steel Institute*, vol. 2 (1898), esp. discussion pp. 124–25; Carr and Taplin, op. cit, p. 191.

71. Alfred Chandler, *Scale and Scope: The Dynamics of Industrial Capitalism* (Cambridge, Mass., 1990), p. 284.

72. On the £2 million Dunderland Iron Ore Co. venture in Norway in the

decade before 1914, see Flinn, op. cit., pp. 42–45.

73. McCloskey, op. cit.; Allen, op cit. (1975, 1979); Elbaum, op. cit. (1982), esp. pp. 260–26.

74. After 1900 in Germany, open-hearth steel generally attracted a premium of 2 to 5s extra per ton on top of quoted prices because of its superior quality (Burn, op. cit., p. 112).

75. Carr and Taplin, op. cit., p. 53.

76. McCloskey, op. cit., pp. 94–125.

77. Robert C. Allen, "The Peculiar Productivity History of American Blast Furnaces, 1840–1913," *Journal of Economic History*, vol. 37 (September 1977): 605–33, esp. p. 606.

78. Peter Berck, "Hard Driving and Efficiency: Iron Production in 1890," *Journal of Economic History*, vol. 38 (December 1978): 879–900, esp. p. 880.

79. Allen concludes that the main sources of the productivity spurt in the United States were not technical innovations but growth in the average product of fuel "and that improvement was specific to the United States for the simple reason that the Europeans had already taken advantage of the source of growth." Allen, op. cit. (1977), p. 622.

80. Berck, op. cit., pp. 892–93.

81. Carr and Taplin, op. cit., p. 153.

82. Harold C. Livesay, *Andrew Carnegie and the Rise of Big Business* (Boston, 1975), pp. 88–89.

83. Berck, op. cit., p. 880.

84. See, for example, the detailed comparison of Bell Bros.' Clarence furnaces with the Edgar Thompson works by Lowthian Bell. *Journal of the Iron and Steel Institute*, special volume, 1890.

85. A common confusion is that the use of large amounts of raw materials per ton of output should increase the incentive to mechanize handling apparatus. In fact, large volumes of material require the furnace to undertake increased reduction and therefore to work more slowly. The slower working of the furnace restricts the rate of charging. Hence manual charging was adequate for the throughput demands of blast furnaces working on lean ores. Rich ores meant that the blast furnace became hungrier for raw material, inducing the adoption of mechanized charging.

86. Cf. Axel Sahlin, "The Economic Significance of High Silicon in Pig Iron for the Acid Steel Process," *Journal of the Iron and Steel Institute* (1901), describing his work in the U.S. industry.

87. Allen, op. cit. (1981), Appendix 2.

88. Alexander Field, "Land Abundance, Interest/Profit Rates and 19th century American and British Technology," *Journal of Economic History*, vol. 43, no. 2 (June 1983): 412–13. This conclusion is very similar to that of Carr and Taplin, op. cit., pp. 51–53.

89. Carr and Taplin, op. cit., p. 171.

90. Ibid., p. 193. When demand warranted, this output could be stretched by hard driving. In 1912 one of the Cardiff furnaces attained 2,800 tons per week, probably the largest output of any furnace in Europe at the time.

91. Burnham and Hoskins, op. cit., pp. 296–97.

92. Allen, op. cit. (1981), p. 45; Burnham and Hoskins, op. cit., p. 146.

93. Carr and Taplin, op. cit., p. 209.

94. National Federation of Iron and Steel Manufacturers, *Annual Statistics,* various years.

95. In 1913 the U.K. produced 1.2 m tons of wrought iron, accounting for 12% of total iron and steel production. Germany produced only 210,000 tons or 1%. The persistence of this sector was *not* a sign of backwardness. The wrought iron sector in the United States maintained its level of output and the German sector grew from the 1890s to 1914. Wrought iron retained numerous special uses, notably in shipbuilding or rolling stock for wet cargoes where it resisted corrosion better than steel; in chains and cables; and horseshoes. There was considerable modernization and technical improvement in wrought iron in the 1890s.

96. A furnace making forge or foundry iron has only half the output it would have if *the same furnace* were changed over to making basic or hematite iron (Burnham and Hoskins, op. cit., p. 147). The U.K. exported over 1 million tons per annum of foundry pig iron before World War I, with around 25% of this going to Germany.

97. On the peculiarities of the Scottish coal/iron sector see Tolliday, op. cit., pp. 83–85.

98. It should also be noted that the German figures exaggerate weekly output since U.K. figures are annual figures divided by 52 while German figures are annual figures divided by "number of furnace weeks in operation," (Allen, op. cit. (1981), p. 45). Since it was common for a blast furnace to be out of commission for an average of 5–8 weeks per year for repairs and relining over its life, the German average is perhaps inflated by some 10%.

99. Geoffrey Tweedale, "Transatlantic Specialty Steels: Sheffield High-Grade Steel Firms and the U.S.A., 1860–1940," in Geoffrey Jones (ed.), *British Multinationals: Origins, Management and Performance* (Aldershot, 1986), p. 75.

100. Geoffrey Tweedale, *Sheffield Steel and America: A Century of Commercial and Technological Interdependence, 1830–1930* (Cambridge, 1987), pp. xii–xiii.

101. A.L. Levine, *Industrial Retardation in Britain, 1880–1914* (London, 1967), p. 40; Burnham and Hoskins, op. cit., p. 185.

102. Tweedale, op. cit. (1987), pp. 46–57.

103. Ibid., pp. 60–61.

104. David Hounshell, *From the American System to Mass Production, 1800–1932* (Baltimore, 1984), pp. 218–19.

105. Tweedale, op. cit. (1987), p. 100.

106. Ibid., pp. 87–126; Tweedale, op. cit. (1986); Mira Wilkins, *The History of Foreign Direct Investment in the United States Before 1914* (Cambridge, Mass., 1989), pp. 255–64.

107. Tweedale suggests that there were also neglected opportunities for Sheffield to tap U.S. and European high-income markets by linking Sheffield's technical prestige to consumer marketing, rather as the Swiss and some German regions did with edge-tools and knives. Tweedale, op. cit. (1987), pp. 167–80.

108. Carr and Taplin, op. cit., p. 160.

109. Jonathan Zeitlin, "Between Flexibility and Mass Production: Product, Production and Labour Strategies in British Engineering, 1880–1939," in C. Sabel and J. Zeitlin (eds.), *Flexibility and Mass Production: Towards a History of Industrial Possibility* (forthcoming); S.B. Saul, "The Market and the Develop-

ment of the Mechanical Engineering Industries in Britain, 1860–1914," *Economic History Review,* vol. 20, no. 2 (1967): 110–30.

110. Boyce, op. cit.

111. Carr and Taplin, op. cit., pp. 59–60; Burn, op. cit., pp. 57–58. On important design innovations in flexible rolling-mills designed to deal economically with lesser standardization, see L.D. Whitehead, "The Continuous Rolling Mill," *Proceedings of the Staffordshire Iron and Steel Institute* (1924–25).

112. H.J. Skelton, "The Competitive Outlook for the British Iron Trade," *Iron and Coal Trades Review,* 13 June 1900; A. Ladd Colby, "Comparison of American and Foreign Rail Specifications," *Journal of the Iron and Steel Institute,* vol. 71, no. 3 (1906).

113. J. Puppe, "Rolling Mill Practice in the U.S.," Part 1, *Journal of the Iron and Steel Institute,* 1912, Part 2 *JISI,* 1913 gives the perspective of German firms on U.S. practice.

114. Carr and Taplin, op. cit., p. 209.

115. Carr and Taplin's analysis concludes that this was reasonable: "A clear case could not be made that it (the by-product oven) was more profitable than the beehive oven." op. cit., p. 154.

116. British Iron Trade Association, *Annual Reports;* Carr and Taplin, op. cit., p. 210.

117. Carr and Taplin, op. cit., pp. 159–60 and 214.

118. D. Selby-Bigge, "The Development of Electricity in the Iron and Steel Industries with Special Reference to its Latest Application to Reversing Rolling Mills of High Power," *Journal of the Iron and Steel Institute,* vol. 68 (1907).

119. J. Lamberton, "Electric Power in Rolling Mills," *Journal of the Iron and Steel Institute* (1913), pp. 293–314.

120. Walter Dixon in discussion in *Journal of the Iron and Steel Institute* (1912), p. 248.

121. Burnham and Hoskins, op. cit., p. 79; Burn, op. cit., pp. 11–12; Charlotte Erickson, *British Industrialists: Steel and Hosiery, 1850–1950* (Cambridge, 1959), p. 42.

122. P.W. Musgrave, *Technical Change, the Labour Force and Education: A Study of the British and German Steel Industries, 1860–1964* (London, 1967).

123. Cf. Tariff Commission, *Report on the Iron and Steel Industry* (London, 1904).

124. Tweedale, op. cit. (1987), pp. 32–33.

125. Harry Brearly, *Knotted String: The Autobiography of a Steelmaker* (Sheffield, 1941), p. 145.

126. Tweedale, op. cit. (1987), pp. 58–59.

127. Michael Sanderson, "The Professor as Industrial Consultant: Oliver Arnold and the British Steel Industry, 1900–1914," *Economic History Review,* 2nd Series, vol. 31 (November 1978).

128. Edgar Jones, *A History of GKN, Volume 1: Innovation and Enterprise, 1759–1918* (London, 1987), pp. 320–21.

129. See *Journal of the Iron and Steel Institute,* passim; Carr and Taplin, op. cit., pp. 51–53.

130. Sanderson, op. cit., p. 598.

131. In Germany too, however, science-based research clustered in firms which produced the most complex steels, notably the Krupp laboratories.

72   S. Tolliday

132. Bernard Elbaum and Frank Wilkinson, "Industrial Relations and Uneven Development: A Comparative Study of the British and American Steel Industries," *Cambridge Journal of Economics*, vol. 3 (1979); Frank Wilkinson, "Collective Bargaining in the Steel Industry in the 1920s," in Asa Briggs and John Saville (eds.), *Essays in Labour History, 1918–39* (London, 1977).

133. By the 1920s there was a tendency for earnings to run away with technical changes; but this was less marked before 1914 (Wilkinson, op. cit.).

134. Elbaum, op. cit. (1982), pp. 149–50.

135. Big innovations in steelmaking after 1900 such as Talbot furnaces and the introduction of hot-metal practice were usually accompanied by renegotiation of bonus rates. Partly for this reason, in 1908 the larger employers rejected proposals for an industry lock-out to introduce tonnage rates that would decrease on a regressive basis with output (Elbaum, op. cit. (1982), p. 152).

136. H.A. Clegg, A. Fox, and A.F. Thompson, *A History of British Trade Unions since 1889*, vol. 1 (Oxford, 1964), pp. 21–23; Elbaum, op. cit. (1986), pp. 69–71; idem (1982), pp. 150–55, 163–64.

137. Elbaum, op. cit. (1986), p. 51.

138. Tolliday, op. cit.

139. A.J. Sykes, *Tariff Reform in British Politics, 1903–13* (Oxford, 1979).

140. Ingvar Svennilson, *Growth and Stagnation in the European Economy* (Geneva, 1954), p. 120. In 1913 Britain produced 7.6 and Germany 17.32 million tons of finished steel; in 1937 the respective figures were 12.9 million and 19.8 million. Thus Britain produced 43% of German output in 1913 but 65% in 1937. Unlike Svennilson's figures, quoted in the text, these are not adjusted for territorial changes.

141. Ibid., pp. 124-25.

142. H.A. Brassert & Co., "Report on the Properties of GBAG, Deutsch-Luxemburg and Bochumer Verein to Dillon Read & Co," 15 December 1925 (Baker Library, Harvard University).

143. Feldman, op. cit. (1977), pp. 4, 214, 385.

144. Chandler, op. cit., p. 561.

145. William C. McNeil, *American Money and the Weimar Republic: Economics and Politics on the Eve of the Great Depression* (New York, 1986), p. 2.

146. Paul Tiffany, "Opportunity Denied: The Abortive Attempt to Internationalize the American Steel Industry, 1903–29," *Business and Economic History*, vol. 16 (1987); McNeil, op. cit., p. 41.

147. Wilfried Feldenkirchen, "Big Business in Inter-War Germany: Organizational Innovation at Vereinigte Stahlwerk, IG Farben and Siemens," *Business History Review*, vol. 61 (Autumn 1987): 421.

148. Feldenkirchen, op. cit. (1988), p. 125.

149. Harold James, *The German Slump: Politics and Economics, 1924–36* (Oxford, 1986), pp. 146–47.

150. Feldenkirchen, op. cit. (1988), p. 125–26.

151. James, op. cit., pp. 149–52; Feldenkirchen, op. cit. (1987), p. 425.

152. Feldman, op. cit. (1977), p. 12.

153. Svennilson, op. cit., p. 131; on the British catch-up see Tolliday, op. cit., esp. pp. 18–156.

154. Alan Milward, *The German Economy at War* (London, 1965), pp. 182–84; Fritz, op. cit., pp. 93–94.

155. For this period, see Tolliday, op. cit.

Comment

Takamoto Sugisaki

Professor Tolliday's detailed and stimulating paper succeeds in casting new light on the causes and course of the "decline" of the British iron and steel industry. His well-fabricated logic illuminates the pattern of comparative advantage between Britain and Germany. At the same time, he is rather polemic in his emphasis on the excellence of British technical power, its particular demand pattern, and its natural resources, with which Tolliday defends British industrialists from the traditional criticism of their being entrepreneurial failures.

Before raising any questions, we should review a brief history of the works published in Japan on the decline of the British iron and steel industry before World War I. Keiichirō Nakagawa suggested that the shift of puddling into open-hearth furnaces caused the organizational structures of steel production in Britain to become small and fragmented.[1] Tsuneo Mori emphasized the gradual development of private companies into joint-stock companies that had weak liaisons with the banks.[2] Etsuo Abe showed the organizational failure in top management of the British iron companies.[3]

Tolliday supports his ideas of the shift of comparative advantage mainly through a detailed study of metallurgical and technical factors, but on the other hand, within a limited space, the relation of corporate strategy and institutional factors, which constrained transformations from one stage to another in industrial and business structure, might become obscure. No evidence against his cogent metallurgical explanation is at hand, but still I am doubtful. How far can we define the comparative advantage from cost performance in a world market under the pressure of German dumping? On which territory should the factor of natural resources be considered, only in Great Britain or in the empire as a whole? Did British manufacturers really recognize the problem fully? Did they choose rationally? Was there not any way to break through the adverse factors systematically? These questions are examined in turn below.

73

First, why did British industrialists not make the most of the British formal and informal empire in order to change demand patterns and secure needed raw materials? On the demand side, low-grade products were exported to the colonies and South America. The British railmakers, however, did not try to sharpen their competitive edge, but to reconcile and harmonize among nations under the international restrictive practices. IRMA (International Railmakers' Association) was organized by the initiative of the British railmakers in 1884, when Britain's quota of export was 60% in the world market. After interruptions of two decades between 1886 and 1904 and of World War I, this cartel was re-organized each time with the participation of newly developing countries. As a result, the quota for Great Britain in 1935 decreased at the bottom to 23.05%.[4] As for raw materials, Britain was able to invest overseas directly, e.g., in Spanish mining concerns. Tolliday discusses Britain's investment in orefields, an important subject that needs further study.

Second, even in England there were some mergers and integrations of companies, such as Dorman Long with Messrs James & Brothers, Bedson Wire Co., Bell Brothers, and North Eastern Steel Co. Why couldn't such vertical integration be developed further? Were there not any restrictive practices among companies? What constrained vertical integration in Britain is open to question. And why were so many old and small types of furnaces still in use even just before World War I? Can such anachronisms be explained simply by market and wage structures?

Third, why did Tolliday, who has expert knowledge of shopfloor organization, not examine at length the issue of industrial relations? He refers to wage structure and the collective-bargaining system in an allusion to Wilkinson's study, but does not go further.[5] I expected him to discuss the internal labor market structure of the industry thoroughly. The absence of managerial control with the advent of subcontracting, the effect of the 1905 agreement on the wage structure, and the delayed introduction of technological innovations were all related to each other.

Finally, as Tolliday indicated, the very concept of the "decline of an industry" may be debatable. Is it a decline, to shift from larger-scale production of more common grades to various kinds of high-grade steel? Was the shift of comparative advantage inevitable? And how did environmental and institutional factors influence the transformation of the industry?

NOTES

1.   Keiichirō Nakagawa, "Daifukyōki no Igirisu Tekkōgyō (The British Iron and Steel Industry during the "Great Depression")," in *Igirisu Keieishi* (Business History in Great Britain) (Toyo, 1986), ch. 4.

2.   Tsuneo Mori, "Teikokushugi-dankai no Sangyō Kōzō: Tekkōgyō (The Industrial Structure in the Stage of Imperialism: The Iron and Steel Industry)," in *Teikokushugiron*, vol. 2 (British Imperialism), S. Endo, ed., ch. 3, 2–2.

3.   Etsuo Abe, "Igirusugata Keiei Soshiki no Kansei: Tekkō Kigyō, Bolckow, Vaughan Co. Ltd. no Top Management Soshiki (The Failure of British Business Organizations: The Case of Top-Management Organization in Bolckow, Vaughan Co., Ltd.)," in *Meiji Daiguku Keiei Ronshū* 32–3 (1984).

4.   Takamoto Sugisaki, "Senkanki ni okeru Kokusai Tekkō Cartel to Igirisu Tekkōgyō (British Steel Industry and the International Steel Cartel between the Two World Wars)," in *Tsuda College Kokusai Kankei Kenkyū* 16 (1989).

5.   Frank Wilkinson, "Collective Bargaining in the Steel Industry in the 1920s," in *Essays in Labour History 1918–1939*, Asa Briggs and John Saville, eds. (London, 1977), ch. 4.

The Growth of the American Steel Industry, 1865–1914: Technological Change, Capital Investment, and Trade Policy

Paul F. Paskoff

Between the end of the American Civil War and the beginning of the First World War, steelmaking in the United States developed from a small, almost insignificant, branch of the iron industry into the largest industry of any kind in the world. As the steel industry's size—measured in terms of tons of steel produced, numbers of workers employed, and millions and then billions of dollars of capital mobilized—rapidly increased, the industry's organization and technology affected almost every sector of the American economy and profoundly influenced the political life of the nation. At the same time, however, political decisions concerning tariffs and, later, antitrust policy exerted a powerful influence on the industry. Especially with respect to the tariff, a special relationship between the industry and the federal government was sought and cultivated by steel producers. What emerged from this relationship and from that between government and the railroad, petroleum, and other industries was a new American political economy.

I. The Economics of Production

Steelmaking in the United States was of relatively little importance prior to 1860 and output that year was negligible compared to the 700,000 to 900,000 gross tons of pig iron made in the nation's furnaces.[1] However, progress during the years immediately after the war was significant and by 1867 steel output had risen to about 20,000 gross tons. Three years later, the nation's steel furnaces produced almost 69,000 tons.[2] During the next 30 years, steel production grew dramatically, reaching just under 1,250,000 tons in 1880, about 4,300,000 tons in 1890, and over 10,180,000 tons in 1900.[3] In 1913, the American steel industry made more than 31,300,000 tons, which represented about 42% of the world's total output.[4]

The Bessemer process was the basis of the steel industry's rapid growth and development from the 1860s until shortly after the turn of the century. More than 80% of the nation's steel in the 1880s was made using it and, even in 1907, half of all steel output came from Bessemer works.[5] But after 1890 the Bessemer process's relative importance diminished as it was eclipsed by the open-hearth process which accounted for just over 513,200 tons in 1890 and almost 3,400,000 tons in 1900.[6] By the 1880s, almost all steel made in the United States was either Bessemer or open-hearth steel. The triumph of these new technologies entailed capital investment on a scale never before known to the industry. These new capital requirements, the drive to realize lower costs through integration, and the desire for stability and rationality in the markets helped to spur the organization of large steel corporations and the subsequent centralization of corporate power through consolidation within the industry during the last quarter of the nineteenth century.[7]

It was probably the fairly centralized demand from an increasingly consolidated railroad industry that first persuaded iron producers to adopt the Bessemer process. Construction of new track and replacement track for worn-out rails, almost halted during the Civil War, revived almost immediately after the war. The revival was something of a revolution, with its origins in the war years, as the railroad corporations embraced the steel rail in preference to the long-used iron rail.[8]

The first Bessemer steel rails rolled in the United States were made in 1864 at Wyandotte, Michigan.[9] The postwar railroad boom in the United States greatly increased demand for both iron and steel rails, and railmakers were quick to respond. In 1873, American mills rolled about 795,000 gross tons of rails, of which only about 115,000 tons were steel. That modest beginning for steel rails was quickly surpassed when the Bethlehem Steel Company and Andrew Carnegie's Edgar Thompson Works began large-scale production of steel rails.[10] By 1877, output of steel rails exceeded that of iron rails by almost 90,000 tons (386,000 tons of steel rails compared with 297,000 tons of iron rails). Four years later, American rail mills produced about three times as much steel rail as iron rail.[11] During the next two decades, the eclipse of the iron rail by the steel rail proceeded at an accelerated rate. In 1884, production of iron rails was only 23,000 tons, while steel rail output reached 999,000 tons. Iron rail production virtually ceased in 1900, when only 1,000 tons were rolled compared with 2,385,000 tons of steel rails.[12]

Although rails accounted for more of the steel industry's output than did any other single product—as much as 64% in 1884 and 23%

as late as 1900—the industry made a variety of iron and steel products
to meet the demands of post–Civil War residential and commercial
consumers.[13] The diversification and growth of demand for steel and
manufactured steel products stimulated a rapid transformation of the
industry as producers directed their energies and capital toward the
goals of producing more steel and doing so at lower unit costs. Their
success in achieving the former is evident in the output figures presented in Table 1, which compares U.S. steel production with that of the
United Kingdom and Germany, America's two most important competitors in steel during the period 1870–1913. With the exception of
the sharp drop in output associated with the general economic crisis of
1907–8, U.S. production grew without serious interruption throughout
the period. Almost all of this increased output was stimulated and consumed at home and, with the exception of rails, exports of steel were
never significant, amounting to less than 1% of production as late as
1895 and only 6.5% in 1913.[14]

TABLE 1   Steel Output of Selected Countries, 1870–1913 (in millions of gross
tons and as percentages of world total, selected years)

Year	U.K. Tons	%	Germany Tons	%	U.S.A. Tons	%	World Tons
1870	0.22	43	0.13	25	0.04	8	0.51
1875	0.71	40	0.32	18	0.38	21	1.79
1880	1.29	31	0.69	17	1.25	30	4.18
1885	1.89	31	1.20	19	1.71	28	6.19
1890	3.58	29	2.10	17	4.28	35	12.28
1895	3.26	20	3.83	23	6.11	37	16.65
1900	4.90	18	6.36	23	10.19	37	27.83
1905	5.81	13	9.51	22	20.02	45	44.22
1910	6.37	11	12.89	22	26.09	44	59.33
1913	7.66	10	17.32	23	31.30	42	75.15

Source: Derived from Ervin Hexner, *The International Steel Cartel*,
Appendix VI, "World Steel Production 1868–1940, in Millions
of Long Tons," (Chapel Hill, North Carolina, 1943), pp.
324–25.

Much the same point may be made with respect to imports of steel
and even of steel rails. The comparatively insignificant role of imports
in the growth of the aggregate domestic supply of steel prior to 1900,
and even until 1913, has often been attributed to the high protective

tariff duties levied on foreign iron and steel. There is an interesting corollary to this assertion that the tariff effectively barred foreign producers from competing in the American market. Presumably, by insulating American producers from the stimulating effects of foreign competition, the protective tariff subsidized American inefficiency, much to the detriment of the general welfare and the technical progress of the industry.[15] This proposition is inherently untestable, but the historical record suggests that there is reason to doubt its validity.

The data presented in Table 2 for blast furnaces and in Table 3 for steelworks and rolling mills require little explanation. Each table traces the increase in the scale of operations within the steel industry from about the middle of the 19th century until 1914. Immediately apparent from even a cursory inspection of the data is the rapid growth, both relative and absolute, in the size of steelmaking facilities, as measured in terms of capitalization, use of power machinery, including steam engines, and numbers of employees.

TABLE 2 Iron and Steel Blast Furnaces: The Changing Scale of Production, 1849–1914 (selected years)

Year	Number of establishments	Number of wage earners	Primary horsepower	Capital [a]	Wage earners per establishment	Horsepower per establishment	Capital per establishment [a]
1849	404	21,054	—	16,648	52	—	41.21
1859	286	15,927	—	24,673	56	—	86.27
1869	386	27,554	63,900	56,145	71	165.54	145.45
1879	341	41,695	—	89,531	119	—	262.55
1889	304	33,415	248,928	129,547	110	818.84	426.16
1899	223	39,241	497,272	143,159	176	2,229.92	641.97
1904	190	35,078	773,278	236,146	185	4,069.88	1,242.87
1909	208	38,429	1,173,422	487,581	185	5,641.45	2,344.13
1914	160	29,356	1,222,273	462,282	183	7,639.21	2,889.26

[a] Capital and capital per establishment are measured in thousands of dollars.
Source: U.S. Department of Commerce, Bureau of the Census, *Abstract of the Census of Manufactures, 1914*, Table 223, "Summary for Industries: Comparative for the United States, by States for 1914," (Washington, D.C., 1917), p. 640.

TABLE 3   Steelworks and Rolling Mills: The Changing Scale of Production,
1869–1914 (selected years)

Year	Number of establish-ments	Number of wage earners	Primary horse-power	Capital [a]	Wage earners per establish-ment	Horsepower per establish-ment	Capital per establish-ment [a]
1869	422	50,001	—	65,627	118	—	155.51
1879	451	99,103	—	120,374	220	—	266.90
1889	415	137,766	535,430	276,224	332	1,290.19	665.60
1899	445	183,249	1,100,801	430,232	418	2,473.71	966.81
1904	415	207,562	1,649,299	700,182	500	3,974.21	1,687.19
1909	446	240,076	2,100,978	1,004,735	538	4,710.71	2,252.77
1914	427	248,716	2,706,553	1,258,371	582	6,338.53	2,947.00

[a] Capital and capital per establishment are measured in thousands of dollars.
Source: U.S. Department of Commerce, Bureau of the Census, *Abstract of the Census of Manufactures, 1914,* Table 223, "Summary for Industries: Comparative for the United States, by States for 1914," (Washington, D.C., 1917), p. 641.

These gains were accompanied by comparable increases in the levels of capitalization of both blast furnaces and steelworks. The most significant aspect to this pattern of growth in both sectors of the industry is that it occurred even as the number of firms dropped sharply in the blast-furnace sector and leveled off in the steelmaking and fabricating sector. In other words, the steel industry grew intensively, as each installation became more heavily mechanized and capitalized, more than it grew extensively, that is, by additions to the number of firms engaged in production. The character of this intensive growth is made plain when we examine various measures of productivity for the blast-furnace and steelmaking sectors of the industry.

As almost every measure in Table 4 suggests, the growth of pig-iron output was primarily the result of productivity advances. Improvements in blast-furnace design and in furnace equipment permitted the construction of larger furnaces which could make more pig iron and operate at higher temperatures and with greater fuel efficiency. The most direct means of increasing the average furnace output of an individual firm, or of the entire industry, was simply to build new furnaces that were taller in the stack and bigger across the bosh, the widest part of the furnace's interior. Furnaces with larger interior volumes had greater daily capacities, and the construction of the larger furnaces between the late 1870s and the turn of the century yielded impressive results. The largest furnace in 1878 was Andrew Carnegie's "Lucy" which had a stack of just over 70 feet, a bosh of 20 feet, a volume of 15,400 cubic feet, and a daily output in excess of 90 tons.[16] Large furnaces built at the Carnegie Company's works during the 1880s were, on average, bigger than "Lucy" and had daily output capacities that were two and even three times what "Lucy" could manage. By the turn of the century, the capacity of the typical large furnace was almost six times that of "Lucy," about 530 tons of pig iron per day.[17]

TABLE 4 Some Measures of Productivity at U.S. Iron and Steel Blast Furnaces, 1889–1914 (selected years)

| Year | Output [a] | Tons of output per | | | Horse-power | Horsepower per worker | $ Capital per ton of output |
		Estab't.	Furnace	Worker [b]			
1889	7.6	—	—	—	—	7.45	17
1899	13.6	68,161	36,715	387	30	12.67	11
1904	16.5	95,263	42,191	516	23	22.04	14
1909	25.8	137,019	60,897	742	24	30.53	19
1914 [c]	23.3	161,250	57,206	879	21	41.64	20

[a] Output is measured in millions of gross tons (one ton=2,240 pounds).

[b] These are wage earners, that is, production workers.

[c] For reasons discussed elsewhere in the paper, production levels during this year were substantially below those of 1913 when blast furnaces in the United States made almost 31 million tons.

Source: Output figures are from Abraham Berglund and Philip G. Wright, *The Tariff on Iron and Steel* (Washington, D.C., 1929), Appendix B, "Production Data," Table I, pp. 220–21; all other data are from U.S. Department of Commerce, Bureau of the Census, *Abstract of the Census of Manufactures, 1914*, Table 223, "Summary for Industries: Comparative for the United States, by States for 1914" (Washington, D.C., 1917), p. 640.

All of this productivity advance cannot be attributed solely to the increased size of the furnaces. In fact, the erection of progressively larger furnaces in the absence of other critical improvements in design and equipment would have run up against a wall of physically dictated limitations on production, as had already occurred in Great Britain.[18] The solution, pursued in the United States during the early 1870s, lay in the installation of high-pressure blowing engines which almost doubled blast pressures within the furnace from four or five pounds to eight or nine pounds per square inch.[19] The use of more powerful blasts of super-heated air increased the number of cubic feet of air injected each minute into the furnaces. This practice, called variously "rapid blowing," "fast driving," and "hard driving," had the beneficial effect of dramatically increasing pig-iron output, such that a doubling of the blast rate could result in as much as a 50% increase in production.[20]

There were, however, two unfortunate consequences to hard driving. The first of these to be noticed was the higher rate of fuel consumption over that experienced using the standard practice, that is, hard-driven furnaces burned more coke per ton of pig iron produced. The second problem presented by hard driving a furnace was the accelerated rate of corrosion of the furnace's lining as it was subjected to higher temperatures and pressures. One authoritative contemporary estimate of the life of a furnace lining under hard driving was 2.5 years, compared with a 12-year life expectancy for the lining of a standard-practice furnace.[21] Did American furnace operators worry about this result of hard driving and the attendant greater capital expense incurred to re-line the stacks? The answer is no and was almost exuberantly given in 1887 by M.R. Potter of the North Chicago Rolling Mill Company who, comparing the American hard-driven furnace with standard-practice British furnaces, agreed with the view, expressed elsewhere, that "our furnaces lead a short life, but a merry one."[22] His point was that American furnaces could produce more pig iron with greater efficiency than British furnaces could manage in the same time.

Potter's enthusiasm notwithstanding, hard driving initially presented some serious problems, especially when one considers that the cost of re-lining a furnace—estimated by Potter in 1887 to be about $15,000—represented a substantial capital outlay.[23] The problems were, however, solved in the mid-1880s by modifying the internal architecture of the furnace and reducing the temperature of the refractory bricks of the furnace lining by backing it with water-cooled metal.[24] Hard driving and the solutions to the problems it presented entailed progressively higher levels of capitalization, as Tables 2 and 4 indicate. In fact, the capital needed in 1890 for a hard-driven furnace ($253,365) was almost 50% above that required for a standard furnace ($170,125).[25]

Other innovations that contributed to greater furnace productivity took the form of labor-saving machinery such as the skip-hoist for filling the furnace and railroad dumper cars for bringing the inputs from their distant storage areas at the plant to the furnace. These practices were widely used by the mid-1890s[26] and represented a response to the physical problem of sheer scale created by the construction of the larger furnace and increased competition. Much of what has been said, in a general way, concerning productivity advance in the blast-furnace sector of the steel industry is also pertinent to the industry's steelmaking and fabricating sector. The history of the technical progress of this part of the industry is, if anything, better known than is that of the blast furnace and is wrapped in the glamor of names such as Bessemer and Siemens of Europe and Kelly, Holley, and Carnegie of the United States. Not as well known, but of considerable importance, is the steelmaking sector's remarkable record of productivity increases, indicators of which are presented in Table 5.

TABLE 5 Some Measures of Productivity at U.S. Steelworks and Rolling Mills, 1889–1914 (selected years) *

		Tons of output per				
Year	Output a	Estab't.	Worker b	Horse-power	Horsepower per worker	$ Capital per ton of output
1889	3.4	8,000	25	6	3.89	81
1899	10.6	24,000	58	10	6.01	41
1904	13.9	33,000	67	8	7.95	50
1909	24.0	54,000	100	11	8.75	42
1914 c	23.5	55,000	94	9	10.88	54

* All measures are rounded off to the nearest whole unit of measure. Thus, output per establishment is rounded off to the nearest 1,000 tons, output per worker and output per horsepower are each rounded off to the nearest ton, and capital per ton is rounded off to the nearest dollar.

a Output is measured in millions of gross tons (one ton=2,240 pounds) and is rounded off to the nearest 100,000 tons.

b These are wage earners, that is, production workers.

c For reasons discussed elsewhere in the paper, production levels during this year were substantially below those of 1913 when steelworks in the United States made more than 31.3 million gross tons.

Source: For output figures, see Berglund and Wright, *The Tariff on Iron and Steel*, Appendix B, p. 222; all other data are derived from U.S. Department of Commerce, Bureau of the Census, *Abstract of the Census of Manufactures, 1914*, Table 223, "Summary for Industries: Comparative for the United States, by States for 1914" (Washington, D.C., 1917), p. 614.

The progress by steel producers was achieved with two very different technologies, the British-originated Bessemer converter and the newer open-hearth furnace which had been developed in Britain and France. The success of the original Bessemer process—the so-called acid process—in the United States depended initially on the availability of eastern ores with a low phosphorus and sulfur content. After about 1880, the introduction of the "basic process," in which the converter's interior surface was coated with an alkali, effectively neutralized the acidic content of the far more plentiful and economical ore from the Great Lakes ranges. The rapid spread of the Bessemer process in its initial "acidic" form until 1880 and from then until the first years of the 20th century in its "basic" form is traced in Table 6, which also shows the even more rapid adoption by steelmakers of the competing open-hearth process.

TABLE 6 Distribution of Steel Output by Process, 1870–1914 (in gross tons and % of total output for selected years) [a]

Year	Bessemer Process (tons)	(%)	Open-hearth process (tons)	(%)	Total[b] (tons)
1870	38	55	1	1	69
1875	335	86	8	2	390
1880	1,074	86	101	8	1,247
1885	1,519	89	133	8	1,712
1890	3,689	86	513	12	4,277
1895	4,909	80	1,137	19	6,115
1900	6,685	66	3,398	33	10,188
1905	10,941	55	8,971	45	20,024
1907	11,668	50	11,550	49	23,363
1908	6,117	44	7,837	56	14,023
1910	9,413	36	16,505	63	26,095
1913	9,546	30	21,600	69	31,301
1914	6,221	26	17,175	73	23,513

[a] Total percent may not equal 100 due to rounding.
[b] Total includes tonnage produced by the crucible process and all other processes.
Sources: For 1870, 1875, and 1880, see Peter Temin, *Iron and Steel in Nineteenth-Century America* (Cambridge, Mass., 1964), Appendix C, Table C.4, p. 270; for all other years, see Berglund and Wright, *The Tariff on Iron and Steel*, Appendix B, Table II. A, p. 222.

The open-hearth technology became available in the late 1860s and early 1870s and potentially offered three distinct advantages over the Bessemer converter. One was the furnace's ability to use abundant phosphoric American ore to make steels of high quality. Another was the open-hearth furnace's greater fuel economy. The third major advantage of the open-hearth furnace over a Bessemer steel plant was that, because one could build an open-hearth furnace on a smaller scale, its capital cost was 25% to 50% lower. This consideration put the open-hearth process within reach of aspiring steelmakers of comparatively modest means and, therefore, helped to spur its adoption.

Unfortunately, early models of the open-hearth furnace presented two significant problems which limited the technology's appeal. One of these problems was familiar to users of Bessemer converters and involved the acid-induced deterioration of the furnace's interior which, consequently, required frequent re-lining. The other disadvantage to the open-hearth technology was that, for several years after its introduction, the furnaces required charging with solid materials, unlike the Bessemer converter, which took a molten mass. This meant that, unlike the Bessemer converter, the open-hearth furnace had to be hand-charged which entailed higher per-ton labor costs. Both problems were solved by the late 1880s when the inherent advantages of the open-hearth process became evident. As Table 6 indicates, from 1885 until 1910, output of open-hearth steel doubled every five years, while Bessemer steel production slowed and then, after 1913, declined.

Two interesting, but by no means remarkable, aspects to the spread of open-hearth steelmaking in the United States are evident in Table 7. Immediately apparent is the rapid development of the furnace technology, represented here by increases in daily capacity. As late as 1909, less than 14% of American open-hearth furnaces could produce more than 70 tons per day. Five years later, more than 23% of the furnaces had that output capacity. The increase was due to the construction of larger furnaces, the perfection of mechanical charging, and, probably, also to the reduction in the capital cost per ton of output that accompanied the standardization and widespread acceptance of the furnace design. In other words, as operators became more familiar with open-hearth technology, much of the risk that had once characterized open-hearth furnace construction and operation dissipated. This is essentially what the experienced steelman, Charles M. Schwab, said would happen when he predicted the eclipse of the Bessemer process by the open-hearth.[27]

Also clearly indicated in Table 7 is the considerable disparity between open-hearth furnace capacities in the United Kingdom, where the technology originated, and the United States. British furnaces not only tended to be smaller, perhaps because of higher capital costs, but the small design persisted until the outbreak of World War I and put the open-hearth sector of the British steel industry in 1913 behind the level of development reached by American producers at the turn of the century. The American producers' edge over their British counterparts in the adoption and construction of large open-hearth furnaces is, by itself, far from being conclusive evidence against the proposition that the protective tariff encouraged complacency and backwardness in the American steel industry. For that matter, none of the American innovations in furnace construction and operation, including hard driving, or steelmaking methods, or steel plant design by itself can be used to negate the assertion that the tariff subsidized American production inefficiency. When taken together, however, these individual instances of technological progress and productivity advance undermine the proposition.

TABLE 7   Open-hearth Steel Furnaces in the U.K., 1913, and the U.S.A., 1909 and 1914: Number and Percentage Distribution by Capacity Ranges (in gross tons)

Capacity range	U.K., 1913 (number)	(%)	U.S.A., 1909 (number)	(%)	U.S.A., 1914 (number)	(%)
under 50 tons	394	72.2	367	52.0	346	40.0
50–59 tons	115	21.1	137	19.4	189	21.9
60–69 tons	17	3.1	105	14.9	127	14.7
70–79 tons	3	0.5	51	7.2	92	10.6
80–89 tons	3	0.5	44	6.2	43	5.0
90–99 tons	0	0.0	0	0.0	14	1.6
100 tons and over	14	2.6	2	0.3	53	6.2
Total	546	100.0	706	100.0	864	100.0

Source: U.K. figures are derived and adapted from Committee on Industry and Trade, *Survey of Metal Industries: Iron and Steel, Engineering, Electrical Manufacturing, Shipbuilding, with a Chapter on the Coal Industry, Being Part IV of a Survey of Industries* (London, 1928), table, p. 24. U.S. figures are derived from Department of Commerce, Bureau of the Census, *Abstract of the Census of Manufactures, 1914* (Washington, D.C., 1917), Table 71, p. 110 .

There were, of course, other technological developments within the American steel industry that increased steel output and production efficiency. One of the most important, especially in terms of its significance for the years after the war, was the introduction of the use of electrical motors to drive machinery at rolling mills. Although electric power did not come into its own in the steel industry until the mid-1920s, its use increased rapidly before World War I. The 270,000 electrical horsepower put to work in 1914—about 10% of the total installed horsepower at rolling mills in that year—was, by itself, not particularly impressive.[28] More impressive was electrical horsepower's 37.5% share of the industry's total horesepower on line that year. Still more impressive was the substantial increase that this figure represented over that for only ten years earlier when electrical horsepower accounted for only 12.7% of the total.[29] This high rate of growth may seem unusual, but probably it was not. It was more or less duplicated within the rolling mill sector of the industry between 1905, when only 10,600 horsepower of electric main roll drives were installed, and 1914, when electrical horsepower installed that year reached 42,775.[30]

Not surprisingly, the spread of the innovation of electric power within the steel industry did not proceed without setbacks. An electric motor's initial cost before any of it was recovered through use was roughly three times that of a steam engine of comparable power.[31] As was true of any substantial capital outlay, investment in electric drives for rolling mills was acutely sensitive to the fluctuating business conditions within the industry. The influence of the state of the larger economy on the timing of new installations of electromotive power for rolling mills was only one manifestation of a more general relationship among capital investment in steelmaking facilities, steel output, and the business cycle.

Charles M. Schwab, president of the Bethlehem Steel Corporation, alluded to this relationship in the course of his extensive testimony before the Committee of Ways and Means of the House of Representatives on December 15, 1908. According to Schwab, the useful term of service of a blast furnace was five years, during which time it would be used intensively. Thereafter, it would be torn down in favor of a newer, better model.[32] Although this ferocious pace of depreciation probably was not characteristic of the steel industry as a whole, it was generally so of the larger firms, such as U.S. Steel and Schwab's own concern, Bethlehem Steel. Its effect was to spur the adoption of best-practice techniques by important segments of the industry that were intent on improving the quality and increasing the quantity of their output without incurring higher unit costs. Known as the "American practice," this effort to realize greater and greater efficiency through modernization had its precedent in the hard-driving furnaces of the last decades of the 19th century. It involved the scrapping of "anything from a steam engine to a steel works whenever a better piece of apparatus was to be had, no matter whether the engine or works was new or old" and "involved the expenditure of enormous sums of money."[33]

The goad to this Schumpeterian process of "creative destruction" was primarily domestic competition as American firms fought one another in ever larger, consolidated forms during the 1880s and 1890s in an effort to dominate a rapidly growing home market. Upon the formation of the United States Steel Corporation in 1901 the economic and political environment in which the industry operated fundamentally and irrevocably changed. Still, even after 1901, large integrated concerns, such as Bethlehem Steel, were organized and existing ones, such as Republic Steel, thrived, as firms, large and small, continued to pursue and adopt innovative production methods. The persistence of this corporate behavior probably was driven by continuing competition and the changing character of demand due to the requirements of automobile manufacturers and the rapidly expanding use of structural steel forms. The combined effect of these influences was to urge ever higher levels of capital expenditure, though the course of investment was anything but smooth.

Just as the introduction of electromotive power reflected business conditions within the industry, the level of overall investment in steel-making facilities fluctuated, as did output and production capacity, with the ebb and flow of the business cycle and, after 1907/08, declined as the pace of overall economic activity slowed.[34] This is only what one would expect in view of the complexity and magnitude of the physical plant necessary for steelmaking. For example, the average cost of a new blast furnace installed at a U.S. Steel Corporation works in 1902 was just under $400,000.[35] Capital improvements on this scale were major undertakings, even for a corporation as large as U.S. Steel, which spent that year almost $9.75 million on additions and improvements to its iron and steel manufacturing plants alcne.[36]

The behavior of capital investment in new power technology and in the primary production technologies of the Bessemer and open-hearth processes was only one facet of a complex set of responses by steel producers to their industry's larger operating environment. Considerations other than the economics of production informed their decision-making between the wars, and none was more powerful than the highly charged perennial debate over the protective tariff. This was politics, though hardly politics pure and simple.

II. The Tariff and the Political Economy of Steel

The campaign for and against protection after the Civil War had its roots in earlier campaigns that had been waged with varying degrees of incivility since 1789. Until the Civil War, protectionists had become much more familiar with defeat than with victory. Secession and the outbreak of fighting in 1861 meant an end to southern opposition to and obstruction of protectionist legislation and the speedy passage of a succession of higher tariffs, culminatig in a rate of 47% in 1869. This protectionist victory was built on a prewar foundation of support for protection among northern and western congressional delegations which continued through and after the war, thanks in large part to the energetic efforts of the American Iron Association. Founded in 1855 and re-organized in 1864 as the American Iron and Steel Association (AISA), the organization was the iron and steel industry's very effective lobby in Congress.

By 1873, tariff rates were still protectionist, but they had fallen from their high levels of 1869. The decline reflected the Republican Party's preoccupation with the political rehabilitation of the defeated southern states, the party's general political difficulties, and probably also a degree of complacency within the industry because of the postwar business boom. The eruption of the Panic of 1873 shattered the complacency and stimulated new calls for protectionism. The result was a succession of tariff acts aimed at discouraging importations of foreign, especially British, iron and steel products. And yet, as Table 8 indicates, these laws imposed progressively lower duties in terms of dollars on pig iron and steel. However, in part because of the changing international price structure for key products, especially steel rails, low nominal rates actually amounted to considerable ad valorem duties. This was especially true of the most important steel product of the day, steel rails. The per-ton rate on these, although sharply down to $20.16 from the $28.00 level, nevertheless gained ground in ad valorem terms because of a decrease in the price of British steel rails.

Further offsetting the reduction of the specific duty on rails, and the reduction on pig iron as well, was the natural tariff imposed by geography on importers who had to charge a price for their product high enouver to the cost of shipping it to the Pittsburgh region, which, by 1890, produced about 40% of the nation's pig iron and steel.[37]

TABLE 8 Duties on Specific Products under the Various Tariff Acts,
1883–1913

Product [a]	Tariff Act of					
	1883	1890	1894	1897	1909	1913
Iron ore						
Rate in $	0.75	0.75	0.40	0.40	0.15	free
Ad valorem % rates						
Initial rate	33	30	30	30	6	0
Final rate	30	50	30	17	4	0
Pig iron						
Rate in $	6.72	6.72	4.00	4.00	2.50	free
Ad valorem % rates						
Initial rate	48	40	23	22	16	0
Final rate	40	36	22	24	11	0
Steel rails						
Rate in $	20.16	13.44	7.84	7.84	3.92	free
Ad valorem % rates						
Initial rate	61	34	54	35	18	0
Final rate	79	62	35	29	16	0
Structural shapes						
Rate in $	1.25	0.90	0.60	0.50	0.40	10%[b]
Ad valorem % rates						
Initial rate	89	63	35	26	31	10
Final rate	98	65	24	32	28	10
Tinplate						
Rate in $	1.00	2.20	1.20	1.50	1.20	15%[b]
Ad valorem % rates						
Initial rate	29	76	50	68	42	15
Final rate	29	83	51	57	38	15

[a] The duties on iron ore, pig iron, and steel rails were in terms of dollars per
gross ton (ton=2,240 pounds); the duties on structural shapes and tinplate
were in terms of dollars per hundred pounds.
[b] The duties on structural shapes and tinplate were computed on an ad valorem basis under the act of 1913.
Source: Adapted from Berglund and Wright, *The Tariff on Iron and Steel*
(Washington, D.C., 1929), table, p. 110.

Thus, in order to get foreign rails to the center of domestic rail production, from which the foreign and domestic varieties would have
equal access to the lucrative railroad construction market, an importer
would have had to charge enough to absorb a trans-Atlantic freight bill

of about $2.50 to bring one ton from Great Britain to Philadelphia and an additional railroad freight charge of $5.00 per ton to transport it from there to western Pennsylvania.[38]

The competitive advantages bestowed by a somewhat fickle Congress in 1883 and a more faithfully protectionist geography on most American iron and steel producers did not quiet their demand for greater tariff protection. With the exception of iron-ore and pig-iron producers (again, see Table 8), they got much of what they wanted and more than they could reasonably have hoped for when Congress passed a tariff bill in 1890, called the McKinley Tariff after its energetic sponsor, Congressman William McKinley, an Ohio Republican who was destined for greater things.

One should bear in mind, when considering the rates of the protective tariffs, that their decrease from 1878 to 1883, and from 1883 to 1890, as well as subsequent reductions in 1913, occurred while production and export levels generally increased and while imports of competing foreign iron and steel products generally decreased or at least failed to increase appreciably. This curious lack of a demonstrable relationship between the health of the domestic iron and steel industry, on the one hand, and the erosion of tariff rates, on the other, did not go unnoticed by opponents of protectionism and even became a source of embarrassment for a handful of the industry's leaders who admitted that large segments of the industry no longer needed protection.

As early as 1882, the iron and steel pioneer and then congressman, Abram S. Hewitt, conceded to the U.S. Tariff Commission that in his opinion, "everybody admits that the duty upon steel is out of all reason."[39] Not quite everybody. Although the case for a protective tariff on iron and steel was no longer self-evident in 1882, the industry could still make it without undue embarrassment. By 1890, the difficulty of doing so had significantly increased. Steel ingot and rail producers found themselves in an especially awkward position. The need to maintain the strength of AISA, which was then conducting a strenuous campaign for increased rates, moved them to support the lobby's position, even as the volume and efficiency of their production had all but driven imports from the domestic market.

Both protectionists and their opponents invoked the national interest, patriotism, and the welfare of the American worker to support their respective positions, which amply demonstrates the truth of the dictum that a fact is a double-edged sword. The protectionists warned that congressional action to lower tariff rates would force producers to reduce costs by imposing sharp wage cuts on their workers. The basis for their assertion was the pronounced and long-standing disparity between American wage levels and the generally lower wages paid to British iron and steel workers.[40] This emphasis on comparative wage rates had figured prominently in AISA's lobbying effort for higher tariff duties in 1871. That year, the organization's annual report to its members informed them of a resolution passed at its annual meeting which warned that a lessening of protection for American industry would inevitably disrupt the national economy because industrial workers would be "thrown into idleness or into agriculture."[41]

Such arguments became more forceful and more sophisticated as the industry matured. By early 1894, as the general economy slid further into an acute depression, bound up, as had been the crisis of 1873–78, with systemic problems within the railroad industry, important segments of the iron and steel industry suffered. Steel-rail production was particularly hurt and anticipated the general contraction by about three years as rail output declined in response to a falling off of orders from railroad corporations.[42] Production had peaked in 1887 when the mills had rolled more than 2.1 million tons. After a drop of almost 30% over the next two years, production had climbed to almost 1.9 million tons in 1890. Thereafter, however, output had fluctuated along a generally descending path and had bottomed out at a little more than a million tons in 1894.[43] Significantly, the railmakers turned to foreign markets to find buyers of rails which they could not sell at home. Their tactic was almost certainly the very one of which they had so loudly complained for decades and which they had so often cited before Congress in support of their demand for a high tariff: they dumped their surplus abroad in the hope of sustaining prices at home.[44]

The severe conditions of the depression were the backdrop in early 1894 for the U.S. Senate's consideration of a tariff bill named for its sponsor, William Lyne Wilson. The Wilson bill called for substantially lower general rates and could not have come up at a more difficult time for protectionist forces. Less than two years earlier, Henry Clay Frick had precipitated the Homestead Steel strike by Andrew Carnegie's workers and had engineered their bloody defeat and the destruction of their union. The strike and its suppression were still fresh in the minds of the public and many members of Congress and had won the industry few friends. The nation's money supply was once again the subject of impassioned debate by partisans, both informed and lunatic, and the economy was about to enter the second debilitating year of the depression that had begun the previous May. These were some of the considerations at work on the Senate as a Democratic congress began to consider the Wilson bill.

As had been congressional practice for almost fifty years when tariff legislation was pending, the Senate's Finance Committee in December 1893 had sent out a detailed questionnaire on business affairs to "merchants, manufacturers, and producers" to learn their views concerning the most appropriate tariff rates for a large number of specific goods.[45] The members of committee could not have been surprised by the lines along which the responses divided.

Even in the 1820s, the iron industry had split more or less cleanly, but not amicably, on the issue of a protective tariff.[46] In the years after the Civil War, a much larger iron and steel industry had perpetuated the pattern. Primary producers, that is, the producers of basic products such as pig iron, steel rails, and structural iron and steel, had long called for as much tariff protection as they thought they might be able to induce Congress to provide. Secondary producers, or manufacturers of wrought (bar) iron and hardware, and importers of the products made by the primary producers were generally anti-protectionist. Before the Civil War, even the great railroad corporations, because of their preference for British iron and, later, steel rails, were often to be found on the side of the anti-protectionists.[47] More recently, however, the interlocking of directorates between steel corporations and railroad corporations and the latter's dependence on the former as shipping customers had converted the railroads into fervent believers in protectionism.

For the most part, the iron and steel industry sang a paean to the virtues of protectionism which, to naive members of its audience, must have seemed miraculous for a near perfect harmony, marred only by the dissonance of some secondary manufacturers and a few mavericks among the primary producers. R.T. Crane, president of the Crane Iron Company of Chicago, was one of the latter. He responded to the Senate's questionnaire with a blunt essay in which he dismissed the necessity and even the desirability of continued high tariff rates for iron and steel. Ridiculing the purported connection between tariff rate reductions and reductions in wages, he observed that "in any event, low wages mean cheap goods."[48] He reserved his harshest comments for his fellow producers who had "not been forced by competition to work out the economies that are accomplished in other lines."[49] Moreover, if they were not "nearly ready for free trade [their businesses] must be in incompetent hands, and they should certainly no longer be more than moderately protected."[50] Although other

voices within the industry echoed Crane's opinions concerning production efficiency, his anti-protectionist view was not widely held and,
even as late as the mid-1890s, was far outside the industry's consensus
on the tariff.

Far more representative of the opinions of producers were those
which blamed "the continued and unprecedented tinkering with the
tariff" for the depression.[51] The remedies proposed by these critics of
the Wilson tariff bill varied greatly in tone, ranging from the intemper-
ate to the almost clinically dispassionate, but all advocated defeat
of the bill and most urged a prolonged period during which the
McKinley Tariff's rate structure would remain in force and unchanged.[52]
Perhaps the most succinct expression of these sentiments was that
offered by the pig-iron producer, Clare, Duduit & Co. of Ohio, whose
recommendation was, simply, "Kill the Wilson bill."[53] No less caustic
was the concluding observation to a long reply by the venerable
Cambria Iron Company of Johnstown, Pennsylvania. Founded in 1850
and capitalized in 1893 at $14 million, Cambria was a vertically inte-
grated firm of considerable importance as a producer of pig iron and
steel rails and, also, as a member of AISA. The Senate Finance
Committee could not have failed to recognize that Cambria's views
represented those of a significant part of the industry. After asserting
that no "civilized country has adopted free trade," Cambria's statement
closed by saying that "[g]enerally the affairs of nations have been managed by men of affairs, and no country other than the United States
has ever given control of its fiscal legislation to theorists."[54]

Such sentiments and the producers' thinly veiled threats to slash
wages if tariff rates fell did not persuade. In August 1894, Congress
passed the Wilson-Gorman Tariff, the additional name on the act
being that of Senator Arthur Gorman of Maryland. Thanks to his tinkering with the Wilson bill's proposed rate structure and his maneuver-
ing of the revised bill through the Senate, the tariff that went to
President Grover Cleveland for his signature was not the rate-slashing
measure that Senator Wilson had intended it to be. Comparing the
tariff legislation that bore his name to the bill that he had drafted,
Wilson asked, "Is this a government by a self-taxing people or a government by trusts and monopolies?"[55]

Wilson's irritation had been aroused by the special protection given
to the sugar trust by the Wilson-Gorman Tariff. He could at least derive
some measure of satisfaction from the act's treatment of the iron and
steel industry. Tonnage rates and their ad valorem equivalents suffered
deep cuts (see Table 8) which, according to the industry's jeremiads,

should have had a profoundly harmful effect on domestic iron and steel production. They did not. One reason behind the lack of effect of the rate reductions of 1894 was that the fall in American pig-iron and rail prices from their high levels in 1880 had been accompanied by little change in British prices, thereby narrowing the international price disparity and severely eroding the competitive position of British products. In fact, beginning in 1894, imports of British pig iron, steel rails, and steel ingots and castings fell off sharply. Of course, this dramatic decline had to do, in part, with reduced American demand arising from depressed domestic business conditions. But, as many producers pointed out, the foremost cause of decreased American demand for foreign iron and steel, as well as of falling American prices, was the fierce competition among domestic producers as they struggled for shares of a market awash in surplus production.[56] A spokesman for the Spang Steel and Iron Company of Pittsburgh put it well, saying that foreign competition was not a problem for the firm. Rather, the challenge came from "the home competition" which had driven prices down "to such a point that it keeps out foreign goods such as we make."[57]

Severe domestic competition had arisen primarily because production capacity had expanded faster than demand. As we have already seen, this rapid growth of capacity had occurred because of the industry's technological advances and its mobilization of progressively greater concentrations of capital. The resulting fierce competition stimulated further efforts to increase productivity and operational efficiency by all segments of the industry, including small merchant blast furnaces as well as large integrated steel firms.[58] The Cambria Iron Company found the domestic competition "so severe that it [had] enforced the utmost economy of production . . . not only by reduction of wages, but by activity of invention in improving machinery and large outlays of capital in the improvement of plant."[59] The larger Illinois Steel Company of Chicago experienced equally harsh conditions and reported that the most striking feature of its operating environment had been the reduction in the per-ton cost of labor due to "an absolutely marked decline in all wages, the end of which it is impossible to foresee."[60] The company attributed the drop in unit labor costs partly to reductions in wages and the cost of raw materials, but found that "by far the greatest decrease [had] been brought about by improved methods of manufacture, by the introduction of automated machinery, by development of new processes by which waste and loss have been saved, and by economies of various kinds."[61]

The continuing introduction of new techniques and equipment was the other reason for the American steel industry's immunity to foreign competition in its home market, despite the lower rates of the Wilson-Gorman Tariff. The new and well-placed confidence of major American steel men was evident in Joseph Wharton's testimony in 1894 before the House of Representatives, which was considering the then-pending tariff legislation of that year. Wharton, president of Bethlehem Steel Company, the forerunner of the Bethlehem Steel Corporation, was blunt, almost arrogant, as he told the congressmen:

We are not pleading the baby act. We have grown to a stature where we can fight our own battles, and we merely demand of our legislatures to give us a fair showing [that is, the lowest necessary tariff rate] and let us in on equal terms.[62]

The American market remained the preserve of domestic producers during the rest of the 1890s, through the depression and the recovery from it that began in 1897. In that year, the newly inaugurated president, William McKinley, called for a new tariff with somewhat higher rates to generate needed revenue for the federal government. Congress quickly obliged that year with the Dingley Tariff which held most rates on iron and steel products at their Wilson-Gorman levels, but raised the duty on tinplate, the manufacture of which the McKinley Tariff of 1890 had specifically (and successfully, as it turned out) sought to stimulate (see Table 8).[63] This solitary instance of post-1880 tariff protection having nurtured a nascent branch of the steel industry strengthens rather than weakens the argument that the late 19th-century tariff on iron and steel products was largely unnecessary after 1880.[64] Certainly, it was unnecessary by the late 1890s, the years when the first great wave of business consolidations got under way and began to transform the steel industry and much of the general economy of the United States.

The great merger movement, and even its culmination within the steel industry in 1901 when the United States Steel Corporation was organized, did not end the calls by producers and AISA for tariff protection.[65] By then, of course, AISA's declaration of only a decade earlier that "Protection is the enemy of trusts" was embarrassingly anachronistic.[66] The lobby's point had been that protection insured the maintenance of competition against the ever more pronounced tendency within the industry toward agglomeration and, if only for a brief interval, there had probably been some truth to AISA's assertion.

By keeping out dumped foreign iron and steel, the tariff likely permitted small, unconsolidated firms, such as merchant blast furnaces, to find their niche in the domestic market as suppliers of pig iron and more specialized products to larger firms. The next ten years, however, were a period of expansion for many firms and consolidation of many of them into still larger concerns. By 1901, many of the most influential members of AISA were among the nation's largest corporations. That these firms or, for that matter, their industry, should still have required protection from foreign competition is not credible. Why, then, did many of them, including U.S. Steel, and AISA continue to call for high tariffs? Although part of the answer probably has to do with corporate greed or, in less highly charged terms, the drive to maximize market share and profits, the more satisfactory explanation is both more subtle and complex and has a great deal to do with the activities of U.S. Steel.

As the largest trust or holding company of its day, U.S. Steel dominated the American steel industry. Upon its creation in 1901, it accounted for almost two-thirds of all domestic steel ingot output and considerably greater shares of the industry's manufacture of other steel products, as well as about 29% of worldwide steel output. Its subsidiaries conducted manufacturing in eight states, from Massachusetts to Wisconsin, and mining operations in others. The trust's involvement in the steel markets extended to virtually every product line from primary steel, such as ingots and castings, to finished goods, such as rails and fence wire. Although U.S. Steel's share of domestic steel ingot production fell to just under 54% by 1911, the year the U.S. Department of Justice sought its dissolution under the Sherman Anti-trust Act, the corporation still enjoyed price-fixing power in a large number of product lines, but especially steel rails, for which it had imposed a price of $28 per ton in 1902. Little had changed by 1914 as the anti-trust suit moved tortoise-like through the federal judiciary.[67] On the eve of World War I, U.S. Steel still accounted for more than 50% of steel ingot production and was still able to sustain its $28 price for rails.

The existence of U.S. Steel and about a dozen smaller but still very large firms represented a concentration of capital and production and market power that profoundly altered the character of the industry and the manner in which its constituent firms conducted business. There had obviously been differences in capabilities and behavior between large, integrated firms and smaller, non-integrated concerns even before the merger wave of the late 1890s. But the disparity between the two undoubtedly became more pronounced after the drive for consolidation began. Table 9 presents a comparison of the per-ton total costs and per-ton labor costs incurred by large and small firms in the production of various types of primary steel. It is evident that the larger firms, a grouping which, of course, includes U.S. Steel, enjoyed considerable advantages in total costs and labor costs in every product line. Typically, non-labor costs per ton and total costs per ton for large firms were between 13% and 20% less than they were for small firms. The difference was even greater with respect to per-ton labor costs which for large firms were between 38% and 46% less than for the smaller concerns.

There were three readily identifiable sources of the cost advantage enjoyed by the large firms. In attempting to account for the per-ton labor cost disparity in the production of large Bessemer billets between large and small firms, the Commissioner of Corporations in 1913 emphasized technological change, saying: "The chief cause for [the] difference is probably due to differences in average output per mill, but partly to differences in labor-saving devices."[68] Another reason for the disparity, in this instance having to do with non-labor cost components, undoubtedly stemmed from the very largest firms' and especially U.S. Steel's facilities for railroad and waterborne transportation of iron ore and other raw materials. Finally, there were the advantages that were intrinsic to integration and sheer size—tighter coordination and scheduling of operations, economies of scale, and better facilities.

The advantages that accrued to the larger concerns as a group were, of course, enjoyed by U.S. Steel, the largest of the large firms. Its initial ownership of strategically important ore deposits and coking facilities and its capital depth which enabled it to make acquisitions of additional properties, including the fateful purchase in 1907 of the Tennessee Coal, Iron, and Railroad Company, augmented the benefits to the trust of size and managerial efficiency. Given these advantages, as well as the recovery of prices from their long secular decline during the last third of the 19th century, U.S. Steel could scarcely have avoided the handsome profits which it made during its first decade.

Depending on the cost-accounting method one chooses to employ, the trust's profits were either acceptable or prodigious. In its presentations to various investigative bodies of the federal government, including the Bureau of Corporations from 1911 to 1913 and the Temporary National Economic Commission (TNEC) of the 1930s, the Steel Corporation used the "book cost" for such items as ore, coke, pig iron, and other intermediate goods, all of which were produced and transported by its various divisions or subsidiaries. A consequence of this bookkeeping practice was that the tabulated cost incurred in making steel ingots, for example, was substantially higher than the true cost or "integration cost" to the corporation and, instead, actually approximated the cost borne by much smaller and less integrated firms. The

TABLE 9 Per-ton Cost of Labor in the Production of Selected Steel Products According to Size of Firms, 1902–6 [a]

	All companies	Large companies	Small companies
	Bessemer pig iron		
Output (gross tons)	44,311,530	40,873,250	3,438,280
Labor cost per ton ($)	0.73	0.69	1.26
Total cost per ton ($)	12.10	11.93	14.21
Labor as % of total cost	6.03	5.78	8.87
	Basic pig iron		
Output (gross tons)	9,161,685	8,466,492	695,193
Labor cost per ton ($)	0.60	0.57	1.06
Total cost per ton ($)	11.82	11.65	13.90
Labor as % of total cost	5.08	4.89	7.63
	Bessemer billet ingots		
Output (gross tons)	29,099,783	27,519,174	1,580,609
Labor cost per ton ($)	0.57	0.55	0.89
Total cost per ton ($)	15.47	15.26	19.12
Labor as % of total cost	3.68	3.60	4.65
	Large Bessemer billets		
Output (gross tons)	17,151,389	15,722,275	1,429,114
Labor cost per ton ($)	0.53	0.51	0.76
Total cost per ton ($)	17.90	17.56	21.69
Labor as % of total cost	2.96	2.90	3.50
	Bessemer rail ingots [b]		
Output (gross tons)	15,495,210		
Labor cost per ton ($)	0.55		
Total cost per ton ($)	15.75		
Labor as % of total cost	3.49		

[a] Excludes "transfer profits," i.e., profits tabulated by an integrated concern as a raw (ore or coke) or semi-finished material (pig iron) moved through the concern's system of production from one subsidiary or subdivision of the firm to another. When included with the basic costs of production, they raised the total or "book" cost of production of any product. Such "transfer profits" were generally unavailable to non-integrated firms.

[b] No small companies made Bessemer rail ingots during the period 1902–6.

Source: U.S. Commissioner of Corporations, *Report on the Steel Industry, Part II: Cost of Production, Full Report* (Washington, D.C., 1913), pp. 287, 294, 305, 314, 311.

TABLE 10   Estimated Profits and Rates of Return on Investment of U.S. Steel
in Selected Product Lines, 1910

Product group	Price	Cost of production	Estimated profit	Profit as % of cost	Capital investment	% Rate of return
Bessemer pig	15.50–		5.29–	51.8–		13.6–
iron a	19.90	10.21	9.69	94.9	39.00	24.8
Large Bessemer						
billets	24.00	14.45	9.55	66.1	53.00	18.0
Bessemer rails	27.45	16.67	10.78	64.7	65.00	16.6
Open-hearth						
plates	32.00	22.72	9.28	40.8	83.00	11.2
O-H structural						
shapes b	32.57	22.50	10.07	44.8	79.00	12.7

General note: All dollar amounts represent dollars per-ton.
a The price range given for Bessemer pig iron is conjectural because U.S. Steel
sold little or no pig iron. The price range therefore indicates the probable
bounds within which U.S. Steel would have sold pig iron. Consequently, the
figures for estimated profit, profit as a % of cost, and the % rate of return are
also conjectural.
b The abbreviation O-H stands for "open-hearth."
Source: Adapted   from   figures   presented   in   U.S.   Commissioner   of
Corporations, *Report on the Steel Industry, Part III: Cost of Production,
Full Report* (Washington, D.C., 1913), pp. 527, 529, 530, 532, 533.

contrast between the "book" and "integrated" costs is reflected in Table
9. U.S. Steel's profits and rates of return on investment for specific
products in 1910, a normal business year, are presented in Table 10,
and it is clear that the corporation did very well, well enough to satisfy
Charles M. Schwab's stipulation that "in the manufacture of steel
unless a man can see a profit of 20 or 25 per cent a year he had better
keep out."[69]
    Such profits were undoubtedly beyond the reach of most firms
within the industry and that fact, in conjunction with the great cost
advantages enjoyed by U.S. Steel and other very large steel firms, suggests one reason why, after 1901, the industry increasingly began to
speak with more than one voice on the tariff question. The industry's
structure clearly was very different from what it had been only a
decade before and it would have been surprising had the interests of
large consolidated and integrated firms and much smaller, non-inte-

grated firms coincided. The two groups could still make common cause for the tariff, but the reasons each had for wanting continued protection were no longer the same.

Critics of big business and opponents of the protective tariff on steel often made the same mistake of casting their particular bête-noire in simplistic form. Thus, big steel was a conspiracy of firms run by ruthless, rapacious men whose private interest was inimical to the public good. Similarly, the protective tariff was a tool of these large steel firms to rob small businesses and American consumers by keeping out foreign steel products which, if allowed into the country, would drive down domestic prices. However much truth there was—and there was some—to these charges, the historical record indicates that enough fundamental error attached to each indictment to distort the understanding by contemporaries of the relationship between big steel and the protective tariff.

Charles M. Schwab, appearing on December 15, 1908, before the House Ways and Means Committee on the question of tariff revisions, encountered a considerable body of such thinking when the subject of steel-rail prices came up at the very end of his lengthy testimony. A member of the committee posed a question to which no simple answer was possible and to which no such answer could have been expected from the president of the nation's second largest steel corporation. The congressman, having already been interrupted by Schwab, persisted, saying

> Let me finish my question. And the great corporations are so blended and dovetailed and interwoven together that they, pursuing their various functions, controlling their various interests, combine and plunder the common people? When I say plunder, I mean by charging a higher price than they could without such combination.

At this point, other members of the committee jumped in and demanded of Schwab, "Answer yes or no." Exasperated, he replied, "I give up. I do not even understand the question."[70]

Such moments have not been rare in the long record of congressional committee hearings. What makes this particular colloquy valuable is its conflation of the demonologies of the tariff and big business. To a certain degree, Schwab had encouraged the committee's hostility by his blithe dismissal of the possibility of any collusion among major steel producers to fix prices. For example, when a congressman asked him,

"How does it come about that steel rails have for the last five years remained at $28 [per gross ton] without any collusion with anybody else?", Schwab's reply was disingenuous to the point of bare-faced lying. He assured the committee that the remarkable price stability of steel rails was due to the fact that the $28 price "seems to have been recognized by all rail manufacturers as a fair price, and [one] giving a fair profit" and that any unilateral price reduction would trigger a "steel war" which would ruin all rail makers.[71] When the congressman pressed him to say whether he really believed that "absolute uniformity for the last few years in price [sic] of steel rails at $28 is without agreement", he replied, simply, "Absolutely."[72]

Schwab was similarly certain and unbending when the committee asked him whether American steelmakers could operate successfully without a tariff. He told the committee that if the tariff were reduced, steel companies would have to cut their workers' wages to bring them down to levels comparable to those paid to workers in Great Britain and Germany.[73] This was the traditional argument of AISA and its members, trotted out in late 1908 by someone whose corporation enjoyed a cost structure and rate of return on investment which made the tariff a matter of little direct consequence. Why, then, did Charles M. Schwab seek to perpetuate this view? The answer may well be that, after thirty years' involvement in the steel industry, first at Carnegie Steel, then with U.S. Steel, and, most recently, as head of the company he had created in 1904, Bethlehem Steel Corporation, he still saw the tariff issue in the parochial terms that he had first come to understand it.

When the committee questioned Judge Elbert H. Gary, chairman of the board of U.S. Steel, three days later, he also gave them arguments in favor of a protective tariff. It quickly became evident, however, that Gary had a remarkable view as to the ultimate value of protectionism. Asked if he believed that "the iron manufacturers cannot control the American market without the help of the tariff", he replied with considerable understatement that "the United States Steel Corporation would endeavor to take care of itself; but I think that many, if not most, of our competitors would soon be out of business, and we would have the field." This prompted the logical next question: "Then, from a selfish standpoint, it would be to the interest of the United States Steel Company to take the tariff off?" In his answer to this question, Gary demonstrated the qualities of mind that made him not merely a powerful steel man but an industrial statesman, as well.

You might think so, but I do not think so. I think it would be the worst thing that could happen to United States Steel, because the people would not stand it. We do not want those conditions, and instead of trying to bring about such conditions as that, we have done what we could, fairly and justly, to prevent it and to assist our competitors.[74]

Gary had said essentially the same thing on other, less public occasions. At his celebrated "Gary dinners" in 1907 and 1908, he had advanced the idea of "cooperative competition," by which he meant that U.S. Steel and other major steel firms would agree not to engage in destructive price cutting to undermine one another.[75] Because the winner in any such exercise would necessarily have been U.S. Steel, the latter's restraint must have been deliberate. This suggests that Gary wanted a rationalized competitive environment which would provide U.S. Steel with a shield against an anti-trust suit to which his corporation was vulnerable.[76] Although some members of the committee were not persuaded of Gary's sincerity when he said that U.S. Steel wanted a tariff because it would sustain the corporation's competitors, the historical record suggests that he meant what he said.

The sort of self-restraint, however self-interested, practiced by U.S. Steel required a safety valve by which it could dispose of a part of its prodigious and increasing steel output. Had the corporation attempted to sell domestically all that it produced, the result would have been a collapse of prices and the ruin of its competition. The formation in November 1903 of the U.S. Steel Export Company provided the means by which surplus production could be safely and profitably removed from the domestic market and sold abroad. From the inception of this venture, the corporation intended the opening to foreign markets to be more than merely an arrangement by which to dump steel abroad, though it certainly lent itself to that purpose.[77] From 1904, the first full year of its operation, through the end of 1910, the U.S. Steel Export Company typically accounted for about 80% of all American steel exports and as much as 8% to 10% of U.S. Steel's production.[78]

Irrespective of its purpose, the formal establishment of U.S. Steel's export business and the active interest taken in foreign markets by other large firms, notably Bethlehem Steel, caused considerable domestic controversy. The sharp tone of certain exchanges between congressmen and industry leaders at the House Ways and Means Committee's tariff hearings of 1908 and 1909 was due, in part, to the

belief of many committee members (and, presumably their constituents) that an industry which could sell steel abroad at a lower price
than at home and still make a profit did not need tariff protection
from foreign competition. This point came up repeatedly during the
hearings, and both Gary and Schwab attempted to defuse it when they
testified. Schwab explained, for example, that American steel firms did
not encounter competition from foreign producers of steel rails in this
country because "buyers of rails in this country want to get their rails
from the people who patronize their railroads" even if it meant paying
a bit more than the price of foreign rails.[79] He went on to say that
American rail producers met foreign competition in peripheral markets, "in countries where we [American and foreign rail producers]
have a mutual field of competion—South America, Siberia, or similar
countries."[80]

Gary, for his part, had tried to explain how and why American steel
producers sold some of their products in foreign markets for less than
they sold them in the United States. The question had come up when a
congressman had asked him to account for the flurry of steel exports
to the United States from Germany. Gary said that the German steelmakers were not doing anything untoward. "When business is dull [at
home], they do in Germany what we do here—to keep their mills running and the men employed, they dump the surplus."[81] This portrayal
of the export policy of U.S. Steel as a seemingly expedient tactic rather
than a carefully planned and executed strategy was probably politically
wise but, as we have seen, it was at best a half-truth.

The involvement of U.S. Steel in foreign markets was a part of the
corporation's plan for operating in a domestic market where Judge
Gary's "cooperative competition" prevailed in key product lines. The
firm's support of a protective tariff was stimulated by its realization
that, despite progressive reductions in rates over the preceding
decades, the duties on imports helped it to keep its domestic competitors in business. They were appropriately grateful.[82]

The committee heard other witnesses, including 73-year-old Andrew
Carnegie, to whom it listened with a respect bordering on awe. In the
end, the bill that emerged from its deliberations and went to the new
president, William Howard Taft, in 1909 kept steel products on the
protected list but at substantially reduced rates. For all practical purposes, the battle over tariff protection for steel was over, although the
last salvo was not fired until passage of the tariff of 1913, the so-called
Underwood-Simmons Tariff, which put iron ore, pig iron, and steel
rails on the free list and slashed all other steel rates.

The irony to this protracted struggle over protection was twofold. In the first instance, the opponents of protection during the 1890s and early 1900s were mistaken in their view that it had fostered monopoly. At most, one could have fairly said that, after 1901, it temporarily shielded U.S. Steel from the unwanted attentions of the Justice Department's anti-trust lawyers by sustaining the corporation's smaller competitors. The other ironic aspect to the victory of the anti-protectionists lay in the very timing of their triumph. Long before their legislative victory over the protectionists, the steel industry's material and organizational development had enabled its most important segments and firms to fend off foreign competition without a tariff. Coming when it did, the removal of tariff protection for steel mattered very little, if at all. The steel industry had needed protection in the years before 1880, perhaps as late as 1890, and had fought hard to get it from Congress. But thereafter, because of the industry's continuing technological advances and organizational change, and because of a favorable geography of production, it could have readily dispensed with the tariff. Doing so almost certainly would have improved the industry's political standing at home. The refusal or inability of leading steel firms to take that step was the result of many considerations, including ideological inertia. In the end, however, it proved not to matter. The steel industry had transformed itself and, in the course of doing so, had become suited to the new American political economy of big business and big government which its growth had helped to stimulate.

NOTES

1.   William T. Hogan, S.J., *Economic History of the Iron and Steel Industry in the United States*, vol. I, Parts 1 and 2 (Lexington, Mass., 1971), pp. 6, 11. Unless otherwise stated, all tonnages are given as gross tons. A gross ton equals 2,240 pounds.

2.   Peter Temin, *Iron and Steel in Nineteenth-Century America: An Economic Inquiry* (Cambridge, Mass., 1964), Appendix C, Table C.4, p. 270.

3.   Ibid., Appendix C, Table C.4, pp. 270–71.

4.   Ervin Hexner, *The International Steel Cartel* (Chapel Hill, N.C., 1943), Appendix VI, "World Steel Production 1868–1940, in Millions of Long Tons," pp. 324–25.

5.   Temin, op. cit., Appendix C, Table C.5, pp. 272–73.

6.   American Iron and Steel Association (1880–86), *Annual Statistical Report*, 1940, p. 15 (1887–1900), photostat; see also Temin, op. cit., Appendix C, Table C.4, pp. 270–71.

7. Paul F. Paskoff (ed.), *Iron and Steel in the Nineteenth Century*, a volume in William Becker (gen. ed.), *Encyclopedia of American Business History and Biography* (New York, 1989), p. xxxi.

8. Much of the following discussion of the early production and use of steel rails and other steel products is adapted from ibid., pp. xx–xxi, xxxi.

9. Kenneth Warren, *The American Steel Industry, 1850–1970: A Geographical Interpretation* (Oxford, 1973), p. 93.

10. Output figures are from Temin, op. cit., Appendix C, Table C.6, pp. 274–75. See Warren, op. cit., p. 94, for a discussion of the involvement of the Bethlehem Iron Company and Carnegie Company in the production of steel rails.

11. Temin, op cit., Appendix C, Table C.6, pp. 274–75.

12. Ibid.

13. Hogan, op. cit., chapter 15.

14. Percentages are derived from Abraham Berglund and Philip G. Wright, *The Tariff on Iron and Steel* (Washington, D.C., 1929), p. 126. Exports of American rails were inconsequential until 1897 when they accounted for about 9% of domestic production. By 1904, that proportion had increased to just over 18% but had fallen back to about 13% by 1913. Ibid., pp. 119–20.

15. For a classic statement of this view, see Frank W. Taussig, *The Tariff History of the United States*, 8th ed. (New York, 1931), p. 134.

16. Hogan, op. cit., pp. 232–313.

17. Ibid., p. 213.

18. J.C. Carr and W. Taplin, assisted by A.E.G. Wright, *History of the British Steel Industry* (Cambridge, Mass., 1962), p. 53.

19. Ibid. A figure for the pressure of the hard-driven furnace's blast as high as 17.5 pounds per square inch is given in Robert C. Allen, "The Peculiar Productivity History of American Blast Furnaces, 1840–1913," *Journal of Economic History*, vol. 37, no. 3 (1977): 605–33.

20. Hogan, op. cit., p. 213. For a more rigorous analysis, see Peter Berck, "Hard Driving and Efficiency: Iron Production in 1890," *Journal of Economic History*, vol. 38, no. 4 (1978): 879–900.

21. See Berck, op. cit., p. 884.

22. Quoted in ibid., p. 880.

23. Ibid., pp. 885, 895.

24. Hogan, op. cit., p. 213.

25. Berck, op. cit., Table 1, p. 886.

26. Hogan, op. cit., pp. 214–15.

27. U.S. Congress, House of Representatives, *Tariff Hearings before the Committee on Ways and Means, 1908–1909*, 60th Cong., 2d Sess., 1909, Doc. 1505, "Statement of Charles M. Schwab," December 15, 1908, p. 1669.

28. See Table 3 for the total horsepower installed at rolling mills in 1914 and Hogan, op. cit., vol. II, part 3, p. 434, for the installed electrical horsepower in 1914.

29. Ibid.

30. Eldon S. Hendriksen, *Capital Expenditures in the Steel Industry, 1900 to 1953* (New York, 1978), Table XII, "New Installations of Electric Main Roll Drives, 1905 to 1931 and 1939 to 1945," p. 110.

31. Hogan, op. cit., vol. II, p. 433.

32. U.S. Congress, House, 60th Cong., 2d Sess., op. cit., p. 1669.

33. H.H. Campbell, *The Manufacture and Properties of Iron and Steel*, 4th ed. (New York, 1907), pp. 470–71. Quoted in Bela Gold, William S. Peirce, Gerhard Rosegger, and Mark Perlman, *Technological Progress and Industrial Leadership: The Growth of the U.S. Steel Industry, 1900–1970* (Lexington, Mass., 1984), p. 634.

34. Arthur F. Burns and Wesley C. Mitchell, *Measuring Business Cycles* (New York, 1946), Chart 10, "Frickey's Standard Pattern of Short-Term Fluctuations in American Business Activity, 1866–1914," p. 112.

35. United States Steel Corporation, *First Annual Report to Stockholders of United States Steel Corporation [for 1902]*, April 6, 1903, "Property Account," pp. 15–17. Reproduced in Richard Vangermeersch (ed.), *Financial Accounting Milestones in the Annual Reports of United States Steel Corporation: The First Seven Decades* (New York, 1986), pp. 13–15.

36. Total capital expenditures by U.S. Steel in 1902 were almost $16.8 million. Ibid., p. 15.

37. Berglund and Wright, op. cit., p. 133.

38. Ibid. Freight rates published by railroads during the late 1880s and, especially, the 1890s were notoriously unreliable because of such cut-throat competitive tactics as rebates to large-volume shippers. Still, as Peter Temin has observed, "They are all we have." Temin, op. cit., p. 255. One might reasonably contend that a tariff was necessary only so long as the geographical center or concentration of the U.S. iron and steel industry put producers within inexpensive reach by rail of east coast ports, such as New York, Philadelphia, and Baltimore. This geographical vulnerability had been substantially eliminated by 1890.

39. Quoted in Temin, op. cit., p. 213.

40. This contention by American producers with respect to British wages antedated the Civil War. See Temin, op. cit., pp. 115–16; also see Paul F. Paskoff, *Industrial Evolution: Organization, Structure and Growth of the Pennsylvania Iron Industry, 1750–1860* (Baltimore, 1983), p. 77. For more recent expressions of the same sentiments, see U.S. Congress, Senate, Committee on Finance, *Replies to Tariff Inquiries*, "Schedule C, Metals and Manufactures of," 53d Cong., 2d Sess., 1894 (various report numbers, bulletins, and replies).

41. Hogan, op. cit., vol. I, p. 175.

42. See, for example, Temin, op. cit., pp. 222–23.

43. Berglund and Wright, op. cit., table, p. 119.

44. Ibid., p. 122.

45. U.S. Congress, Senate, *Replies to Tariff Inquiries*, 53d Cong., 2d Sess., Report No. 418, "Circular Letter of Inquiry," p. 3.

46. Paskoff, op. cit., pp. 76–77.

47. Ibid., p. 78.

48. U.S. Congress, Senate, 53d Cong., 2d Sess., *Replies to Tariff Inquiries*, Reply No. 1197, p. 10.

49. Ibid.

50. Ibid.

51. Ibid. See, for example, Reply No. 1223, Bristol Iron and Steel Company; Reply No. 1224, E. & G. Brooke Iron Company; Reply No. 1230, Dunbar Furnace Company; Reply No. 1234, George J. Fritz; Reply No. 1235, Globe

Iron Company; and Reply No. 1300, The Spang Steel and Iron Company. Almost all other replies were in a similar vein.

52. Ibid. These replies were augmented by those of some of the industry's more substantial firms, including Reply No. 1312 of the Colorado Fuel and Iron Company, a pig-iron and steel-rail producer.

53. Ibid., Reply No. 1227.

54. Ibid., Reply No. 1311.

55. Quoted in Page Smith, *The Rise of Industrial America: A People's History of the Post-Reconstruction Era*, vol. 6 in the series *A People's History* (New York, 1984), p. 531.

56. U.S. Congress, Senate, 53d Cong., 2d Sess., *Replies to Tariff Inquiries*, Reply Nos. 1222, 1300, 1311.

57. Ibid., Reply No. 1300.

58. For the strides made after the late 1880s and early 1890s by merchant blast-furnace concerns, see U.S. Department of Labor, Bureau of Labor Statistics, Bulletin No. 474, Miscellaneous Series, *Productivity of Labor in Merchant Blast Furnaces*, December 1928 (Washington, D.C., 1929), especially Appendix 2, "Individual Plant Studies in Early Years."

59. U.S. Congress, Senate, 53d Cong., 2d Sess., *Replies to Tariff Inquiries*, Reply No. 1311.

60. Ibid., Reply No. 1313, p. 28.

61. Ibid., p. 31.

62. Quoted in Temin, op. cit., p. 213.

63. Presumably, the additional protection accorded tinplate makers under the Dingley Tariff was intended to restore some of what the Wilson-Gorman Tariff had stripped away. Under the latter, the duty on tinplate had fallen from the $2.20 per 100 pounds (2.2 cents per pound) provided under the McKinley Tariff (1890) to $1.20 per 100 pounds (1.2 cents per pound). The rate had been only slightly lower—$1.00 per 100 pounds—under the act of 1883, a level generally considered to be virtually non-protective. But during the first full year under the Wilson-Gorman Tariff's lower level of protection, domestic tinplate production had increased from about 74,000 gross tons to 114,000 tons, a gain of 40,000 tons or about 54%. These facts have prompted William Hogan to "wonder how far the [tinplate] industry actually was indebted to the McKinley Tariff." Hogan, op. cit., vol. I, p. 353. He has concluded that although "the tariff gave it impetus . . . this impetus was perhaps more psychological than material." Ibid., p. 355. Output figures are from Berglund and Wright, op. cit., table, p. 131.

64. For two rigorous treatments of the role of tariffs in fostering the growth of the American iron and steel industry see: V. Sundararajan, "The Impact of the Tariff on Some Selected Products of the U.S. Iron and Steel Industry," *The Quarterly Journal of Economics*, vol. 84, no. 4 (1970): 590–610; and Bennett D. Baack and Edward John Ray, "Tariff Policy and Comparative Advantage in the Iron and Steel Industry: 1870–1929," *Explorations in Economic History*, vol. 11, no. 3(1973): pp. 3–23. Sundararajan argues that, during the 1870–1914 period, technological advances and the availability of "new sources of raw materials [p. 604]" more than the protective tariff "were the main factors explaining the prodigious advance of the industry [p. 604]." Baack and Ray are critical of Sundararajan's methodology and conclude that "tariff policy did play a signifi-

cant part in promoting domestic production in the iron and steel industry," especially before 1900 [p. 23].

65. The phrase is from Naomi R. Lamoreaux, *The Great Merger Movement in American Business, 1895–1904* (Cambridge, Mass., 1985). The organization and early years of U.S. Steel, often called, simply, "the Corporation" by federal investigators of the steel industry after 1901, has been the subject of considerable detailed study. Three fine studies of U.S. Steel's role in the industry and larger economy are: ibid.; Gertrude G. Schroeder, *The Growth of Major Steel Companies, 1900–1950*, in *The Johns Hopkins University Studies in Historical and Political Science*, Series LXX, Number 2 (Baltimore, 1953); and U.S. Commissioner of Corporations, *Report on the Steel Industry, Part I: Organization, Investment, Profits, and Position of the United States Steel Corporation* and *Part III: Cost of Production, Full Report* (Washington, D.C., 1911 and 1913).

66. American Iron and Steel Association, *Bulletin*, 23 (October 23, 1889), p. 290, quoted in Hogan, op. cit., vol. I, p. 346.

67. The federal government's attempt to force the dissolution of U.S. Steel ended in March 1920 when the United States Supreme Court upheld the judgment in favor of the corporation of a federal district court in New Jersey. The matter was finally laid to rest that May when the Justice Department's bid for a rehearing of the matter was denied. See Schroeder, op. cit., p. 100.

68. U.S. Commissioner of Corporations, op. cit., Part III, pp. 314–15 and p. 288.

69. U.S. Congress, House, 60th Cong., 2d Sess., *Tariff Hearings*, Doc. 1505, p. 1658.

70. Ibid., p. 1678.

71. Ibid., p. 1650.

72. Ibid., p. 1651.

73. Ibid., p. 1657.

74. Ibid., "Statement of Elbert H. Gary," December 18, 1908, p. 1706.

75. Schroeder, op. cit., p. 45.

76. Ibid. The tactic worked. During the trial of the government's anti-trust suit, U.S. Steel's competitors testified that the corporation had always behaved "fairly, had not engaged in price cutting, and had never sought to force them out of business."

77. Hogan, op. cit., vol. II, p. 780; U.S. Congress, House, *Tariff Hearings*, "Statement of Elbert H. Gary," Doc. 1505, p. 1718.

78. Export percentages are derived from Hogan, op. cit., vol. II, Table 23-1, p. 781; output percentages for U.S. Steel are derived from United States Steel Corporation, *United States Steel Corporation T.N.E.C. Papers: Comprising the Pamphlets and Charts Submitted by United States Steel Corporation to the Temporary National Economic Committee*, in three volumes, vol. II, *Chart Studies* (United States Steel Corporation, 1940), p. 142.

79. U.S. Congress, House, *Tariff Hearings*, "Statement of Charles M. Schwab," Doc. 1505, p. 1653.

80. Ibid.

81. U.S. Congress, House, *Tariff Hearing*, "Statement of Elbert H. Gary," Doc. 1505, p. 1718.

82. Schroeder, op. cit., p. 45.

Comment

Etsuo Abe

In the first section of his paper, Professor Paskoff alludes to the small role steel imports played in the United States between 1865 and 1914. Some scholars maintain that high protective tariffs were responsible. If this is the case, the question arises whether such high tariffs subsidized American inefficiency. Paskoff denies this and reasons as follows. As exemplified in Carnegie's "Lucy" furnace and later developments, the American iron and steel industry became highly mechanized and its equipment and technology were always state-of-the-art. The result was very high productivity. In addition, the renowned hard-driving process helped to raise the productivity of blast furnaces to prodigious levels. Despite the hard-driving blast furnace's higher productivity, it *initially* had two disadvantages: a higher rate of fuel consumption and an accelerated corrosion of the furnace lining. However, these disadvantages were before long overcome by technical innovations. Therefore, it seems that the key to the success of the steel industry in the United States was technology. It was necessary to have a certain sense of the tremendous potential in a technological breakthrough and not be deterred by problems inherent in the new technology. The adoption of the LD converter in Japan during the 1950s presented problems similar to those of the hard-driving blast furnace. An LD converter damages the lining of the furnace by charging oxygen. But engineers at NKK, a leading Japanese steel company, surmounted this technical difficulty, and as a result NKK became a pioneer in the introduction of the LD converter. The point is that technological choice must be made with a view not to short-term costs and existing technical possibilities but rather to the potential for future development.

Likewise, American steelmakers exploited the open-hearth furnace more successfully than their British counterparts. This was due to the larger, more cost-effective size of the American hearths, but the larger scale was made possible in part by the chemical nature of the American hearths. They were basic rather than acidic like the British hearths and basic open-hearths can be built on a much larger scale. Moreover, basic hearths were able to neutralize the acidic content of ores that were more plentiful and economic. So in the technological choice of a steel-making process, the Americans showed the right judgment.

In general, American steelmakers followed a policy of "creative destruction," what came to be known as the "American practice," which is the "effort to realize greater and greater efficiency through modernization." This made the industry very competitive indeed. Yet today the industry seems to have made an about-face. Have American entrepreneurs changed? And if so, why?

During the period under consideration, however, there were a number of technologically innovative corporations. How were techno-logical innovations diffused among corporations and among engi-neers? Through professional associations of engineers? Or were trade secrets jealously guarded? I think it would be useful to know the degree of technology transfer between them. Another question is relat-ed to the demand side. Paskoff refers to a "rapidly growing home market." Faced with such a vigorous market, steelmakers must have become "bullish." However, what sort of market did they anticipate, particularly in the post-railroad age?

In the second section Paskoff discusses the effects of tariffs. Tariff duties decreased over time. At first, railroad companies objected to the tariffs, but later changed their attitude because of interlocking interests with the steel companies. At the same time, intense domestic competi-tion made the industry immune to foreign competition by encourag-ing continual technological improvements. But the disparity between integrated and non-integrated firms gradually became more pro-nounced, and their respective interests were not necessarily in har-mony with each other. Why did many big corporations nevertheless continue to call for high tariffs? This question is raised by Paskoff, and the logic of his answer is cogent: If a cut-throat war between integrated and non-integrated firms took place, most non-integrated firms, i.e., relatively small companies, would be driven out of business. In the absence of smaller firms to give the lie to their defacto monopoly, large corporations feared anti-trust laws, and under the present arrangement they were able to enjoy handsome profits by overseas dumping and at the same time maintain high domestic prices at the expense of the consumer. This was the reason large corporations adopted the strategy supporting high tariffs. What judgment can we give on this strategy, from the viewpoint not only of economic policy but also of management efficiency? Coincidentally, this strategy resembles a strategem of Japanese firms called "the way of the convoy" (*gosō sendan hōshiki*) during the post–World War II period, though there is a difference in that the lead in Japan is often taken by the government.

The German Iron and Steel Industry in the 19th Century

Rainer Fremdling

I. Introduction

At the turn of the century, the iron and steel industry was regarded not only as a major sector in modern industrialized countries, but also quite often as the very symbol of a nation's cultural achievement. In those days, no one could draw on the rather sophisticated set of national accounts for different countries, which would have allowed a more precise comparison of the achievement of nations, thus enabling us to assign their rank in the international league table more accurately. The rough yardstick of contemporary observers, however, is probably best put forward in this statement by the German technical historian Ludwig Beck: " . . . the progress of the iron industry is so closely connected with any progress in modern culture and civilization, that the very consumption of iron per capita presents the proper yardstick of industry, welfare, and the power of nations."[1]

In this evaluation, the fact that America and Germany surpassed Britain's iron and steel production has often been seen as symbolic of the British decline. By 1890, the United States had taken the permanent lead in producing pig iron and steel, while Germany had surpassed Britain concerning steel in 1893, and pig iron in 1903. Producers in the United States mainly confined themselves to meeting the enormously growing demand in their own protected market, but their German counterparts challenged the British dominance of the world market ever more powerfully. By 1910, German exports of iron and steel had outstripped Britain in third markets, and producers from the Ruhr were even selling some of their products on the British home market itself.[2] The supremacy of the "workshop of the world," so palpably demonstrated at the Crystal Palace world exhibition in 1851, was clearly forfeited on the eve of World War I. The turning point lies precisely in the last third of the 19th century, which Landes labels the "age of steel."[3]

Looking back from 1913, it is tempting to see the British relative
decline as background for Germany's successful emulation, which led
to a closing of the gap and ultimately an overtaking. These elements
can be traced indeed, and the evidence seems unambiguous. However,
in such a simplified view, producers in the leading country always represent the best-practice standard, which producers in other countries
try to imitate. This does not only apply to techniques in use, but also to
business and market organizations and other institutional arrangements. Concerning the best-practice standard, Britain undoubtedly was
the leader until the last third of the 19th century, and later on the
United States or Germany followed. Perhaps a more appropriate concept is that of convergence and divergence.[4] This new paradigm allows
a better explanation of the economically viable coexistence of various
practices in different countries (or even regions and firms). The traditional lead-lag or best-practice paradigm fits into the broader new
paradigm as a special case—mainly incorporated in periods or elements of convergence. Many phenomena (e.g., non-adoption of the
seemingly best practice), which in the old paradigm would have been
labeled as a "failure," could in the new paradigm be regarded as an
appropriate adaptation to a different socioeconomic environment.
(This does not apply to all cases, to be sure.) Similarly, a mere trans-
plantation of best practice techniques from a highly developed to a less
developed country might be labeled as a "failure" in the new
paradigm.

This article will concentrate on the development of the German iron
and steel industry, but it cannot refrain from contrasting some aspects
with the British case. Finally some of the recent arguments concerning
the German and British performance in this sector shortly before
World War I are sketched.

II. The Adoption of Mineral-fuel Techniques

The modern iron and steel industry developed in Germany during the
middle decades of the 19th century. Since the speed of adopting the
then new mineral-fuel techniques differed widely in the various
branches of the iron industry, it is necessary to distinguish between the
two stages of primary iron production. First there is the smelting process in a coke blast furnace, and second, the refining/shaping process
(puddling and rolling), for which hard coal is used. The transition
from charcoal to hard coal as fuel was demand induced, brought about
mainly by railway construction.[5] When Germany began building railways around 1835, the indigenous iron industry was not capable of pro-

viding rolled rails in sufficient quantities at competitive prices. Some coke blast furnaces had already been erected in remote Upper Silesia as early as the end of the 18th century. But these endeavors, undertaken mainly by the Prussian state, were commercially unsuccessful. In most respects they could not compete, even in their area, with ironworks that employed traditional methods. Furthermore, puddling and rolling had barely been adopted in that region, even up until the mid-1830s. In western parts of Germany, attempts to introduce coke smelting had failed altogether for a long time. This was not a technical problem, but rather a question of economic feasibility. The most successful entrepreneurial strategy in the West turned out to be a combination of traditional techniques with modern British ones. As early as the 1820s, some rural ironworks introduced puddling, and thus hard coal, to refine the high-quality charcoal pig iron. Some still shaped their wrought iron traditionally through the use of the hammer, but others already applied rolling. Thus a high-quality wrought iron was produced which could compete in traditional markets at lower costs. With puddling requiring hard coal, the expensive charcoal was reserved for the first stage of primary iron production. In principle, this partly modernized production might have included rails as well, which actually happened at times. On the whole, however, a low-quality iron sufficed for rails, but then in previously unknown quantities. The German iron industry, dispersed in small rural firms, was not able to meet this demand.[6] Thus, in spite of an import duty, the first German trains ran almost exclusively on rails made in Britain.[7]

The German iron industry's response to railway demands had been somewhat restrained in the second half of the 1830s, but a quick import substitution took off in the early 1840s. At that time many iron-processing plants using modern British technology were established in the coal districts, and existing firms switched over to the new technology, thus enlarging their capacities. This enabled domestic producers to meet a growing proportion of local demand for rails and other finished iron products. By the 1850s, most of the rails were produced in Germany. In 1853, roughly half of the stock of rails on Prussian railways were still of British origin, but by 1863, this proportion declined to nearly 10%.[8] The import substitution proceeded so rapidly that it took no more than two decades to reverse the relation between domestic- and foreign-produced rails on Prussian or German railways. The German iron-processing industry, almost incapable of producing rolled rails at the beginning of the railway era, experienced an astonishing increase in capacity from the 1840s to the 1860s. Not only did it supply the expanding domestic market with railway iron, but more iron products, including rails, were exported than imported. (Annual growth rates for bar iron, including rails, in Prussia:[9] 1841–50= 5.7 (puddled iron alone=12.9), 1851–60=6.6 (10.0), 1861–70=9.0; Zollverein's imports and exports of rails in 1000 metric tons:[10] 1860–65=10.2 and 23.6 1866–71=23.6 and 149.9.)

This transitional period, with its peculiar sequence of import substitution, requires an explanation: Before the new demand for railway iron had arisen, there were rather weak economic incentives for conversion to the British model. Traditional and partly modernized ironworks were then very well capable of meeting the demand for high-quality wrought iron. British-produced iron was no perfect substitute and could only compete on the German market when Britain endured slump years with extremely low iron prices. In contrast to France, the German market was in principle open to foreign competition. Furthermore, rising charcoal prices induced powerful productivity increases. Without any basic changes to a firm's other work processes or organization, hard coal using puddling, being a handicraft after all, could be integrated into traditional firms, and fuel-saving devices could be utilized on traditional blast furnaces. In retrospect it is clear that such a motley iron industry was doomed to die, though this was not obvious before the end of the 1850s. It would therefore be rash to describe the transitional period from the 1820s to the 1850s as just an Indian Summer. In the finally obsolete branch a fuel-saving tradition was created which was later adopted by the modern German iron and steel industry. A good example of this is the hot blast developed by the Scot Neilson in 1828, widely praised as the most important innovation in the iron industry during the first half of the 19th century. In some British regions, e.g., South Wales, this innovation was adopted reluctantly, though many charcoal blast furnaces on the Continent implemented this device promptly.[11] An additional innovation was developed within the charcoal iron industry, namely heating the hot blast with the waste gases of the furnace.[12] Later this became a powerful device for saving fuel in coke blast furnaces.

Quite a number of firms with a traditional background (e.g., Hoesch, Gutehoffnungshütte) built puddling and rolling mills for railway needs. In remote coal districts, such as Upper Silesia and the Saar, modern rail mills possessed coke blast furnaces of their own, while ironworks in the Aachen-Düren district and the Ruhr initially had none. For firms close to the Belgian border or in the Ruhr district, which were inexpensively connected with Britain over the Rhine and the North Sea, it was economically feasible to import pig iron from abroad and to work it up to rails. In doing so, these firms simply followed the rules of comparative advantage. This advantage was reinforced by the peculiar tariff structure, which encouraged the import of pig iron by renouncing any import duty, and discouraged the import of bar iron and rails by levying a duty, though moderate (i.e., 60 M per ton in 1835, 40% ad valorem). Therefore, imported pig iron that had been smelted with coke played a major role in this period, and the substitution of foreign rails was accompanied by increased imports of pig iron (ratios of net imports to the production of the Zollverein, bar iron: 1841–50=0.26, 1851–60=0.05, 1861–70=–0.03, pig iron: 1841–50=0.37, 1851–60=0.35, 1861–70=0.11).[13] Domestic pig iron output, which continued to be produced mainly in charcoal-using blast furnaces, stagnated in the 1840s. Not until 1851–60 did the domestic production of coke-smelted pig iron accelerate and eventually dominate the industry. (Annual growth rates for pig iron in Prussia: 1841–50=2.5 (coke pig iron alone=4.6), 1851–60=11.5 (27.0), 1861–70= 9.6 (12.6)).[14] Since the productivity of bar iron production increased only slightly (if at all) in Britain from 1830 to 1870, it is plausible that the German puddling and rolling mill equipment did not fall behind the best British standards.[15] And, given the higher growth rates in the German refining sector, it also seems plausible that German forges on the average possessed more modern equipment than their British counterparts. This is confirmed by the report of a German iron master who visited the most important British iron districts in 1860: "Who has ever seen the larger Westphalian, Rhenish and Belgian rolling mills will find little if any noteworthy in most of the English and Scottish mills. The rolling mill equipments, so magnificent they might appear, are out of date, however, in nearly every respect."[16] As against this, most reports stressed the higher productivity of British puddlers and rollers.[17] Given the lower wages in Germany, the costs of working up pig iron into bar iron and rails probably did not differ much in both countries. Thus the cost advantage the British rolling mills still possessed in the 1860s was mainly due to the input of cheaper pig iron. Transportation costs and import tariffs were high enough to protect German firms from the cheaper British bar iron on their internal market.

The growing demand for pig iron in Germany and the huge quantities imported had shown indigenous firms their market opportunities. It is not surprising that there was a time lag in the building of coke blast furnaces in the Ruhr district, given the aforementioned comparative advantage on the second stage of primary iron production. Until recently however, there was no satisfactory explanation as to why the smelting branch in the Ruhr did not gain momentum prior to the 1850s.[18] When looking at supply side factors, it seems fairly clear that by the middle of the 1840s no limitations existed anymore. Hard coal suitable for coke was available, as were iron-ore deposits, either in the Ruhr district itself or in its vicinity. Furthermore, there could no longer be the question of a lack of capital, skilled workers, technicians, or entrepreneurs as limiting factors, because the industry's expansion in the early 1850s actually relied heavily on the import of foreign capital and men. In principle these developments would have been possible some years earlier, as it actually was regarding the establishment of puddling and rolling mills. In fact, the contemporary observer Oechelhäuser reported that in the boom year of 1847 numerous plans were made to erect coke blast furnaces.[19] But the downswing of the business cycle in 1848 delayed the realization of these plans until the following upswing of the business cycle in the 1850s. From then on the Ruhr area was the most dynamic iron- and steel-producing district in Germany. While its mainly charcoal iron had comprised barely 5% of Germany's pig iron production in 1850, the Ruhr supplied a quarter of it by 1870.[20]

III. Further Expansion: The Adoption of Liquid-steel Techniques and Cartels

At the end of the 1860s, the traditional charcoal-based techniques had become obsolete at both stages of iron production, and a modern iron industry had emerged. It formed part of a broader industrialization process, which no longer depended solely on the demand for railway construction. On the German market even the smelting branch, at least in its most important part—the production of pig iron for puddling and rolling mills—no longer needed to fear British competition. The import duty on pig iron had long been reduced and was completely abolished in 1873, but even in the following slump years, British pig iron barely acquired more than a stopgap function in this market segment up to 1913. Imported British pig iron primarily served foundry purposes and was also utilized as input for Bessemer converters.[21]

Some steel firms opposed the re-introduction of a duty on pig iron for the above reason. As Germany possessed only a few deposits of iron ore with a low phosphoric content, not enough pig iron could be produced which was suitable for the newly introduced Bessemer process of refining pig iron to steel.[22] Despite that well-founded opposition, a duty of ten per ton was levied in 1879, i.e., roughly 20% ad valorem.

Protected by the reintroduced tariff, the smelting branch made moderate profits during the brief period of three years. But thereafter, from 1883 to 1890, the relative losses per ton of pig iron were even higher than they had been in the slump years from 1874 to 1879, when iron masters had rallied against the abolition of iron duties.[23] It seems quite obvious that neither the lack nor introduction of a pig iron tariff brought about a fundamental change in the conditions under which the smelting branch existed during the so-called Great Depression.[24] It was the disproportion between excess capacity and the demand on the German market which caused the losses between 1874 and 1890. The already mentioned low propensity to import pig iron for refinery purposes throughout this period is a good indication that the problems were internal and not a result of dumping practices by foreign competitors.[25] The difficulties that arose from 1874 on were caused by investment decisions during the preceding boom period begun in 1868. Since then, numerous independent investment decisions had led to an enormous increase in blast-furnace capacity. Due to the long gestation period, the available capacity reached its peak after the Gründerboom had faded. In 1868 the "Oberbergamtsbezirk Dortmund" (Ruhr district) possessed 63 blast furnaces, 55 of which were in blast. And in 1875, 46 out of 71 furnaces were in blast. Idle capacity was even worse in 1876–77: In the Ruhr area, 39 out of 69 (and 38 out of 68) furnaces were in blast.[26] The worst year for Germany as a whole was 1876, when 220 out of 466 blast furnaces lay idle.[27] These wide gaps between capacity and operating unit use, however, did not lead to an equally drastic decline of pig iron production. The situation in the Ruhr district was typical: In 1874 output had dropped by nearly 14% below the peak level of 1873, but by 1877 it had not only increased but had also surpassed the former peak level, although approximately 45% of the capacity lay idle. This implies that only the most modern and thus most productive blast furnaces were used. While the average output per unit had been 9,425 tons in 1872, it increased to about 15,000 tons in 1878.[28] In other districts similar developments occurred, but they ensued with some delay. The German pig iron output of 1873 was slightly surpassed in 1879, although the average output per furnace increased from 5,900 to 10,600 tons in those years.[29]

The outcome of the business cycle downswing has been described here in some detail in order to reveal the basic behavior pattern for the time span of the so-called Great Depression until the 1890s. Between 1871 and 1892 the output grew threefold though it fluctuated heavily. Actual production decline seldom occurred. Thus a backward demand shift was mainly compensated for by declining prices. The falling export quotas since the 1880s indicate that there was no alternative to the domestic market. A forward shift of demand was mainly met by production increases rather than by higher prices. Thus a long-term downward trend in prices ensued.[30] The asymmetric fluctuation of prices and output indicates that tough competition and structural excess capacity caused the aforementioned losses during this period. As a consequence of these market conditions, constant pressure weighed on firms either to leave the market or to increase productivity on a massive scale. And indeed Krengel's analysis shows that the number of firms declined from 249 in 1871, to 103 in 1893, and remained so until 1913. But the average output per firm increased from 6,761 tons to 52,233 tons between 1871 and 1893. Krengel's calculation of total factor productivity yielded a yearly growth rate of 1.16 between 1873 and 1893, which means that technical progress contributed to the growth of production in this period by nearly one-third.[31] Krengel explains the abstract notion of "technical progress" by describing various measures which were implemented in order to improve the productivity of the smelting process. One group is related to several fuel-saving devices: In 1871, 1.52 tons of coke were necessary for smelting one ton of pig iron, and in 1893 the amount was reduced to 1.15, with a slight increase to 1.27 in 1913. The volume of the furnaces was augmented from roughly 220 cubic meters in 1870 to 450 in 1890. Furthermore the furnaces were driven harder and a number of mechanized devices were applied. The sequence of operation was improved in tandem with the steelworks in order to attain a continuous and heat-saving flow between the two stages of production. More and more engineers were educated at technical universities, where they were enabled to gain a theoretically based insight into the chemical and physical foundations of iron smelting.[32]

According to Krengel, most of these improvements had taken place before the mid-1890s so that the last period before World War I experienced rather low technical progress. Between 1893 and 1913, total factor productivity grew by just 0.29% per year and accounted for only 4.3% of the increase in production.[33] But during the boom years from 1893 to 1913, demand for pig iron increased rapidly. Accordingly, production grew with rather high and steady rates, ultimately raising output fourfold. Despite low productivity growth, high prices were demanded. In making high profits the fruit were reaped, which had been sown in the period before.

The second stage of primary iron and steel production, i.e., refining and rolling, was dominated by puddled iron until 1889. It then reached its peak with a production of nearly 1.7 million tons. Thereafter the output of puddled iron declined more or less steadily, amounting to no more than about 350,000 tons in 1911. By then, products refined by means of liquid-steel processes comprised nearly 11 million tons. This type of iron or steel had surpassed puddled iron for the first time in 1890.[34] At the second stage of primary iron and steel production there were few drastic changes in the rolling mills, whereas important changes occurred in the refining branch. Puddling was replaced by the new processes of Bessemer, Siemens-Martin (open-hearth), and Thomas. It should be kept in mind that substituting liquid-steel processes for puddling depended on economic considerations (cost and price difference), as well as on the physical properties of the new steel products. In the last respect only the basic variant of the open-hearth process rendered a steel which was a perfect substitute for the soft puddled iron.[35]

Until the early 1880s the German iron and steel industry had developed along the same lines as its British counterpart. This changed thereafter, transforming that convergence into a period of divergence.

In contrast to the diffusion of coke smelting or puddling and rolling, the new liquid-steel processes spread in Germany without considerable time lag from Britain. Krupp (1862) was the first firm to introduce the Bessemer process. Although Bessemer steel was orginally meant as a substitute for the expensive crucible steel (Tiegelstahl), it soon turned out that the properties of the hard Bessemer steel were not suited for that purpose. Instead, only one segment of the market that had been created by puddled iron, namely rails, caused the breakthrough for the new technology. Krupp, who formerly had not produced rails at all, now turned to this market. The capacity of the Krupp steelworks increased rapidly. The two small two-ton converters of 1862 were supplemented by two five-ton converters in the following year, and an additional nine were installed by 1865. When Krupp relinquished the exclusive rights of the Bessemer patent in Germany, other German works joined in the introduction of the Bessemer process. Bochumer Verein (which, like Krupp, had made its fortune with crucible steel products rather than rails), entered the market for steel rails in 1865. The first major traditional rail producer to switch over to steel rails was Hörder Verein in 1864. Both of its mills installed new equipment at the end of the 1860s comprising the now usual five-ton converters.[36]

By the beginning of the 1860s, it had already been proven that the stronger Bessemer rails would last much longer than the softer pud-

dled rails. Due to higher production costs, the new rails were considerably more expensive, however. Initially railway companies were only
willing to pay the higher price for replacement rails on heavily used
tracks. Thus Krupp, with its extended capacity of 13 converters, faced
sales problems in 1866. However, by the end of the 1860s, the price of
Bessemer rails had generally fallen to close to that of puddled rails,
and the demand increased. The remaining price difference gave
British railmakers the option of either producing the cheaper rails for
overseas railway companies (where the traffic density was low), or of
supplying railways at home (where traffic was intense) with the more
expensive product. Since German rail mills had barely established contacts with overseas markets, they could expect that their main customers, i.e., German railway companies, would demand more and
more Bessemer rails. Thus these specific market conditions forced
Germany to adopt the modern technology. Therefore at the end of the
1860s, before the Gründerboom of 1872–73 was perceptible, independent investment decisions had widened the capacity of the Bessemer
industry enormously. This was evidenced with a time lag. Only a few
new railmakers entered the market, and the increased capacities could
not be attributed to an overreaction in the boom phase of the business
cycle. Rather, Wengenroth ascribes it to the defensive strategy of
replacing the puddling furnace capacity.[37] Entrepreneurs had anticipated the vast increase in domestic demand for the Bessemer rails the
new tracks and replacements would create. And indeed investment in
railways reached previously unknown heights between 1872 and 1877,
with an absolute peak in 1875, when nearly one-third of Germany's
total net investment went into railway construction.[38] In addition to
new investment, widespread replacement of the old, puddled rails took
place.

    In contrast to Britain, domestic demand for railway iron fluctuated
heavily, and in the second half of the 1870s it was clear that the
increased capacity had outstripped the internal demand. One solution
was to increase exports—indeed from 1875 onward a growing proportion of rails was sold on third markets.[39] In spite of that relief, many of
the large steel mills faced severe financial difficulties and did not pay
any dividends at all.[40] Another solution for an individual enterprise was
to try to increase its efficiency. By reducing costs it could obtain a competitive advantage in both the internal and external markets. If such a
strategy is followed by all firms, however, it generates even more of an
overcapacity, given a limited demand. This individual behavior was one
reason why the original investment decisions, however reasonable, led
to a severe overcapacity.

A major obstacle to an increase in efficiency lay in the converter itself: "The converter only worked a small percentage of the time because of the technical characteristic of the production, the difficulty of moving the metal from place to place, and the time needed to rebuild the converter lining consumed in the extraordinarily high heat of the process. The bottom of the converter would wear out after one or three heats, the converter would have to be cooled, and a man would climb inside and repair the lining of the converter. Having two converters kept the machines employed more of the time, but the original plan was not satisfactory."[41]

Most of the technical improvements on the original plan were invented and first applied in Britain and in the United States. But Wengenroth points out that all of these innovations were implemented in Germany without any significant delay.[42] Holley's American innovation, for example, which made the bottom of the converter removable, was developed in 1869–70 and patented in 1872.[43] In Britain, Holley's innovation was introduced in 1874, and in Germany in 1875 (Hörder Verein). At the end of the 1870s, the new bottoms were common in Germany. In a case study on Krupp's Bessemer plant, Wengenroth demonstrates the effects of modernizing a first-generation Bessemer plant in one step. From 1875 to 1878, new equipment was installed in all three Krupp plants. In 1875, the first plant was modernized within a few months, and from then on a speedy mass production of steel was possible. The Dowlais company in Great Britain and American fast-driving methods served as models. Labor productivity increased from 98 tons in 1873 to 236 tons in 1878. In each plant the converters could be used 25 times instead of the former capacity of only ten times per day.

The costs of the refining process declined by nearly 50%. Thus the cost-reducing effect was accompanied by a vast increase in productivity and capacity. The rising capacity at Krupp's and other German steel mills did not depend on new equipment alone, but also on a better organization of the work process. Due to economies of scale, this higher throughput reduced costs even further. In this respect, the German mills of the late 1870s possessed an advantage over their counterparts in Britain, where organizational improvements were introduced only in the new plants at the beginning of the 1880s. On the other hand, some of the new British plants erected in the mid-1870s boasted of newer equipment. Moreover, they used the method whereby pig iron went directly from the blast furnace to the converter. In Germany the standard practice was to melt down the pig iron in a special cupola furnace. This was necessary because German firms had to import Bessemer pig iron to a large degree. An important condition for determining the competitive position of German and British firms is thus provided. The latter could draw on significantly cheaper pig iron supplies, affording them a competitive advantage after all.

Individual efforts to cut costs by enhancing efficiency could not solve the problems of overcapacity; rather they aggravated it, as was shown. Given the cost advantage of British firms, the question arises as to why German steel mills were not challenged on their domestic market and why, on the contrary, they succeeded in undermining British exports by penetrating into third markets.

German firms compensated for their shortcomings, i.e., higher input costs, by creating a different market organization and a specific sales strategy. This could be done because a protective wall of customs reserved the German market for domestic suppliers. Since the 1860s tariffs had declined and eventually were abolished in the 1870s, though they were reintroduced by 1879. The specific tariffs on iron and steel products reached 15% to 25% ad valorem and with few alterations remained in effect until 1914.[44] During the brief episode of free trade the German state and private railway companies yielded precedence to domestic steel firms.[45]

Although there had been regional cartels prior to the 1870s, it was during that decade that the specific pattern of a national cartel emerged for the first time, developed behind protective tariffs and export dumping.[46] Since 1868, Krupp, Bochum, and Hörde had already decided on production quotas for Bessemer rails. When submitting offers to railway companies, the three suppliers agreed upon the firm which should bid the lowest. They channeled the demand according to their quotas. High demand in the boom years up to 1873, and the limited number of competitors, guaranteed full employment in the Bessemer steel companies. In the "Gründerjahren," arrangements had been made about prices rather than production, but this changed toward the end of that period. The increased number of firms made the formation of a cartel more difficult. Nevertheless, in 1874 the great Rhenish-Westphalian Bessemer works formed the cartel "Vereinigte Stahlwerke." Krupp joined it with some hesitation and reached a quota of 25%. Having improved his Bessemer plant through massive investment, Krupp left the cartel after a few months in early 1875. His withdrawal resulted in heavy price competition. It was clear that a national cartel would not function without the vast capacity of the Krupp plant. Thus, the other firms, which had joined into a railmakers association, tried to lure Krupp into the cartel. According to Wengenroth's analysis, it was finally the power of the great banks that forced Krupp into the cartel. The Dortmunder Union, a creation of the Disconto-Gesellschaft, threatened Krupp with cut-throat competition by the railmakers association. Due to his capacity and the high productivity of his Bessemer plant, Krupp did not have to fear any competition based solely on productive power. As he was not backed by any major bank, he would have lacked the financial power to survive cut-throat competition, so he finally joined the cartel in 1876. This national cartel, "Schienengemeinschaft," lasted with some interruption and under different names until 1914.[47] It also made arrangements with cartels in other countries, culminating in the international cartel (International Railmakers Association) of 1884 which lasted only two and a half years.

With a declining rail demand, the German rail cartel lost its significance for the steel industry and was finally merged into a multi-product cartel, the "Stahlwerksverband" of 1904. Its predecessor, the "Schienengemeinschaft," however, was more than just a forerunner of the powerful multi-product cartels. In the 1870s it controlled more than three-quarters of the domestic sales in steel,[48] and moreover, it promoted the introduction of specific sales strategies and an entrepreneurial behavior alternating between cooperation and competition. The cartel did not prevent efforts to increase productivity through improved techniques and organization. At that time, however, it could not guarantee high profits but mere survival. This is one reason why the still-profitable British firms did not regard the German market organization as a model to be emulated. In spite of the German cartel, roughly half of the Bessemer plants were out of blast in 1877. But the remaining plants were used intensively. The entrepreneurs and managers were well aware that the average costs of producing steel declined with the enlargement of the operating scale in a certain plant. The domestic market, however, could not absorb all the steel produced, and exports presented a solution. But the German steel exporters faced severe competition from British and Belgian suppliers. As many observers have noticed, German export prices for rails were considerably lower than internal prices. But this dumping did not necessarily mean that export sales resulted in losses for German firms.[49] During the 1870s those firms complained about losses, indeed, because export prices did not cover the average costs they had calculated. On the other hand, they knew that the profits of domestic sales depended on the cost-reducing effect of large-scale production. The concept of marginal costs determining the lower limit to prices was yet unknown. Some firms, however, had neglected several items of fixed costs in their calculations, and thus approached their marginal costs. Comparing export prices with those approximate marginal costs, Wengenroth concludes that export prices certainly lay above the real marginal costs. Wengenroth's detailed evidence lends strong support to the argument put forward by Webb.[50]

The German steel firms survived the crisis of the 1870s by applying both individual and collective strategies. Individually they quickly adopted the newest techniques and organizational reforms in order to cut back costs. As already mentioned, this increased their capacities enormously. They could only survive as a group by taking collective actions toward a national cartel which was sheltered from external threats through a protective tariff. This in turn allowed a price discrimination between the domestic and foreign market. With the export market absorbing the surplus production at prices close to marginal costs, large-scale production with low average costs was possible.

In Germany, the production of Bessemer steel reached its peak in 1882. But it rapidly lost its significance with declining railway demand and with the advent of the Thomas process. The phase of convergence between the German and British steel industries ended with the development of this new liquid-steel process, which allowed phosphoric pig iron to be converted into steel.[51] In contrast to Britain, the price difference between Bessemer and Thomas pig iron was high enough for many firms in Germany to switch over to the Thomas process. Although economically the new process could mean a much higher profitability, technically, it was only a slight modification of the Bessemer process. In fact, the Thomas process is just the basic version of Bessemer's invention, wherein the converter is now lined with basic dolomite, and basic limestone is added to the molten iron in order to combine with the phosphoric acid in slags.

Converters which had been shut down during the rationalization period of the 1870s were used for trials. The profitability of the new process was most pronounced in the German Southwest, with its rich minette-ore deposits. Bessemer mills there had not been profitable, and as early as 1880 the extant plants switched over to the new process. Thomas steel was originally regarded as a mere substitute for Bessemer steel rails. But in the very center of German steel production, Rhineland-Westphalia, the cost difference was not clearly in favor of the new process and existing orders for rails led to a slight delay in its diffusion. However, as early as 1880 Hörder Verein succeeded in producing a soft steel with the Thomas converter. The trials in Hörde had also shown that the hitherto useless piles of slags from the puddling process could be utilized in the blast furnace to smelt pig iron for this soft steel. Charging the blast furnace with old slag and suitable domestic iron ores made the pig iron serving as input for the Thomas process cheaper than the input for the Bessemer converter.

The resulting soft steel allowed a diversification of end products. In producing merchant iron, wire, tubes, pipes, and sheet metal out of Thomas steel, the steelworks could either abandon their puddling furnaces or enter anew into the market which had previously been reserved mainly for puddled iron. It was for these reasons that as early as 1881 most of the Rhenish-Westphalian steelworks converted at least parts of their Bessemer plants into units producing Thomas steel. (Initially no new plants were erected.) In contrast to Britain, the German Thomas steel was barely threatened by open-hearth steel, the only perfect substitute for puddled iron. Thus in the 1880s the German steel mills concentrated all efforts on improving the production of Thomas steel. Beyond a temporary device to make use of the limited stocks of slags from puddling, this turned out to be a long-term strategy which was feasible because the rich minette deposits offered a long-term guarantee for sufficient domestic iron ore supplies. At that time it was not yet perceptible that the Ruhr would switch primarily to Swedish iron ore imports in the 1890s.[52] Although the Bessemer plants could easily be converted into Thomas plants, the introduction of ten-ton converters and the greater product variety demanded a new organization of the work process. In the compact Bessemer plant everything had been done in one building: melting down the pig iron, converting, casting, and repairing. In Hörde and Peine a new concept was realized in 1882. Most importantly, converting and casting were separated in two buildings, thus allowing an independent change in the size and amount of equipment. This afforded greater flexibility in the mix and volume of output, which led to an advantage over the compact plants of the older type, rather than lowering costs. Thus two types of plant designs coexisted.[53]

Around 1890, when most technical and organizational improvements in producing Thomas steel had been achieved, the aforementioned steel type dominated the German market. For merchant iron, wire, and semi-finished products, the quality of Thomas steel sufficed and had a price advantage. In general, German steel consumers were content with medium qualities, for which Thomas steel was adequate.

Germany had fewer shipyards demanding high-quality open-hearth steel, and there was a smaller demand for Bessemer rails there than in Britain.[54]

TABLE 1   Liquid-steel Production, 1880–1900 (%)

	Open-hearth	Bessemer	Thomas
1880	4.9	92.6	2.5
1884	27.4	34.1	38.5
1890	17.4	15.7	66.9
1900	32.3	3.4	62.3

Source: Wilfried Feldenkirchen, *Die Eisen und Stahlindustrie des Ruhrgebiets 1874–1914* (Wiesbaden, 1982), p. 187. See also note 34.

With regard to finished products, the German statistics do not allow a clear distinction between liquid steel or puddled iron. But quantitative evidence on the different inputs is available. Liquid-steel products combined had surpassed puddled iron (Schweißeisen) by 1887. Within the category of liquid steel, the shares shifted as shown in Table 1. These figures make clear how fast Bessemer steel was replaced by Thomas steel during the 1880s.[55] Whereas Bessemer steel had become insignificant by 1900, open-hearth steel had gained a remarkable share of total production by that time.

The open-hearth process (Siemens-Martin) was first applied successfully in 1864 by Martin in France. He used a hearth constructed by Wilhelm Siemens. Pig iron, iron ore, and scrap iron were suitable for input. In an open-hearth furnace, like in a puddling furnace, the input was melted down, but due to the high heat, the refining process took place without the help of a puddler. The yield was liquid steel, which was processed in the same manner as steel obtained from the converter. Open-hearth refining took a very long time; it was even slower than puddling, though this slowness had distinct advantages. During the several hours of refining, the composition of the molten mass could be tested and altered in order to acquire a desired steel quality in a specific range, a process not possible in the converter. Furthermore, the liquid steel could be cast into more homogeneous products, as it comprised fewer undesired gas bubbles than converter steel. Like the Bessemer converter, the open-hearth initially had an acid lining, but with the invention of Thomas a basic lining was also possible. Due to technical problems, however, this was not achieved before the end of the 1880s. With this basic variant in the open-hearth process, the last domain of the puddling process could be replaced, both in respect to output (steel qualities) and input (type of pig iron). Two features led to the distinct advantage of this process in the long run: Firstly, scrap recycling gained more importance, and secondly, the minimum size of an efficient open-hearth plant was far smaller than that of a converter steel plant.[56]

The open-hearth process spread more slowly in Germany than in Britain, where shipbuilding in particular demanded shipplates and angles made from this slowly produced steel.[57] In the late 1860s Krupp had already introduced this process in Germany, but as late as the end of the 1870s only two firms in Germany applied it: Krupp and the Bochumer Verein. Initially, open-hearth steel was supposed to compete with Bessemer steel in the market for rails. Unfortunately, sufficient information is not available about cost differences. Even if it were, the two processes are difficult to compare. In the 1870s when Bessemer plants were likely to have increased their productivity much faster than plants with open-hearth furnaces, Bessemer steel was probably only slightly cheaper. The advantage was obviously not great enough to encourage widespread production of open-hearth rails. Instead, open-hearth steel became a cheaper substitute for the high-value crucible steel (Tiegelstahl) in some market segments. This production could be carried out in relatively small plants with low investment costs. An open-hearth plant was complementary to the large Bessemer mills because it could process scrap, a by-product of rail production. Such enlargements were carried out in the 1870s by Krupp, Bochumer Verein, Dortmunder Union, and Phönix.[58]

In 1879, Krupp and Bochumer Verein dominated this branch of the steel industry with roughly 90% of the market. They were strong in both the markets for Bessemer rails and crucible steel. Unlike Britain, the expansion of Germany's open-hearth steel had not yet taken off during the 1880s. Without mass markets for shipplates and tinplate bars, open-hearth steel was mainly restricted to working up scrap from rail production. Although it was used for a variety of products, it could not replace puddled iron in a mass market. The largest market for puddled iron around 1890 was merchant iron. It was Thomas steel that became cheaper than puddled iron and eventually replaced it from 1890 onward. After the turn of the century, however, open-hearth steel increasingly substituted for Thomas steel because domestic and foreign consumers demanded more of this high-quality steel for many different purposes.[59] Furthermore, German shipyards expanded rapidly in the two decades before 1913 and used more and more German steel plates, produced with the open-hearth process.[60] In contrast to the German Southwest, with its minette deposits, all the new steel mills in the Ruhr after 1900 were open-hearth plants. In 1913 nearly 50% of all liquid steel was produced with this process there; in the entire German Empire this share was 40%.[61] The contrast with Britain is striking: In 1907 (the year of the first census of production) 70% of all British steel ingots were produced with the open-hearth process.[62] This indicates the divergent structure of the steel industry in both countries, with the Germans specializing in the lower quality branch and the British engaging in the higher quality range.

Toward the end of the 19th century, all major technological innovations were spread within Germany, leaving narrow room for further technical improvements up to 1913. Thus increased efficiency and profitability could mainly be obtained from organizational reforms of both markets and firms. The most obvious features were an increased propensity toward cartels and vertically integrated firms. Vertical integration minimizes transaction costs, and continued uncertainty about future price developments created a powerful incentive of vertical integration.

Before resuming an analysis of the formation of cartels for semi-finished and finished steel products, a brief discussion of pig iron cartels is necessary.[63] Although there are earlier examples, it was not until the 1870s that organized sales cartels emerged in this branch. Each of the pig iron-producing regions formed a cartel of its own. Since 1896 these regional cartels had made arrangements on a national level, but it was not until 1911–12 that a full-scale national cartel came into being without the threat of outsiders.[64] There were several reasons why the cartels were unsuccessful in controlling prices on the German market: prices fluctuated wildly along with the business cycle because the incomplete cartels always broke apart during slump years. This was not solely due to disturbances from outsiders, but also to the peculiar setup of the cartel. Pig-iron output used by the large integrated works themselves was not counted in the cartel quota, and the members were not obliged to deliver their quota to the central sales organization. Thus, in boom years they sold almost nothing through the cartel, while in slump years they insisted on their quota. Such a cartel among integrated firms and pure pig-iron producers could not function when it was most needed. Even in those years when the cartel organization did work, its price policy was limited because the competition of imported and old iron enforced competitive pricing. Imported pig iron, mainly destined for foundries, played a role in the 1870s, whereas scrap iron became increasingly important with the diffusion of the open-hearth process. The pig-iron duty of ten M per ton seemed to be irrelevant right at the outset. Even the domestic German price for foundry pig iron was well below the price at which British foundry pig iron reached German ports.[65] By and large, pig iron was sold at competitive rather than cartel prices.[66]

The pig iron cartels were probably of primary importance in speeding up the overall tendency toward large vertically integrated iron and steel mills. This tendency has often been explained by technical economies in handling material and saving fuel. But these factors produce effects independent of any cartel policy. To avoid cartel price fixing above competitive levels would be a good reason to integrate blast furnaces. This is emphasized by Webb, who explains the fact that around 1900 steel mills, more than other branches of iron processing (foundries, puddling works), had their own blast furnaces, as follows: Through integration they avoided high markups (cartel price fixing) for Thomas pig iron, which was a heavy burden as against the low value added in producing heavy steel products.[67]

This reasoning, however, is rather weak, because empirical evidence does not support continuous price fixing above competitive levels by the cartels.[68] On the other hand, the cartels aggravated the uncertainty about future price developments by yielding to price volatility. In the peak years of 1899–1900, steel mills without their own blast furnaces barely got the pig iron they required. In order to avoid such future shortages, they made long-term contracts at high prices and piled up large stocks of pig iron. With the slackening of the business cycle, prices fell drastically, but the cartel insisted on these contracts.[69] Thus cartels increased transaction costs, which could be reduced through vertical integration.

The formation of a cartel for rails has already been described. Other cartels concerning railway products came into being, and were related to the Railmakers Association. The stability of the association and the related cartels was endangered, however, when Thomas steel increasingly entered into new markets other than railway needs (e.g., half-rolled ingots, bar iron, wire, etc.). Here Thomas steelworks faced not only the competition of similar steel mills, but also that of traditional puddling works. A successful cartel for wire was formed in 1886 when it was clear that steel wire could be cheaper than wire produced from puddled iron.[70] During the 1890s, the number of cartels for certain products increased, half-rolled steel among them. Most however, were rather loosely organized and agreed upon prices rather than on production quotas and had no central sales organization.[71] This changed in 1904, when 27 vertically integrated firms formed a multi-product cartel—the "Stahlwerksverband." This Steel Mill Federation comprised all major producers of heavy steel products. These products (half-rolled ingots, rails, ties, and beams) were sold successfully through a central organization on both the domestic and foreign markets. Production quotas were allocated according to the capacity of the cartel members. An effective control of light products (bars, sheet, wire, and pipe) failed. Here the cartel faced competition both from pure rolling mills and from an increased number of small firms producing open-hearth steel. Furthermore, the cartel members concentrated more and more on light products, because an expansion in heavy steel products was restricted by the quotas. From 1909 on, light product sales outnumbered heavy steel product sales. This efficient cartel for heavy products undermined the existence of pure rolling mills by entering the competition for light products, and by fixing cartel prices for their input. Thus the need for vertical integration became urgent. A monopolistic price fixing for heavy products was limited, though, because roughly 20% of such products were supplied by non-members. Restricted competition in one field sharpened the competition in other fields, such as light products. The struggle for production quotas, which always occurred when the cartel contract was to be renewed (1907, for example), led to increased investment or the overtaking of firms.[72]

IV. Concluding Remarks

The supposition that "the tariff-cartel system did reduce the innovative lag in Germany by increasing the incentive for vertical integration" is doubtful.[73] Concerning the major innovations in steelmaking, any noticeable lag toward Britain had been rectified as early as the 1860s. The marked propensity toward vertical integration was surely accelerated. The tariff-cartel system had made itself felt already in the 1870s: Resulting price discrimination between the domestic and foreign market guaranteed an efficient use of the capacity, and thus assured low average costs. The success of German steel products on export markets even in Britain has very often been regarded as an indication of higher productivity of the German steel industry, as compared to that of their British counterparts. The productivity difference was explicity measured by Allen and Webb.[74] Both of them found higher productivity in Germany, which they measured by using prices. But such an approach would yield reliable results only if the product mix in both countries had been similar. This was simply not the case. The divergent developments of the German and British steel industries resulted in a different specialization: Thomas steel in Germany and open-hearth steel in Britain. And it was precisely the low-quality Thomas steel with which German firms entered the British market.[75] Rather than a more efficient production it was the tariff-cartel system, supported by the state and enforced by the banks, that made Germany's exports more competitive on the world market than those of their British counterparts.

NOTES

1.   Ludwig Beck, *Die Geschichte des Eisens in technischer und kulturgeschichtlicher Beziehung* (Braunschweig, 1899), pt. 4, p. 3. See also Arthur Spiethoff, *Die wirtschaftlichen Wechsellagen* (Tübingen, 1955), pp. 38 f. passim, who used pig-iron consumption as the best indicator available for detecting business cycle fluctuations, and David S. Landes, *The Unbound Prometheus. Technological Change and Industrial Development in Western Europe from 1750 to the Present* (Cambridge, 1969), p. 250, states: ". . . the consumption of iron *per capita* has always been one of the most accurate measures of industrialization."
2.   Ibid., p. 269.
3.   Ibid., p. 249.
4.   It is one of the main aims of Wengenroth's seminal book to show divergent developments in the British and German steel industries after 1880. Ulrich Wengenroth, *Unternehmensstrategien und Technischer Fortschritt, Die deutsche und die britische Stahlindustrie 1865–1895* (Göttingen, 1986), p. 16, chapter 5.
5.   Rainer Fremdling, *Eisenbahnen und deutsches Wirtschaftswachstum 1840– 1879* (Dortmund, 1985), pp. 74, 78–83; idem, "Railroads and German Economic Growth: A Leading Sector Analysis with a Comparison to the United States and Great Britain," *Journal of Economic History*, vol. 37 (1977): 587–93; idem, *Technologischer Wandel und internationaler Handel im 18. und 19. Jahrhundert, Die Eisenindustrien in Großbritannien, Belgien, Frankreich und Deutschland* (Berlin, 1986), pp. 326–37; Horst Wagenblass, *Der Eisenbahnbau und das Wachstum der deutschen Eisen- und Maschinenbauindustrie 1835 bis 1860* (Stuttgart, 1973), passim; Reinhard Spree, *Die Wachstumszyklen der deutschen Wirtschaft von 1840 bis 1880* (Berlin, 1977), pp. 273–94.
6.   A good example is given by Wagenblass, op. cit., pp. 20 ff. There were no German factories which could have delivered the 5,650 tons of rails necessary for the first major railway built between 1836 and 1839 from Leipzig to Dresden. This amount would have required 30% of the production of wrought iron in Prussia, and the task was far beyond the capacity of the few rolling mills. On the other hand, the largest British factory, the Dowlais Company of

South Wales, would have been able to do the job within two months.
7. In 1843, nearly 90% of Prussian railway tracks were furnished with British rails. Fremdling, op. cit. (1986), p. 330.
8.   Ibid.
9.   Ibid., p. 361.
10.   Max Sering, *Geschichte der preussisch-deutschen Eisenzölle von 1818 bis zur Gegenwart* (Leipzig, 1882), pp. 292f., 300f.
11.   Charles K. Hyde, *Technological Change and the British Iron Industry 1700–1870* (Princeton, 1977), pp. 154f., 157, 159.
12.   Gottfried Plumpe, *Die württembergische Eisenindustrie im 19. Jahrhundert* (Wiesbaden, 1982), pp. 104ff.
13.   Fremdling, op. cit. (1986), p. 355.
14.   Ibid., p. 361.
15.   "The performance of the refining sector after 1829 is less clear because reliable cost data are scarce. Forge productivity stagnated or increased slightly between 1830 and 1870." Hyde, op cit., p. 209. Similarly, Philip Riden, "The Iron Industry," in Roy Church (ed.), *The Dynamics of Victorian Business,* (London, 1980), pp. 77ff.: "Once puddling had been adopted there were no spectacular innovations in either the forging or rolling of iron comparable with the hot blast in smelting."
16.   Scharf, "Bericht über eine im Herbst 1860 unternommene Bereisung der wichtigsten Eisenhüttenbezirke Englands und Schottlands," *Zeitschrift für das Berg-, Hütten- und Salinenwesen,* vol. 9 (1861): B289.
17.   Fremdling, op cit. (1986), pp. 190–200.
18.   See the discussion in ibid., pp. 343–48.
19.   Wilhelm Oechelhäuser, *Vergleichende Statistik der Eisen-Industrie aller Länder und Erörterung ihrer ökonomischen Lage im Zollverein* (Berlin, 1852), pp. 25 ff. His report has obviously been neglected by economic historians.
20.   Wilfried Feldenkirchen, *Die Eisen- und Stahlindustrie des Ruhrgebiets 1879–1914* (Wiesbaden, 1982), p. 27
21.   Jochen Krengel, *Die deutsche Roheisenindustrie 1871–1913* (Berlin, 1983), pp. 146–62.
22.   Feldenkirchen, op. cit., p. 37f. In the 1870s, however, the import of Bessemer pig iron declined. See also Karl W. Hardach, *Die Bedeutung wirtschaftlicher Faktoren bei der Wiedereinführung der Eisen- und Getreidezölle in Deutschland 1879* (Berlin, 1967), p. 35f.
23.   See the average prices and costs in Krengel, op. cit., p. 102.
24.   Hardach, op. cit., pp. 46–49.
25.   Ibid., pp. 34ff.
26.   Feldenkirchen, op. cit., tables 3, 9.
27.   Krengel, op. cit., p. 68.
28.   Output in 1,000 tons: 1873=537, 1874=465, 1875=468, 1876=498, 1877=552, 1878=632. Feldenkirchen, op. cit., table 9, p. 42f.
29.   Krengel, op. cit., pp. 39, 68.
30.   On prices and production see ibid., pp. 39, 75. On export quotas see Feldenkirchen, op. cit., table 66.
31.   Krengel, op. cit., pp. 42, 111.
32.   Ibid., pp. 55, 112–22.
33.   Ibid., p. 111.

34. Feldenkirchen, op. cit., table 54. On (ibid., p. 187) Feldenkirchen gives the year 1887.

35. A thorough description of these methods is to be found in Wengenroth, op. cit., pp. 30–43.

36. Ibid., pp. 49 f. For the following analysis see also this outstanding book by Wengenroth.

37. Ibid., p. 53.

38. Fremdling, op. cit. (1985), p. 31; Walther G. Hoffmann, *Das Wachstum der deutschen Wirtschaft seit der Mitte des 19. Jahrhunderts* (Berlin, 1965), p. 259. Hoffmann's faulty railway investment figure for aggregate total investment has not been corrected.

39. Wengenroth, op. cit., pp. 128–31.

40. Feldenkirchen, op. cit., pp. 51–56.

41. Peter Temin, *Iron and Steel in Nineteenth-Century America* (Cambridge, Mass., 1964), p. 135.

42. Wengenroth, op. cit., pp. 72–118.

43. Temin, op. cit., p. 136.

44. Steven B. Webb, "Tariffs, Cartels, Technology and Growth in the German Steel Industry, 1879 to 1914," *Journal of Economic History*, vol. 40, (1980): 310.

45. Wengenroth, op. cit., p. 145. Steel rails were allowed to enter duty-free for one and a half years. Ibid., p. 136; Feldenkirchen, op. cit., p. 39.

46. On the following see Wengenroth, op. cit., pp. 136 ff.

47. Webb, op. cit., p. 329.

48. Wengenroth, op. cit., p. 139.

49. Ibid., pp. 146ff.

50. Webb, op. cit., p. 324f.

51. On the following see Wengenroth, op. cit., pp. 176ff.

52. Feldenkirchen, op. cit., pp. 161ff.

53. The last plant erected in Germany according to the Bessemer-Holley concept in 1883 had operated for nearly 80 years. Wengenroth, op. cit., p. 204.

54. Ibid., p. 207.

55. Major exceptions were the Osnabrück steel mill, which possessed iron ore suitable for Bessemer pig iron in the vicinity and Krupp, who shared ownership of this type of iron ore fields in Spain. With a new plant in the mid-1890s, he also switched over to the Thomas process. Wengenroth, op. cit., pp. 210ff.

56. Ibid., pp. 37ff.; see also Temin, op. cit., pp. 138ff.

57. Donald N. McCloskey, *Economic Maturity and Entrepreneurial Decline, British Iron and Steel, 1870–1913* (Cambridge, 1973), pp. 50ff.

58. Wengenroth, op. cit., pp. 217ff.

59. Ibid., pp. 222–25.

60. Feldenkirchen, op. cit., p. 81.

61. Ibid., p. 143.

62. "Census of Production, Final Report on the First Census of Production of the United Kingdom (1907)," *Part I, General Report* (London, 1913), p. 101f.

63. On the following see Krengel, op. cit., pp. 34–37, 176–80; Feldenkirchen, op. cit., pp. 118–20; Arthur Klotzbach, *Der Roheisen-Verband* (Düsseldorf, 1926), passim.

64. Ibid., pp. 157ff.

65. On the prices see Krengel, op. cit., p. 177.

66. See the contrary statement by Webb, op. cit., p. 311. See also p. 316f. where he estimated the realized tariff which of course assumes higher prices in Germany than on the world market. Unfortunately he presents no price data.

67. Ibid., p. 319. Here again the reader is left with scanty information.

68. Prices and production costs calculated by Krengel (op. cit., pp. 102, 179) suggest a much lower markup than the 33% calculated by Webb. This markup was only reached in peak years such as 1899 and 1900, if at all. See Feldenkirchen, op. cit., p. 184f., table 51.

69. Ibid., p. 118; Fritz Blaich, "Ausschließlichkeitsbindungen als Wege zur industriellen Konzentration in der deutschen Wirtschaft bis 1914," in Norbert Horn and Jürgen Kocka (eds.), Recht und Entwicklung der Großunternehmen im 19. und frühen 20. Jahrhundert, (Göttingen, 1979), p. 328f.

70. Wengenroth, op. cit., p. 209.

71. On this and the following see Feldenkirchen, op. cit., pp. 120–24.

72. Ibid., pp. 143, 264.

73. Webb, op. cit., p. 323.

74. Robert C. Allen, "International Competition in Iron and Steel, 1850–1913," Journal of Economic History, vol. 39 (1979): 932; Webb, op. cit., p. 322f.

75. Wengenroth, op. cit., pp. 288ff.

Comment

Takeshi Fukuoh

By contrasting the divergent structures of the iron and steel industries of Britain and Germany in the late 19th century, Professor Fremdling carried out an appropriate approach to an international comparison. On the whole, I have no distinct disagreement with his skillfully detailed and very informative argument concerning the international steel rivalry debates. However, I would like to raise several aspects to promote discussion.

In the conclusion of his paper, Fremdling stressed the function of the German tariff-cartel system, and the role of the state government and banks in Germany. According to his account, Germany's success with the low-quality, mass-produced basic Bessemer products was an excellent fruit which could not have been yielded if not for the afore-mentioned systematic seedbed. Nevertheless, we are told very little about the essential part it played in the period of the German iron and steel industry's development. Therefore, more detailed explanation is necessary in this respect.

Financial aspects may be taken up as the first problem. How could the growing demand for a considerable amount of capital to invest in new plants, equipment, and so forth during the rapidly expanding years (especially in the 1860s and afterwards) be met? Moreover, the formation of vertical integration following the expanding phase required measures for solving difficult finance problems. As many prior studies indicate, joint-stock companies and banks had been essentially involved in this matter, which needs further detailed examination.

Secondly, the relation between cartel formation and banking interests is to be considered. In the case of the Bessemer cartel, the role of banks in luring Krupp into the cartel is mentioned, but the question remains yet unanswered as to whether or not German banks usually acted to promote cartels, possibly to guard their investments in the iron and steel industry.

Thirdly, the implication of cartels in building up vertical integration by steel firms should be considered further. Although the cartel's function of promoting vertical integration in the German iron and steel industry is often referred to, the case of the "Stahlwerksverband" indicates that many vertically integrated firms had already created their organizations prior to the formation of this multi-product cartel. It seems to me that reasons other than the mere existence of the cartel alone are possible for the German propensity toward vertical integration. Regarding the relationship between the cartel and vertical integration, one should bear in mind the German—especially the Ruhr—coal industry, where the cartel developed in a typical fashion. Hard coal, constituting one of the most important cost factors, had played a definitive role in the establishment of vertical integration in the German iron and steel industry. In this manner, the exercise of the Rhenish-Westphalian Coal Syndicate is worthy of discussion. As is well known, the combination of coal and steel was the most striking feature of the large integrated German steel firms.

German iron and steel industry entrepreneurs were recognized as being very conscious of—and at the same time very active in—market organization from the early phase of modern development. The reason why they were so sensitive to this point, while their British counterparts were not, deserves further examination as the fourth point. If tough competition, as Fremdling suggests, was characteristic of the German industry and its entrepreneurs, the origins or causes of this toughness in competition are to be explained more fully.

Lastly, we need to inquire about the intention of the German state government in encouraging the iron and steel industry through tariffs, cartels, and other measures. Regarding this point, attitudes of the iron and steel entrepreneurs toward government behavior should also be a matter of investigation. This point may extend somewhat into the political and social history of German business, but one could anticipate a fruitful discussion from this side of the issue.

Response

Rainer Fremdling

Professor Fukuoh has raised some important questions which are not dealt with sufficiently in my paper. The first concerns finance. Most enterprises were founded as joint-stock companies in the 1850s. Banks functioned as intermediaries in issuing stock capital, or as shareholders themselves. In addition, they provided short-term and long-term loans. In the formative years those banks also channeled foreign capital (French and Belgian) into those firms. The further expansion of firms was financed from profits, loans, or additional share capital. In the long run, loans increased faster than the finance from profits or additional share capital. Family-owned enterprises, even when they were run as joint-stock companies, relied more on internal resources of finance. During the two decades before World War I, long-term investment was prefinanced increasingly by short-term loans. Vertical integration was mainly financed by external sources, either additional share capital and bonds, or loans from banks. Because most of the vertical integration took place during the boom years from the 1890s onward, raising these funds was not that difficult and the banks actively supported this process by supplying funds and technical expertise.

This relates to the second question. As shareholders as well as creditors of both long-term and short-term loans, the banks regarded cartel formation as a device to secure their interests, and thus actively promoted it.

The third question deals with the coal cartel. The powerful Rhenish-Westphalian Coal Syndicate was founded in 1893. It possessed a central sales organization and fixed prices above competitive levels. By a backward integration through acquiring coal mines, steel mills could avoid price fixing by the coal cartel. However, it is not entirely clear whether or not price fixing by the cartel was the main motive for integrating backward. Some observers claim that prices were fixed rather moderately above competitive levels (Feldenkirchen, op. cit., p. 114). In any case, risk of unsecured coal supply and the need for piling up large stocks of coal could be reduced by integrating backward. Thus steel mills saved transaction costs.

Concerning the fourth question, one has to bear in mind that the German iron and steel industry was much more hit by the "Great Depression" than its British counterpart. Structural overcapacity in the 1870s and 1880s forced German entrepreneurs into this mixture of tough competition and collusive behavior, as I described. In stable markets more or less close to equilibrium, where entrepreneurs can reap sufficient profits, there is no need for turning to such extreme devices as tough competition or cartel formation. Both are nothing more than two sides of the same coin.

The last question raises a crucial point in the history of the German Empire. As has frequently been pointed out by political historians, there was a coalition between the traditional ruling elite, the Prussian nobility ("Junker"), and the new elite, the industrialists, dominated by heavy industry. They joined in their anti-democratic and anti-union attitudes. In giving up challenging the political power of the traditional elite, the industrialists were by and large assured that the state would not interfere unfavorably with their enterprises in return. The re-introduction of tariffs in 1879 (the coalition of "rye and iron") has to be understood in this context, which moreover resulted in a general policy favoring production over consumption. Government toleration or even promotion of syndicatization should be regarded as an instrument of national economic policy. Within the ruling elite, the opinion prevailed that the moderate pricing policies of cartels created stability and helped to maintain high employment—thus protecting the national labor. In contrast to the legal system of Anglo-Saxon countries, cartel agreements in Germany were confirmed as binding in law by the central court in 1897. If the state interfered with cartel forming at all, it enforced it (Potash Law 1910). And the steel industrialists boasted of having no need of state intervention in organizing their cartels.

The Evolution of Structures in the Iron and Steel Industry in France, Belgium, and Luxemburg: National and International Aspects, 1900–1939

Eric Bussière

Our main aim in this study is to analyze, in a historical and comparative context, the relations between international competition and the structures of the iron and steel industry in France, Belgium, and Luxemburg during the period 1900–39. The structures of the industry at the beginning of the century were determined by the very different nature of the markets (a small domestic market and an open economy in Belgium, and a large domestic market and protectionism in France), but also by an important technical factor: the common development of the Thomas process based on the iron ore of Lorraine. This development explains the convergence of the two models in the interwar period, largely abetted by the political consequences of the war. The early 1920s, a period of strong competition, were characterized by a dependence of French and Belgian industry on foreign markets. In both cases, the evolution of structures reveals attempts to adapt to these new conditions and a movement toward a common model. Its features, promoters, and external sources will be examined here. We will also consider the impact of its failure in the late on the competitiveness of the industry, as well as the impact of cartelization during the thirties.

I. The Prewar Structures

In 1913, the region presented striking differences in market strategy. There was a fundamental opposition between the iron industry in France, almost entirely oriented toward its domestic market and exporting comparatively little (11.03% of production), and Belgium, which exported the greater part of its output (63.15% in 1913).

The German iron and steel industry, which was dominant on the Continent due to its massive production, shows an intermediary position as regards its markets (29.83% exported in 1913).[1] The importance of the German market was enhanced by the fact that Luxemburg

141

and the most productive areas of Lorraine belonged to the Zollverein. Thus German Lorraine sold in the Zollverein 1,190,000 of its 3,870,000 metric tons of pig iron and 88% of its 2,280,000 tons of steel, while Luxemburg sold 1,040,000 of its 2,548,000 tons of pig iron and 91.8% of its steel.[2] Microeconomic studies on French firms corroborate the marginal role of exports. Denain-Anzin, based mainly in the north of France, exported only 1.38% in weight and 1.15% in value of its production in 1913.[3] The role of exports was in fact limited to easing pressures on the domestic market when surpluses were driving down prices. Exports, on the contrary, played a major role for Belgian firms such as Espérance-Longdoz (based near Liège), which exported 74.3% of its merchant bars and plates in 1913.[4]

The form of producers' organizations in France as well as Belgium seems to be strongly connected with the market structure, especially when compared with their German counterparts. In Germany, the Stahlwerksverband (Association of Steelworks) succeeded, between 1904 and 1907, in regrouping the major part of steel production and itself controlled sales (except finished products after 1912).

The success of this model was favored by the concentration of production and a domestic market that offered (before 1914) a base large enough for such an organization.[5] Many prewar and postwar publications in France insisted on the advantages of the flexible features of the French producers, syndicates, or *comptoirs*.[6] But these features betray in fact the weak concentration of structures in the French iron and steel industry, and that too within the framework of a rather narrow and protected market. The French *comptoirs* controlled in fact a restricted number of products and were weakened by important dissidents, that is, firms which did not participate. Only one of these syndicates was stable and efficient—the Comptoir des Poutrelles (structural shapes), founded in 1896. It was formed by the major producers, with only one dissident, de Wendel, and succeeded, from 1896 to the war, in maintaining a great stability of prices and establishing a normalization of production. Other attempts to create *comptoirs*, however, failed due to a large number of dissidents and their inherent instability. The dispersal of structures (26 makers of structural shapes at the beginning of the *comptoirs*) and the conflicts of interest among factories, steelmakers, and rerollers in the Comité des Forges testify to this weakness of organization. In spite of this, professional organizations tried to preserve the existing structures, especially in small units. Finally, the weakness of commercial organization of the producers and the major influence of iron merchants on the market also contributed to maintaining the status quo.[7]

International competition had, for a long time, negative effects on the organization of the French steel industry. In the 1860s, the main role of the Comité des Forges was to organize the protection of the French market against competition. The laws and ordinances of 1888, 1892, and 1910 were regarded as victories for this body. Moreover, export organization always played a role subordinate to that of the domestic market and was principally used to preserve the latter equilibrium. Thus the Comptoir des Poutrelles governed the entire production of central and southern France, where production was lowest, but only part of the output of the highly productive northern and eastern works. So the surplus had to be exported. The Comptoir d'Exportation des Produits Métallurgiques was finally founded in 1905, ten years after the Comptoir des Poutrelles, partly, it seems, at the request of German producers, but also, as we shall see, because of the burgeoning production of the northern and eastern works.

In Belgium, producers' syndicates were more directly connected to export markets than in France because of the weakness of the domestic market and low tariffs. The establishment of the Syndicat Belge des Rails d'Acier (1880) seemed to inspire foundation of the first rail producers' syndicate in 1884. The Comptoir des Aciéries Belges in 1905 included the whole range of A products, and in the same year enabled Belgian industry to participate in international syndicates. In Belgium, unlike France, export strategies were instrumental in the foundation of producers' syndicates.[8]

This comparison between France and Belgium reveals a strong diminishing at the begining of the 20th century. The increasing use of the Thomas process after 1895 and the growing need of French industry for coke created among France, Belgium, and Germany an interdependence in terms of supply, one consequence of which was a partial internationalization of the firms. France and Belgium depended on Germany for their supply of coke (respectively about 2,500,000 and 1,000,000 tons in 1913). This dependence, considered dangerous at the time, explains the interest taken by industrialists of French Lorraine and Luxemburg in the Aix-la-Chapelle and Westphalian areas. Likewise we can mention the association between ARBED (Luxemburg) and Eschweiler Bergwerksverein (Aix) in 1913, and the business interests of de Wendel, Marine-Homécourt, Micheville, Aciéries de Longwy, and Pont à Mousson in Aix-la-Chapelle and the Ruhr before 1914.[9]

Belgian industrialists associated themselves with French ones (Marine, Pont à Mousson, Micheville, and Schneider) in the development of the Campine coal mines. In return, we had Belgian interests

in iron mines in French Lorraine. In 1913 67% of Belgian imports
of iron ore came from France. This interdependence in raw materials
was added to the internationalization of production of several
firms. ARBED was based in Luxemburg, the Saarland, and the Aix
area. The Belgian firm la Providence (Charleroi) possessed two important works in northern and eastern France. Ougrée Marihaye's production was based chiefly on the three main continental markets:
Belgium, France (with its important subsidiary of the Hauts-Fourneaux
de la Chiers since 1905), and the Zollverein (since 1905 in Rodange).[10]
Though internationalization was less important in the case of
France, there were the financial links between the Forges et Aciéries
du Nord et de l'Est and the Usines Métallurgiques du Hainaut
(Belgium).

The beginning of internationalization, the convergence of structures, and the increasing solidarity between French and Belgian industrialists in the face of the growing competitiveness of Germany show
that the importance of the rupture represented by the First World War
must not be exaggerated. A similar remark can be made about the role
of the German Lorraine (after 1871) in the Zollverein. Studies at the
time indicated that German Lorraine, specializing in semi-finished
products, complemented the Ruhr, which specialized in highly finished goods. This view according to P. Zahlen is not entirely correct. If
this specialization existed until the 1880s, the introduction of the
Thomas process and the building of integrated works progressively
transformed German Lorraine into a competitor of the Ruhr (the production of rolled steels increased 24 times between 1880 and 1913 in
Lorraine and 6 times in the Ruhr). Moreover, a progressive trend
toward highly finished products can be noted in Lorraine. So Lorraine
had become a competitor of the Ruhr within the Zollverein itself by
1913.[11]

The distinguishing features of the French iron and steel industry
before the war, in comparison with the German and Belgian industries,
must be clarified. Can the minor place of exports and the relatively
strong protectionism be explained by high costs of production and an
inferior competitiveness?

Until the First World War, pig iron was considered the fundamental
product of the iron and steel industry. Table 1 shows that the most productive foundries were situated in the Zollverein (Luxemburg and
Lorraine), and the less productive in France.[12]

This analysis has, however, to be amended. Though nationwide

TABLE 1 Production of Pig Iron per Blast Furnace (thousand tons)

Year	France	Belgium	Luxemburg	Lorraine
1905	26.5	37.5	44	47.2
1907	29.5	35.3	46	46.5
1909	32.2	42.5	46	49.2
1911	37.3	44.5	46	53.2
1913	39.7	46.0	57	60.4
1920	36.3	42.9	53	
1925	57.1	63.6	69	
1927	64.6	67.4	71	
1929	66.9	71.0	82	
1931	90.5	76.1	87	
1933	68.9	84.7	90	
1935	70.8	81.9	93	
1937	75.4	80.9	103	
1939	68.8	76.5	–	

statistics for 1912 seem to confirm it (average daily production: 89 tonsin France, 170 tons in Germany), a study of 52 foundries in France and 34 in Belgium shows, on the contrary, figures not so very different from the German ones (138.5 tons a day in France, 159.5 tons a day in Belgium).[13] The fact is global statistics in France include rather small foundries in central and southern France where low outputs adversely affect the averages. Microeconomic studies at our disposal show that the output of the plants established at the beginning of the century in eastern France are equivalent to their competitors in the Zollverein. Thus, the Homécourt works in 1913 produced 376,000 tons of pig iron with five blast furnaces in action. In France as in Belgium investment in the industry was considerable from the beginning of the century and the machinery was largely renewed.

In Lorraine, the Neuves-Maisons works were built between 1900 and 1903, and two new blast furnaces were built in 1910; at Homécourt, five new furnaces were built between 1903 and 1913. In the North of France, where the blast furnaces were smaller, Denain-Anzin possessed six furnaces in 1900 with a daily output of 100 tons each; two more were built in 1906–7 (200–220 tons each) and still two more in 1913 (275–300 tons). In Normandy the blast furnaces of Caen, whose construction began in 1912, were slated to produce 375–400 tons a day.[14]

It seems, then, that the Thomas process was the source of a successful technical model that was soon adopted throughout the Continent.

In Belgium the works of Ougrée-Marihaye were re-organized in 1894 according to the German model, as a result of a journey of their managing director, G. Trasenster, to Ruhrort; the works of Neuves-Maisons were built with the technical assistance of German engineers; and the earliest departmental managers (steelworks and rolling mills) were a German and a Belgian.[15]

If technical and organizational processes were relatively similar on the Continent, other factors could influence competitiveness. French industrialists, in particular R. Pinot, the general secretary of the Comité des Forges, regularly refer to the high cost of coke, imported from Germany for the most part, and a difference in terms of cost price of 9 F per ton between France and Germany, and 5 F per ton between France and Belgium.[16] P. Zahlen's analysis plays down the importance of this disadvantage. A comparison of the cost prices of pig iron between the Ruhr works (Friedrich-Alfred Hütte in Essen) and the Southwest works (Esch-Arbed in Luxemburg) reveals that the low cost of iron ore largely counterbalanced the high cost of transporting coke from Westphalia, with an advantage of nearly 20% for Esch-Arbed.[17] This over-cost seems, in the present case, higher than the amounts usually mentioned in France. Another analysis shows that German coke imports into France helped to stabilize prices in the domestic market (coke shipped from northern France to the Lorraine).[18] Moreover, in Belgium industrialists increased their imports of German coal and coke, which cost less than Belgian coal and coke, between 1900 and 1913, and a few of them even abandoned their coal interests in Belgium.[19]

All this suggests that the growing power of the French iron and steel industry between 1900 and 1914 obliged it to increase its exports. Its performance between 1903 and 1913 confirms this conclusion, with a growth of 152% in steel production (Germany 118%).[20]

Investments made just before the war also support this view. In 1914 French steel production increased by approximately 1,000,000 tons because of the opening of two new works. Investments planned by Denain-Anzin for the 1914–18 period projected a significant growth of steel production (between 400,000, and 700,000 tons per year). This forecast was corroborated by F. Sermier, who observed an investment cycle of ten years in the French iron industry, with peaks in 1901 and 1911. The reconstruction of the early 1920s was actually, then, part of a continuous development.[21] From a global point of view, the period preceding the First World War revealed an increase of competition between industrial areas of Western Europe and a partial internationalization of firms. The French iron and steel industry was clearly affected by this movement, even though somewhat belatedly. Transformations due to the war, in fact, only accentuated this process.

II. Competition and Structures in the 1920s

1. Changes Due to the War

Most business historians recognize that the First World War was an opportunity for French industrialists and politicians to realize fully the industrial gap between France and Germany. Victory, they hoped, would enable them to close it, especially in the iron and steel industry. This objective was furthered by the recovery of Lorraine, by acquiring business interests in Luxemburg and the Saarland, and by forming cartels with the Belgians. As a result, the French steel production was able to increase from 4.6 to 8.9 million tons, with perhaps an additional 2 million tons in Saarland and 1.5 in Luxemburg. These projects had counterparts in Belgium, whose aim was an economic annexation of Luxemburg. The projects were, however, developed more in political or ministerial circles than in industry. In France, though the Foreign Office and the Ministry of Industry were in favor of them, industrialists, with a few exceptions (E. Schneider in France and G. Barbanson in Belgium), were much more cautious, realizing how difficult it would be for the domestic market to absorb these new quantities of steel.[22] Thus in France the Comité des Forges was in favor of an annexation of Luxemburg by Belgium, but in Belgium the Groupement des Hauts-Fourneaux opposed economic union with Luxemburg in 1920–21. The Treaty of Versailles finally ceded Lorraine to France, and the Saarland also for a period of 15 years. Economic union between Belgium and Luxemburg was ratified in 1922.

These transformations induced in fact real changes in the prewar equilibrium between the national iron and steel industries. Luxemburg had partly to transfer its exports from Germany to other markets, and France became a major exporter (from 630,000 tons in 1913 to 3,875,000 tons in 1925).[23] The necessity of an increasing competitiveness to win new markets and of replacing equipment destroyed by the war offered an opportunity for radical change in industrial structures. These possibilities were debated in France and Belgium after the war and in the following years.

The structure of the industry in France and in Belgium was very scattered. In France, 14 firms quoted in the stock exchange held in 1912 81% of the assets of the iron and steel industry. In Belgium, 13 producers were responsible for 95% of the pig-iron production in 1913.[24] In both cases we are in the presence of an oligopoly of average-sized enterprises which contrasts with the industrial concentrations of Germany and the United States. The official literature in France reported for a long time that this state of affairs was a deliberate choice. A book published in 1914 by the Comité des Forges favorably contrasts the French system, which respects the independence of enterprises, with the American trust or the "high-handed" German cartel. H. Flu, in his book of 1924, perpetuated this self-serving description. The firms enter into a trust "willy-nilly" and this can as easily land them into intolerable difficulties as achieve the much-vaunted progress they hope for. As for the German cartel, it constitutes a "rigid" agreement, and disregards the interests of its members.[25] This type of analysis revealed in fact a strong resistance to a concentration and rationalization of structures. In fact the principal efforts in this matter came from the banks.

The Société Générale de Belgique attempted, in 1918 when their forges were being rebuilt, to promote a global renovation of the structures in the Belgian steel industry. The main idea was "to americanize completely our steel industry" according to the model of United Steel, by means of an amalgamation of all existing enterprises. Each would specialize in one type of product. This scheme would have permitted a rapid and more coherent reconstruction to take place. The banks, and the Société Générale in particular, were ready to support it. The failure of this attempt can be traced to rivalries between industrialists, the reluctance of some of them to compromise their independence (especially Cockerill, whose mechanical-engineering divisions were important), and the lack of investment by the banks in the Belgian iron and steel industry just after the war.[26] Such projects were, it seems, also attempted in France. So the archives of Denain-Anzin reveal that "the commission, informed of alliance projects between some French metallurgic societies, thinks there is no reason for the Société de Denain et d'Anzin to seek that sort of combination."[27] The crisis of 1921 and difficulties that some enterprises fell prey to in the following years stimulated new initiatives. They came from the Banque de Paris et des Pays-Bas. In a series of reports in 1922, 1924, and 1926, one of the directors, L. Wibratte, proposed that they take advantage of the financial difficulties of the steel industry and the expected recession due to the recovery of the French franc to effect a complete renewal of structures in the French steel industry. His program was to close the western works, to specialize the central foundries in high-quality steel, and to form three large groups in the North and the East. He maintained that such a concentration alone would permit them to compete with the recently formed Vereinigte Stahlwerke and U.S. Steel. The failure of this new attempt can be attributed in part to the steady fall of the franc until 1926 and the establishment of the European steel cartel in 1926.[28] Furthermore, in France as well as Belgium the banks proved unable to exert any influence because they had invested so little in the industry.

2. Forms of Concentration

The failure of the banks left the industrialists the responsibility of themselves managing the changes brought about by the war. The territorial and political changes (sequestration of German enterprises) encouraged a movement toward internationalization. This continued tendencies which began at the end of the 19th century, and in which firms extended their operations first to other regions of the country and, after the war, throughout Western Europe. Marine-Homécourt's case was typical. Established in the mid-19th century in central France, it extended its operations to the Southwest in 1881, a period when the market was still regional. The opening of works in the North and in the East (Homécourt) in 1903 completed its multiregional features and gave it a nationwide sphere of operations. The war extended this movement. Marine formed a partnership with the Aciéries de Micheville to rebuild itself, and purchased the former German works of Rombas in Lorraine. In Luxemburg it participated in the establishment of HADIR (Hauts-Fourneaux de Differdange, St-Ingbert, and Rumelange) with Micheville, Pont à Mousson, and Belgian interests. In Saarland it acquired a major interest in the Dilling works. All of these investments increased the national and, even more, the international dimension of the group, with its far-flung operations and the necessity of exporting a major part of its 2,500,000 tons of iron and steel.[29] A similar development took place in the Forges et Aciéries du Nord et de l'Est, which had interests in Basse-Loire (Trignac), Lorraine (Uckange), and Saarland (Neunkirchen and Hombourg).[30] The internationalization of enterprises in Belgium and Luxemburg also flourished during this period. ARBED and Schneider created the Société des Terres Rouges (Luxemburg and Lorraine), and Ougrée-Marihaye entered into agreements with Rombas and Trefileries et Laminoirs du Havre.

All these developments led to the formation of European groups whose productive capacity increased from 1.5 million to 2.5 million tons: Marine, Ougrée, de Wendel, ARBED, and Nord et Est.[31] However, this process rarely led to amalgamations. In France especially, it led to conglomerates in which several industrial firms were associated. Marine-Homécourt's structure is typical of this model (Fig. 1).[32]

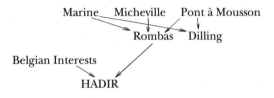

FIG. 1 The Marine-Homécourt Group (or Group Laurent).

We can find the same type of structures in Nord et Est, where new subsidiaries in western France, Lorraine, and Saarland maintained their identity, or in the ARBED–Schneider–Terres-Rouges case. In the Ougrée case, La Chiers, a French subsidiary, did not forfeit its legal independence.

Therefore, though these new groups were rather strong on paper, they had no integrated structure of management. However, to be able to compete in national and international markets they were obliged to innovate. In fact, the new commercial structures that emerged after World War I developed largely as management strategies. In the French case especially, the internationalization of operations and markets was the instigator of an evolution of great corporations.

The Marine-Homécourt case is a good example of the strengths and limitations of the new commercial structures created in the twenties. It is a conglomerate of five major enterprises without any common instrument of management. After the postwar rebuilding was accomplished, it limited itself to turning to account the few existing complementary characteristics of output in the different works by means of an internal market: Homécourt, Rombas, and Dilling supplied St-Ingbert with billets between 1925 and 1935. However, this type of support often failed due to the lack of an integrated management.[33]

In fact, the only genuine attempt to create an integrated structure of management was the establishment of a commercial subsidiary, DAVUM; it was originally oriented toward the French market and, after the establishment of a sister company devoted to exports in 1927, toward the international market. The chairman of these two firms was T. Laurent (chairman and general director of Marine) and on its board sat directors of every major enterprise of the group. Marketing policy was discussed at a biweekly conference of works directors. So

DAVUM was instrumental in integrating the Marine group, due to the productive capacity at its disposal and the possibility of specializing progressively each works' production. DAVUM in effect played this role simply by the assignment of orders. Homécourt specialized in semi-finished products and Rombas in more highly finished good. A policy of series was implemented by Micheville, Rombas, and HADIR with regard to export markets. In 1927–28 DAVUM could be expected to coordinate a large European industrial group constituted by Marine, Aciéries de France, and Fabrique de Fer de Maubeuge (northern France), and Angleur (a Belgian firm). However, limits to DAVUM's scale of activities soon became apparent: Angleur refused to associate itself with DAVUM, and the products of the northern partners often competed for the same markets as Marine's. Above all, DAVUM suffered from an inability to impose its decisions on the works: it could control neither prices nor output. So one could say DAVUM was an attempt to integrate the group which had still not succeeded in the early thirties.

The process is similar but more advanced in the case of Ougrée-Marihaye. In 1922 Ougrée entered into partnership with a Dutch steel-trader who had operations in Germany and England; this association helped to establish the Socobelge (Société Commerciale Belge) in 1924. It became the trader for every works in the group and for a few national and international cartels (a wire producers' association and a hoops and strips producers' association). A very close collaboration between Socobelge and Ougrée took the form of a permanent committee that permitted them to define the group's strategy jointly. In this case, the strong subordination of the subsidiaries to Ougrée strengthened Socobelge's position.[34]

This type of commercial subsidiary became widespread in France, Belgium, and Luxemburg during the interwar period: Columeta for the ARBED and Ucometal for enterprises under the Société Générale de Belgique. However, the process of integration through a commercial subsidiary did not in every case succeed. It was rather successful in Columeta and Socobelge, but less so in Ucometal (works of the S.G.B. group remained autonomous for the most part) and DAVUM. None of them, except perhaps Columeta–ARBED, were as successful as the Vereinigte Stahlwerke model, which was created at the same time. In the latter, the amalgamation was undertaken at the bank's request and the bank authorized a more radical transformation of structures.[35] The process of integration by the market was, however, not fated to failure in France. In the French tubes and pipes industry, the foundation of

Vallourec initiated a progressive amalgamation of the whole of the industry.[36] The question remains whether the cartels that appeared in 1925 in France and Belgium did not constitute a major impediment to this evolution.

3. The European Steel Cartel

The origins of the European steel cartel are well known thanks to numerous studies on them.[37] It developed after a short but severe period of competition in which many factors contributed to the intense competitiveness of the industry: tariffs imposed on Germany in the Versailles treaty, obstacles to the supply of coke, strong fluctuations of the currencies, and political factors such as the Ruhr invasion in 1923. Competition during these years affected not only commerce between Germany and its former enemies, but also trade among the former allies themelves. Between 1919 and 1922, the fall of the German mark and large investments in the Ruhr area permitted German industry to exert strong pressure on export markets. The French and the Belgians were not able to agree to a cartel in 1919 (with Saarland and Luxemburg); and in 1921 the competition was particularly intense and protectionist pressures arose in France. The Belgians prevented the establishment of French *comptoirs* in 1921 when their French subsidiaries chose not to participate, but French industrialists exerted pressure on the Belgians through their allies in Luxemburg.[38]

In 1924, the monetary recovery in Germany and the fall of the French and Belgian francs reversed the positions. After the summer of 1924, products from Lorraine were sold at favorable prices on the markets of southern Germany.[39]

The marketing advantage of Lorraine was even more pronounced in 1925; in July the average prices at the works for bars were: Ruhr, 127.5 marks/ton; and Lorraine, 104.7 marks/ton. The cartel formed in September 1926 can be explained by the desire of German industry to protect its own market and by the eagerness of the French to consolidate their rather good position before the monetary recovery. These agreements were in fact composed of two parts. The first established a quota system which permitted France, Luxemburg, and Saarland to sell products in Germany under the control of the Stahlwerksverband. The second (the Entente Internationale de l'Acier) established a general control of production (in quantity) between countries (France, Belgium, Luxemburg, and Germany) or rather between regions that competed with each other for the same markets, especially since the rebuilding period.[40]

Belgian industry found itself isolated in these transactions. No arrangement could be worked out with Luxemburg in spite of the customs union between the two countries. So the Luxemburgian industrialists acted as intermediaries between the French and the German, and the Belgians finally had to join the arrangement.

The conditions under which the syndicates were formed in 1925 and 1926 reveal the importance of the changes that the French iron and steel industry underwent since the war. Until 1914, French *comptoirs* had as their primary aim the organization of the domestic market. Their re-emergence after 1925 was promoted by the E.I.A and I.R.M.A (International Railmakers Association) and also by the international market. In fact, the model of organization of the Belgian and French industries during the twenties is largely based on the German model of the Rohstahlgemeinschaft (Steelmakers Association). The E.I.A. can be considered, for the most part, as a further development of national syndicates formed on this model. It remained unchanged until 1931, when it was broken up. In spite of the existence of a few specialized *comptoirs*, attempts to form syndicates for the main products (A products) failed in 1927 and 1930. Similar attempts in the French market also failed or proved to be inefficient. These fluid conditions permitted the development of the commercial organization of firms in the twenties; the fluidity and incompleteness of the system also encouraged other attempts at rationalization between 1926 and 1929.

The *comptoirs* at the end of the twenties favored the external development of firms by a process of purchase or amalgamation that permitted them to grow by increasing their quotas. A few operations took place in France (purchase of the Aciéries de France by Chatillon-Commentry),[41] and a few more in Belgium (amalgamation of Angleur and Athus, Chatelineau and Sambre et Moselle, and the purchase of Alliance-Monceau by Ougrée).[42] In Belgium this process was favored by the Société Générale, which bought major interests in Cockerill and Sambre et Moselle. In Luxemburg, ARBED and Terres Rouges were amalgamated in 1926. This process also had its equivalent on an international level. In 1928 and 1929 the Société Générale established closer relations with ARBED by an acquisition of stocks on the Dutch market. This first step was followed in the autumn of 1929 by an amalgamation on a European scale between a German group (Vereinigte Stahlwerke, Gelsenkirchen, and Phoenix), a Belgian group (the Société Générale and ARBED), and a French group. If it had succeeded, it could have rationalized all the existing works and have made massive new investments. In France, in spite of the consent of Marine-Homécourt, the project was defeated by the refusal of de Wendel, whose participation was thought to be indispensable.[43] In fact, this project was the equivalent, on an international scale, of the Vereinigte Stahlwerke in Germany. It can be described as an attempt to create on the Continent a sort of "European Steel" along the lines of the American model.

III. Markets and Organization: Developments in the Thirties

1. The International Steel Cartel

The nature of the international steel cartel can be best described by the evolution of its predecessor. During the twenties the aim of the Belgian steel industry was to organize the export markets in order to defend itself against its German competitors, especially in the event of an economic recession in Germany. They feared in fact the practice of dumping by French and German industries, a result of their larger domestic markets. The failure of the two attempts (1927 and 1930) to organize specialized *comptoirs* originated in this conflict of interests between countries with large domestic markets and countries with small home markets. The decisions of the Düsseldorf meeting (13 July 1928) anticipated the evolution of the thirties: The German group agreed to a limitation its exports in exchange for a reduction of penalties for exceeding its quotas. At the same time (early 1928), the Belgians agreed to stop their exports to the German market. So, by the end of the twenties, only French-Belgian trade was unorganized.[44]

The dissociation between domestic and export markets during the thirties was due, first, to the ability of the industry in countries with large domestic markets to maintain higher prices and, second, to the absolute necessity in Belgium and Luxemburg of accepting low prices in their export markets.[45]

Under these circumstances, Germany and France were able to preserve their advantage and to separate the domestic and export markets in the new cartel. In the case of France, industry was supported by the government, which was determined to use the threat of quotas to help it, as in the case of the Franco-Belgian agreement of 1932. The peculiar form of the organization of the international steel cartel in 1933 was a consequence of this evolution: The export markets alone were organized.

From a national and international point of view, the cartel organization was a much more constraining system than its predecessor, especially in France. The extent to which it influenced the industrial and commercial structure of the steel industry is the question we want to address here.

The Comptoir Sidérurgique de France (C.S.F.) was founded on a permanent basis at the beginning of 1932 and lasted until the end of the thirties. It controlled virtually all production in France and enlarged its sphere of influence by agreements with re-rollers in 1935–36 and steel traders in 1936. So it was understandably considered by a few authors as the instrument of management of the industry. Its effect on the structure of the industry, however, was certainly to impede its evolution. The main role of the C.S.F. was to determine production quotas for each works and for each type of product. In 1932, the quotas were fixed according to the production statistics of the late 1920s; in 1935, according to the new machinery and its theoretical productive capacity. These allotments were not to be modified for a period of five years. Such agreements between works were obtained by the creation of equalizing funds between the main products and between domestic and export markets.[46]

The consequences of this system, a stabilization of structures in the steel industry in France,[47] are shown in Table 2.

TABLE 2   The Largest Firms as Percentage of National Production (1929: actual production; 1937–38: relative production in *comptoirs*)

	1929	1937–38
Chiers	4.1	5.342
Denain-Anzin	5.1	5.890
De Wendel	16.8	17.546
Knutange	6.3	6.234
Longwy	5.3	6.421
Marmiche	8.0	9.681
Chatillon-Commentry	3.9	5.728
Nord et Est	5.4	8.366
Normande	3.8	4.491
Pompey	4.2	3.253
Providence	?	5.392
Rombas	6.6	8.430
Senelle-Maubeuge	4.3	4.618

This general analysis must, however, be clarified. The identity of the industrial groups was not eclipsed completely by the C.S.F.'s authority. In Marine-Homécourt's case, negotiations with the C.S.F. were conducted for the group as a whole, and Homécourt and Micheville were considered as a single contracting party. Moreover, the integration of the industry was favored by C.S.F. rules that encouraged this type of acquisition. On the whole, the cartel's rules permitted the major enterprises to preserve part of their commercial autonomy. For instance, DAVUM remained the commercial instrument of the Marine group, and about 87% of DAVUM-Exports's orders in 1938 were directed to it.

The same analysis could be made in the Belgian case. Though Cosibel (Comptoir de Vente de la Sidérurgie Belge), founded in May 1933, was an official member of the steel cartel, its orders were handled by the commercial organs of the firms: Socobelge and Ucometal.[48] However, as in France, the cartel system was not favorable to a further integration of the groups. The enterprises under the control of the Société Générale de Belgique kept their autonomy, and the evolution of the Ougrée-Marihaye group was directed toward greater autonomy of the major units. In this particular case, the market situation favored this process.

2. Competitiveness: From Prosperity to the Depression
The principal question we will address here is the the relation between cartels, competitiveness, and the structure of enterprises.

Competitiveness in the twenties depended on factors such as the general level of prices, the level of wages, and the cost of raw materials—all largely influenced by monetary and political policies—but it cannot be assessed by production statistics alone. Such figures are, moreover, difficult to obtain because of the lack of detailed studies on the subject.

In France and Belgium, the steel industry was largely rebuilt according to prewar models. This can be explained by the refusal of industrialists to introduce structural changes, the desire for a rapid reconstruction to exploit the high demand for steel products, and, especially in Belgium, the eagerness to recover, as quickly as possible, one's share of the export market. This program was also favored by the recovery of German equipment in Lorraine, ceded to France at Versailles. Such was the case in France, for instance, for the firm Nord et Est in Valenciennes.

In the late 1920s, the French and Belgian steel industry was characterized by medium-sized plants. In Belgium the average output of pig iron per plant in 1929 was 250,000 tons (about 300,000–600,000 tons for the largest works);[49] in France nearly all the works produced over 250,000 tons, and half of them over 400,000 tons a year. So it compared favorably with the British industry (where only 8 plants out of 56 produced over 250,000 tons of lingots a year), but unfavorably with the larger German works (half of the production of lingots came from plants whose individual outputs exceeded 800,000 tons in 1929), especially after the rationalization of production by the Vereinigte Stahlwerke in 1926.[50]

In general, reconstruction did not hinder the introduction of modern equipment. The works of Denain were nearly completely rebuilt with new equipment, as were the Homécourt works. However, in the majority of cases, new equipment was combined with recovered equipment.[51]

If we consider the first stage of production, Table 1 reveals a steady increase of pig-iron production, due for the most part to the growth of the size of blast furnaces.[52] In France, for instance, the new blast furnaces of Denain had a capacity of 300 tons each, instead of the 200 tons of the older furnaces.[53] Table 1 also shows that French production after the war nearly equaled that of Belgium, due partially to the recovery of Lorraine, where the furnaces were more capacious. Table 3 reveals the excellent position of Belgian industry in this stage of production, and the effects of German rationalization since 1926. The same conclusion can probably be advanced in the French case according to Table 1, whereas Luxemburg's case can be considered rather similar to the German one.[54]

TABLE 3 Output per Man per Year (in tons)

Year	U.K.	Germany	Belgium
1924	281	240	534
1927	365	470	525
1928	348	590	543
1929	399	600	525

TABLE 4 Cost Price per Ton in 1927 (gold francs)

	Pig iron	Merchant bars
Burbach	63.26	134.68
Esch	67.86	102.32

However, the second and third stages of production (smelting and rolling) became more important in terms of cost reduction during the interwar period. For instance, a comparison between the Burbach (Saarland) and Esch (Luxemburg) plants of the ARBED shows the effects of the good productivity in rolling mills in the latter (Table 4).[55]

Here also, statistics quoted by D.L. Burn highlight the impressive performance of Belgian industry, with an annual output per man of 98 tons in 1929, compared to 58 tons in England and 96 tons in Germany (smelting and rolling).[56] A close analysis of French firms confirms the role of machinery in high productivity, especially at the rolling stage of production. At Denain-Anzin and Homécourt the mills were entirely reconstructed, as were part of the mills at Valenciennes.[57] However, most of them were oriented toward semi-finished products to be sold on export markets. For this type of product, high productivity strengthened by the low wages in France[58] yielded high profits in the late twenties.[59]

So by the end of the 1920s, the French iron and steel industry was able to produce semi-finished goods, on a rather large scale. This result can be considered an achievement of the model created at the end of the 19th century, as studies on investment at Denain-Anzin and Nord et Est confirm. If these plants had worked under normal conditions between 1913 and 1927, investment would have reached nearly the same levels as it did with the postwar reconstruction.[60]

Investment in Belgium during the 1930s passed through three phases: a very high level in 1929–32 as a result of high profits in the period 1928–30, a period of low investment in 1933–37, and a short resurgence in 1938–39 after high profits in 1936–37.[61] This pattern was reflected in France, although the amount of investment in new technology seems to have been lower than in Belgium, with 319 million francs-Poincaré invested in 1927–31.[62] Case studies confirm this general movement with, for instance, a virtual drying up of investment at Nord et Est in 1932–35 and a very low level at Denain-Anzin.[63]

The nature of the investment lends credence to the idea that the structures of this industry were immobile in the thirties. In France expenditures in 1928–31 were used to finance a completion of reconstruction rather than technical innovations aimed at new products. In Belgium the preference for simple steel products for export remained dominant in the late thirties. So the most important investments of Ougrée-Marihaye in 1937–39 simply refurbished the existing equipment at Ougrée and Rodange.[64] However, some innovations on the part of French and Belgian firms can be cited. In France, Denain-

Anzin and Nord et Est developed their production of high-quality steel. In Belgium, Espérance-Longdoz increased its production of sheets and phased out the production of semi-finished goods, while La Chiers developed the production of sheet steel for the automobile industry in 1931–32.

The statistics of this period show a decline in the productivity of blast furnaces, more acute in France than in Belgium (Table 1).[65]

Figures published by the inquiry commission of 1939 reveal the increasing difference of productivity during the thirties vis-à-vis German industry.[66] According to the commission, 60 of the 90 blast furnaces in activity were modern ones in 1939. The equipment in the steelworks was adequate, except for the capacity of the open-hearth furnaces, which were generally smaller than German or American furnaces (5 out of 90–100 tons). The major weakness was in the rolling mills, in which only a third of the equipment was on the German level and perhaps an additional 25% was considered adequate. In general, heavy mills for semi-finished products were new or modernized plants, while small mills for finished goods were too numerous and revealed overcapacities. Basically, the absence in France of investment in continuous strip mills and cold rollers on the American model, which was followed in Germany and England, revealed the problem of structures in the steel industry. The conclusion of Guillaume and Huberson in their report of 1939 pointed to the necessity of a major overhaul of these structures.

The years 1895–1930 were a period of great development in the Belgian and especially the French steel industry, based on the iron ore of Lorraine and on the Thomas process. On the lines of this technical and organizational model, largely inspired by Germany, were built the large plants of Lorraine, Luxemburg, and Belgium. A major consequence of this development was the growing role of exports for the French steel industry, a role originating at the turn of the century and strongly increased by the political consequences of the war. The competitiveness of this model was due to its technical efficiency, the low cost of iron ore, and low wages.

However, the model did not find, in France and Belgium, very favorable ground. The French and Belgian structures were narrow ones, with insufficient processing industries. So the important steel plants were specialized in semi-finished products and largely oriented toward export markets. Similarly, the general structure of the industry in France and Belgium, mostly represented by medium-sized enterprises, was not large enough to accommodate this model.

In spite of this, during the twenties attempts were made to correct these disadvantages by developing new commercial structures, and the period also illustrates the importance of internationalization in the evolution of structures, especially in the French steel industry. The failure of these attempts and the inability of the banks to impose radical change of structure by amalgamation according to the American or German model largely accounts for the immobility of industrial structures. It was also responsible for the bad choice of investments in 1929–32 and their later decline. For the French and Belgian steel industries, the cartel formed during the thirties, was at best a makeshift solution.

NOTES

1.   S.D.N., *Memorandum sur l'industrie du fer et de l' acier* (Geneva, 1927).
2.   Banque de Paris et des Pays-Bas, "Note sur l'industrie du fer et de l'acier après la guerre," unpublished.
3.   O. Hardy-Hemery, "Industries, patronat et ouvriers du Valenciennois pendant le premier vingtième siècle," Thesis, Paris, 1981, pp. 738–39.
4.   L. Willem, *La Société d'Espérance-Longdoz, 1905–1960*, p.439, unpublished.
5.   H. Rieben, *Des ententes de maîtres de forges au plan Schumann* (Lausanne, 1954), pp. 109–14.
6.   Comité des Forges de France, *La sidérurgie française, 1864–1914* (Paris, 1920), pp. 505–25; H. Flu, *Les comptoirs métallurgiques d'après guerre, 1919–1922* (Paris, 1925) pp. 17–35; A. Piettre, *L'évolution des ententes industrielles en France depuis la crise* (Paris, 1936).
7.   Hardy, op. cit., pp. 738–43.
8.   C. Reuss, E. Koutny, and L. Tychon, *Le progrès technique en sidérurgie: Belgique, Luxembourg, Pays-Bas* (Louvain, 1955), pp. 92–95.
9.   P. Zahlen, *La sidérurgie de la région Sarre, Lorraine, Luxembourg dans les années vingt* (Florence, 1988), pp. 184–85.
10. E. Bussière, "La sidérurgie belge durant l'entre-deux-guerres: le cas d'Ougrée-Marihaye," *Revue belge d'histoire contemporaine*, vol. 15, no. 3–4 (1984): 304–5.
11. Zahlen, op. cit., pp. 272–81.
12. Reuss et al., op. cit., pp. 386, 427, Chambre syndicale de la sidérurgie française, *Bulletin*, no. 1 (1945).
13. Hardy, op. cit., p. 536.
14. Ibid., pp. 535–37; *T. Laurent 1863–1953* (Paris, 1955), pp. 53–58; R. Bühler, *Die Roheisenkartelle in Frankreich, 1876–1934*, (Zurich, 1934), p. 48; Archives Nationales 175 AQ 14, Cie de Chatillon, Commentary, Neuves-Maisons.
15. Bussière, op. cit., p. 305; Archives Nationales 175 AQ 14.
16. Bühler, op. cit., p. 4.

17. Zahlen, op. cit., pp. 247–49.

18. Ibid., pp. 186–88.

19. Reuss, op. cit., pp. 88–89.

20. Bühler, op. cit., p. 3.

21. Ibid., p. 11; Hardy, op. cit., p. 620; F. Sermier, "Les investissements de la sidérurgie française, 1919–1973," Thesis, Paris XIV, 1981.

22. G.H. Soutou, *L'or et le sang: les buts de guerre économiques de la première guerre mondiale* (Paris, 1989); J. Bariéty, *Les relations franco-allemandes après la première guerre mondiale* (Paris, 1977); E. Bussière, "Les relations entre la France et la Belgique dans les rivalités économiques et financières en Europe, 1919–1935," Thesis, Paris IV, 1988.

23. S.D.N., op. cit.

24. J. Bouvier, F. Caron, "Structure des firmes, emprise de l'Etat," in Braudel et Labrousse (eds.), *Histoire économique et sociale de la France*, vol. 4 (Paris, 1980), p. 784; Reuss, op. cit., p. 299

25. Flu, op. cit.

26. Bussière, op. cit., pp. 306–8.

27. Hardy, op. cit., pp. 1468.

28. Banque de Paris et des Pays-Bas, Dossier 507/25.

29. E. Bussière, "Stratégies industrielles et structures de management dans la sidérurgie française: le cas de Marine-Homécourt durant l'entre-deux-guerres," *Revue historique* (1989/1).

30. Hardy, op. cit., pp. 1476–81.

31. C. Prêcheur, *La Lorraine sidérurgique* (Paris, 1959), pp. 208–28.

32. Bussière, op. cit. (1989).

33. Ibid.

34. Bussière, op. cit. (1984), pp. 332–33, 342–44.

35. W. Feldenkirchen, "Big Business in Interwar Germany," *Business History Review*, vol. 61, no. 3 (1987): 417–53.

36. C. Omnes, *De l'atelier au groupe industriel, Vallourec* (Lille, 1982), pp. 205–6.

37. Rieben, op. cit.; E. Hexner, *The International Steel Cartel* (Chapel Hill, N.C., 1943).

38. Bussière, op. cit. (1988), pp. 118–30.

39. Zahlen, op. cit., pp. 225–56.

40. Ibid., pp. 259–64.

41. Archives Nationales 175 AQ.

42. Reuss, op. cit., p. 107.

43. Bussière, op. cit. (1988), pp. 504–8.

44. Ibid., p. 493.

45. Rieben, op. cit., p. 203.

46. Hardy, op. cit., p. 2347.

47. Bussière, op. cit. (1989), p. 39.

48. Bussière, op. cit. (1984), p. 350.

49. Reuss, op. cit., p. 386.

50. D.L. Burn, *The Economic History of Steel Making*, (Cambridge, 1946), pp. 432–33.

51. Hardy, op. cit., pp. 1458–60; T. Laurent, pp. 58–60.

52. Ruess, op. cit.; Burns, op. cit., p. 417.

53. Hardy, op. cit., p. 1458.
54. Reuss, op. cit.; Burn, op. cit.
55. Zahlen, op. cit., p. 149.
56. Burn, op. cit., p. 427–34.
57. Hardy, op. cit., pp. 1458–68; Burn, op. cit., p. 409.
58. Burn, op. cit., p. 422; Zahlen, op. cit., p. 153.
59. Zahlen, op. cit., p. 242; Archives Nationales 139 AQ 135 (Marine-Homécourt).
60. Hardy, op. cit., p. 1577.
61. Reuss, op. cit., p. 336.
62. Archives Nationales 62 AQ 7, Commission d'études sidérugiques (1938–39), reports by Guillaume and Huberson, Jordan, and Cornu-Thenard, unpublished.
63. Hardy, op. cit., p. 2046.
64. Bussière, op. cit. (1984), p. 364.
65. See note 52.
66. Archives Nationales 62 AQ 7.

Comment

Toshikatsu Nakajima

Based on original sources, Dr. Bussière has analyzed the structure and functions of producers' organizations in the Franco-Belgian steel industry before 1939. *Ententes* and *comptoirs*, compared to their German and American counterparts, were formerly considered fragile and obsolescent. It is certain that, both in France and in Belgium, all attempts to introduce American-style trust organizations failed in the early twenties because of bankers' small interest in the industry. But French and Belgian industrialists, in order to complement lax cartels, tightened the interconnections of their firms and created commercial subsidiaries in common. Thanks to these measures, each firm, organized in one of the five industrial groups (Marine, Ougrée, de Wendel, ARBED, and Nord et Est), could specialize its activity, while the level of production was efficiently controlled. Thus big blast furnaces in Lorraine could compete in productivity with their German rivals, though the desire of industrialists to maintain their independence prevented large-scale investments, especially in the rolling process.

Bussière explained precisely the logic of interfirm relationships *within* the steel industry. To clarify the points of the argument, the financial side of the problem could also be treated concretely.

Bankers had little interest in the steel industry of France and Belgium. It is well known that the industrialists of Lorraine financed mostly by themselves the development of their steelworks. Before 1914, some 300 million francs were invested in steel production in Lorraine. The banks financed only 20 million (less than 7%) of this investment. The rest was collected either in the security market or by plowing back the steelmakers' own profits. According to Omori Hiroyoshi, who examined the balance sheets of the main steelmakers in Lorraine before 1914, more than 60% of their investment was self-financed.

What, then, made this enormous self-finance possible? Capital previously accumulated? Or the high price of products supported by a pro-

163

tectionist government? In short, with what financial assets did the industrialists maintain their independence?

The problem of vertical integration also remains to be analyzed. Firms combining steelmaking with mechanical engineering (Cockerill in Belgium and Schneider in France, for example) disturbed the formation of stable cartels in steel products. As Bussière argues, the heterogeneity of these metalworking enterprises can be attributed to the lack of dynamism in the steel market. But it is also true that their metal-processing and engineering activities corresponded to the consumer-oriented industrialization strategy pursued by the French in the growing international division of labor. The downstream diversification of large-scale enterprises in the interwar period should be explained in this context.

Bussière analyzed in detail the creation of some Franco-Belgian industrial groups before 1939. Did those groups play a positive role in the growth of heavy industry during and after World War II? Or did they rather obstruct recent structural changes? In any case, only a detailed study of postwar growth will clarify the historical meaning of the turbulence of the interwar period.

Response

Eric Bussière

There was a definite evolution in the way the industrialists financed their investments, especially in France. Before World War I high prices partly permitted by *ententes* and protection, and profits in mechanical engineering or the armaments industry were the major sources of financing heavy equipment in Lorraine. During the twenties the sources were state indemnities, indebtment, and inflation, profits made during the war by firms situated partly in central France, and, especially between 1927 and 1929, the high prices permitted by the European steel cartel. In Belgium the links between the bankers and industrialists were stronger before the war; in the absence of war profits, debit financing was essential and bankers increased their interests between 1927 and 1935.

The problem of industrial groups combining steel and mechanical-engineering industries must be examined. This integration was only partial; large firms in Lorraine utilized in their mechanical-engineering departments, which were situated in central France, steels of high quality produced in the same area. As for their semi-finished products from Lorraine, they accepted cartels mainly in the thirties. The problems were more difficult with independent re-rollers; investments from large firms in rolling mills during the thirties were mainly defensive ones encouraged by the cartels from 1932 to 1936. As a result, there were general agreements with re-rollers and iron merchants in 1936.

As for the Franco-Belgian groups before World War II, their role in postwar growth and European integration must not be overestimated. In France the major mergers were initiated by the state in this period, and were carried out in the national interest. Indeed, some of the most important Franco-Belgian industrial groups were dismantled in the 1950s and the 1960s.

Import Substitution and Competitiveness in the Prewar Japanese Iron and Steel Industry

Tetsuji Okazaki

I. Introduction

This paper aims to clarify the process and causes of import substitution in the pre–World War II Japanese iron and steel industry with a focus on international competitiveness.[1] The international competitiveness of a specific industry here denotes the degree to which production costs are low in an international context. The study, therefore, first necessitated a comparative analysis of various countries' cost data. The following points should be kept in mind. International competitiveness as defined above is generally determined according to comparative costs based on real conditions such as production factors and technology, and on nominal conditions such as exchange rates and general price levels.[2] This is a standard approach, but it is especially useful in showing that a given industry's competitiveness is based not simply on intra-industry conditions but is also connected to the entire economy. Industrial development/decline under the pressures of international competition should be placed in the context of the historical evolution of the whole economic structure.

Historical studies of the prewar Japanese economy, which have proliferated in recent years,[3] to some extent take note of the issue of international competitiveness, but they do not fully bring out the above points. As a result, the mechanism for the change of the industrial structure has not been sufficiently explained. Meanwhile, great importance is attached to World War I as an epoch of rapid changes in industrial relations, the capital market, etc., as well as changes in industrial structure.[4] These changes should be placed in the standard analytical framework of international competitiveness.

In selecting that framework, this study seeks to explain import substitution in the Japanese iron and steel industry as one aspect of structural economic change as well as provide some insights into historical structural change in the Japanese economy.

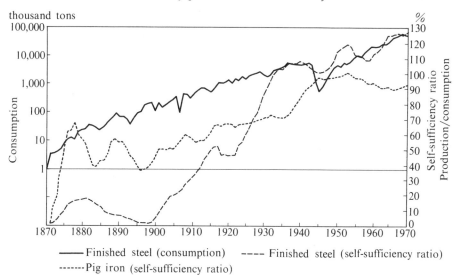

FIG. 1 Consumption and Self-sufficiency Ratio of Iron and Steel.
Sources: Tekkō Tōkei Iinkai, *Tōkei kara Mita Nihon Tekkōgyō 100 Nenkan no Ayumi* (100 Years of the Japanese Iron and Steel Industry viewed through Statistics) (1970); Shōkōshō, "Seitetsugyō Sankō Shiryō" (Reference Materials on the Iron and Steel Industry).
Note: Until 1945, consumption in Korea was included.

II. Introduction and Diffusion of Modern Technology

Japanese consumption of iron and steel was extremely low in the 1870s, but it began to increase at a rapid pace after the start of industrialization (Fig. 1). This consumption created a level of demand favorable to the development of the iron and steel industry. This industry, like several others in prewar Japan, grew successfully through import substitution in an expanding domestic market.[5] As early as 1900–1904, production of pig iron and finished steel exceeded 200,000 metric tons (t) and imports fell to 40% (pig iron) and 60% (finished steel) of the total consumption.

Most of the production took place at the state-owned ironworks (Yawata Seitetsujo), which began operation in 1901 (Table 1). It should be noted, however, that already before World War I, several private enterprises also produced iron and steel. Most of these made forged or founded steel with open-hearths, but Tanaka Kōzan (Tanaka Mining) and Nippon Kōkan (Nippon Steel Pipe Co.) were mass producers of iron and steel that substituted for imports on a large scale. Moreover, the former produced iron and steel in a continuous process, and the latter was the first iron and steel enterprise established with funds raised in the capital market.[6]

TABLE 1 Output of Iron and Steel (thousand tons)

	1914	1919	1929
Pig iron			
Total	300	674	1,241
Yawata Seitetsujo	222	281	646
Private	79	393	594
Tanaka (Kamaishi) Kōzan	40	64	99
Wanishi Seitetsujo	24	116	117
Mitsubishi Seitetsu	0	78	154
Others (over 5,000 tons)	14	134	225
under 5,000 tons	14	101	13
Finished steel			
Total	283	553	2,034
Yawata Seitetsujo	230	281	899
Private	52	272	1,135
Tanaka (Kamaishi) Kōzan	14	11	71
Nippon Kōkan	3	52	223
Kawasaki Zōsenjo	0	50	186
Others (over 5,000 tons)	35	158	655
under 5,000 tons	23	64	98

Source: Shōkōshō, *Seitetsugyō Sankō Shiryō* (Reference Materials on the Iron and Steel Industry).

TABLE 2 Profit Rates on Invested Capital by Firm (% per year)

	1914	1918	1922	1925	1928	1931	1933
Pig-iron producers							
Yawata Seitetsujo	16.1	112.6	0.0	1.0	15.5	2.9	31.5
Tanaka (Kamaishi) Kōzan	7.0*	32.5	0.0	−1.4	4.6	−4.5	17.6
Mitsubishi Seitetsu	−	12.1	−11.2	1.0	5.3	−2.3	8.2
Others							
Nippon Kōkan	1.6	43.0	3.0	3.2	12.9	−2.8	45.1
Asano Kokura Seikō	−	−	3.7	2.5	4.2	6.2	66.0
Osaka Seitetsu	−	31.5	0.1	12.0	22.5	12.8	56.8
Fuji Seikō	−	15.2	−0.2	1.1	1.7	1.6	35.0
Kawasaki Zōsenjo	10.6	53.7	8.7	5.2	−25.0	−12.5	0.2
Kobe Seikōjo	13.0	45.7	6.8	5.3	3.5	−3.2	13.0
Nihon Seikōho	1.7	32.8	14.2	3.6	4.9	−0.7	9.8

*Estimated from a report of a student of Tokyo Imperial University (Utoro Shingo), 1910.
Sources: Business reports of each firm.

These facts suggest that iron and steel production grew to a business on the commercial level. As a matter of fact, just before World War I Yawata Seitetsujo was earning an annual profit of 16% on invested capital, and private enterprises (including the two mentioned above) were also reaping profits, although they had begun operation in the red (Table 2). Tanaka Kōzan's profits around 1910 are estimated to have been 7% on invested capital. Nippon Kōkan's low profit rate in 1914 can be explained by the fact that it only commenced operation in the latter half of 1914. From mid-1914 to mid-1915, it earned a profit of 5.5%. The major reason the government planned to establish the state-owned ironworks in the 1890s was that it did not expect private investment in the iron and steel industry at that time. Under the promising circumstances explained above, however, privatization of Yawata Seitetsujo was considered as early as 1909.[7]

It is striking that owing to an import tax of only 15% or so,[8] the newly born Japanese iron and steel industry achieved some profitability. One of the factors that made this possible was the fact that a global economic depression came to an end in the 1890s. However, there were also conditions peculiar to Japan. Since the Japanese monetary system was on a de facto silver standard until 1897, the fall of the foreign iron and steel prices was alleviated by a decline of the relative price of silver to gold.[9] In other words, as the yen depreciated almost in parallel to iron and steel prices in Europe and the United States, prices in terms of the yen remained almost constant from the 1870s to the 1890s (Fig. 2). Iron and steel prices in Japan fell until the middle of the 1880s because Japanese prices approached prices abroad as foreign trade expanded. After an initial decline, Japanese prices stayed constant, and then rose to a high level after the turn of the century, influenced by the rise in prices abroad.

Meanwhile, the cost data of the iron and steel industry in pre–World War I Japan, as shown in Tables 3–5, are notable in some respects. First, the cost level was markedly lower than the price of iron and steel in Japan. The average price-cost margin is calculated at 106% (pig iron) or 24% (finished steel) at Yawata Seitetsujo, and 64% (pig iron) or 9% (finished steel) at Tanaka Kōzan. Needless to say, this margin formed the basis of the comparatively high profit rate mentioned before. At the same time, it suggests that the iron industry was competitive with foreign products in the Japanese market at least in certain kinds of products. In fact, as shown in Tables 3 and 5, the cost of pig iron in Japan was almost equal to that in developed countries (without transportation costs). It is true that the cost of finished steel differed considerably between Japan and the developed countries, but that difference is sufficiently compensated for if transportation costs to Japan (about ¥20) and tariffs are taken into account.[10] With this in mind, a second fact becomes apparent, namely that the Japanese iron and steel industry at that time was more competitive in pig iron than in steel, and that the cost of finished steel was higher in spite of the low cost of pig iron.

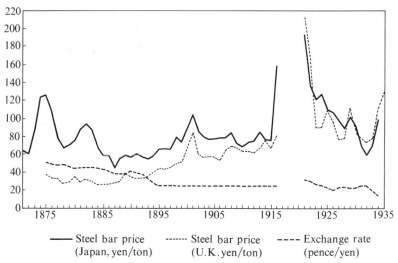

—— Steel bar price   ······ Steel bar price   ---- Exchange rate
(Japan, yen/ton)   (U.K. yen/ton)   (pence/yen)

FIG. 2 Steel Bar Price and Exchange Rate.
Sources: Kin'yū Kenkyūkai, *Waga Kuni Shōhin Sōba Tōkei Hyō* (1937); Tōyō Keizai Shinpōsha, *Nihon no Keiki Hendō* (Business Cycles in Japan) (1931); Shōkōshō, op. cit.

These will be examined in detail. The breakdown of the cost of pig iron shows that the industry compensated for its low productivity with the low price of its inputs,[11] particularly in the case of Tanaka Kōzan. Its coke ratio was extremely high, and labor productivity was as low as one-fifth or one-third that of developed countries. Conversely, the price of iron ore was lower than that in Lorraine, one of the cheapest ores in the developed countries, and Tanaka Kōzan's wage rate was only one-seventh or one-fourth that of the developed countries. As a result, the cost of pig iron at Tanaka Kōzan was lower than in the United Kingdom. At that time all Tanaka ore came from its own mine, so the low price of iron ore was due to Tanaka's own low wage rates.

The low productivity was the result of poor production facilities. In

TABLE 3 Cost of Pig Iron (yen/ton)

	Yawata				Tanaka (Kamaishi)			
	1914	1922	1928	1931	1909	1922	1928	1931
Cost								
Total	21.2	37.8	36.1	27.4	26.6	55.8	36.7	26.8
Coke	7.0	19.1	14.7	11.3	16.8	29.5	22.4	16.0
Iron ore	9.2	13.8	14.9	11.8	4.0	9.0	8.2	8.4
Labor	1.0	2.8	1.6	1.7	1.3	5.0	2.6	1.1
Input-output coefficient								
Coke/pig iron	1.03	1.04	1.06	1.00	1.60	1.43	1.07	0.94
Iron ore/pig iron	1.67	1.59	1.45	1.47	2.20	1.74	1.66	1.62
Labor/pig iron	1.40	1.57	0.84	0.90	2.60	3.26	1.53	0.85
Price								
Coke	6.8	18.4	13.9	10.6	10.5	20.6	20.9	16.9
Iron ore	5.5	8.7	10.3	8.0	1.8	5.2	4.9	5.2
Labor	0.7	1.8	1.8	1.9	0.5	1.5	1.7	1.3

Sources: Satō Shōichirō, "Senzen Nihon ni okeru Kangyō Zaisei no Tenkai to Kōzō" (Development and Structure of the Account System of State-owned Business in Prewar Japan) III, *Keiei Shirin*, vol. 4, no. 7 (1967); Fujii Nobuyuki, "Shōwa Shoki Yawata Seitetsujo no Seisanhi Dōkō" (The Production Costs of Yawata Ironworks in early Shōwa), *Shakai Keizai Shigaku*, vol. 50, no. 6 (1985); Okazaki Tetsuji, "Ryō Taisen Kan Ki ni okeru Nihon Tekkō Gyō no Hatten Kikō" (The Mechanism of the Development of the Japanese Iron and Steel Industry between the Two World Wars), Ph.D. diss., University of Tokyo, 1986.

TABLE 4 Costs of Steel Ingots and Steel Bars (yen/ton)

	Yawata Seitetsujo				Tanaka (Kamaishi)				Osaka Seitetsu		
	1914	1923	1928	1931	1908	1924	1928	1931	1923	1928	1931
Cost											
Steel bar	58.1*	108.6	83.8	75.5	66.1	106.9	81.2	57.3	114.6	86.8	54.5
Steel ingot	29.9	53.5	51.5	38.3	41.1	77.2	57.7	36.9	68.9	58.8	36.5
Input-output coefficient											
Pig iron/steel ingot	0.44	0.82	0.68	0.68	0.52	0.55	0.63	0.61	0.13	0.32	0.26
Scrap/steel ingot	0.51	0.26	0.36	0.35	0.70	0.53	0.49	0.52	1.04	0.91	0.96
Coal/steel ingot	0.32	0.32	0.24	0.24	0.86	0.36	0.22	0.22	0.51	n.a.	0.32
Labor/steel ingot	1.09	1.43	1.32	1.14	8.40	2.44	1.59	1.05	n.a.	1.45	1.47
Labor/steel bar	3.42	2.99	2.24	2.32	10.00	2.48	1.39	1.14	n.a.	1.27	1.09
Input price											
Pig iron	27.0	40.0	39.0	29.2	24.0	44.4	32.3	26.8	54.6	46.3	27.6
Scrap	25.6	30.5	34.3	22.6	23.3	n. a.	n. a.	n. a.	33.2	29.0	16.6

Sources: Same as Table 3; "Osaka Seitetsujo Enkakushi" (The History of Osaka Seitetsujo), ms. in Nihon Seitetsu Kabushikigaisha Shashi Hensan Shiryō.

* Average cost of finished steel.

TABLE 5 Costs of Pig Iron in the Developed Countries (yen/ton)

	U.K.		Lorraine		U.S.A.	
	Before WWI	1921	Before WWI	1921	Before WWI	1921
Cost						
Total	32.1	43.1	19.6	27.7	28.3	54.2
Coke	8.8	14.2	11.1	18.2	8.2	21.9
Iron ore	18.7	20.2	5.5	4.7	15.0	19.8
Labor	2.0	3.6	1.5	3.1	1.3	3.6
Input-output coefficient						
Coke	0.93	0.92	1.15	0.99	n.a.	n.a.
Labor	0.56	0.45	0.71	0.81	n.a.	n.a.
Price						
Coke	9.5	15.4	9.7	18.4	n.a.	n.a.
Domestic ore	2.6	7.5	1.9	3.5	n.a.	n.a.
Imported ore	9.8	15.8	–	–	n.a.	n.a.
Labor	3.6	8.1	2.1	3.9	n.a.	n.a.

Source: *Tetsu to Hagane* (July 1923).

1910, the capacity of the blast furnace at Tanaka Kōzan was only 25 or 60 tons per day,[12] while average daily production per blast furnace was about 270 tons in United States and about 80 tons in the United Kingdom,[13] where facilities were rather old-fashioned compared to other developed, advanced countries. Moreover, Tanaka Kōzan had no by-product coke oven. Operation of these facilities depended largely on manual labor. For example, raw materials were put into blast furnaces by handcart, and coke was raked out of the ovens by workers and extinguished with fire hoses.[14] The steelmaking process saw much the same conditions. The capacity of the open-hearths at Tanaka Kōzan was less than ten tons per charge, much smaller than that in the developed countries. More important, though it produced both pig iron and steel, blast-furnace gas and coke-oven gas were not utilized for steelmaking and rolling.[15] This is considered to have been a major cause of the large difference between the cost of pig iron and that of finished steel.

In the case of Yawata Seitetsujo, which was designed by German engineers and whose equipment was imported from Germany, the situation was rather different.[16] The scale of the plant was much larger than that of private enterprises, almost on a par with the developed countries.[17] Yawata also introduced by-product coke ovens as early as 1907.[18] Owing to such advanced facilities, productivity at Yawata generally exceeded that of Tanaka Kōzan. It was the coke ratio particularly that reached the same level as in developed countries. Therefore, the cost of pig iron, with its cheap inputs, was almost as low as that in Lorraine.

However, Yawata had features in common with Tanaka Kōzan. As is evident in the fact that the process of raw material input was not mechanized until 1914,[19] operations depended highly upon manual labor, and labor productivity was low, roughly one-third or half of that in developed countries (Tables 2 and 4). Additionally, blast-furnace gas and coke-oven gas were not utilized for steelmaking and rolling; therefore coal consumption per ton of finished steel was 3.3 t,[20] compared with a maximum of 2.7 t in Europe.[21] In short, the Japanese iron and steel industry combined modern Western technology with an extremely low wage rate, and thus could achieve competitiveness in the Japanese market so early. To put it in a more general perspective, the successful introduction of Western technology into the iron and steel industry in an underdeveloped Japanese economy enabled this industry to raise its position in the comparative cost structure.

It was not necessary for the Japanese iron and steel industry to catch up with the top level of Western technology. This made the introduction of technology somewhat easier. The introduction of an unknown technology was, nevertheless, very difficult. To overcome that difficulty, state-owned enterprises played an important role, although it was not Yawata Seitetsujo but Tanaka Kōzan that succeeded in operating a modern blast furnace for the first time. Tanaka Kōzan was established originally by purchasing the state-owned ironworks at Kamaishi. An attempt by that state-owned enterprise to produce iron ended in failure, but valuable technological information and experience was gained. Tanaka Kōzan hired engineers working at the state-owned ironworks, and its success was due largely to these experienced engineers.[22] The technical skills of steelmaking were also developed at military factories.[23] That technology was diffused to private enterprises either directly or indirectly by Yawata Seitetsujo. It is well known that Yawata was ready to move skilled workers "embodying" technology to private enterprises. Before World War I many engineers and skilled workers moved between enterprises,[24] contributing to the diffusion of technology.

III. Expansion in Non-international Competition—World War I

It is well known that during World War I European products retreated from the Asian market including Japan, and that this gave Japanese industries an opportunity to expand rapidly.[25] Demand for iron and steel increased tremendously, five to ten times larger at the end of the war than it had been at the beginning in nominal terms.[26] Because iron and steel imports were rigidly limited, almost all the increased demand resulted in price rises and domestic production increases particularly by private enterprises. The remarkable rise of the profit rate caused by a drastic rise in prices stimulated production strongly (Table 2).

At that time, iron and steel production by small-scale works, with an annual production under 5,000 t, rapidly increased. In other words, the wartime production increase was accompanied by the entry of many small-scale enterprises into the industry. But more important, existing large enterprises expanded their production to a great extent and some leading companies entered the industry. Of the wartime production increase, 70–80% was produced by large enterprises whose annual production was over 5,000 t (Table 1). The same held true in facilities expansion. While many small-scale blast furnaces and open-hearths were built, the number of relatively large-scale facilities also increased. Before the war, the largest blast furnace was that at Yawata with a daily capacity of 200 t. By 1921, Yawata had built four blast furnaces over 200 t including one of 300 t capacity.[27]

Expansion of scale, however, was even more remarkable in private enterprises, whose largest blast furnace had had only 60 t capacity before World War I. By the end of the war, they had seven blast furnaces of over 100 t capacity.[28] Leading private enterprises caught up with the level of the prewar Yawata Seitetsujo in terms of the scale of their furnaces. Because operation of blast furnaces smaller than 100 t was halted as soon as the war ended, the average capacity of operating blast furnaces reached 180 t at the beginning of the 1920s. Although this level was lower than that of the United States (over 300 t),[29] it was almost equal to Germany's (about 200 t) and exceeded that of the United Kingdom (about 100 t).[30]

As for open-hearths, while 25 t per charge became the standard scale at private enterprises, Yawata Seitetsujo raised its standard scale to 50 t per charge from 25 t.[31] At that time 50 t in the United States[32] and 40–50 t in the United Kingdom[33] were standard. Therefore, during the war Yawata expanded its scale of facilities to keep up with those of developed countries, and private factories overcame their extreme backwardness. The temporary suspension of international competition during World War I was in effect a greenhouse, contributing to rapid growth and a closing of the technological gap.

It should be emphasized that this rapid growth of the iron and steel industry was accompanied by irreversible structural or institutional changes which significantly influenced later trends in the industry's international competitiveness. Among them were changes in the markets of production factors (labor and capital), which entailed a structural change of the Japanese economy as a whole.

First, growth of private enterprise was supported by the development of the new mechanism of fund-raising. All the leading iron and steel enterprises newly established during World War I took the form of joint-stock companies, and almost all the enterprises which had been privately owned before the war were turned into joint-stock companies. This happened mainly because accelerated economic growth caused a rapid rise of savings rate, and the accumulation of financial assets expanded the capital market during World War I.[34]

The implications of joint-stock company formation and capital market expansion were quite clear in the case of those enterprises not affiliated with zaibatsu. The number of stockholders of Nippon Kōkan and Kawasaki Zōsenjo (Kawasaki Shipyard Co.) increased greatly, and newly established enterprises from their inception collected rather small amounts of money respectively from widely spread stockholders.[35] Thus direct financing from the capital market became an important fund-raising tool for the iron and steel industry. Among these enterprises Tōyō Seitetsu (Oriental Ironworks Co.), Nippon Kōkan, and Kawasaki Zōsenjo were listed at both the the Tokyo and the Osaka stock exchanges, and Osaka Seitetsu (Osaka Ironworks Co.) was listed at the Osaka stock exchange.[36]

Meanwhile, increasing their investment in the iron and steel industry, zaibatsu established or changed their business to joint-stock companies, which they controlled by holding more than 50% of the stock. This made it easy for zaibatsu not only to evaluate and control their businesses but also to keep their assets liquid and raise funds in the capital market. In fact, the expansion of Asano Kokura Seikōjo (Asano Kokura Steel Co.) and Asano Zōsenjo (Asano Shipyard Co.) created a demand for funds greater than Asano's holding company could afford, and so funds were raised in the capital market.

Second, nominal wage rates rose drastically. Following upon rapid inflation, from 1917 labor disputes over wages increased.[37] In the iron and steel industry almost all the major enterprises including Yawata Seitetsujo experienced serious labor disputes.[38] Since there was a labor shortage, workers obtained large raises. The rise of the nominal wage rates was a phenomenon common to Europe and the United States, but was much larger in extent in Japan. The nominal wage rate at the end of World War I was three times as high as the prewar level in

Japan, while it had about doubled in Europe and the United States (Tables 6 and 7). Needless to say, large wage differences still remained, for, as seen in Section II, the nominal wage rate in Japan had been only one-seventh to one-fourth that of the developed countries before the war. Japanese wages relative to foreign wages, however, rose more than 50%. In other words, inflation and the labor movement weakened the prewar basis of the competitiveness of the Japanese iron and steel industry.

TABLE 6 Index of Relative Price System (1910–14=100)

	Nominal wage rate	Nominal interest rate	User cost of capital I	User cost of capital II	Coal price	Steel-bar price	Pig-iron price
1910	95	80	123	75	96	95	88
1914	108	119	131	118	109	98	106
1918	166	91	-664	198	294	484	915
1922	348	131	402	225	238	156	139
1926	364	125	283	177	219	127	115
1930	327	93	269	117	197	89	99
1934	307	78	-74	107	222	132	118

Notes: User cost I = $(i_t - 1/3 \sum_{k=0}^{2} \pi_t\text{-k}) \times P_t$
 User Cost II = $i_t \times P_t$
 i_t =nominal interest rate
 π_t = inflation rate
 P_t = price of investment goods
Sources: Okawa Kazushi, *Chōki Keizai Tōkei* (Long-term Economic Statistics) *(LTES), Bukka* (Tokyo, 1967); Tōyō Keizai Shinpōsha, *Keizai Nenkan* (Yearbook of Economic Statistics); Shōkōshō, op. cit.

Third, and specific to the iron and steel industry, was the establishment of the Iron and Steel Institute of Japan, whose purpose was to "improve and develop the iron and steel industry in Japan through study and research of all the problems relating to iron and steel, including science and economy."[39] It was designed to disseminate technological information. According to the membership list in 1928, engineers and research staff members of all the leading iron and steel enterprises, military factories, and universities participated in this institute. Its major activities were publication of a monthly journal, *Tetsu to Hagane* (Iron and Steel), and holding lectures and study meetings. As seen in the next section, the Iron and Steel Institute of Japan came to

TABLE 7 International Relative Prices, Wages, and Exchange Rates

	Wholesale prices*		Nominal wage rates†		Exchange rates‡	
	U.S.A	U.K.	U.S.A.	U.K.	U.S.A.	U.K.
1910	92	99	95	97	100	100
1914	100	96	102	104	100	100
1918	104	85	99	83	96	70
1922	144	122	178	162	103	95
1926	127	120	162	177	105	105
1930	113	112	145	164	100	101
1934	143	139	175	160	167	173

Notes: * Index of Japanese prices/foreign prices (1910–14=100)
　　　† Index of Japanese nominal wage rate/foreign nominal wage rate
　　　 (1910–14=100)
　　　‡ Index of exchange rate in terms of the yen (1910–14=100)
Sources: *LTES* vols. 8, 14; B.R. Mitchell, *European Historical Statistics 1750–1970*
　　　 (London, 1975); U.S. Bureau of Census, *Historical Statistics of the*
　　　 United States: Colonial Times to 1970 (Washington, D.C., 1975).

play an important role in formulating and solving technological problems after World War I.

Fourth, a law promoting the iron and steel industry (Seitetsugyō Shōrei Hō) was enacted in 1917. By this law iron and steel enterprises were remitted business taxes and import tariffs on their equipment for a certain number of years.[40]

IV. The Renewal of International Competition and the Rationalization of the Industry

As soon as World War I ended, European countries resumed exports of iron and steel to the Japanese market. In addition, Asian regions such as India and Manchuria expanded their iron and steel industries, especially pig-iron production, which made intensive use of their abundant natural resources and manpower.[41] Thus the Japanese iron and steel market after the war became a field of competition between newly developing Asian producers including Japanese and well-established producers in the developed countries. As a result, the iron and steel prices returned approximately to the prewar level (Table 6).

Conversely, the rise of the nominal wages during the war was persistent. Despite the postwar depression, the nominal wage rate was not adjusted to a lower level, remaining three times higher than the prewar level throughout the 1920s. The persistence of nominal wage rates resulted in high coal prices, which was labor intensive and involved large transportation costs. While European and American coal prices were 1.4 to 1.9 times higher than their prewar levels, in Japan they stayed at about 2.2 times higher than the prewar level. In other words, a remarkable change in the Japanese price system had taken place (Table 6). High wages and high coal prices pushed up the cost of iron and steel. Moreover, owing to the large foreign exchange holdings accumulated during World War I and capital inflow,[42] the yen did not depreciate in spite of relatively high prices and wages (Table 7).

In the case of pig iron, both at Yawata Seitetsujo and Tanaka Kōzan, each expense in pig-iron production (coke, iron ore, and labor) rose to 1.5 to 3.8 times the prewar level, and thus the total cost increased about two times (Table 3). It is clear that the major cause of cost increases was the rise of input prices, which in turn was due to the rise of wage rates. At the same time it should be noted that productivity growth was stagnant and sometimes, like labor productivity, actually declined. The lack of productivity increases is supposed to have been caused by the shortage of skilled labor and the maladjustment of auxiliary equipment owing to extremely rapid wartime expansion. It was impossible to balance the rise of input prices with productivity growth. As a result costs at Yawata Seitetsujo, which had ranked in the lowest class of the developed countries prior to the war, rose to the middle class, and that at Tanaka Kōzan beyond the highest class. Moreover, the Indian iron and steel industry, which had developed during the war, produced pig iron at the cost of about ¥15 per ton on the basis of extremely low wages, roughly one-third of the wage in Japan.[43] Thus the iron and steel industry of Japan, which had come to be a relatively high-wage country, was threatened by competition from low-wage developing countries.

That competition particularly threatened the private enterprises which supplied pig iron to the market. It should be noted, however, that Japanese enterprises were not forced to reduce pig-iron costs to the same level as Indian import costs, because India varied its export destinations according to the relative prices of various countries' markets.[44] In this way India played the role of arbitrager in world pig-iron pricing. Thus, if the price of pig iron in the Japanese market fell to that in Europe or the United States, the large pig-iron consumers, the Indian menace was removed from Japan. Therefore, the Japanese iron and steel industry virtually competed with European and American producers through the intermediary of Indian pig iron, and therefore the significance of the development of the Indian iron and steel industry lay in the fact that it removed the effect of transportation costs from Europe and United States, which protected Japanese pig-iron producers as a non-tariff barrier. In this context, it is important that pig-iron costs at Japanese private enterprises rose above the highest level in the developed countries.

The cost of steel ingots and finished steel at enterprises producing iron and steel in a continuous process rose from 1.7 to 1.9 times the prewar cost (Table 4). With stagnant labor productivity, the rise of wage rates and coal prices pushed up the cost of steel directly or indirectly through the pig-iron costs, as explained above. However, the situation was not the same in enterprises that did not have continuous process, and which contributed to a major part of the wartime steel production increase. The market price of pig iron or scrap was not much higher than the prewar level, and thus a relatively favorable price system was formed for non-continuous processing. Adequate data on the cost of non-continuous processing are not available, but the cost of steel ingots was estimated at ¥46 per ton when Nippon Kōkan was established.[45] The cost of steel ingots at Osaka Seitetsu, a represen-tative non-continuous steelmaker like Nippon Kōkan, was in 1923 about 1.5 times as high as that of prewar Nippon Kōkan (¥46). As a result, the non-continuous processing cost of finished steel came to almost the same level as that of continuous processed steel. Because of lower investment per production unit, non-continuous process enter-prises enjoyed more favorable conditions than continuous-process works. In other words, under the price system and the technology after World War I the non-continuous process was the optimal one for the iron and steel industry. In fact, the profit rates in invested capital in the 1920s were relatively higher in such enterprises (Table 2).

At either type of enterprise, however, the cost of finished steel was higher than in Germany, a major competitor of Japan in finished steel, even if transportation cost and tariffs are taken into account.[46] Therefore, even for the steelmaker using the non-continuous process, profits on invested capital fell to 2 to 3%, and enterprises with continu-ous process or producing only pig iron sustained losses. Thus the Japanese iron and steel industry was faced with the need to overcome its declining competitiveness.

Some members of the the Iron and Steel Institute of Japan clearly recognized this problem. A Mitsubishi Seitetsu (Mitsubishi Ironworks Co.) engineer vistited Europe and the United States in 1910–20 and delivered a lecture entitled "A Method of Saving Fuel for Making Iron and Steel" to the institute soon after he returned to Japan.[47] He stressed the importance of saving fuel and labor, and presented fuel-saving devices that were being developed in the West, such as a by-products coke oven, utilization of coke-oven gas and blast-furnace gas in steelmaking and rolling, etc. This lecture can be interpreted as a proposal to adapt the Japanese iron and steel industry to the new relative price system by means of technological change.

TABLE 8 Statement of Source and Application of Funds I (1920–31) (¥1,000)

	Nippon Kōkan		Osaka Seitetsu		Fuji Seikō	
	Application	Source	Application	Source	Application	Source
Ordinary accounts		9,862		1,583	618	
Ordinary profit		7,745		762	638	
Depreciation		2,280		821		20
Others	163					
Financial accounts		9,012	1,420			794
Paid-up capital		8,725		540		5,326
Bonds		4,000				
Borrowing		197	1,140			451
Bills payable	100		933		3,797	
Others	3,810			113	1,186	
Other accounts	18,875		162		94	
Fixed assets	6,303			249	1,411	
Liquid assets	7,131			362		1,412
Dividends and bonuses	4,882		773		98	
Others	559					

Source: Okazaki, op. cit.

The introduction of new technology necessitated investment in facilities and equipment. The fund-raising mechanism which had developed during World War I played a major role in raising the capital for this investment. First, several non-continuous processing enterprises, whose profits were relatively high, adopted the joint-stock company structure in an attempt to reduce capital and thereby restore financial strength.[48] Nippon Kōkan, a representative example, reduced its capital by half in 1921, and appropriated all the gains from the stock retirement to depreciate its assets. This measure created incentives to new investment for the capital market, because it raised profit per share through depreciation and a decrease in the number of shares. At the same time, Nippon Kōkan issued an equivalent amount in new stocks (preferred stocks), the payment of which became a core source of funds for the company in the 1920s (Table 8). Such measures as reducing capital, depreciating assets, and then raising funds in the capital market were taken by Osaka Seitetsu and Fuji Seikō (Fuji Steel Co.) as well.

TABLE 9 Statement of Source and Application of Funds II (1920–31) (¥1,000)

	Kamaishi Kōzan		Wanishi Seitetsu		Mitsubishi Seitetsu	
	Application	Source	Application	Source	Application	Source
Ordinary accounts		250		656		5,373
Ordinary profit	3,190			362	2,469	
Depreciation		2,496		294		6,978
Others		944				864
Financial accounts		11,832		5,206	434	
Paid-up capital						
Bonds		1,475				
Borrowing		1,005		5,206	3,400	
Bills payable		11,834				5,796
Others	2,482				2,830	
Other accounts	12,083		5,863		4,939	
Fixed assets	12,055		5,501		3,830	
Liquid assets		772			1,109	
Dividends and bonuses	800		362			

Source: Same as Table 8.

Enterprises with continuous process or pig-iron producers which earned no profit, however, could not take the measures explained above. Yet it was these enterprises whose international competitiveness particularly declined, and they needed considerable funds for rationalization. In place of the capital market, the zaibatsu system and the government acted to fill that need. In 1921, Tōyō Seitetsu entrusted Yawata Seitetsujo with the management of its ironworks, and in 1924 Mitsui Zaibatsu bought Tanaka Kōzan. As a result, all enterprises using continuous process or producing pig iron came under state ownership (management) or Mitsui/Mitsubishi Zaibatsu ownership. Until 1926, Yawata Seitetsujo handled funds for fixed capital to be paid from the government general account separately from the working balance of the ironworks.[49] Under this system, a gross fixed capital of ¥135 million (with an annual average increase of 12%) was formed during the 1920–26 fiscal years.[50] Mitsui/Mitsubishi Zaibatsu supplied funds for iron and steel enterprises under their control in the form of loans

(Table 9). Kamaishi Kōzan (Kamaishi Mining Co., successor of Tanaka Kōzan) borrowed more than ¥10 million from four companies: Mitsui Kōzan (Mitsui Mining Co.), Mitsui Bussan (Mitsui & Co.), Mitsui Ginkou (Mitsui Bank Co.), Mitsui Shintaku (Mitsui Trust Co.). As for Wanishi Ironworks, it belonged to Nihon Seikōsho (The Japan Steel Works, Ltd.), which was in turn affiliated with Mitsui Zaibatsu, Nihon Seikōsho, Mitsui Kōzan, and Hokkaido Tankō Kisen (Hokkaido Coal Mining and Shipping), who established a kind of partnership to which was entrusted the management of Wanishi Seitetsujo. They acted as guarantors of the obligations incurred by the partnership. And Mitsubishi Seitetsu borrowed money directly in the form of a bill payable by Mitsubishi Gōshi, the holding company of Mitsubishi Zaibatsu.[51] It was because the zaibatsu had access to more information on the enterprises and business under their control than ordinary investors in the capital market, that they played such an entrepreneurial role in carrying out this seemingly risky investment.[52]

What were the effects of the investment of these funds? First, as to the pig-iron production process, the scale of blast furnaces continued to increase rapidly despite the economic depression. Yawata Seitetsujo built a new furnace with a daily capacity of 500 t, equivalent to the average scale in the United States, while private enterprises, whose largest blast furnace at the beginning of the 1920s was a single 200 t furnace, came to have seven furnaces over 200 t, including a 420 t furnace at Kamaishi Kōzan.

Second, with the increase in scale of the blast furnace, arrangements for auxiliary equipment were made and the profiles of the blast furnaces were improved. Among the auxiliary equipment, the change in the ore loading system was particularly notable. The very symbol of the backwardness of the Japanese iron and steel industry, namely the handcarts with which the raw materials were put into the furnace, disappeared.[53] Meanwhile, the furnace was changed to the "wide-hearth, low-bosh" type, which was appropriate for the production of basic pig iron and which also kept pace with the worldwide trend.[54] Third, the use of the by-product coke oven spread throughout the industry.[55]

Last but especially important was the development of preliminary treatment of raw materials. Kamaishi Kōzan, Wanishi Seitetsujo, and Yawata Seitetsujo introduced sintering machines in the late 1920s. Sintering not only made utilization of powder ore possible, but also served to improve markedly the quality of raw materials. Thus it contributed to fuel-saving by increasing deoxdiizability and eliminating water, and also made quality control of pig iron easy by eliminating sulphur.[56] The technology for producing high-quality basic pig iron was established at Mitsubishi Seitetsu,[57] which first had good-quality iron ore for the production of basic pig iron at its own site early in the 1920s.[58] Yawata Seitetsujo followed suit in the mid-1920s. Preliminary treatment of raw materials, however, made production of excellent basic pig iron possible for all pig-iron producers in Japan.[59]

On the basis of these improvements in the pig-iron production process, the continuous iron- and steelmaking process became efficient, which it hardly was before World War I. Yawata Seitetsujo began to utilize blast-furnace gas and coke-oven gas as fuel in its open- hearths in 1923,[60] and Kamaishi Kōzan built a new open-hearth which used coke-oven gas and coal tar, by-products of coke ovens, as fuel in 1927.[61] These measures were specific to enterprises with continuous process, but other improvements in the steelmaking process were useful to those with the non-continuous process as well. Among them, the standard scale of newly built open-hearths became 60 t per charge at Yawata Seitetsujo, and 30 to 50 t at private enterprises.[62] The standard in private as well as public enterprises had caught up with that of developed countries by the beginning of the 1930s. Moreover, the use of waste-heat boilers and the mechanization of open-hearth operations progressed.[63]

Information on those improvements was reported in *Tetsu to Hagane,* and the Iron and Steel Institute of Japan held annual study meetings with engineers from each enterprise to exchange information on technological innovations. Thus the circulation of technological information, from facilities design to daily operating methods, was rapid.

The effects of this technological improvement were clear (Tables 3 and 4). The coke ratio, including that at Kamaishi Kōzan, which had been very high at the beginning of the 1920s, fell below 1.0 by 1931. The input coefficient of coal in the steelmaking process fell by 20% to 40% during the 1920s, while labor productivity increased 1.3 to 3.8 times in pig-iron making, steelmaking, and rolling processes. Labor/fuel-saving technology progressed greatly, and enabled the industry to adapt to a drastic rise of wages and coal prices. The coke ratio and labor productivity approached the levels of developed countries by the beginning of the 1930s.

Naturally the cost declined remarkably too. The cost of pig iron at Kamaishi Kōzan had caught up with that at Yawata Seitetsujo by the end of the 1920s, and it reached the same level as Vereinigte Stahlwerke Aktiengesellschaft in Germany.[64] As discussed above, the entry of India into the pig-iron industry forced the Japanese iron and steel industry to realize the same production costs as Europe and United States. And the industry in fact achieved this objective by the end of the 1920s. Moreover, the cost of finished steel fell below the cost of German imports to the Japanese market. In short, it can be concluded that the Japanese iron and steel industry recovered its competitiveness in the Japanese market by the end of the 1920s.

Based on its renewed competitiveness and supported by the government,[65] the Japanese iron and steel industry attempted to eliminate imported products from the Japanese market in 1926. Yawata Seitetsujo adopted a price policy for finished steel called "principle of following foreign price." This meant monitoring and slightly undercutting import prices from Europe.[66] Thus the self-sufficiency ratio of finished steel in Japan rose steadily (Fig. 1). As for pig iron, which needed more time and funds for the improvement of its production process, a cartel composed of private enterprises in Japan and Manchuria adopted the policy, in tacit cooperation with the trading company importing Indian pig iron and Indian producers, to maintain prices higher than those in Europe and the United States in the latter half of the 1920s. Subsequently the cartel conducted a thoroughgoing "following foreign price" policy to eliminate Indian products under the Great Depression. At first, Indian producers reacted to Japan's strategy by cutting prices, but afterward shifted their export focus from Japan to the United States and the United Kingdom, because prices in the Japanese market fell to the price levels in these countries. Thus the self-suffiency ratio increased toward the beginning of the 1930s.[67]

Productivity growth in the iron and steel industry was considerable relative to other Japanese industries.[68] The iron and steel industry raised its position in the comparative cost structure. It is well known that the yen depreciated greatly when Japan abandoned the gold standard to adopt a floating currency, and that the profits of the iron and steel industry climbed to very high levels in the 1930s. The reason for this was the relatively high productivity growth in the iron and steel industry described here, and the relatively low productivity growth of other industries.

V. Conclusions

Several basic points emerge from this study. First, Japan's iron and steel industry prior to World War I had already achieved considerable competitiveness vis-à-vis foreign imports, largely because low wages helped to counteract the influence of underdeveloped technology on productivity. Japan's competitive strength was directly related to pig iron, which unlike finished steel was labor-coal intensive. The technology, introduced from Western countries, did not need to be state-of-the-art since labor was cheap, and this made the introduction itself easier. It could be interpreted as an example of the adaptation or selection of borrowed technology.[69] The government supported the private sector mainly by supplying human resources developed in the state-owned factories, including military ones. Taking macroeconomic adjustment into account, the successful introduction of modern Western technology raised the iron and steel industry to the upper ranks of the comparative cost structure.

Second, the drastic wage rise during World War I, an aspect of the structural change of the Japanese economy, pushed up the production costs of the iron and steel industry, whose technology had been predicated on a low wage rate. Japan's wage increase, seen in the international context, was relatively quite large, and this in conjunction with the development of the industry in other Asian countries based on their abundant labor and natural resources caused the Japanese iron and steel industry's ranking in the comparative cost structure to fall. Moreover, despite the increase in nominal wages, the yen did not depreciate in the 1920s because of a wartime accumulation of foreign exchange, and as a result the competitiveness of the industry was reduced, especially in pig iron, which was more labor-coal intensive.

In an effort to counteract the debilitating impact of the rise in wages and coal prices, the industry embarked on a program of aggressive rationalization, implementing labor-coal saving technological changes. It was the new fund-raising mechanism developed during the war, in other words, the capital market and the zaibatsu system, that provided the funds for this venture. Thus the wartime structural economic changes were not only the cause of a declining international competitiveness, but also served as one of the solutions. Another institutional change that played an important role in postwar rationalization, was the establishment of the Iron and Steel Institute of Japan. It pinpointed problems facing the industry and circulated technological information in order to solve them.

Lastly, as a result of the abovementioned rationalization measures, the iron and steel industry raised its productivity and renewed its competitiveness in the Japanese market. On this basis, it pursued from the late 1920s a policy of undercutting import prices, and improved the self-sufficiency ratio. At the same time, the iron and steel industry raised its rank in the comparative cost structure. Therefore, the yen depreciated sufficiently after it floated in 1931 to raise the iron and

steel industry's profit rate remarkably high. In sum, owing to technological changes coupled with the adjustment of the exchange rate, the
Japanese iron and steel industry adapted itself to the drastic changes in
the relative price system that occurred during World War I, and was
established as a new leading sector in the industrial structure.

NOTES

I would like to thank every participant at the Fuji Conference, members of the
Keizai Hatten Kenkyūkai at Hitotsubashi University, and my colleagues at the
Faculty of Economics, University of Tokyo, Professors H. Takeda, K. Ueda, and
H. Yoshikawa, for their helpful comments. All errors are, of course, my own
responsibility.
    1.   Matsumoto Kazuyuki and Hanazaki Masaharu, *Nichi Bei Ajia NIEs no
Kokusai Kyōsōryoku* (International Competitiveness of Japan, the United States,
and Asian NIEs) (Tokyo, 1989), p. 41.
    2.   Amano Akihiro, *Bōeki Ron* (International Trade Theory) (Tokyo, 1986),
pp. 14–15.
    3.   Hashimoto Jurō, *Dai Kyōkō Ki no Nihon Shihonshugi* (Japanese Capitalism
during the Great Depression) (Tokyo, 1984); Nakamura Takafusa and Odaka
Konosuke, ed., *Nijū Kōzō* (The Dual Structure) (Tokyo, 1989). Tsurumi Seiryō
explained this by the comparative cost structure. However, he did not sufficiently investigate the cause of the change. See "Nihon Shihonshugi no Hatten
to Gaikoku Bōeki" (Development of Japanese Capitalism and International
Trade), in Morita Kiriro and Motoyama Yoshihiko, eds., *Sekai Keizai Ron o
Manabu* (A Study on the World Economy) (Tokyo, 1980).
    4.   Hashimoto, op. cit, Chap. 1–2; Takeda Haruhito, "1920 Nendai Shi
Kenkyū no Hōhō ni Kansuru Oboegaki" (A Note on Methods for the Study of
the 1920s), *Rekishigakyu Kenkyū* (Journal of Historical Studies), vol. 486.
    5.   This pattern of industrial development is named "gankō keitai" (a pat-
tern of flying wild geese). See Yamazawa Ippei, *Nihon no Keizai Hatten to Kokusai
Bungyō* (Japanese Economic Development and International Division of
Labor) (Tokyo, 1984).
    6.   Iida Ken'ichi, Ōhashi Shūji, and Kuroiwa Toshirō, eds. *Gendai Nihon
Sangyō Hattatsushi* (History of Industrial Development in Modern Japan), vol. 4
(Tokyo, 1969), pp. 174–84.
    7.   Ministry of International Trade and Industry (MITI), ed., *Shōkō Seisaku
shi* (History of Industrial Policy), vol. 17, pp. 75, 141–43.
    8.   Ibid., pp. 147–48.
    9.   Nakamura Takafusa, *Meiji Taishō Ki no Keizai* (The Economy in the Meiji
and Taishō Eras) (Tokyo, 1985), pp. 42–61.
    10.   MITI, ed., op. cit., p. 222.
    11.   Kojima Seiichi, *Nihon Tekkō Shi* (History of the Japanese Iron and Steel
Industry), volume for Meiji Era (Tokyo, 1981), pp. 458–59; MITI, ed., op. cit.,
pp. 158–63.
    12.   *Kamaishi Seitetsujo 70 Nen Shi* (70 Years of the Kamaishi Ironworks)
(Tokyo, 1955), p. 70.

13. Kojima Seiichi, *Tekkōgyō Ron* (The Iron and Steel Industry) (Tokyo, 1943), p. 67.

14. A report by Utoro Shingo to Tokyo Imperial University, Faculty of Engineering, Department of Metallurgy, 1910.

15. Ibid., by Yamagata Kinji.

16. Iida et al., op, cit., pp. 106–22.

17. Ibid., pp. 147–48.

18. *Yawata Seitetsujo 50 Nen Shi* (50 Years of Yawata Seitetsujo) (Tokyo, 1950), p. 66.

19. Ibid., p. 80.

20. Kojima, op. cit., volume for first half of the Taishō era, p. 326. With regard to Yawata Seitetsujo, another factor was pointed out: that is, its large variety of products with small lots. See Satō Shoichirō "Senzen Nihon ni okeru Kangyō Zaisei no Tenkai to Kōzō" (Development and Structure of the Account System of State-owned Business in Prewar Japan)III, *Keiei Shirin*, vol., 4 no.7.

21. Kojima Seiichi, *Tekkōgyō Hattenshi Ron* (Development of the Iron and Steel Industry) (Tokyo, 1925), p. 407.

22. Iida et al., op. cit., pp. 56–63.

23. Ibid., pp. 63–66.

24. Ibid., pp. 256–59.

25. For example, Hashimoto, op. cit., Chap. 1.

26. Shōkōshō (Ministry of Commerce and Industry), "Seitetsugyō Sankō Shiryō" (Reference Materials on the Iron and Steel Industry) (1937).

27. Ibid.

28. Ibid.

29. Mori Takashi, "Ryō Taisen Kan Ki no Amerika Tekkōgyō" (The American Iron and Steel Industry Between the Two World Wars), *Keizaigaku Kenkyū* (Hokkaido University), p.173 (1960).

30. Duncan Burn, *The Economic History of Steelmaking, 1867–1939* (Cambridge, 1961), p. 367.

31. Shōkōshō, op. cit.

32. Ishizaki Teruhiko, "Ryō Taisen Kan Ki no Amerika Tekkōgyō" (The American Iron and Steel Industry between the Two World Wars), *Shō kei Ronsō* (Kanagawa University), vol. 3, no. 4, p. 83.

33. Burn, op. cit., pp. 362–64.

34. Proportion of savings to GNP rose from 14.1% in 1910 to 30.7% in 1917 Ōkawa Kazushi, *Kokumin Shotoku* (National Income), (Tokyo, 1974), p. 248). For the expansion of the capital market, see Takeda Haruhito "Nihon Teikokushugi no Keizai Kōzō" (Economic Structure of Japanese Imperialism), *Rekishigaku Kenkyū*, special number (1979), pp. 146–48.

35. Business report of each enterprise.

36. *Tokyo Kabushiki Torihikijo 50 Nen Shi* (50 years of the Tokyo Stock Exchange), (Tokyo, 1928); *Daikabu 50 Nen Shi* (50 Years of the Osaka Stock Exchange) (Osaka, 1928).

37. Takeda Haruhito, "Rōdōryoku" (Labor Force), in Ōishi Kaichirō, ed., *Nihon Teikokushugi Shi* (History of Japanese Imperialism), vol. I (Tokyo, 1985), pp. 288–89.

38. Ōhara Shakai Mondai Kenkyūjo, *Nihon Rōdō Nenkan* (Japan Labor Annual) (Tokyo, 1919–21).

39. *Nihon Tekkō Kyōkai 50 Nen Shi* (50 Years of the Iron and Steel Institute of Japan) (Tokyo, 1965), p. 37.

40. MITI, ed., op. cit., p. 192.

41. Nagashima Osamu, *Nihon Tekkōgyō no Kōzō Bunseki* (An Analysis of the Structure of the Japanese Iron and Steel Industry) (Kyoto, 1987), pp. 156–64; Nagura Bunji, *Nihon Tekkōgyō Shi Kenkyū* (A Study on the History of the Japanese Iron and Steel Industry) (Tokyo, 1984), pp. 208–81.

42. Hashimoto, op. cit., pp. 121–22.

43. Sugiyama Kōji, "Indo Tekkōgyō Shisatsu Dan" (A Report on the Observation of the Indian Iron and Steel Industry), *Tetsu to Hagane* (Iron and Steel) (Jan. 1923).

44. Okazaki Tetsuji, "Sentetsu Kyōdō Kumiai" (Pig Iron Association), Hashimoto Jurō and Takeda Haruhito, eds., *Ryō Taisen Kan Ki Nihon no Karuteru* (Cartels in Japan between the Two World Wars) (Tokyo, 1985), pp. 32, 82.

45. *Nihon Kōkan Kabushikigaisha 30 Nen Shi* (30 Years of Nihon Kōkan Co.) (Tokyo, 1942), p. 140.

46. MITI, ed., op. cit., p. 249.

47. *Tetsu to Hagane* (June 1921).

48. Okazaki Tetsuji, "Ryō Taisen Kan Ki ni okeru Nihon Tekkōgyō no Hatten Kikō" (Mechanism of the Development of the Japanese Iron and Steel Industry between the Two World Wars), Ph.D. diss., University of Tokyo (1986).

49. MITI, ed., op. cit., p. 249.

50. Ministry of Finance, *Sainyū Saishutsu Kessan Sho* (Statement of Accounts).

51. Okazaki Tetsuji "1920 Nen Dai no Tekkō Seisaku to Nihon Tekkōgyō" (Policies on the Japanese Iron and Steel Industry in the 1920s), *Tochi Seido Shigaku* (Journal of Agrarian History), vol. 103, p. 14.

52. Zaibatsu could be seen to function as a "miniature capital market." See Oliver E. Williamson, *Markets and Hierarchies* (New York, 1975), Chap. 8.

53. Reports by Kawamura Ginji to Tokyo Imperial University, Faculty of Engineering, 1923; by Murase Tetsuzō and Oikawa Zenjirō, Tohoku Imperial University, Department of Metallurgy Faculty of Engineering, Department of Metallurgy, 1929, 1930.

54. Horikiri Yoshio, *Nihon Tekkōgyō Shi Kenkyū* (A Study on the History of the Japanese Iron and Steel Industry) (Tokyo, 1987), pp. 73–74.

55. Kuroda Taizō, "Seitetsu Yō Gaitan ni tsuite" (On Cokes for Making Pig Iron), *Tetsu to Hagane* (Jan. 1928).

56. To produce high-quality basic pig iron, it was necessary to operate the blast furnace at low temperature, and for that large deoxidizability and low sulphur content of the raw materials were necessary. See Kodama Yukimasa, *Tetsu, Kō Kōzai* (Iron, Steel, and Steel Products) (Tokyo, 1942), pp. 167–68.

57. Okazaki, op. cit. (1985), p. 48.

58. Horikiri, op. cit., pp. 67–68.

59. Horikiri, op. cit., is misleading in that he does not mention this technological progress.

60. *Yawata Seitetsujo 50 Nen Shi*, p. 56.

61. *Kamaishi Seitetsujo 70 Nen Shi*, p. 91.

62. Shōkōshō, op. cit.

63. Kōzan Konwakai, *Nihon Kōgyō Hattatsu Shi* (History of the Development of the Japanese Mining Industry), vol. 2 (1932), pp. 94–128.

64. The pig-iron cost at Vereinigte Stahlwerke in Germany was 66–67 RM (¥34–35) at the end of the 1920s. See Kudō Akira, "Nachisu Taisei ka no Tekkō Shihon" (Iron and Steel Firms under the Nazi Government), in *Nachisu Keizai to Nyū Diiru* (Nazi Economy and the New Deal), Institute of Social Science, University of Tokyo (Tokyo, 1979), p. 97.

65. In 1926, tariffs on finished steel were revised to 18%, and a subsidy for pig iron was set up (¥3–6 per ton). See MITI, ed., op. cit., pp. 242–46.

66. Iida et al., op. cit., p. 293.

67. Okazaki, op. cit. (1985), pp. 56–60, 72–81.

68. MITI, *Kōgyō Tōkei 50 Nen Shi* (50 Years of Census Manufactures) (1961).

69. Minami Ryōshin, *Nihon no Keizai Hatten* (Economic Development in Japan) (Tokyo, 1981), pp. 115–21; Kiyokawa Yukihiko, "Nihon no Gijutsu Hatten" (Technological Development in Japan), in Minami Ryōshin and Kiyokawa Yukihiko, eds., *Nihon no Kōgyōka to Gijutsu Hatten* (Japanese Industrialization and Technological Development) (Tokyo, 1987), pp. 290–93; MITI, ed., *Kōgyō Tōkei 50 Nen Shi* (50 Years of Manufacturer Censuses).

Comment

Osamu Nagashima

Japanese scholars studying the history of Japan's iron and steel industry have emphasized its backwardness prior to World War I since its most important problem was to catch up with the developed countries. In contrast to the old thinking, Professor Okazaki stresses the high level the Japanese iron and steel industry had attained before World War I. Focusing on production costs, he demonstrates the international competitiveness of the industry and explains how this competitiveness changed as the structure of Japan's economy was transformed during World War I.

I agree with the general argument of Okazaki's paper, but there are a few points that should be examined.

(1) Although I agree with Okazaki that before World War I the cost of pig iron in Japan was lower than in developed countries, pig iron is a semi-finished product for integrated steelworks and should not be analyzed in isolation. I think it is necessary to focus on the total cost of the finished products, for example steel rails, which were the principal output of Yawata before World War I. About half of the pig iron produced by Yawata was consumed by Bessemer converters in the form of molten pig iron. Yawata had until 1927 produced Bessemer rails, into which they then rolled Bessemer steel ingot. But due to unsuitable Bessemer rails, Yawata had to adopt what is called a duplex steelmaking process (where both the Bessemer converter and the open-hearth furnace are used). Therefore, the cost of these rails was higher. It is necessary to compare both the price and the quality of the rails produced by Yawata with that of the imported rails.

(2) Okazaki failed to mention that the government played an important role in the development of this Japanese industry. Yawata was protected by government subsidies. Before World War I, the Railway Ministry, and the Army and Navy bought about half of the steel products (bars, rails, plates, castings, etc.) which Yawata, the state-owned steelworks, produced; for example, the rails produced by Yawata, the

advantage to which the Railway Ministry gave over imported rails, were the greatest output of steel products of Yawata before World War I. But the rails of Yawata did not meet the standards of the Railway Ministry. Yawata could not produce high-quality rails until the latter half of the 1920s because Yawata could not acquire iron ore suitable for the Bessemer converter. If Japan's iron and steel industry had not developed under the umbrella of the protectionist policies of the government, the industry could not have competed so successfully with foreign products for the domestic market before World War I.

(3) Okazaki also neglects to mention the use of scrap iron. Before the 1920s Yawata used the scrap process of steelmaking, in which basic open-hearth furnaces consumed as much scrap, which originated from plants within the integrated steelworks, as pig iron. Other steelmaking firms, private enterprises possessing both basic open-hearth furnaces and rolling mills, increased the output of rolled steel after World War I. These firms produced 50–60% of the rolled steel in the 1920s. They could increase the output of rolled steel due to cheap pig iron from India and scrap, both domestic and imported. They used more scrap than pig iron, in the ratio of 1.5 scrap to 1 pig iron, and scrap was the most important raw material for them. In the latter half of the 1930s, Japan imported scrap from the United States with which it fed its growing output of steel.

(4) Japanese steelmaking firms that possessed basic open-hearth furnaces could lower the cost of steel ingots and finished steel due to the low price of pig-iron imported from India. The imported pig-iron forced pig-iron producers in Japan to lower their market price. Okazaki, however, says that the Japanese pig-iron cartel adopted policies in tacit cooperation with the trading companies importing pig iron from India and Indian producers, in order to maintain their prices. The pig-iron cartel, on the contrary, confronted the trading companies—Kishimoto Shōten and Nichiin Tsūshō. The members of the cartel, the Japanese pig-iron producers, still saw their own market share diminish in the latter half of the 1920s. Therefore I do not agree with Okazaki that there was tacit cooperation between Japanese pig-iron producers and the trading companies importing Indian pig iron.

The Postwar Japanese Iron and Steel Industry: Continuity and Discontinuity

Seiichiro Yonekura

I. Introduction

It is impossisble to consider the post–World War II development of Japan without considering the extraordinary development of its iron and steel industry. Japan's heavy industrialization and its rapid economic growth depended on this industry's development. The other large Japanese industries, such as shipbuilding, automobiles, machinery, and consumer electronics, developed largely based on steel. From 1946 to 1970, the industry increased crude steel production from 0.56 to 93.3 million metric tons (the third largest in the world). This dynamic development, adapting to the external environment despite limitations in resources and unfavorable terms of trade, demonstrated remarkable entrepreneurial innovations. This paper will focus on how such strides were made and who was responsible for them in the postwar period. As a background for the argument, let us take a brief look at the international context of the industry.

1. A Quantitative Survey

Prewar crude steel production peaked at 7.65 million tons in 1943. Production fell to as low as 0.56 million tons in 1946, but rose to 4.84 million tons in 1950, 9.40 million in 1955, and 22.14 million in 1960, in fact doubling every five years. In 1973, production reached a record high of 120 million tons (see Fig. 1). Japan's share of world production moved from 6.5% in 1960 to 15.6% in 1970. More important than its quantitative expansion was the increase in its share of world exports of steel. In 1955, the United States exported 14.2% of the world's steel, West Germany 9.9%, the Soviet Union and Eastern Europe 10.6%, and Japan a mere 6.6%. Japan's share rose to 16.1% in 1965 and 28.6% in 1973, becoming the world's largest exporting country. Thus, the Japanese iron and steel industry not only achieved quantitative expansion, but also competitive advantage in the world's markets.

million tons

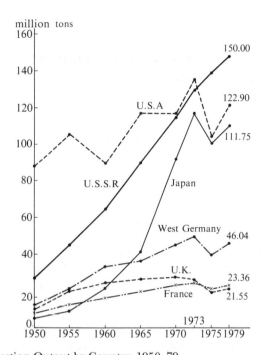

FIG. 1 Production Output by Country, 1950–79.
Source: Shin Nittetsu Sōgō Chōsabu, *Sengo 35 Nen Nihon Tekkōgyō Hatten no Rekishi* (35-year History of the Postwar Japanese Steel Industry) (Tokyo, 1970), p. 3.

In considering the postwar development, three interrelated factors must be examined: productivity, economies of scale, and technological innovations.

Productivity. Donald Barnett and Louis Schorsch's detailed research on productivity illuminates the conspicuous rise in Japan's productivity, compared to other nations in the postwar period.[1] As shown in Table 1, the ratio between the United States and Japan of man-hours needed by integrated steelmakers to produce one ton of hot-rolled sheet steel was 9.16:27.03 in 1958, 7.85:14.40 in 1964, 6.22:6.17 in 1972, and 5.36:4.42 in 1980. As for cold-rolled sheet steel, the same turnover happened by 1980. This clearly shows the tremendous gains in productivity that Japanese integrated iron and steel producers made by the 1970s. What brought about such gains in productivity? Barnett and Schorsch stress the interaction between the high rate of market growth and high investment.[2] In other words, Japanese producers were able to achieve a high rate of investment because there existed a great demand for steel in postwar Japan. In contrast, they emphasize the turning of a vicious circle of low growth and low investment in the United States (calculations based on 20-year straight line depreciation); by 1980 the United States was investing $38.6 billion in the industry whereas Japan was investing $70.4 billion. This proves that there was a twofold difference in the net capital stock even though both countries had nearly the same production capacity. However, there are two problems with Barnett and Schorsch's interpretation. One problem with their argument is that in order to attribute the high level of investment and high productivity to the external factor of market growth, they are forced to equate market growth with investment expansion. In so doing, they neglect the investment-driven growth pattern evident in the Japanese economy as early as the 1950s: That is, the dynamic interaction in which investment begets investment and market growth. Thus, before we conclude merely that investment occurs because there is growth, we have to look closely at the contents of investment and the relation between investment and growth. The second problem with Barnett and Schorsch's argument is that a high level of investment does not necessarily lead to high productivity. It is necessary to consider the type of investment.

TABLE 1   Productivity by Product among Integrated Steelmakers, 1980 (man-hours per ton)

	1958 U.S.A.	1958 Japan	1964 U.S.A.	1964 Japan	1972 U.S.A.	1972 Japan	1980 U.S.A.	1980 Japan
Hot-rolled sheet	9.16	27.03	7.85	14.40	6.22	6.17	5.36	4.42
Plate	10.89	28.64	9.73	15.70	8.33	6.89	7.73	5.26
Cold-rolled sheet	11.58	35.65	10.01	19.12	8.07	8.21	7.21	5.84
Hot-rolled bar	12.50	32.10	11.50	17.49	9.50	6.91	7.60	4.65
Wire rod	12.28	27.73	10.80	14.03	8.32	5.73	6.45	4.24

Source: Donald F. Barnett and Louis Schorsch, *Steel: Upheaval in a Basic Industry* (Cambridge, Mass., 1983), p. 119.

Economies of Scale. Muller and Kawahito have gathered very interesting data in the context of Japanese investment.[3] As shown in Table 2, between 1957 and 1976 Japan, the United States, and the European

Community (the original six countries) invested the same amount, $27 billion, in their steel facilities (no depreciation calculated). Their total capacity was nearly the same at 150 to 160 million tons. However, the type of investments which they pursued were surprisingly different. In terms of the rate of growth of production capacity, the United States increased 134% and the EC 283%. In contrast, Japan achieved an amazing 1,079% capacity expansion. Behind this statistic lies the fact that nearly all of Japan's postwar capacity expansion (71.5%) lay in building new factories, so-called greenfields. In the United States only 25.0% and in Europe only 29.4% of investment capital went into greenfields. In 1976, Japan's ten largest factories were responsible for 76.2% of its total production, whereas in the United States only 37.1% and in the EC only 29.4% were produced in the ten largest facilities. Muller and Kawahito's data support the contention that Japanese steelmakers were able to achieve tremendous expansion in scale.

TABLE 2 Comparison among the United States, Japan, and the EC: Investment and Capacity

	U.S.A.	Japan	EC*
Approximate amounts invested in steel-making capacity (excluding investments in non-steel, mining, and sales activities), 1957–76	$27 bill.	$27 bill.	$27 bill.
Productive capability[†] in 1956 (in million net tons)	119	14	59
Productive capability in 1976	159 (134%)	151 (1,079%)	167 (283%)
Productive capability added, 1956–76	40	137	108
Capacity added since 1956	44	151	119
(of which greenfield capacity)	(11)	(108)	(35)
Capacity added since 1967	6	107	74
Capacity of the largest ten plants in 1976	59	115	64

*Original Six: West Germany, Italy, France, Belgium, Netherlands, Luxemburg.
†Productive capability (sustainable capacity) = 90% of maximum usable capacity.
Source: Hans Mueller and K. Kawahito, *Steel Industry Economics* (New York, 1978), p. 1.

Data presented by Barnett and Schorsch also show that with the exception of the electric furnace, Japan's average amount of produc-

tion in the principle manufacturing processes surpassed that of the
United States by 1980.[4] Moreover, McCraw and O'Brien show in Table
3 how much larger in scale were Japan's largest ten facilities than those
in the United States. The United States' largest factory would be comparable to Japan's ninth largest. By concentrating capital expenditures
in large-scale and new facilities, the Japanese iron and steel industry
was able to make large gains in productivity. In other words, Japanese
steel firms demonstrated economies of scale. However, the Japanese
steel industry did not gain the competitive advantage merely by enlarging the size of the factory unit. Economies of scale were also achieved
by adopting important technological innovations.

TABLE 3 Crude Steel Capacity of Individual Plants, 1977–78 (millions of net
tons)

Japan		U.S.A.	
Fukuyama (NKK)	17.6	Indiana (Inland)	8.5
Mizushima (Kawasaki)	14.0	Gary, Ind. (USS)	8.0
Chiba (Kawasaki)	10.0	Sparrows Pt., Md. (Bethlehem)	7.0
Kimitsu (Nippon Steel)	10.5	Great Lakes, Mich. (National)	6.6
Wakayama (Sumitomo)	10.2	E. Chicago, Ill. (Jones & Laughlin)	5.5
Kashima (Sumitomo)	9.9	Burns Harbor, Ind. (Bethlehem)	5.3
Yawata (Nippon Steel)	9.7	S. Chicago, Ill. (USS)	5.2
Ōita (Nippon Steel)	9.3	Fairless, Penn. (USS)	4.4
Nagoya (Nippon Steel)	8.3	Cleveland, Ohio (Republic)	4.4
Kakogawa (Kobe)	7.1	Wierton, W. Va. (National)	4.0
Total	106.5		58.9

Source: Thomas McCraw (ed.), *America vs. Japan* (Boston, 1986), p. 87.

Technological Innovations. There were two technological innovations that
helped the postwar Japanese iron and steel industry achieve economies
of scale and cost competitiveness. These were the basic oxygen furnace
(hereafter BOF), an innovation in the process of steelmaking, and the
continuous caster (CC), an innovation in the process of ingot manufacture.

The BOF was invented in Austria in 1952 as a steel-refining furnace
that could take the place of the open-hearth furnace (OHF). The BOF
used pig iron as its principal raw ingredient and decreased the percentage of scrap needed until finally no scrap at all was necessary. It
reduced refining time to a tenth of what it had been, thereby increas-

ing the efficiency of the furnace, and it saved half the construction cost. As shown in Table 4, the rate with which Japan introduced the BOF was much faster than the rate with which the United States, the EEC (nine countries), or Canada introduced it. By 1981 the OHF had completely vanished from Japan.

TABLE 4 Adoption of New Technologies

	U.S.A.		Japan		EEC (9)		Canada	
	%	m tons	%	m tons	%	m tons	%	m tons
BOF								
1960	3.4	3.3	11.9	2.9	1.6	1.8	28.1	1.6
1965	17.4	22.9	55.0	24.9	19.4	24.3	32.3	3.3
1970	48.1	63.3	79.1	81.2	42.9	65.1	31.1	3.8
1975	61.6	71.8	82.5	92.9	63.3	87.2	56.1	8.0
1981	60.6	73.2	75.2	84.1	75.1	103.6	58.6	9.4
BOF plus electric furnace								
1960	11.8	11.7	32.0	7.1	11.5	12.4	40.4	2.3
1965	27.9	36.7	75.3	34.1	31.5	39.5	45.1	4.6
1970	63.5	83.5	95.9	98.4	57.7	87.6	45.9	5.6
1975	81.0	94.5	98.9	111.3	82.6	113.7	76.4	10.9
1981	88.8	107.3	100.0	111.9	98.6	136.0	86.5	13.9
Continuous casting								
1971	4.8	5.8	11.2	11.0	4.8	6.7	11.5	1.4
1976	10.5	13.5	35.0	41.4	20.1	29.7	12.0	1.7
1981	21.1	25.3	70.7	79.0	45.1	62.3	32.2	5.3

Source: Same as Table 1, p. 55.

Continuous casting was important because it shortened the conventional pattern of manufacture, making possible continuous production of slabs, blooms, and billets directly from the steel-refining process. In comparison with the conventional process where refined steel was cooled into ingots and then reheated to make slabs, blooms, and billets, the CC reduced energy cost, and increased yield and productivity. As seen in Table 4, by 1981 continuous casting had spread at the rate of 21.1% in the United States, 45.1% in the EC, and 70.7% in Japan. By 1986, it exceeded 95% in Japan. In addition to the BOF and the CC, innovations were made to improve surface treatment through the introduction of continuous annealing and galvanizing techniques, and through computerized process control. By the 1980s the Japanese iron and steel industry has become the most efficient and cost competitive in the world.

The next question that comes to mind is how the large-scale investments necessary to produce such innovations were made possible, and who made the decision.

2. The Question of MITI-led Growth

As we have seen, in order to achieve consistent increases in productivity, Japanese iron and steel producers invested large sums in new facilities and technological innovation. By 1965 they had surpassed the production capacity of West Germany and Great Britain, and by 1970 they had put Japan next to the United States and the Soviet Union. This rapid industrial development was not limited to the steel industry; it extended to textiles, shipbuilding, electronics, automobiles, and even computers. Considering that Japan had lost all its empire and 25% of its wealth after World War II, such development is phenomenal. Beginning in the late 1960s, this achievement began to attract the attention of the world. Those who sought the key to Japan's success tended to focus on the role of the government and in particular that of the Ministry of International Trade and Industry (hereafter MITI). This is the "Japan, Inc." interpretation which presumes that the government (which is synonymous with MITI) played the role of corporate headquarters, managing Japan's principal industries. The first statement of this viewpoint appeared in a volume by the U.S. Department of Commerce, *Japan: The Government-Business Relationship* (1972) which was translated into Japanese as "Kabushiki-kaisha Nihon" (Japan Inc.). Thereafter, even more detailed research appeared in Magaziner and Hout's *Japanese Industrial Policy* (1981) and in Chalmers Johnson's *MITI and the Japanese Miracle* (1982), which features a historical analysis. If one reads these three representative works carefully, one will notice that in analyzing the relationship between business and the government in connection with Japan's industrial development, they do not say that Japan was simply an absolutely state-led economy. However, the strong impression left by the terms "Japan, Inc." and "miracle," combined with an absence of thorough detailed studies of Japanese industries, has led to the conception that Japanese economic development was synonymous with government-led growth.[5]

The Japanese iron and steel industry has not escaped that bind. Although in their report on the Japanese iron and steel industry for the Department of Commerce, Hout and his co-authors at Boston

Consulting Group disclaimed direct government intervention after the 1960s as follows:[6]

As this report will suggest, however, government's cooperation with industry over the last decade has been neither economically decisive nor operationally mysterious. It is easy to overestimate the government's impact on Japan's competitive position.
    A more accurate explanation of Japan's success would emphasize a modern physical steelmaking capacity resulting from the highly effective raw material acquisition and logistic systems, and productivity gains which overcome rapidly rising labor wages and lowered actual unit labor cost over the 1960s.

The impression that the government directed the steel industry remains strong. For instance, McCraw and O'Brien put great emphasis upon MITI's role in the industry's development:[7]

During the immediate postwar years, the government's primary objective was simply to rebuild the country's devastated economy. Because Japan had few natural endowments, it depended on external sources for necessities such as food and raw materials. Reindustrialization also required the importation of expensive technology and heavy machinery. In order to earn the foreign currency to pay these large import bills, Japan needed a correspondingly large volume of exports, preferably of the high-value-added variety. Thus, MITI targeted several industries for potential export growth: steel was one of those. . . .
    As MITI bureaucrats grappled with this question, one aspect of their strategy began to emerge clearly. For the eventual export strategy to work, the Japanese domestic market must play a vital function: it must become a greenhouse where the essential factors of competition—supply, demand, and price—could be carefully controlled. Like sunlight, temperature, and humidity, they might be adjusted up or down, in order to nurture the development of Japanese steel companies. Through this strategy, MITI would alter the economic environment in which Japanese steel managers made investment decisions.

They go on to say that the Japanese government nurtured the steel industry by (1) protecting the domestic steel industry by excluding most foreign steel imports, (2) controlling overcapacity and competitive price cutting, and (3) allocating the right to increase capacity based on each company's demonstrated efficiency. MITI certainly played an important role in the development of the Japanese steel industry. However, the claim that it turned the Japanese domestic market into a greenhouse to cultivate Japanese firms is clearly an exaggeration. There are two problems with this kind of interpretation. First of all, it is very doubtful whether a government can manipulate the domestic market in order to cultivate the export competitiveness of its firms just by protecting and subsidizing the domestic companies. Protecting the domestic market from imports and nurturing the iron and steel industry through the imposition of tariffs was certainly not first practiced in postwar Japan. From the end of the 18th century such protective measures have been used in Britain, the United States, Germany, France, Belgium, and the developing countries. For example, the French government has applied very similar measures or sometimes more direct intervention to promote its iron and steel industry.[8] Moreover, developing countries and the more heavily planned countries in the socialist sphere have all protected their own industries. However, despite such efforts, protection of the steel industry has not always worked so well.[9] It is not enough, therefore, to point to the governmental aid as the reason for the successful development of the Japanese industry. Futhermore, it should be noted that such protectionist measures often hindered the development of other industries, such as shipbuilding, automobiles, and so on.

The second problem with the greenhouse hypothesis is closely related to the first. No matter how well conceived the government's plans might have been, it was private firms that carried them out. It was not the government but private firms that invested tremendous sums of money into systematic innovations and achieved clear productivity and quality gains. Not considering the receptivity of the private firms to technology or their organizational capability may lead to overlooking the true essence of the industry's development. As Alfred D. Chandler, Jr., makes clear in his detailed study of the development of the modern corporation, an organizational capability is an absolute prerequisite to achieving competitiveness in captial-intensive industries, where economies of scale and scope play a significant role.[10] It is impossible to achieve the economies of scale associated with large-scale expansion and continuous coordination without developing the organizational capability to forecast demand, coordinate output and input, and operate plants and equipment continuously. In addition, it is necessary to have strategic planning capability, resource allocation capability, a managerial hierarchy, and an organizational structure. Without considering such organizational capability, is is naive to say that when governments change the investment environment, firms achieve economies of scale.

Moreover, as Rosenberg has shown, "the successful transfer of technology is not a matter of transporting a piece of hardware from one geographic location to another."[11] No matter how hard a government or other institutions try to foster industries, if the receiving side has not built up a social, economic, and organizational foundation which can accept technology and capital, then technology transfer will not succeed. For instance, the World Bank, which made an important contribution to Japan's rationalization program, had by 1960 supplied a much greater amount of financing ($159 million) to India's two steel firms than to Japan's largest six producers ($144 million). The 1960 World Bank report evaluated the Indian steel industry as follows: "Rich deposits of iron ore, coal, manganese, and limestone, allied to a plentiful supply of labour, enable India to produce steel at costs as low as any in the world."[12] However, it is well known that in comparison to the industry in resource-poor Japan, the Indian steel industry, to which the World Bank gave its approval and which the Indian government strived to foster, did not develop as successfully.

Leonard Lynn was the first to undertake a thorough investigation of the organizational capability of the Japanese steel industry in his book *How Japan Innovates* (1982). He conducted a comparison of the United States and Japan, focusing on the way in which the BOF was adopted, and attempted to interpret Japan's organizational response to innovation. He diligently sought to perceive the role of MITI, individual firms, trade associations, and related companies. He made it clear that the introduction of the BOF into Japan and not into the United States was not accidental, but was based on Japan's organizational and institutional superiority. Although Lynn went a bit too far in trying to apply his organizational theory, it nonetheless is a ground-breaking work.

In order to understand the technological and organizational capability of the industry, it is then necessary to look at its historical development.

3. Purpose and Framework: Continuity and Discontinuity
As we have seen above, the Japanese iron and steel industry has developed very systematically in terms of quantity, quality, productivity, economy of scale, and technological innovations. Although the role of the

government and MITI has attracted the attention of the world, one cannot understand the dramatic development of Japan's iron and steel industry during the postwar period by looking at the role of the government alone. Past studies, in focusing on quantitative expansion and the role of MITI, have overlooked the central role of private firms. In particular, since the productivity increases achieved by the Japanese iron and steel industry were due to the systematic use of production innovation (i.e., large integrated works on greenfield sites) and technological innovations (i.e., the BOF, the CC, and the computerized process-control technology), we must not avoid touching upon the receptiveness to technology and the organizational capability that enabled the industry to realize those gains. Accordingly, the main concern in this paper is to analyze the technological and organizational capabilities of the industry and its competitive structure, and how they contributed to the extraordinary development of the industry. In addition, the paper will examine the role of the government, not from the government side, but in terms of its interaction with the receiving firms, and will clarify under what conditions and in what ways the government intervention was effective.

An important key to examining the above two issues is a historical approach. In particular, the paper calls attention to the dynamism between continuity and discontinuity through the prewar and postwar periods. There is a tendency to separate the prewar and postwar periods when analyzing postwar Japanese economic development. Many tend to underevaluate the prewar development of Japanese industries as, for instance, Kawahito did when he said that "the Japanese steel industry was almost nonexistent at the end of World War II, but its position as one of the world leaders was clearly established by the end of the 1960s."[13] Throughout the pre–World War II period, however, the industry accumulated both technological and organizational skills at quite a high level when compared with the world standard. Although at its prewar peak Japanese steel production had only reached one-tenth that of the United States, it had attained 57.8% that of Great Britain, 36.9% that of Germany, and 149.2% that of France. The continuities of these technological and organizational foundations of the industry should not be neglected.

In the field of industrial policy and government-business relations, the importance of the continuity from the prewar period has been already pointed out. Chalmers Johnson discovered the "striking continuities" between the prewar Ministry of Commerce and Industry and the postwar Ministry of International Trade and Industry.[14] Nakamura

Takafusa has stated that "the greatest inheritance from the wartime controlled economy is the heavy industrialization in the postwar period."[15] However, as these continuities were not well connected with the continuities of industries and firms, only the role of the government in the rapid development has been spotlighted. Furthermore, as these literatures did not emphasize the discontinuity after the war, they neglected what really changed in the government as well as in industries. In order to understand the essence of the remarkable development of the Japanese industries, we should examine the kinds of discontinuities that were carried out by the government, industries, and individual firms. This paper will seek to analyze the development mechanism of the iron and steel industry in view of the dynamic interaction between continuities and discontinuities of the prewar and postwar period.

II. Discontinuities Brought by SCAP

On August 15 of 1945, Japan surrendered to the Allied Powers. Japan was stripped of its empire and lost 25% of its national wealth. The iron and steel industry, the most essential industry for the war economy, became the target of criticism and of reparations. In 1945, few people foresaw that the industry would revive within a few decades. Immediately after the war, Japan was confused and tired. In this atmosphere of despair, no one anticipated the amazing growth the Japanese iron and steel industry would undergo in the next few decades. Interpretations such as "MITI targeted several industries for potential export growth: steel was one of them," were only made in hindsight.[16]

Rather, in the defeated mood of the postwar period, there appeared to be almost no hope for the iron and steel industry. Even Nagano Shigeo, director of the Iron and Steel Control Association, was no exception. He later recalled:[17]

> I heard the Emperor's announcement of Japan's defeat on the radio in Hokkaidō. I thought that everything had gone and that my twenty years dedicated to the steel business were in vain. . . . Thus, I decided to be a farmer in Hokkaidō. Actually I bought two rice fields, a small starch factory, and a self-sufficient salt mill with ¥200,000, my whole savings.

At that time, ¥200,000 was not a small amount at all. For the managers of the industry, the war defeat left them in such despair that they could not even dream that the industry would be targeted as strategic.

1. "Japan does not need its costly iron and steel industry"
In fact, during the immediate postwar years, MITI was not yet established, and the Japanese government hardly possessed a targeting policy. The situation of the industry at that time was much closer to what Asada Chōhei, president of Kobe Steel, later recalled:[18]

After the war, I was a vice chairman of the Kansai Economic Federation and often had arguments with the Osaka-based cotton spinning businessmen. At that time, as every industry suffered from a lack of coal and electricity, they said: "Since Japan does not have any iron ore or coal, it does not need its costly iron and steel industry. Our cotton-spinning firms will rebuild the Japanese economy through exports; there is no need for the iron and steel industry." I was so angry that I countered by saying that as iron and steel were basic for all other industries, Japan must have it even if it were to eliminate the cotton industry. It was February of 1947. Thus, the general view of the public was that Japan should eliminate the iron and steel industry since the country had no natural endowments. It was said, rather, that it should import the iron and steel it needed and should go for the light industries.

When we look at the production figures at that time, we can understand that Asada's recollection was not an exaggeration. In 1945, the Japanese iron and steel industry was literally destroyed. Iron and steel production had declined to 0.42 and 0.68 million tons, respectively, from 5.22 million and 6.77 million tons in 1943, the peak year of wartime production. The number of working blast furnaces and open-hearth furnaces had decreased to only 3 and 22 from 35 and 208 in 1943. These declines were not caused by the American Air Force's strategic bombing or by the disappearance of munitions demand. The main reason was that the Japanese iron and steel industry had lost its resource base: the scrap from the United States and the mines in its former colonies or dependencies in Manchuria, China, and Southeast Asia. In 1943, Japan depended on imports for 61% of its iron ore and 38% of its coal.[19] By the end of the war, the Japanese iron and steel industry had lost almost all its resources in Asia and its cargo ships as well. In addition, the Supreme Commander for the Allied Powers (SCAP) had come down hard on the zaibatsu and the munitions industries. On October 31, 1945, the Preliminary Statement of the U.S. Reparations Mission to Japan recommended that Japan should "be left with industries which do provide her with a minimum of export goods, for the purpose of obtaining exchange for necessary and approved imports, such as food."[20] Edwin W. Pauley, ambassador of the United States and personal representative of the President on reparations, recommended removal of the iron and steel capacity as follows:[21]

(3) All steelmaking capacity in excess of 2,500,000 tons per year. Japan's admitted present steel capacity is in excess of 11,000,000 tons, as compared with 1930, when Japan produced 2,300,000 tons of ingots and consumed only 1,700,000 tons of finished steel.
(4) All capacity for the production of pig iron in excess of 500,000 tons per year.

The Pauley Mission recommended that the Japanese iron and steel industry be downsized to 500,000 tons in annual ironmaking capacity (plus 1,000,000 tons imports), 2,250,000 tons in steel ingots, and 1,500,00 tons in finished steel. According to its calculations, the production level of steel ingots would be reduced to that of 1930. However, due to the fact that the population had increased by 1945, this figure would make the level of steel consumption per capita that of 1915. In order to insure that Japan would not again become a menace to world peace, SCAP tried to eliminate the possibility of the revival of the munitions industries. Thus during the Occupation, steel managers could hardly dream that iron and steel would later be chosen as a strategic exporting industry. Rather, they were concerned solely with how to survive.

Obviously the Japanese iron and steel industry could not agree with Pauley's report and made a formal protest on the grounds of economic efficiency. The industry argued that in order to import 1,000,000 tons of pig iron, ¥90 million would be required, while it would cost only ¥58 million if Japan produced the same amount of pig iron itself by importing 2,000,000 tons of iron ore and 600,000 tons of coal.[22] This calculation revealed that there was a strong consensus in the industry that it was more economical to make pig iron than to buy it. In other words, the industry recognized that integrated iron and steel production was more economical and efficient. This consensus had developed as a result of the industry's bitter experience during the war. However, as SCAP did not allow any resource imports, the industry had to make production plans based on domestic resources. Right after the war, for example, the Japan Steel Corporation had to scale down its production plan based on domestic natural resources, because of SCAP's ban on imports. The plan expected that the annual production of pig iron and finished steel would be 400,000 tons and 360,000 tons, respectively.[23] Compared with the production level of the company in 1943 (3.65 million tons of pig iron and 2.51 million tons of finished steel), the plan was considerably smaller.

In addition to SCAP's severe occupation policy, there was the fact that the Japanese economy was wracked by inflation and food shortages. An officer to SCAP's political advisor wrote to the Secretary of State: "A famine in Japan of two or three months duration would in all probability result in widespread civil disturbance; would seriously retard achievement of the purpose of the occupation."[24]

Coal production, in particular, became the bottleneck for industrial revival. Because of the release of Korean miners, coal production rapidly declined to one-tenth of the prewar level. The coal shortage impeded the energy supply and the normal activities of the basic industries. The shortage of basic goods impeded coal mining in turn.

At the end of 1946, it was widely rumored that the Japanese economy would pass the point of no return by March or May of 1947. It was this economic crisis that gave hope to the iron and steel industry. In December 1946, in order to stop the further decline of the Japanese economy, the Economic Stabilization Board of the Japanese government announced a new economic policy: the so-called priority production system (*keisha seisan hōshiki*) proposed by Arisawa Hiromi, professor of Tokyo University. To stem the vicious cycle of coal and steel shortages, the priority production system was envisioned to provide coal to the iron and steel industry and then provide the increased steel to the coal mining industry. The industry decided to concentrate its production on Japan Steel's Yawata Works at the beginning. Coal allocation to the iron and steel industry was increased by 57%. As a result, the total output of coal reached 29.3 million tons (a 33% increase) in 1947. This priority production system was no more than the application of the principles of the wartime controlled economy.[25]

In addition to giving the industry priority in coal allocation, the priority production system had two important side effects on the Japanese iron and steel industry. One was that the industry was recognized as still being important for economic development. The other was that SCAP, which had been against resource imports, allowed the industry to import 13,000 kiloliters of diesel oil, 2,000 tons of coal, and 250,000 tons of hard coal per month from the United States and Asia. The permission to import resources encouraged the leaders of the industry who had been discouraged by previous threats to liquidate the industry. Thanks to the priority production system, the iron and steel firms which had barely maintained themselves by making pots and kettles could begin true production.

However, the priority production system was only planned to overcome the economic crisis, so the full restoration of the iron and steel industry was still uncertain. In fact, SCAP announced the Interim Directive Regarding Advance Transfers of Japanese Reparations in April 1947, and 30% of the total assets of the iron and steel industry were designated as part of Japan's first reparation.[26] In addition, in order to democratize the Japanese economy, SCAP dissolved the zaibatsu firms and introduced the Antimonopoly Law and the Deconcentration of Execessive Economic Power Law in December 1947. Under these laws, the zaibatsu and many large industrial firms were designated as having excessive economic power and were ordered to be split. Thirteen iron and steel firms including Japan Steel, NKK, Kawasaki Heavy Industries, Sumitomo Metal Industries, and Kobe Steel were selected for dissolution.

With the outbreak of the Cold War, particularly after the Greek Rebellion of 1947, the government of the United States began to change its occupation policy from one which emphasized punishment to one which aimed at supporting the Japanese economic recovery. The United States decided to aid in Japan's economic development to prevent the spread of communism in East Asia. As a result of this change the Antimonopoly Law and the Deconcentration Law were applied less strictly. Easing its occupation policy, the U.S. government sent a new industrial reparation survey mission to Japan, the Strike Mission. The mission of 20 industrial experts surveyed Japan's industrial structure and decided that Japan needed at least 2,500,000 tons of annual capacity of pig iron, 3,500,000 tons of steel ingot, and 2,650,000 tons of finished steel. The mission's calculations provided hope and a great deal of relief to the industry.

2. The Dodge Line as a Paradigm for Change
In 1948, due to the priority production system and the Strike Mission's report, the Japanese iron and steel industry began to increase operation. For the Japanese government, then, it was an urgent object to establish a concrete economic policy for the industry. However, the Ministry of Commerce and Industry (MCI), which was re-established in August 1945 as a successor of the Ministry of Munitions, continued using the old methods of the wartime economy. These were (1) price control and (2) subsidies to offset price differentials. Since 1939, the

Japanese government had fixed prices and subsidized the differentials between production cost and sales price to carry out wartime production. After the war, in order to stabilize the postwar economy, it again fixed sales prices at eight times those of 1939 and subsidized differentials. The prices of pig iron and the average price of finished steel per ton were fixed at around ¥1,300 and ¥2,600, respectively. However, the production cost of pig iron, for example, was already ¥2,287 and as the postwar inflation progressed rapidly, the firms suffered tremendous losses. They lost over ¥50 million in 1946.

In order to help these firms keep operating, MCI created an innovative device in 1947: the Reconstruction Finance Bank (Fukkō Kin'yū Kōkō). The Reconstruction Finance Bank supplied about ¥13.5 billion to basic industries (coal mining, iron and steel, electric power, and fertilizers), of which during the first two years the iron and steel industry received ¥3.53 billion. This governmental loan was totally different from the old control methods such as subsidy and the control association, since it was an indirect and very private and voluntary-oriented involvement when compared with the prewar involvements of the Japanese government. It was the result of learning from the bitter experiences during the war economy.[27]

In July 1947, because of rapid inflation and a thriving black market, the government again had to increase the fixed prices to 65 times the average prices in 1934–36. In spite of the increase, the government had to subsidize iron and steel sales prices 53% and 43%, respectively, to make up the difference with the cost of production. Thus, the industry could maintain its operation and sales activities only with huge governmental assistance.

However, it would be exaggerating to say that this governmental aid brought about the international competitiveness that the industry would enjoy later. Although the governmental support was significant in that it enabled the industry to get its production started in the difficult times after the war, there was no relation between these protectionist measures and international competitiveness at all. These measures—tariff, price control, subsidy, and preferential finance—were well-worn devices to foster basic or infant important industries around the world. There are few examples where these measures have been successful. On the contrary, such measures not only often impede healthy competition among private firms, they often retard proper economic development for the nation as a whole.[28] In fact, the huge amount of Japanese governmental assistance accelerated the postwar inflation and pushed the economy to the brink of bankruptcy in 1948.

This situation thus necessitated more American aid and induced criticism of SCAP and its occupation policy in the United States. Americans complained that U.S. tax money was going down the drain in Japan.[29] In reaction, the U.S. government, easing its occupation policy, decided in February 1949 to send Joseph M. Dodge, former president of the Bank of Detroit, to supervise Japan's economic recovery. Analyzing the Japanese economy, Dodge announced his economic reforms in what came to be called the "Dodge Line." The Dodge Line had four basic goals: (1) to achieve a true balance in the consolidated budget, (2) to abolish government subsidies, (3) to terminate loans from the Reconstruction Finance Bank, and (4) to establish a single exchange rate ($1=¥360).

The severity of the Dodge Line astonished not only the Japanese government and industries, but also the staff of SCAP. For the government, a truly balanced budget meant that it had to carry out a deflationary policy. For the Japanese industries, the abolishment of subsidies and governmental loans and the imposition of a single exchange rate meant that they had to be self-supporting without governmental aid. This seemed especially harsh, because the industries, depending on imported materials, would have to earn the foreign currency to purchase these materials by themselves.

In the uncertain environment of postwar Japan, the Dodge Line was a paradigm for change from a war economy to a self-supporting one. More importantly, it directly linked the creation of a self-supporting economy to international competitiveness. To carry out a truly balanced budget, the government could not spend more than what it earned. Therefore, in order to expand the economy beyond its limited natural resources, Japan had to earn money through trade and export, and to export successfully, Japan's industries had to become internationally competitive, which meant carrying out rationalizations. The Dodge Line made the direction in which Japan should go very clear. Following the paradigm for change inaugurated by the Dodge Line, the Japanese government, stressing international trade to earn foreign currency, reorganized the Ministry of Commerce and Industry into the Ministry of *International Trade* and Industry in April 1949.

In reality, the Dodge Line posed a serious challenge to the iron and steel industry. As mentioned above, the industry had been protected by subsidies and loans. In addition, the government had applied multiple exchange rates toward certain priority imports to lower production costs. For example, imported iron ore per ton was U.S. $17.26 on the world market, but was sold to the iron and steel producers for ¥2,402 per ton. This meant that the exchange rate applied to iron ore was about $1=¥140, while the acceptable rate was supposed to be around $1=¥360. The single exchange rate meant that the industry would lose the preferential import prices. The single exchange rate $1=¥360 was adopted in April 1949, and the subsidies were scheduled to be gradually abolished by July 1950. Thus, the Dodge Line pushed up production costs as well as sales prices.

The imposition of the Dodge Line once more raised the question of whether Japan really needed such a vulnerable and costly industry such as the iron and steel industry. Even among the officials on the Economic Stabilization Board, some questioned whether it was efficient to keep investing in the iron and steel industry, considering investment efficiency and the international division of labor.[30] Paul M. O'Leary, a member of the Dodge Mission, was of the opinion that the Japanese iron and steel and aluminum industries were not necessary. To defend its existence, the industry strived to rationalize its facilities with the help of a technological mission sent by the U.S. government to improve the obsolete technologies. However, it was impossible for the industry to gain international competitiveness in such a short period. Japan's steel prices were the most expensive in the world. In January 1950, Japanese steel sold at $77 per ton while bar steel sold for $73 in Britain, $57 in Germany, $59 in France, and $66 in Belgium. With the final termination of subsidies on July 1 of 1950, the industry fell into chaos.

It was nothing more than superb luck, then, that the Korean War broke out at nearly exactly the same time: on June 25, 1950. Procurement by the U.S. military and a sudden price rise radically changed the deflationary environment created by the Dodge Line. The Japanese economy began to boom. By September, military procurement of steel reached 78,000 tons and the industry's financial situation quickly improved. However, although the Korean War improved the short-term profit of the industry, it did not solve any of the basic problems the Dodge Line dictated to the industry. Attaining international competitiveness through vigorous rationalization and modernization remained the number one item on the agenda.

III. The Innovation of Kawasaki Steel: The Entrepreneurship of Nishiyama Yatarō

In addition to the Korean War, 1950 witnessed two other very important events that would spark the industry's response to the Dodge Line. One was the split-up of the Japan Steel Corporation and the other, more important, was the establishment of Kawasaki Steel Corporation.

Japan Steel was Japan's largest iron and steel firm with market shares of 78.2% (3.56 million tons) in pig iron and 48.2% (3.75 million tons) in crude steel in 1943. After the war, SCAP designated Japan Steel as a munitions company with too much power and ordered it to split up into two purely private companies. After the outbreak of the Cold War, the U.S. government altered its occupation policies, and SCAP eased its deconcentration policy of large corporations. However, even though SCAP subsequently released the other designated large steel firms from the breakup order, Japan Steel was forced to split into two integrated firms which became Yawata Steel and Fuji Steel Corporations in April 1950.

Yawata Steel took over the Yawata Works, while Fuji Steel inherited the Hirohata, Kamaishi, Wanishi, and Fuji Works. Miki Takashi became the first president of Yawata Steel and Nagano Shigeo assumed the presidency of Fuji Steel.

In the same month, Kawasaki Steel became independent from Kawasaki Heavy Industries (KHI). In contrast to Japan Steel, the order to split KHI was retracted in 1949 and there was no obligation for the company to spin off its steel division. However, Nishiyama Yatarō, chief engineer and director of KHI's steel division, who was one of the top five managing directors of KHI after the war, wanted to set up his division as an independent corporation. KHI's main business had been shipbuilding and its steel division had been regarded only as a means toward backward integration. During the desperate postwar years, while conventional managers in the shipbuilding division became negative and tried to downsize the company's activities, Nishiyama saw an extraordinary business opportunity. Right after the war, he made a speech to his people at the steel factory:[31]

Eventually, steel will become less expensive than lumber. Yes, we will make it cheap. Lumber takes decades to make, but steel can be produced any time. And a 100-meter piece of lumber is impossible to produce, but with steel, it is simple. Before long, more houses will be made with steel than with wood.

The Japanese iron and steel industry must cut costs and develop the ability to compete internationally by switching to the American mode of scale production and away from the European mode of small-based productivity. It is necessary, therefore, to construct an integrated iron and steelworks that has blast furnaces.

Nishiyama was determined to achieve not only independence for the steel division, but also the integration of pig-iron production.

As early as September 1950, he announced that the newly born Kawasaki Steel would build a state-of-the-art integrated works in Chiba. The plan called for two 500-tons-per-charge (tpc) blast furnaces, six 100 tpc open-hearth furnaces, matching slab mills, and hot and cold strip mills with annual capacities of 350,000 tons of pig iron and 500,000 tons of crude steel.

To the industry, MITI, and the Bank of Japan, the decision seemed ridiculous. First, as the total output of crude steel in 1950 was only 2,500,000 tons, Kawasaki's anticipated annual capacity of 500,000 seemed excessive. Second, as only 12 out of 37 existing blast furnaces were in operation, Kawasaki's two new blast furnaces were regarded as an unnecessary investment that would cause oversupply. Particularly after the split of Japan Steel, the plan seemed excessive. Following Japan Steel's split into Yawata and Fuji, the market structure had already changed into an oligopoly controlled by the three large integrated firms of Yawata, Fuji, and NKK. The entrance of Kawasaki Steel, therefore, was seen as an unnecessary threat, especially to newly born Fuji Steel headed by Nagano Shigeo.

Since the split of Japan Steel had been carried out according to an artificial partitioning plan dictated by SCAP, Fuji had to start its operation with lopsidedly large pig-iron and small steel production facilities. To Fuji, therefore, Kawasaki's planned pig-iron production seemed to presage oversupply. MITI and the Bank of Japan had also opposed Nishiyama's proposal on these grounds.

To Nishiyama, the main reason for entrance into integrated production was, ironically, the split of Japan Steel. During the war, the main task of Japan Steel had been to provide cheaper and better iron and semi-finished steel under the strict control of the government. In this sense, Japan Steel had never been a real competitor to the private non-integrated steel firms, such as Kawasaki, Sumitomo, and Kobe. Rather, it had played the role of a stable provider of inexpensive pig iron and semi-finished steel. After the war, however, SCAP divided Japan Steel and created two purely private firms to bring healthy and free competition into the industry. Therefore, the split meant that Yawata and Fuji not only became Kawasaki's competitors in the steel market but also tough negotiators when Kawasaki wanted to purchase pig iron.

In addition, Nishiyama had experienced tremendous difficulties as a non-integrated steelmaker during the war period, being hampered by the lack of American scrap in particular. Nishiyama saw entering the field of pig-iron production as a measure of self-defense. From the viewpoint of industrial organizational theory, the split of Japan Steel meant its first mover advantage and resulting high-entry barrier were reduced by an order of SCAP. Therefore, it became easier for Kawasaki Steel to enter integrated production in its economic rationale.

The construction cost of Nishiyama's plan, ¥16.3 billion, seemed out of the question to the Bank of Japan, which was struggling to achieve the balanced budget mandated by the Dodge Line. Kawasaki Steel had only ¥500 million in paid-in capital, and it had no way of achieving its plan without borrowing money from the government or other sources. The fact that KHI's steel division had concentrated its steelmaking operations in open-hearth furnaces and thus had no experience with blast-furnace operation increased the perceived riskiness of the plan. Understandably then, Nishiyama's plan was regarded as an impossible dream, and was opposed by MITI, the Bank of Japan, and the industry.[32] Ichimada Hisato, president of the Bank of Japan, said, "I will grow *pen-pen gusa* (weeds) over Kawasaki's Chiba, if they construct it against my better judgment." To them, it seemed more reasonable and efficient to restore unused blast furnaces and to rationalize obsolete rolling mills rather than build a new integrated works.

To Nishiyama, it did not seem enough gradually to renovate obsolete facilities to gain international competitiveness. From his bitter wartime experience, he had learned that integrated iron and steel production was far more efficient and productive. However, resource-poor Japan had to import raw materials for integrated production. Considering the conditions imposed by Dodge, it was therefore urgent for integrated production to gain the power to earn foreign currency to import. This meant that the facilities had to be state-of-the-art. In fact, the rationality of Nishiyama's decision would be proved later by the fact that the other firms followed his lead.

1. Nishiyama's Three Innovations

Nishiyama's decision was innovative in three ways. First, the proposed Chiba Works was an innovation itself. It was to be equipped with the world's most advanced technologies in the best factory layout. In 1951, Nishiyama sent the first postwar private technical mission to the United States to research state-of-the-art technologies in the field of iron and steel. After it returned, the mission revised the first proposed plan, and the estimated construction cost was increased to ¥27.3 billion. Since Nishiyama recognized the technological importance of the Chiba Works, he did not hesitate to lavish money on it. In addition, the loca-

tion of the works was also innovative. The Chiba Works were constructed on the shore of Tokyo Bay near the capital, Japan's largest market
for steel, an area well-designed to facilitate seashore loadings for material imports and product exports. A well-known technological historian
described the innovativeness of the Chiba Works as follows:[33]

> Compared with any other plants, Kawasaki's Chiba Works had the
> best layout. In the prewar period, the plant with the best layout
> was the Hirohata Works of Japan Steel, but even Hirohata was no
> comparison with Chiba. While the total length of railroad within
> Chiba plants was approximately 60 kilometers (about 38 miles),
> that of the Yawata Works, Japan's largest steel works, was over 500
> kilometers. Before the war, people were astonished and moved by
> the fact that the mileage of Yawata's internal railroad was equal to
> the distance between Tokyo and Osaka. However, this understand-
> ing was not scientific at all. . . . Sixty kilometers is the typical
> mileage for plant railroads in modern steelworks in the postwar
> period. In fact, the Chiba works became the basic model of the
> coastal steel plant in postwar Japan as well as a prototype of the
> world standard for the modern steelworks.

Nishiyama's Chiba Works represented a quantum leap above other
contemporary iron and steelworks.

Nishiyama's second innovation was that it addressed the problem of
the unbalanced development of the Japanese iron and steel industry.
As mentioned before, Kawasaki's entry into integrated production was
a measure of self-defense. Logically, it was inevitable that Kawasaki's
move would affect the decision-making processes of Sumitomo and
Kobe, since they faced a similar situation. In fact, Sumitomo and Kobe
also decided to integrate their blast-furnace operations following
Kawasaki. In 1953, Sumitomo merged with Kokura Steel (the former
Asano's Kokura Steel), a small integrated firm, to acquire blast-furnace
operation. Kobe for its part participated in the management of
Amagasaki Steel, a small integrated firm, in 1954. Later, the two
makers also decided to build their own advanced integrated works similar to Kawasaki's Chiba Works. Soon, the six largest integrated firms,
Yawata, Fuji, NKK, Kawasaki, Sumitomo, and Kobe were producing
about 90% of the pig iron and 80% of the crude steel, and an
oligopolistic market structure emerged (Fig. 2). The historical distortion
between iron and steel production was solved by Kawasaki's initiation.

The final way in which Nishiyama was innovative was the way in

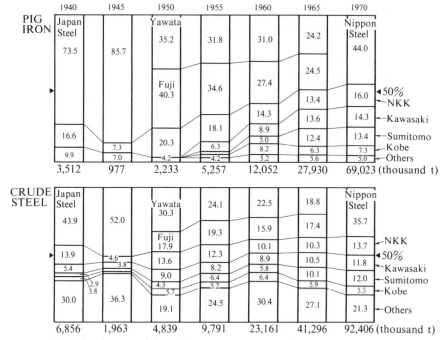

FIG. 2 Market Shares of the Six Largest Companies (percentage).
Source: Seiichiro Yonekura, "Innovative Behavior and Entrepreneurship of
    Kawasaki Steel in the Postwar Period," Discussion Paper #121,
    Institute of Business Research, Hitotsubashi University (1984).

which he sought capital. The proposed budget, ¥16.3 billion, consisted
of a governmental loan for ¥8 billion (49.1%), a company bond issue
of ¥3.1 billion yen (19.0%), bank loans of ¥1 billion (6.1%), and ¥4.2
billion (25.8%) from retained earnings. From the beginning, then,
Nishiyama intended to borrow almost three-quarters of the construction costs from outside. As has been frequently explained by economic
historians of postwar Japan, the high economic growth of postwar
Japan was made possible by overborrowing (or from the viewpoint of
the bank, overloaning) and the indirect finance system.[34] Under the
scarce capital conditions of the postwar period, the Japanese firms had
to overborrow from banks to finance their capacity expansion plans,
and the government backed up these overloans with credit from the
Bank of Japan. Nishiyama pioneered this overborrowing growth pattern. In fact, in order to borrow money and to have close relations with
Daiichi Bank, Nishiyama accepted a financial advisor from the bank
and made him company chairman—above Nishiyama himself. In 1953,

Omori Hisanori, managing director of the Daiichi Bank, thus became chairman of Kawasaki Steel. In addition, Nishiyama also pioneered introducing foreign funds. Kawasaki Steel made a contract to borrow $20 million (¥7.2 billion) from the World Bank in 1953, making Kawasaki the recipient of the first large introduction of foreign funds in the postwar period.

2. Dynamic Interaction between Continuity and Discontinuity
Nishiyama in his decision to construct the Chiba Works as the most advanced integrated plant in Japan thus pioneered the postwar growth pattern of the iron and steel industry and created a competitive paradigm that would rule the industry. It was the dynamics of continuity and discontinuity between prewar experiences and postwar change that led him to such a bold decision. Before the war, Nishiyama had been chief engineer and general manager of KHI's steel division. He won the Hattori Prize, the most prestigious prize in steel engineering, in 1938 and had been known as "Nishiyama of the open-hearth furnace" for his knowledge and expertise in the industry. While accumulating expertise in steelmaking technology and management, he came to perceive the limitations of non-integrated steel production. Although he tried to integrate pig-iron production during the war, he could not succeed because of the deteriorating war economy. His decision to integrate production in the 1950s was, therefore, a continuation of his wartime efforts.

In addition, Nishiyama exploited his accumulated network of contacts and knowledge in the old Japan Steel and Showa Steel. When he planned a blueprint of the Chiba Works, Yamaoka Takeshi, vice president and chief technical officer of Yawata Steel, gave him technological advice. More importantly, when he constructed the Chiba Works, he employed engineers from Showa Steel in Manchuria and made use of their accumulated expertise. Showa Steel had experimented with several advanced technologies. After the war Showa Steel was confiscated by the Chinese government, and the Japanese engineers returned to Japan. Nishiyama hired those engineers. Among them, Asawa Saburō, a disciple of Umene Tsunesaburō, played a most important role as superintendent of the Chiba Works. Umene and Asawa developed an improved method of iron-ore preparation that Asawa brought to the Chiba Works, where it reached fruition. In addition, engineers from the old Japan Steel and the navy also made important contributions to the construction of the Chiba Works.[35] Those continuities were the basis for Nishiyama's bold decision.

While accumulated technological expertise and his network of contacts encouraged Nishiyama's decision, drastic discontinuities after the war also stimulated his entrepreneurship. As mentioned before, the most drastic discontinuity for Nishiyama was the split of Japan Steel. In addition, the purge of the wartime business executives by the Occupation Army was also one of the biggest changes. With SCAP's democratization efforts, top executives of the munitions industries, including iron and steel and shipbuilding, were purged. As a result, Nishiyama was promoted to one of the five top executives of KHI in spite of his youth. The promotion brought him an extraordinary opportunity to achieve his goal. Soon after his inauguration, he insisted upon the independence of the steel division from KHI. Directors at the main corporate office and the shipbuilding division opposed Nishiyama, but he was able to effect the independence of the steel division. Soon after the establishment of Kawasaki Steel, Nishiyama announced his plan for the construction of the Chiba Works. The end of the war and the more democratic economic environment encouraged by SCAP provided him with an opportunity to enhance his technical skills and to put into practice his entrepreneurial ideas.

3. The First Rationalization Program

Other steel companies also proposed expansion plans to respond to the special procurement demands of the Korean War. These proposals were filed at MITI as part of the First Rationalization Program (1951–53) in 1951. The procedure of making the rationalization program was similar to that of the prewar Control Association. The Control Association had been abolished by GHQ–SCAP in February 1946. The Japan Iron and Steel Council, which replaced the Control Association, was also abolished by the government in April 1947, since it still reflected the wartime control organization. Then the Japan Iron and Steel Federation (Nihon Tekkō Renmei), a non-control, purely private trade association, was established in December 1947.[36] The Japan Iron and Steel Federation (JISF) played an important role gathering and compiling information for the industry.

The proposed investment for the First Rationalization Program amounted to ¥667 million. The program was intended to be carried out over three years, from 1951 to 1953, but it was extended for two more years. The total capital expenditure during the five-year period reached ¥128.2 million. However, as MITI encouraged a rationalization of rolling processes, hot and cold strip mills in particular, and as the Bank of Japan opposed Nishiyama's plan, there was no blast-furnace construction included in the plan except at Kawasaki's Chiba Works.

Nishiyama's plan was aloofly regarded by the government as an exceptional case. In April 1951, Kawasaki started the construction of the Chiba Works without MITI's approval. In the First Rationalization Program, therefore, 47.8% of the capital was spent on the rationalization and modernization of rolling processes, while 19.7% went to the ironmaking process.

MITI still did not consider the industry one worth targeting as strategic for international trade, for in 1954, when the Korean War was over and a recession ensued, MITI deemed it inappropriate for export under the New Export Plan.[37] In order to understand MITI and its real industrial policy, it is very useful for us to understand why MITI defined iron and steel as an "inappropiate exporting industry." As mentioned above, under the Dodge Line, it was financially difficult for the government to subsidize iron and steel firms. Even without the Dodge Line, it was not easy for the Japanese government to protect and subsidize industries at that time. First of all, in order to achieve the stability of the Japanese economy, the government was enforcing a tight budget. Subsidization and protectionism would upset the balanced budget and cause a fiscal deficit. Second, as the iron and steel industry was a basic industry for the development of the other industries, the higher price of protected iron and steel might cause the uncompetitiveness of other industries, such as shipbuilding, coal mining, machinery, and automobile manufacture. For MITI, charged with overseeing the development of the nation's economy as a whole, it was not easy to single out one industry as strategic. From an overall economic point of view, we can say that it was rational for MITI to decide in 1954 that the iron and steel industry would not be competitive. The First Rationalization Program, therefore, should be seen as just the beginning of learning by trial and error.

Along with the First Rationalization Program, the government established important systems to facilitate the rationalization and modernization of the industry.[38] Although there were a total of seven measures, two stand out:

(1) The first was the establishment of the Japan Development Bank to supply key industries with low-interest funds. The Japan Development Bank provided ¥9.96 million for the iron and steel industry during the First Program. Although it accounted for only 7.7% of the total investment of the program, it had an important "pump-priming" effect, since the Ministry of Finance asked com-

mercial banks to extend cooperative loans to the key industries. (2) The second consisted of tax measures including permission for rapid depreciation of designated investments for important machinery and the exclusion of strategic machinery from import duties.

The establishment of the Japan Development Bank set up the basis for the overborrowing growth of the postwar economy. In fact, 55.5% of the funds of the First Program consisted of external funding from governmental banks, commercial banks, and corporate bonds. Tax measures also helped firms that suffered from insufficient capital to accumulate funds by transforming profits to expenses in the form of rapid depreciation.[39] MITI began indirectly to prepare an environment where private firms would be able to increase capacity. These measures, however, cannot be considered directly responsible for the international competitiveness that the industry would gain later, because such aids have long been implemented by governments around the world without Japan's success.[40] If we praise these measures as having been successful in Japan, we have to analyze how the Japanese firms exploited these measures to increase their competitiveness. Without analyzing the mechanism by which these measures were exploited, it is easy to fall into the trap of assuming that the governmental aid itself was the source of competitiveness.

IV. A New Competitive Model and Innovations

In 1955, as the American and European economies recovered from the recession of 1954, the Japanese iron and steel industry recovered through its exports. Since the American and British iron and steel industries did not have enough exporting capacity to fill the demands of the recovered European countries, their Japanese counterpart was able to fill the gap through direct and indirect exports of steel.

Japan's total amount of steel exports was expected to reach 2.2–2.5 million tons by the end of 1955. In October of the same year, however, MITI decided to restrict the steel exports to around 2 million tons because it thought that overexporting might cause not only a steel shortage but also price increases and a drain on scrap.[41] This restrictive measure revealed two important things. One was the emergence of the iron and steel industry as an exporting industry. For MITI and the industry, the exporting boom of 1955 marked their first realization that Japanese steel could occupy a place in the world market. The year

1955 was very important because Japan had recorded its first trade surplus ($535 million) without the special demands created by the Korean War. The Japanese economy had begun to be self-supporting as the Dodge Line had required.

Another important realization was the limitation of scrap. Compared with an abundance of scrap in the United States, Japan had few such resources. The worldwide economic recovery made scrap in high demand and had raised its price. It was therefore expected that it would be more difficult for the Japanese industry to import scrap, particularly from the United States. This scrap shortage put the non-integrated steel producers, who depended on imported scrap, at a great disadvantage. Thus the emergence of the iron and steel industry as an export industry and the limited supply of scrap created the setting for the technological shift from a non-integrated to an integrated production system.

In addition, the economic recovery of 1955 unexpectedly developed the largest economic boom in Japanese history. The economic boom was called the "Jimmu boom," so named because the boom was thought to be the biggest since Emperor Jimmu, the legendary first emperor of Japan who was thought to have come to the throne in 660 B.C.

During the boom, the iron and steel companies announced expansion plans, and these plans were compiled as the Second Rationalization Program (1955–60). The Second Rationalization Program was different from the first one in two ways. First, the Second Program was not initiated by MITI as the first one had been, but by the industry. Japan Iron and Steel Federation played a key role in coordinating each firm's individual plan.

Second, and more importantly, the main emphasis of the Second Program was put on the construction of blast furnaces. In other words, the expansion and construction of an integrated production system was the main goal of the Second Program. This contrasted sharply with the First Program, in which Kawasaki was the only firm to construct a new blast furnace.

In the Second Program, Yawata built two new blast furnaces, Fuji one, NKK and Kawasaki two each, while Sumitomo and Kobe each built one. Following Kawasaki's lead, Sumitomo and Kobe decided to build new seaside works similar to the Chiba Works. The companies could no longer ignore the advantage of the integrated production and the modern layout incorporated in the Chiba Works.[42] All of these newly built blast furnaces had a capacity of over 1,000 tons daily, matching the high minimum efficient scale of the newly introduced BOFs, as we will see later.

In 1956 MITI announced that there was a need to develop a long-term supply strategy for raw materials:[43]

Considering the increasing demand for steel worldwide, there are two important issues which the industry must address. One is the need for capacity expansion and the other is the serious shortage of raw materials. In order for the iron and steel industry to continue developing for the long term and to strengthen its status as an exporting industry, it is urgently necessary to establish a long-term supply strategy for raw materials and capital investment.

In response, the industry sent the Scrap Investigation Mission to the United States and started studies in the feasibility of procuring raw materials, iron ore in particular, from India, Malaya, and the Philippines. These studies concluded that even in the United States the supply of scrap was tight, and that the international market of scrap would be very speculative. Thus the industry strongly perceived the advantage of iron ores as raw material. The choice of iron ore as a raw material meant the choice of integrated operations. In the Second Rationalization Program, it was clearly recognized that in order for the Japanese iron and steel industry to circumvent the unstable scrap market, the shift from non-integrated to integrated production was inevitable.

Historically, the Japanese iron and steel industry had been divided into integrated and non-integrated works, and this fact characterized the industry and the industrial policy of prewar Japan.[44] The shift initiated by the Second Program ended the industry's historical imbalance. The total investment of the Second Program reached ¥533.1 billion ($1.48 billion), and 11 new blast furnaces were built. In order to stabilize the resource supply, the industry and the general trading firms Mitsui and Mitsubishi started a joint development of Indian iron-ore mines with a long-term contract. Also, the industry jointly built large cargo ships specialized in iron-ore transportation, since a feasibility study by the Japan Iron and Steel Federation revealed that the specialized large cargo ships would reduce transportation costs by 20%. The role MITI played in the joint development of specialized iron-ore cargo ships characterized MITI's indirect coordinating role in the post-war period.

In 1958, in the middle of the post–Korean War recession, MITI initiated a joint venture between steel and shipping companies. As a joint venture, seven iron and steel firms jointly established the Japan Iron Ore Transporting Company with loans from the Japan Development Bank. Because the company was able to guarantee regular shipments of iron ore to the shipping companies, they jointly ordered five specialized cargo ships from the shipbuilding companies. The orders were compiled into the fourteenth Planned Shipbuilding Schedule that the Ministry of Transportation launched for the promotion of the shipbuilding industry. [45] For the shipbuilding industry, which had suffered from a sudden decline of orders in the post–Korean War recession, the orders of large cargo ships helped them maintain their capacity utilization ratio. Thus MITI satisfied the needs of three industries—iron and steel, shipbuilding, and shipping—with one concrete measure. This kind of activity as a networker and intermediator was MITI's most important role in the postwar era.

1. The Basic Oxygen Furnace (BOF)
With the decision to make the shift to integrated production came the rapid adoption of technological innovations. An early innovation adopted in Japan was the basic oxygen furnace (BOF). The BOF was commercialized by two small Austrian companies in 1952 as a steel-refining furnace which could take the place of the open-hearth furnace (OHF). The BOF used pig iron as its principal raw ingredient and decreased the percentage of scrap needed until finally no scrap at all was necessary. It reduced refining time to a tenth of what it had been in the OHF, thereby increasing the efficiency of the furnace, and it saved half of the construction cost. At first, the BOF had many problems, including tremendous pollution, a narrow scope of applicability in steel production, and problems relating to the durability of bricks within the furnace.

As Leonard Lynn's detailed study has shown, the developers of the BOF wanted to sell the new technology to the American steel firms which were then producing ten times more steel than their Japanese counterparts.[46] Unexpectedly, however, the Japanese firms were more aggressive at adopting the innovation than the Americans. The American firms, with relatively abundant scrap, and confidence and a huge investment in the proven OHF, did not feel the need to try the unproven BOF. The Japanese firms were more willing to experiment because of their greater difficulty in obtaining scrap. The most attractive character of the BOF was lower or no utilization of scrap. The BOF was the furnace for pig-iron users. As it turned out, the introduction of the BOF was well timed, coinciding as it did with the technological shift to integrated production. Therefore, the industry's decision to build new blast furnaces and to employ the BOF simultaneously was quite rational, particularly because a much smaller investment had been made in the relatively new OHF works.

In the Second Program, Yawata, Fuji, NKK, Sumitomo, and Amagasaki (Kobe's affiliate) decided to try the BOFs, since the BOF reduced production costs by 10–20% compared with the OHF. In the program, therefore, 54% of the steelmaking investment went to the construction of the BOFs.[47] Since Kawasaki had just invested in the latest OHFs at Chiba and Nishiyama had confidence in the proven OHF, Kawasaki became the last company among the largest six to introduce the BOF. As the 1960s and 1970s progressed, use of the BOF spread rapidly throughout the industry (see Table 4).

It is sometimes said that MITI initiated or induced the steel industry's technological adoptions.[48] There were, however, very few cases in which MITI initiated or played a direct role in the adoption of new technologies. In the case of the BOF, it should be noted that the introduction of the BOF was initiated by NKK, and that its adoption had been made possible by the continuous efforts of the company since before World War II. During the war, NKK had studied the basic Bessemer furnace, a process of steelmaking that used only pig iron and had discovered the potential of the BOF as early as 1951. In 1955, NKK decided to sign a contract with the Austrian manufacturer of the BOF as a general licensee.

However, Yawata, then Japan's largest iron and steel firm, was also interested in the BOF and tried to set up its own contract with another licenser. At that time, as MITI controlled all foreign transactions (including those covering licensing of technology from foreign firms), it intervened and let NKK sign the contract because its license was cheaper and the terms were more reasonable. MITI arranged for NKK to be the sole licensee, but negotiated a solution in which other companies could introduce the technology through NKK. Also, MITI set up a committee among the private firms to share information, pursue cooperative research on the BOF, and to divide royalty fees. In this technological diffusion, both the Japan Iron and Steel Federation and the Iron and Steel Institute of Japan played central roles. Thanks to MITI's mediation and those information-sharing institutions, the Japanese companies were able to introduce the BOF at half the price required of the American firms.[49] It was true that MITI played an important role as an intermediary and coordinator, but it must be noted that it was the private sector that introduced the superior technology and implemented it. In other words, MITI's technological intervention was successful because of the vigorous initiatives of private firms.

The BOF was more than just a substitute for the OHF; it revolutionized the steelmaking process in both speed and scale. The refining times in the early BOF were roughly one-tenth those required in the OHF. As the average scale of the BOF doubled through the 1950s and 1960s, the BOF reduced production costs by 10–20%. This increased productivity led to increasingly large-scale blast furnaces and other important technological innovations, such as the continuous caster and computerized process-control technology.

The larger and faster production rates which resulted in the 1960s from the large blast furnaces and the BOFs created a technological imbalance between the steelmaking and slabmaking processes. This technological imbalance, in turn, encouraged the Japanese iron and steel industry to adopt the continuous caster (CC).[50] The CC was a revolutionary technology in that it shortened the conventional pattern of manufacture, making possible continuous production of slabs, blooms, and billets directly from the steel-refining process. In comparison with the conventional process, where refined steel was cooled into ingots and then reheated to make slabs and billets, the CC reduced energy cost and increased yield and productivity. Although the CC was conceived of in the nineteenth century, it was not brought to fruition until the 1950s. At first, the CC was beset with many problems in application and quality. It was also considerably more expensive to build. However, Japanese firms, led by Yawata Steel and Sumitomo Metal Industries, began to introduce the technology in 1955, because it enabled makers to cast the large masses of steel produced by the BOF faster and more efficiently than in conventional slab mills. It was quite natural for the Japanese industry, which had pioneered the BOF, to find potential in the CC and to adopt it aggressively. In this way, the Japanese iron and steel industry developed a very fast, large, and streamlined production system from blast furnace to rolling mills.

This streamlined production system required more precise and faster process control at each phase. Another technological imbalance occurred. When using the conventional technologies, engineers themselves were responsible for process control. However, the steelmaking with the BOF and the CC had become so fast and large that it required some artificial control method; that is, the computerized process-control technology. As early as 1962, Fuji introduced the first analog com-

puter system to control the BOF, and after that the computerized process-control technology spread throughout the industry. By the 1980s,
the Japanese iron and steel industry had established a reputation in
this technology. Recently, steel firms have even begun to exploit their
experience in computer technology as part of their strategy to diversify
away from steel production itself.[51] Thus the adoption of the BOF led
to the successive adoption of other innovations in the integrated production system and made the Japanese industry the most efficient and
productive in the world. It must be noted that the introduction and
the implementation of those innovations were carried out not only by
engineers, but also by factory workers. Without the incremental
improvements based on hands-on worker experience, the Japanese
iron and steel companies would not have introduced these new technologies successfully.[52]

2. Following Nishiyama's Model
During the Second Rationalization Program, the industry increased its
crude steel production from 9.4 million tons in 1955 to 22.1 million
tons in 1960 and invested about ¥587.1 billion (the six largest integrated firms invested about ¥500 billion).[53] Following the Second Program,
Prime Minister Ikeda Hayato launched the Income Doubling Plan in
1960, thus beginning a period of rapid growth. The Income Doubling
Plan forecast that crude steel capacity would increase 48 million tons
by 1970, and thus 30 new blast furnaces would be needed. Adoption of
this plan stimulated the industry to expand its capacity, and the steel
companies began to construct new large-scale seaside works that could
exploit the cost advantage of the BOF and successive innovations.
Although these plans were called the Third Rationalization Program,
the plan was merely a combination of the separate expansion plans of
each of the individual firms.

Each of the largest six firms launched new works. These included
Yawata's Kimitsu, Fuji's Oita, NKK's Fukuyama, Kawasaki's Mizushima,
Sumitomo's Kajima, and Kobe's Kakogawa. These were all based on
Kawasaki's Chiba Works prototype. Surprisingly, Kawasaki's new
Mizushima Works was launched because its Chiba Works had already
become too small for the new streamlined and large-scale production
system. In the Third Program, the industry invested ¥1,092 billion ($3
billion), of which ¥740 billion was invested by the largest six. Crude
steel capacity increased to 93 million tons by 1970. These amazing figures raise the fundamental question why and how such a growth was
achieved. It has been well explained that the rapid growth of the

Japanese economy in the 1950s was pulled through by domestic demand, investment in particular, not by export.[54] Iron and steel were no exception. The iron and steel demand for construction, in the industry itself, and for the machine and shipbuilding industries made up a large portion of the demand structure throughout the 1950s and 1960s.[55] The demand from the iron and steel industry itself, consisting of around 20–25%, played a particularly significant role in the growth of the industry. It was clear that the industry was growing in a virtuous circle of "investment calling for investment." Growth was initiated not only by external factors but by the internal aggressiveness of the industry itself, that is "investment-driven growth."

The second question that comes to mind was how the industry could fund such great expansions. In the investments of the Second and Third Programs the external procurements of capital (short-term loans and company bonds) consisted of around 40–50% of total investment. By international comparison, this proportion was very high. In 1959, for instance, the average share of retained earnings in the capital investment of the ten largest American and four largest German firms was 91.7% and 93.1%, respectively, while that of the Japan's six largest was 45.6%.[56] As already mentioned, the Japanese economic growth of the 1950s was based on overborrowing, and the iron and steel industry was no exception. In the industry, the six largest, which produced roughly 95% of the pig iron and 70–80% of the crude steel, constructed their new, large, and highly-equipped integrated works by borrowing almost half of their investments. In other words, the industry followed the competitive model that Nishiyama set at Kawasaki's Chiba Works. Nishiyama's competitive model that was to compete oligopolistically for market share by constructing state-of-the-art works with loans and company bonds became the competitive model of the industry. This model, with its advanced large-scale equipment, achieved a higher minimum efficient scale (MES) and thus made it difficult for the steel manufacturers to operate at a low utilization rate. MES means the scale of operation necessary to reach the lowest cost per unit. In capital-intensive industries such as iron and steel, the more a firm invests, the lower its cost per unit becomes, but the higher its break-even point (BEP).[57] The large-scale and streamlined works built by borrowings and company bonds also set both the MES and the BEP higher and higher, since the companies had to pay interest and dividends periodically. Thus the higher BEP and MES made the competition for the market share all the more fierce. Once firms began to compete within Nishiyama's competitive model, they could only be assured of survival by keeping operation over the BEP and MES and investing in new technologies. Thus Nishiyama's model had competition built into it.

It also should be noted that the World Bank played an important role in funding the Japanese iron and steel rationalization programs. The World Bank loaned $84 million to Kawasaki, Sumitomo, and Kobe for their integrated process expansion.[58] As credit investigations by the World Bank were very strict, the companies had to prove themselves worthy of receiving loans. Besides merely funding their expansion plans, the loans from the bank also strengthened the overborrowing pattern of the Japanese firms.

V. Coordination of Competition

Between 1955 and 1965, the Japanese iron and steel output multiplied four times. Although the vigorous domestic demand for iron and steel absorbed the expanded supply at the beginning of the expansion program, overcapacity and the cyclical price decline soon became serious problems for the industry. In general, because the iron and steel industry, with high fixed costs and cyclical demand, is vulnerable to the business cycle, many countries have developed coordination tactics such as U.S. Steel's price leadership in the United States and cartelization in Germany. In Japan, the state-owned Yawata Works, the only fully integrated enterprise in the prewar period, set up a designated-price system (*tatene-sei*), similar to the price leadership in the United States. During the war the iron and steel prices were controlled by the government. In 1950, the newly born Yawata restored the designated-price system to stabilize market prices. Under the designated price system, Yawata announced the prices of iron and steel two months ahead after consultation with Fuji and NKK. The three largest non-integrated firms, Kawasaki, Sumitomo, and Kobe, would then follow their lead.

However, these large firms produced 70% of Japan's total steel output. The remaining 30% was produced by medium and small-sized firms who sold their output at what was called the sales price. In addition, there was another price called the "market price" that was formed through informal channels or the black market. Therefore, there were three types of prices: the designated price of the six largest, the sales price of the medium and small-sized firms, and the market price of the black market. Although the steel distributed at the market price was a small percentage of the total steel distributed, the market price was so sensitive to the tone of the market that it often influenced designated price quotations. In June 1951 when the economic boom brought about by the Korean War seemed over, the market price began to decline, and the sales price and the designated price followed. As a result, in September 1952, the designated price system was abandoned since it did not work.

In 1955, when the market conditions recovered from the recession, Yawata tried to restore the designated-price system in order to stabilize steel prices again. But the economic recovery had expanded into the Jimmu Boom, and the market price and the sales prices soared to twice the designated price. The designated system thus lost its meaning as a price stabilizer because Yawata was forced to raise the designated price following the market and sale prices. In response, MITI drew up the Steel Supply and Demand Stabilization Law in October 1956, which allowed the formation of a price cartel that penalized non-participants. However, the industry, recalling its bitter experiences during the wartime controlled economy, opposed the law, and MITI was forced to abandon its effort.[59]

In 1957 when the boom was over, the market price fell beneath the designated price and the sales price also began to decline. Consequently, among the six largest, Kawasaki abandoned the designated price as did Fuji. Fuji's withdrawal from the designated-price system effectively destroyed the basic principle of the system, and it was terminated for the third time in November of the same year. The main reason for the abandonment of the system was that under the newly emerged oligopolistic market structure with the integrated firms initiated by Kawasaki, Yawata, which controlled only 20% of total steel output, could no longer play the role of the price leader that Japan Steel had. In addition, compared to Yawata, which enjoyed a monopolistic product mix of higher-end products, and NKK, Sumitomo, and Kobe, which developed specialized product mixes of tubes, pipes, and machinery, Fuji and Kawasaki produced a mix of lower-end products such as plate and structurals and were in direct competition with medium and small-sized companies. They were thus more vulnerable to the fluctuations of the market price.

In 1957, when expanded capacity sent steel prices falling, they dropped far lower than the average commodity price. For MITI, overseeing the economic growth of Japan as a whole, the instability of iron and steel prices seemed extreme. The fierce competition gave MITI room for direct intervention. After the meeting with 33 steel firms and 191 wholesalers, MITI introduced the open-sales system (*kōkai hanbaisei*) to control the price and quantity of iron and steel via administrative guidance (*gyōsei shidō*). Under the open-sales system, firms had to inform MITI of the quantity and price of the plate steel, medium and small-size bars, medium structurals, and wire rod they produced each month. They were required to sell these products at the stated quantity and price at once. In order to avoid violating the Antimonopoly Law, MITI and the industry said participating firms were only declaring the price and quantity of their output voluntarily. In actuality, however, the open-sales system was nothing more than a cartel coordinated by MITI, the industry, and the distributors. Inayama, who had created the joint-sales cartel and Japan Iron and Steel Materials Sales Union during the war, recalled that the open-sales system was basically the same as the joint-sales organization during the war.[60]

In June of 1958, the open-sales system began operating as a kind of recession cartel to stabilize prices and overproduction. In autumn of the same year, however, the economy again recovered from recession and entered another boom even longer and more prosperous than the Jimmu Boom. The mass media called it the Iwato Boom, implying that it was the greatest prosperity Japan had experienced since the even earlier period when the legendary Sun Goddess Amaterasu was enticed to come out of seclusion from a cave (*iwato*). What a sense of humor. The market price recovered and soared beyond the open-sales price. MITI, therefore, had to ease its restrictions on production and permitted a small price increase. As the market price was soaring higher and higher along with the boom, the industry requested further price increases of MITI, but the Fair Trade Committee (FTC) opposed this cartel agitation for an increase. Disputing the FTC's contentions of unfair trade, MITI defended the open-sales system and even took it one step further, announcing that henceforth MITI would recommend (but not order) production increases and price reductions during economic upturns. The open-sales system as a recession cartel, then, changed to a boom cartel (*kōkyō* cartel).

In the late 1950s and early 1960s, MITI began to intervene directly in the industry's activity, thus establishing its notorious reputation for heavy-handed intervention. Because of such activities, it has been said that the industry could invest and expand its facilities without worrying about oversupply.[61]However, as we have seen, MITI's intervention was not the cause of aggressive investment but rather the result of it. In 1959, for example, MITI forecast that the demand for crude steel in 1970 would be 38 million tons (a 150% increase) and asked the industry to prepare expansion plans. The aggregate amount of the entire industry's proposed plan would reach 39 million tons as early as 1965. Because MITI had been accused of causing the steel shortage and soaring prices of the Jimmu Boom, it did not want to take any responsibility for coordinating new capacity investment plans and asked the industry to do so itself. This coordination by the industry itself was known as *jishu-chōsei* (voluntary self-regulation). In voluntary self-regulation, each firm brought its capacity expansion plan and coordinated with the others in terms of timing, turns, and size. This kind of negotiation of firms was impossible in the United States where the Antitrust Law prohibited any kind of negotiation on price and investment.[62] However, it must be noted that voluntary self-regulation was not a device invented by MITI at a moment's notice, but rather was the result of lessons learned from the wartime controlled economy. During the war, the Control Association allocated production quotas and production capacity to the private firms in the form of self-regulation.[63]

Again, Inayama Yoshihiro, managing director of Yawata at that time, took the initiative in coordinating expansion plans, because of his great experience at the Control Association during the war. He proposed a plan based on the market shares of the six largest during the previous ten years. The Japan Iron and Steel Federation provided the last ten years' production data for the firms. However, the proposed plan was unfair to latecomers such as Kawasaki, Sumitomo, and Kobe, since they had just begun integrated production during the previous few years. Not suprisingly, then, they opposed Inayama's plan. Although the industry did not reach a consensus, it was finally able to coordinate plans by 1962, thanks to Inayama's coordinating skills. From then on, Inayama's nickname was "Mr. Cartel." Under the terms of the agreement, construction of three blast furnaces at Fuji, Yawata, and Kobe and two hot strip mills at Sumitomo and Fuji were permitted, but three blast furnaces at Kawasaki, NKK, and Nisshin were postponed. However, the industry's plans were still much more aggressive than what MITI had in mind: construction of just two new blast furnaces and one hot strip mill. Thus, the aggressiveness of the Japanese firms for new capacity investments was promoted by MITI's coordinating power. Such aggressiveness merely needed a little guidance from MITI.

Furthermore, according to Imai Ken'ichi, a leading specialist on industrial organization, *jishu chōsei*, voluntary self-regulation of capacity investment, itself created the aggressiveness of the industry.[64] Since each of the six largest was able to get information about the capacity expansion of the others, the uncertainty behind investment decisions was reduced and homogeneous decision-making on investment was possible.

Oversupply was the industry's most persistent problem, and Japan's prices for bar steel were the most unstable in the world.[65] This aggressive production finally destroyed even the open-sales system promoted by MITI. By the second half of 1962, as the plants built under the Second Rationalization Program began operation, oversupply became obvious and market prices declined 40% from those of the previous year. Through the open-sales system, MITI and the industry tried to reduce production and maintain the price, but all their efforts were in vain.

In December of 1962 when the six largest announced their individual minimum prices, the open-sales system was effectively over. The main reason for the collapse of the open-sales system was Nishiyama's model for competition. As we have explained, starting with the Second Rationalization Program, the six largest invested in extremely large and modern works financed by borrowings and company bonds to compete for market share. Such investments increased the MES of each plant and made it very difficult for anyone to lower its utilization ratio. In contrast to the destruction of the designated-price system that began at the lower end of the product market, this time price declines emanated from the higher end of the market—for example, cold sheet and strip-mill products, output from the new plants that the six had invested in since 1955.[66] The competitive structure formed by Nishiyama's model itself, therefore, was the deep-rooted cause of the collapse of the open-sales system. In order to stabilize the extreme price fluctuation and fierce competition, it was necessary to change the competitive structure of the industry. Neither intervention by the government nor negotiations among the firms could stop the built-in competition of Nishiyama's model.

VI. The 1970 Structural Change: The Sumitomo Rebellion and the Establishment of Nippon Steel

In December 1963, the open-sales system was abandoned, and the iron and steel market plunged into chaos. The presidents of the integrated firms tried to arrange a stronger production reduction agreement and stop the cut-throat competition. MITI also permitted the formation of a recession cartel in the fields of thick plates, axle steel, and stainless steel.

In 1965, however, a serious conflict broke out between Sumitomo Metal Industries and MITI. Sumitomo disagreed with the plans to reduce production and capacity expansion. As part of its voluntary self-regulation, the industry decided that the integrated firms would reduce production by 10% and the non-integrated firms 5%. It also agreed to postpone all capacity expansion in rolling facilities for two years. Sumitomo, led by President Hyūga Hōsai disagreed with the plan. He gave three main reasons for his dissent: (1) The plan did not include the outputs of the latest production term, (2) the plan did not treat exports as exceptions, and (3) the rule setting each company's utilization ratio was unclear and unfair.[67]

Sumitomo had been very aggressive in expanding its capacity since 1955 and by the 1960s it produced the same amount of crude steel as NKK and Kawasaki. For Sumitomo, a latecomer, it would be advantageous if the output calculated for production reduction included the most recent term, because its output had increased the most in the most recent term. Also, Sumitomo argued that the plan should not include exports as the objects of the reduction, since exports did not result in the oversupply of the domestic market. As Sumitomo exported 40% of its production at that time, it would have been fatal for the company if the plan did not permit a special quota for exports. Sumitomo also opposed the plan because it lacked concrete rules. The company said Yawata and Fuji were selfish and unfair since the plan allocated exceptional quotas and additional terms for the two giants of the industry without reason. Hyūga said:[68]

There is no specific rule for the production reduction and utilization ratios, but always an ad hoc way in which the first movers try to control the latecomers. . . .

The major reason why the incident (the so-called Sumitomo Rebellion) was getting worse was Yawata and Fuji's egoistic allocation of the quotas.

Since other firms including NKK, Kawasaki, and Kobe criticized Sumitomo as egoistic, Hyūga's complaints should not be taken at face value. But it became obvious that the "Sumitomo Rebellion" was the end result of voluntary self-regulation. As Figure 2 indicates, in the oligopolistic competition initiated by Kawasaki, Yawata and Fuji were defenders of their market shares on one hand and were also regarded, Yawata in particular, as price leaders on the other. Sumitomo, which became aggressive under the leadership of Hyūga and pursued Kawasaki's model more so than Kawasaki in the 1960s, protested against the hierarchical structure of the industry and the unclear decisionmaking process in voluntary self-regulation.

Finding it very difficult to persuade Sumitomo, the industry asked MITI to intermediate. MITI, led at that time by the strong leadership

of Vice Minister Sabashi Shigeru, one of the strongest proponents of
controlling industrial order, tried to persuade Sumitomo, but
Sumitomo ignored MITI and increased production beyond its quota.
Sabashi was so angry that he tried to punish Sumitomo by diminishing
its quota of imported coal. However, the mass media criticized MITI
saying that it had no right to intervene in the free competition of private firms. MITI's actions, journalists claimed, were a throwback to the
prewar state-controlled economy. MITI was at that time facing the liberalization of foreign investment, and felt it necessary to re-organize
Japan's industries and to increase their international competitiveness. [69] This had led Sabashi to intervene in the "Rebellion" all the
more aggressively. However, it was the economic downturn getting
worse that finally convinced Sumitomo that its lone wolf behavior
would not bring any results, and it acquiesced in its production quota
in December 1965.

The importance of the "Sumitomo Rebellion" was that it revealed
the limits of voluntary self-regulation and MITI's intervention.
Oversupply and fierce competition resulting from Nishiyama's model
led to structural problems of the industry, and it became clear that
there was no effective measure to stop the price decline without alter-
ing the industry's structure.

In 1966, right after the Sumitomo Rebellion, Nagano Shigeo, president of of Fuji Steel, declared there was need for a new iron and steel
business law similar to the prewar Iron and Steel Business Law. His sug-
gestion, which seemed to resemble the prewar law authorizing state
control, was that the industry be concentrated into two major corporations. Even at that time, he was already thinking of a merger of the two
halves of the prewar Japan Steel, Yawata, and Fuji. He later recalled:[70]

In 1966, although I proposed the idea of creating two major corporations in the east and west of Japan, I had the merger with
Yawata in my mind. Instead of the merger of Fuji and Yawata, I
said "the two major corporations." Because voluntary self-regulation of capacity expansion was always in trouble, and the blast furnaces built every single year were destroying the market price, I
thought I had to do something.

Nagano clearly realized the necessity of restructuring the way in which
the industry competed. He believed that it was necessary to create a
large corporation which would have enough market share and power
to be a price leader like the old Japan Steel. Inayama Yoshihiro, presi-

dent of Yawata Steel and formerly Nagano's subordinate in the Japan Steel Corporation and the Control Association during the war, agreed with Nagano and the two of them announced the largest merger ever in Japanese industrial history in April 1968. They named the new company "Shin Nippon Seitetsu" (literally translated as the New Japan Steel Corporation, even though its official name in English is Nippon Steel Corporation). However, as the market shares of iron and crude steel of the new company would be 44.5% and 35.4%, respectively, the FTC formally opposed the merger saying it would violate the Antimonopoly Law. The legal dispute, which even involved the advice of economic theorists, lasted almost two years.

In contrast to the FTC and many academics, the other companies in the industry and MITI supported the merger. The main reason why the other companies including Sumitomo supported the merger was that they were tired of cut-throat competition and wanted the new firm to assume strong price leadership. Akasaka Takeshi, president of NKK, said, "I have been thinking that the best way to control such excessive competition is through the merger of Yawata and Fuji. If they behave well as a leader of the industry in the competition over capacity expansion and sales, we will find a way out of this morass."[71] In fact, the financial situation of the firms had been deteriorating because of the fierce competition and price-cutting. Their sales were growing, but their profits declined.[72] Therefore, the integrated six sought a solution. They did not think, however, that the newly merged company would dominate the industry. Hyūga, for example, commented:[73]

If Yawata and Fuji merge together, their leadership will be strong. In other words, the industry will become more oligopolistic. However, the industry always tries to exploit the oligopoly to its advantage, since it is always a profit-seeking organization, as you know. If we thought the merger would depress competition as well as our firms, we would be opposed. . . .

Because we don't think we will be unable to compete with the merged company and we think, on the contrary, the merger will stabilize the industry, we give an approving "yes" (to the merger).

He was confident that his firm could compete with the merged company. The other companies, NKK and Kawasaki, displayed the same confidence, since they had already invested in new modern works and their greenfield ratios were far better than that of Yawata and Fuji combined. Thus the merger did not threaten the firms which had already built efficient facilities; it merely provided a breath of fresh air from the fierce competition.

The government and MITI also supported the merger, since they faced the liberalization of foreign trade and investment in Japan, and they felt the necessity of fostering world-class companies to compete internationally. Because of its fear of liberalization, MITI had been most aggressive in its intervention tactics during the late 1960s. At the same time, MITI was also trying to concentrate the number of firms into a few groups in other basic industries including automobiles, textiles, and petrochemicals. The merger of Yawata and Fuji was thus a timely development as far as MITI was concerned. In contrast to the FTC, MITI was willing to protect the private firms' interest to achieve its national goal. In this case, MITI's national goal was to increase international competitiveness and the private firms' interest was the merger.

In addition, the merger was facilitated by an international merger movement taking place at the same time.[74] In Britain, the Labor Party government nationalized 14 of the largest private steel firms to form the British Steel Corporation in 1967. In Germany, the three largest groups, Thyssen, Krupp, and Hoesch, were expanded through a merger, and during the severe recession of 1966–67, steelmakers formed four regional cartels to create price stability. In France in 1966, with governmental prodding, the industry agreed to consolidate into two groups, one based in Lorraine and the other in the Nord, to undertake investment and rationalization plans to enhance productivity. Also in Belgium, Cockerill–Ougrée–Providence, the largest firm, with over 60% of the market share, was created through a series of mergers and acquisitions in the 1960s. These merger movements throughout the world no doubt facilitated the merger of Yawata and Fuji in Japan.

Nevertheless, the FTC ordered a legal stoppage of the merger in May 1969, and Yawata and Fuji were forced to revise the plan from scratch. The FTC pointed out four specific products in particular which would violate the Antimonopoly Law: rail, tinplate for cans, casting pig iron, and sheet pile. Finally, Yawata and Fuji were able to get permission for the merger after conceding a certain number of facilities and know-how to other companies. Fuji leased its rail mills to NKK, Yawata sold stocks of Toyo Steel Sheet (Tōyō Kōhan), its subsidiary specializing in tinplate production, to NKK and Toyo Canning, and Yawata conceded one of its blast furnaces specialized in casting pig iron to Kobe Steel. Moreover, Yawata gave its know-how on the sheet pile to NKK and Fuji did the same for Kawasaki.[75] By giving up these facilities, Yawata and

Fuji finally got permission to merge in October 1969, and Nippon Steel, the world's largest private iron and steel firm, was established in March 1970. The Japanese iron and steel industry was now the largest and most well-equipped in the free world, producing the world's most competitive steel.

Had it not been for the 1973 oil crisis, the establishment of Nippon Steel in 1970 would have changed the industrial structure from one characterized by oligopolistic cut-throat competition to one of price leadership. But the oil crisis led to a severe decline in demand for the industry's products, and it raised the costs of production. As a consequence, what occurred was that new measures were taken to reduce costs, and attempts were made to diversify beyond iron and steel. Unexpectedly, the Japanese iron and steel industry was able to adapt well to the new environment throughout the 1970s. In the 1980s, it had diversified into several fields through its accumulated technologies.[76] These developments, however fascinating, are still going on, and are beyond the scope of this paper.

NOTES

The author would like to thank Professor Alfred D. Chandler, Jr., Davie Gross, and N. Danaraj for their helpful comments.

1. Donald F. Barnett and Louis Schorsch, *Steel: Upheaval in a Basic Industry* (Cambridge, Mass., 1983).

2. Ibid., pp.143–45.

3. Hans Mueller and K. Kawahito, *Steel Industry Economics: A Comparative Analysis of Structure, Conduct and Performance* (New York, 1978).

4. Barnett and Schorsch, op. cit., p. 59.

5. As to arguments on the Japanese economic development and the role of the government, see David Friedman, *The Misunderstood Miracle* (Ithaca, N.Y., 1988), and Marie Anchordoguy, *Computers Inc.: Japan's Challenge to IBM* (Cambridge, Mass., 1989), pp. 1–17. Recently, more industry-specific studies such as Friedman's *The Misunderstood Miracle* in the field of the machine-tool industry and Anchordoguy's *Computers, Inc.* in the computer industry began to contribute to multi-cause explanations for Japanese economic development and a more concrete analysis of government-business relations. However, these works still ignored the dynamism of the private firms, and more industry-based studies are needed to draw generalizations from. The Japanese industrial policies differ from industry to industry, and there are tremendous learning effects between them. Before generalizing about the characteristics of Japanese industrial policy and economic development, it is necessary to accumulate more historical and concrete case studies.

6. James van B. Dresser, Jr., Thomas M. Hout, and William V. Rapp, "Competitive Development of the Japanese Steel Industry," in James B. Cohen

238   S. Yonekura

(ed.), *Pacific Partnership: United States–Japan Trade* (Lexington, Mass., 1972), p. 201.

7. Thomas McCraw and Patricia O'Brien, "Production and Distribution," in Thomas McCraw (ed.), *America versus Japan* (Boston, 1986), pp. 93–94.

8. See Thomas R. Howell et al., *Steel and the State: Government Intervention and Steel's Structural Crisis* (Boulder, 1988), pp. 126–40.

9. For world protectionism, see Kent Jones, *Politics vs. Economics in World Steel Trade* (London, 1986); and Howell et al., op. cit.

10. See Alfred D. Chandler, Jr., *Scale and Scope*, (Boston, forthcoming).

11. Nathan Rosenberg, *Inside the Black Box: Technology and Economics* (Cambridge, 1982), p. 249.

12. The World Bank, *The World Bank in Asia: Summary of Activities* (Washington, D.C., 1960), p. 30.

13. Kiyoshi Kawahito, *The Japanese Steel Industry: With an Analysis of the U.S. Steel Import Problem* (New York, 1972), p. 3.

14. Chalmers Johnson, *MITI and the Japanese Miracle: The Growth of Industrial Policy, 1925–1975* (Stanford, 1982), pp. 308–10.

15. Nakamura Takafusa, *Nihon no tōsei keizai* (A Controlled Economy in Japan) (Tokyo, 1974), pp. 163–64.

16. McCraw (ed.), op. cit., p. 93.

17. Nagano Shigeo, *Watakushi no rirekisho* (My memoirs) (Tokyo, 1980), p. 56.

18. A round-table talk among steel executives in Nihon Tekkō Renmei Sengo Tekkōshi Henshū Iinkai (ed.), *Sengo tekkōshi* (A History of the Postwar Iron and Steel Industry) (Tokyo, 1959), Appendix, p. 9.

19. Nihon Seitetsu Kabushiki Kaishashi Henshū Iinkai (ed.), *Nihon Seitetsu Kabushiki-Kaishashi* (A History of the Japan Steel Corporation) (Tokyo, 1959), pp. 334, 361.

20. Financial History Section, Ministry of Finance (ed.), *The Financial History of Japan*, vol. 20: *The Allied Occupation Period, 1945–1952* (Tokyo, 1982), p. 435.

21. Ibid., pp. 443–49. Reparations from Japan—Immediate Program (Pauley Interim Report) on December 18, 1945.

22. Nihon Tekkō Renmei Sengo Tekkōshi Henshū Iinkai, op. cit., pp. 25–27.

23. Nihon Seitetsu Kabushiki Kaishashi Henshū Iinkai (ed.), op. cit., p. 184.

24. Financial History Section, Ministry of Finance (ed.), op. cit., p. 497.

25. During the war, the Iron and Steel Control Association had tried to reorganize and concentrate iron and steel production into several large works, because of the deteriorated resource situation. See Okazaki Tetsuji, "Dainiji Sekaitaisenki no Nihon ni okeru Senji Keikaku Keizai no Kōzō to Unkō," *Shakai Kagaku Kenkyū* 41:4 (1988).

26. Ibid., p. 472. The interim directive did not materialize but added to the industry's insecurities.

27. What the Japanese government learned from the war was how *not* to control the private industry. See Seiichiro Yonekura, "The Japanese Iron and Steel Industry: Continuity and Discontinuity, 1850–1970 (Ph. D. diss., Harvard University, 1990)," Chapter 6.

28. In the late 19th century, the United States, Germany, Belgium, and France used similar measures to foster their iron and steel industries (see Jones, op. cit.). Also, we have good examples in the Indian and Malaysian iron and steel industries of governments failing to protect their industries with these conventional measures. (See K. Moorthy, *Engineering Change, Indian's Iron and Steel*, Bombay, 1984.)

29. Miwa Ryōichi, "Sengo Minshuka to Keizai Saiken (Democratization and Economic Recovery in the Postwar Period)," in Nakamura Takafusa (ed.), *Nihon Keizaishi: Keikakuka to Minshuka* (Tokyo, 1988).

30. Nihon Tekkō Renmei Sengo Tekkōshi Henshū Iinkai (ed.), op. cit., p. 59.

31. Seiichiro Yonekura, "The Entrepreneurship and Innovative Behavior of Kawasaki Steel in the Postwar Period," Discussion Paper #121, Institute of Business Research, Hitotsubashi University, 1984.

32. However, there were a few people in MITI and the industry who supported Nishiyama's decision from the viewpoint of international competitiveness and technological development. Tabata Shintarō, MITI's Steel Section chief, strongly supported Nishiyama's plan and Yamaoka Takeshi, chief engineer of Yawata Steel, was known as a technical advisor to Nishiyama. But they were not the majority.

33. Hoshino Yoshirō, "Sengo Gijutsushi no Jidai Kubun (A Technological History of Postwar Japan)," in Nakayama Shigeru (ed.), *Nihon no gijutsuryoku* (The Technological Potential of Japan) (Tokyo, 1986), p. 87.

34. See Miyazaki Yoshikazu, *Sengo Nihon no Keizai Kikō* (The Economic Institutions of Postwar Japan)(Tokyo, 1966), pp. 33–71; and Takafusa Nakamura, *The Postwar Japanese Economy* (Tokyo, 1981), p. 145.

35. As to the argument on the technological continuity from Manchuria to Chiba, see Yonekura, op. cit. (1990).

36. Nihon Tekkō Renmei Sengo Tekkōshi Henshū Iinkai (ed.), op. cit., pp. 43–45.

37. Ibid., pp. 174–77.

38. There were seven detailed measures to facilitate this rationalization. Ministry of International Trade and Industry (ed.), *Shōkō Seisakushi*, vol. 17, *Tekkōgyo* (History of Commercial and Industrial Policies, vol. 17, Steel Industry) (Tokyo, 1970), pp. 504–5.

39. Tsuruta Masatoshi, *Sengo Nihon no Sangyō Seisaku* (The Industrial Policy of Postwar Japan) (Tokyo, 1982), p. 53.

40. It was well known that the U.S. and German governments promoted rapid depreciation in the iron and steel industry after the war. The Indian government and the World Bank provided low-cost loans to the Indian iron and steel industry, but the industry did not grow as much as they expected. The developing countries have all tried the same government aids as Japan. See Miyazaki, op. cit., pp. 39–43; Moorthy, op. cit.; and Howell et al., op. cit.

41. In fact, the export of crude steel tripled to 366,500 and that of steel materials increased 44% to 1.32 million tons in 1955.

42. Iida Ken'ichi, Ōhashi Shūji, and Kuroiwa Toshirō (eds.), *Gendai Nihon Sangyō Hattatsushi*, vol. 9, *Tekkōgyo*, (History of Industrial Development in Japan, vol. 9, Steel Industry) pp. 447, 451. Kawasaki Seitetsu Shashi Henshū

Iinkai (ed.), *Kawasaki Seitetsu 25 Nenshi* (A 25-year History of Kawasaki Steel) (Tokyo, 1975), pp. 107–9, describes how Chiba Works increased productivity and efficiency of iron and steelmaking.

43. Nippon Tekkō Renmei Sengo Tekkōshi Henshū Iinkai (ed.), op. cit., pp. 204–5.

44. As to the historical imbalance between iron and steel producers, see Yonekura, op. cit.(1990).

45. Kawasaki Tsutomu, *Sengo Tekkōgyō Ron* (The Postwar Iron and Steel Industry) (Tokyo, 1968), p. 334. There was a scheme known as "Planned Shipbuilding" *(keikaku zōsen)* by which a government shipping corporation *(senpaku kōdan)* ordered and bought ships and then leased them to shipping companies. As the shipping companies generated profits, they paid for the leases and the corporation used these funds to order more ships. See Ezra Vogel, *Comeback* (New York, 1985), pp. 35–57.

46. Leonard Lynn, *How Japan Innovates: A Comparison with the U.S. in the Case of Oxygen Steelmaking* (Boulder, 1982).

47. Iida et al. (eds.), op. cit., pp. 452–53.

48. McCraw and O'Brian, op. cit., pp. 97–98.

49. Lynn, op. cit., pp. 67–89.

50. The theory of technological imbalance is from Nathan Rosenberg, *Perspectives on Technology* (Cambridge, 1976). The innovativeness of the continuous casting and process of adopting it from Seiichiro Yonekura, "Recognizing Potential in Innovations: Armco vs. Kawasaki," Discussion Paper #131, Institute of Business Research, Hitotsubashi University, 1988.

51. See Yonekura Seiichiro, "Seijuku Sangyō ni Okeru Datsu-Seijukuka no Rironteki Wakugumi (A Framework for a Dematurization of the Matured Industries)," *Hitotsubashi Business Review* 34: 2 (1987); and Seiichiro Yonekura, "The Winter Age of the Japanese Steel Industry," Harvard Business School Case no. 0-685-050, 1985.

52. When considering the industry's postwar development, the role of the blue-collar worker should not be neglected. The absence of a discussion of labor's role in the industry's development is due to the exigencies of time and space, not to a lack of appreciation of its importance. For further information, see Ikujiro Nonaka and Seiichiro Yonekura, "Innovation through Group Dynamics: Organizational Learning in JK Activities at Nippon Steel's Kimitsu Works," Discussion Paper #124, Institute of Business Research, Hitotsubashi University, 1985.

53. Iida et al. (eds.), op. cit., p. 478.

54. See Nakamura, op. cit. (1981), pp. 111–50.

55. Iida et al. (eds), op. cit., p. 441.

56. Ibid., p. 479.

57. Chandler, op. cit., pp. 23–24. Chandler emphasizes managerial coordination in achieving MES. I agree with his emphasis, but in the Japanese iron and steel industry, in order to understand the fierce competition for market share, we must also consider MES in the context of the relationship of minimum optimal scale to market share. See Chandler's note on MES in ibid., p. 734.

58. Iida et al. (eds.), op. cit., p. 483.

59. Ibid., p. 476.

60. Inayama Yoshihiro, *Watashi no Tekkō Shōwa-shi* (My History of the Steel Industry in the Shōwa Period) (Tokyo, 1986), pp. 32–43, and 122.

61. For example, see McCraw and O'Brien, op. cit., p. 95.

62. See McCraw and O'Brien, op. cit.

63. For the controlled economy and the Control Association during World War II, see Yonekura, "The Japanese Iron and Steel Industry," Chapter 6.

64. Imai Ken'ichi, *Gendai Sangyō Soshiki* (Modern Industrial Organization) (Tokyo, 1976).

65. Japanese steel prices fluctuated more widely than anywhere in the world. See Kawasaki, op. cit., pp. 168–69.

66. To understand how fierce the competition in the higher end was, see Iida et al. (eds.), op cit., pp. 567–68.

67. Tanaka Yōnosuke, *Hyūga Hōsai Ron* (An Essay on Hyūga Hōsai) (Tokyo, 1975), p. 125.

68. Ibid., pp. 148–49.

69. See Johnson, op. cit., pp. 275–304.

70. Mainichi Shinbun Keizaibu (ed.), *Shin-nittetsu Tanjōsu* (The Birth of Nippon Steel) (Tokyo, 1970), p. 29.

71. Ibid., p. 43.

72. Iida et al. (eds.), op. cit., pp. 585–86.

73. Tanaka, op. cit., p. 176.

74. For the merger movement in the world, see Howell et al., op. cit., pp. 55–189.

75. Mainichi Shinbun Keizaibu (ed.), op. cit., pp. 167–87.

76. See Yonekura, op. cit.(1987), (1985).

Comment

Bunji Nagura

Professor Yonekura's paper tells us much about how and why the Japanese iron and steel industry grew so dynamically in the postwar period. In particular, Yonekura stresses "the dynamic interaction in which investment begets investment and market growth." Various and significant technological innovations, such as the BOF, the CC, the construction of large-scale blast furnaces, etc., were adopted one after another. As a result, the productivity of the Japanese iron and steel industry rose steadily and reached the highest level in the world. According to his explanation, the rapid development of the Japanese industry was carried out by a competitive paradigm that he calls "Kawasaki's competitive paradigm." That is, the integrated iron and steel producers competed fiercely in an oligopolistic situation for the market share by constructing state-of-the-art works with borrowed money. He regards this development of the postwar Japanese iron and steel industry as "the dynamism between continuity and discontinuity during the prewar and postwar periods."

Personally I have a great concern in making a comparison between the prewar and the postwar periods with reference to the pattern of development of the Japanese iron and steel industry. In fact, I have done some studies regarding this subject in the prewar period.

I agree with Yonekura in almost all his views. However, I would like to expand on the following three points. Firstly, the causal relation between the split-up of the Japan Steel Corporation and Kawasaki's competitive paradigm. Second, the meaning of "the dynamism of continuity and discontinuity." Third, "the question of Japan Inc." in relation to the development of the postwar Japanese iron and steel industry.

Regarding the first point, Yonekura emphasizes the importance of Kawasaki's competitive paradigm in the rapid growth of the postwar Japanese iron and steel industry. I have no objection to this. However, if we recall the fact that the so-called Kawasaki's competitive paradigm was brought about because of the split-up of Japan Steel Corporation, would not the latter be considered more significant?

As is well known, the zaibatsu dissolution and the Deconcentration of Excessive Economic Power Law made the market very competitive, and consequently, top management became innovative in general. This was true especially in the case of the iron and steel industry. Moreover, two companies, Yawata and Fuji, which were created by the split-up of the Japan Steel Corporation, also became tough negotiators in purchasing pig iron. Accordingly, it was as a means of self-defense that Nishiyama entered into pig-iron production, as Yonekura pointed out. Therefore, we can regard the split-up of Japan Steel Corporation as the direct cause of Kawasaki's competitive paradigm.

Second, the abovementioned point is also concerned with the question of "the dynamism of continuity and discontinuity." The split-up of the Japan Steel Corporation made the structure of the market, the top management, and the conditions of the supply of raw materials utterly different from those in the prewar period. As a result, Kawasaki's competitive paradigm was brought about. We think it is very important that the integrated iron and steel producers grew rapidly in the oligopolistic market through competitive and innovative investments. This competitive and oligopolistic structure is extremely different from that of the prewar period. This is the reason why we can realize that "discontinuity" is more significant than "continuity," while Yonekura includes both meanings within the term of Kawasaki's competitive paradigm.

He points to technological skills, management administration, industrial policies, and so on, as examples of "continuity." On the other hand, he says, "the end of the war and the more democratic economic environment encouraged by SCAP provided the opportunity for him [Nishiyama] to enhance his technological skills and to initiate his entrepreneurial ideas." Namely, Nishiyama's technological skills and his management administration came into full blossom after the war and through the drastic reform made by SCAP. Accordingly, we prefer "discontinuity" to "continuity" as one of the key concepts when we try to explain the rapid development of the postwar Japanese iron and steel industry.

Last, attention should be called to the fact that the Japanese iron and steel industry has not had the characteristics of a public-sector enterprise and has had little direct connection with the government after the split-up of the Japan Steel Corporation and the abolition of subsidies by the Dodge Line, while many other advanced countries have remarkably increased government intervention in the iron and steel industry in the same period. Accordingly, I agree with Yonekura's view that the Japan Inc. theory cannot be applied, least of all in the case of the postwar Japanese iron and steel industry, although we also recognize that the abovementioned phenomenon shows "discontinuity."

We cannot deny, however, that government policies promoted the development of the postwar Japanese iron and steel industry. Examples of government policies are the establishment of the Japan Development Bank and the pump-priming effect of its loans, tax measures including the permission for rapid depreciation, and so on. These helped the capital accumulation of iron and steel firms in the period of the First Rationalization Program, though they did not actually intend to gain international competitiveness, as Yonekura mentioned. Until the 1950s, government policies, including those of MITI, generally paved the way for the development of iron and steel firms.

In any case, the government-business relationship in the iron and steel industry was a dramatic case of "attraction and repulsion." Consequently, we should understand this relationship as it was.

The American Steel Industry in the Postwar Era: Dominance and Decline

Paul A. Tiffany

The post–World War II era has not been particularly favorable to the many firms participating in the American steel industry. This is especially true for the larger integrated carbon steel companies that have long dominated production in America. Emerging from the war with their plants relatively unscathed, these companies and their leaders were universally perceived as key shapers of the "American Century" unfolding before them. Much of the remainder of the industrial world was in ruin; steelmaking assets in both Europe and Japan were destroyed, thus positioning the domestic American firms for global dominance. A popular refrain of the immediate postwar years declared "as steel goes, so goes the nation"—and both American steelmakers and the American nation seemed headed for an unparalleled reign of world leadership.

The decade of the 1980s, however, has been witness to events far less fortunate for the large integrated steelmakers of America. Indeed, steel has in many respects mirrored the plight of the entire American economy in recent times; according to some observers, steel has even led the way into national decline. Both production capacity and output for carbon steel have fallen dramatically during the 1980s (see Figure 1); large portions of the industry's work force have been consigned to permanent retirement; and a litany of financial woes has put some firms into bankruptcy and turned others toward a search for new strategies that more often than not resulted in greatly reduced operations when compared to the more prosperous past. Most symbolic of this turnabout, perhaps, was the restructuring of the United States Steel Corporation—the leading firm in the world in much of the postwar era—into the USX Corporation, a firm that today is essentially an energy company that derives less than 30% of its revenues from steelmaking operations.[1]

While it is still too early to declare with confidence that American

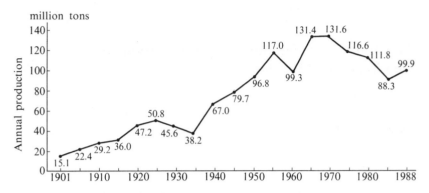

FIG. 1 Crude Steel Production in the United States 1901–88.
Source: American Iron and Steel Institute, *Annual Statistical Report*.

steel is in permanent decline (as some of the restructured and re-invigorated firms have demonstrated admirable resiliency over the past several years), one nevertheless must seriously question whether integrated carbon steelmakers from the United States will ever again be regarded with the respect that often characterized their past competitive position. In this paper, I shall briefly recount the history of how American steelmakers built their industry into such dominance, and then turn to the underlying problems that brought an end to that position. Necessarily, this will encompass a review of the managerial behavior of the steelmakers themselves—their attitudes toward technology, costs, and competition, among other variables. But more importantly, this examination will also require an analysis of steel industry relations with other important interest groups in America, including both government officials and organized labor leaders whose actions affected the industry.

I. Growth Patterns of American Steel in the 20th Century

To understand how the industry was transformed from its position of dominance into one of decline, it is first necessary to recount several factors critical to the development of American steel in the 20th century. Drawing from the data presented in Fig. 1, it is possible to discern several "stages" that characterized this development. In many respects, the pattern that emerges is similar to the well-known "product life cycle" model: (1) an introductory stage in which growth is relatively slow while the product/industry establishes itself with users; (2) a growth stage during which demand grows dramatically and industry leaders emerge; (3) a maturity stage in which the growth rate of demand diminishes as saturation and substitution effects set in; and finally (4) a decline stage during which overall demand actually declines due to a variety of factors. In the 20th century, American steel clearly witnessed both dramatic growth as well as the more recent slow-down. The "introductory" stage was essentially a 19th century phe-nomenon (which will not be addressed in this paper). Whether or not a permanent decline stage can be observed from the activities of the decade of the 1980s is only conjectural at this point, though one must admit that such an outcome is possible.

An important caveat must be asserted before proceeding: we are observing from the vantage point of history. One may impose patterns of growth, maturity, etc., based on after-the-fact knowledge of what actually happened. Yet "real time" managers who had to survey their situations, draw conclusions, and implement responses did not have such a luxury; rather, they had to extrapolate from the past and project into the future as best they could, while surrounded by all of the pres-sures that one associates with management of large firms. Thus when the presumably neutral observer finds "errors" and managerial ineffi-ciencies being committed, and then condemns the individuals (or firm or industry) involved for such behavior, it is especially important that the observer not render ahistorical judgment. Rather, the task of the historian is to comprehend just what led people to take the particular actions they took at the times they were taken. Can we truthfully say that American steelmakers were negligent, irresponsible, perhaps even foolish for not fully anticipating the "inevitable" decline of their indus-try and thus taking preventive actions to reverse such an outcome? Only the most simplistic review would render such conclusions.

1. Growth: 1901–40

In the year 1901, when the great consolidation that led to the creation of the United States Steel Corporation transpired, only slightly more than 15 million tons of crude steel were produced in America.[2] By 1940 the volume had grown to 67 million tons. This latter amount, rep-resenting a recovery from Depression-era declines, allowed the United States again to lead the world in output (as domestic production accounted for 42.9% of global totals in 1940).[3]

Yet even in 1900 the relative position of America as a world steel pro-ducer was strong; the nation turned out 36.8% of global output at that earlier date. With many other nations increasing their volume of pro-duction in the first four decades of the century, the U.S. industry was nevertheless able to maintain the lead that earlier entrepreneurs such as Andrew Carnegie had provided. This was possible due to several factors: for one, the huge internal market of America was rapidly expanding, and with it, steel demand was consistently strong. But growth was also a function of market competitiveness in this period.

In a recent study, the business historians Louis Galambos and Joseph Pratt identified three critical variables that large firms had to balance if they were to achieve sustainable growth and market success: risk control (or stabilization of markets and the surrounding institutional environment); continuous product and process innovation; and manufacturing efficiency.[4] In examining the ability of the American integrated carbon steel producers to meet these criteria, one must differentiate between the several major firms in the market. U.S. Steel was without question the key firm during this growth stage in America (as it has been throughout most of the history of American steel in the 20th century). It began its corporate life with nearly 66% of domestic ingot production, and its share remained at 33% just prior to the start of World War II (when its capacity was two and one-half times more than its nearest rival).[5] Yet while "Big Steel," as the firm was popularly referred to in the press, did indeed remain large, the other players in the industry were far from domesticated during these years. In fact, it was a time of growth and consolidation for a number of other firms that developed large-scale integrated operations of their own, with the result that the near monopolistic conditions that prevailed following 1901 were transformed into oligopoly by the 1930s and beyond. Stabilization, innovation, and efficiency thus took on different levels of significance for each organization.

Clearly it was risk control that motivated the actions of U.S. Steel and its conservative chairman Judge Elbert H. Gary, who presided over the firm from its founding until his death in 1927. Gary perceived that the political activism of the Progressive Era (generally 1900 through 1920) would not be conducive to a corporation as large as his, thus he was willing to compromise market share in order to preserve commercial peace and mollify the suspicious "trust-busting" Justice Department of the federal government. While his regime was decidedly different from the competitive warfare that Carnegie had fostered only a few years earlier, he perhaps had no choice.[6] U.S. Steel was simply too big for government to ignore, and its every move was scrutinized both by Congress and an increasingly aggressive press. Gary's strategy was thus one founded on political more than economic grounds. Through a series of actions that ultimately resulted in the establishment of the

American Iron and Steel Institute, the major industry trade association, he sought to convince his colleagues that ". . . destructive competition is not reasonable, not desirable, and never beneficial in the long
run to anyone."[7] Rather, Gary counseled, cooperation should be the
theme of the industry.

The result was a company that sought success not in market competition, but rather by other means. By virtue of its huge size and vertically
integrated structure, U.S. Steel controlled the chief known deposits of
iron ore and coking coal found in the nation. It willingly sold these
inputs to rival firms, thus allowing them the opportunity to expand.
Moreover, its vast sales allowed Big Steel to dominate price setting in
the industry. The firm's basic strategy was to earn money at the raw
material end of the business (upstream operations), and control competition downstream through its price umbrella—held conveniently
high so that other firms could earn profits even though they did not
have the benefits of scale comparable to U.S. Steel.[8]

U.S. Steel itself, however, did not vigorously pursue innovation or
efficiency under Gary; metallurgical research was given a weak charter,
and individual subsidiary managers were left to operate their fiefdoms
independently, with little coordination or direction from the top.[9]
Other matters—principally political and market stability—were
deemed more pressing. Thus the shift of the industry from its "introductory" stage to one of "growth" was essentially an artificial transition
engineered by the financially oriented Gary, who was more interested
in achieving a stable stream of profits to satisfy his shareholders and
obtaining peace with government, rather than pursuing cost reduction
through innovation and efficiency. Such a strategy would ultimately do
great damage to U.S. Steel, and perhaps by extension the entire
American steel industry.

Other industry entrants, however, were able to thrive under U.S.
Steel's passive attitude toward cost-efficient competition during the
1900–40 interval. The most dramatic growth was registered by
Bethlehem Steel. Only a tiny firm when Charles Schwab took it over in
1904 (he had recently been dismissed as president of U.S. Steel for his
less-than-prudent personal lifestyle), it grew into the second largest
competitor by the 1920s. Not only did Schwab introduce the
entrepreneurial flair that he had learned at Carnegie's side during the
1890s, but he also oversaw a series of mergers and acquisitions during
the 1920s that rapidly expanded both his firm's product line and markets; five companies that had ranked among the top fourteen steelmakers in 1904 were owned by Bethlehem by 1923.[10]

Republic Steel, Jones & Laughlin, and Youngstown Sheet & Tube also gained some ground on U.S. Steel in these years, with Youngstown showing the highest relative profitability of any major firm in the industry over the full span of 1901–30. All three firms grew during these years; Republic, for example, had only 4% of the capacity owned by U.S. Steel in 1904, but by 1940 its capacity had grown to 28% of the industry leader.[11] The most technologically innovative competitor was Armco Steel. Focusing on a strong commitment to research and development, Armco made impressive strides in a number of technical areas such as the development of corrosion-resistant steel and a continuous hot strip rolling mill process.[12] Both Inland Steel and National Steel (the latter formed by merger in 1929) strove for operational efficiency and found it. These were the only two major integrated steelmakers to escape from losses during every year of the disastrous 1930s. Inland achieved this by concentrating its operations in a single large plant in the Chicago area, while National—under the leadership of the cost-conscious Ernest T. Weir—concentrated on lighter steel products aimed at consumer markets that held up better during the Depression years than did demand for the heavy shapes for capital goods markets that were favored by U.S. Steel and Bethlehem at that time.[13]

Thus all of the Galambos and Pratt variables were evident in the major steel firms of the growth era, but no single one seemed to pursue the three simultaneously. In general, this was a period of both market expansion and consolidation by the stronger entrants. The intervention of World War I and its huge demand for steel products ignited a large jump in output, while the destruction of European steelmaking assets during the war left the American firms in a potentially commanding global position. But the hopes of some American steel leaders to convert this temporary advantage into true world domination through direct foreign investment faded when the financial interests behind many of the domestic steelmakers (that is, investment banking firms such as J.P. Morgan & Company) chose instead to rebuild the European rivals rather than take away their markets.[14] As a result, global steel capacity began to expand and pressure was increased on domestic prices, leading to what the industry press termed "profitless prosperity" during the 1920s.

When the Wall Street crash of late 1929 turned into a massive Depression, most of the American producers were unable to avoid financial problems. U.S. Steel, realizing its loose and generally uncoordinated structure was too burdensome in this period, finally began to restructure its manufacturing facilities in 1935. But after more than

30 years of operations, this giant firm could not reorder its "corporate culture" so easily or quickly. It would take another crisis before Big Steel moved significantly in the direction of cost reductions and improved efficiency. The impending world war may have refilled the order books of the large firms, but the problems of the past would linger on for many years to come in this troubled industry.

2. The Postwar Era, 1945–60

The aftermath of the Second World War provides a seemingly inconsistent pattern. With the destruction of steelmaking capacity in both Europe and Japan, American producers emerged with more than half of the world steel trade in their control by 1947. Meanwhile, the dawn of the postwar era brought with it a huge demand for steel to make up for the postponed consumption of the 1930s and 1940s. Crude production jumped from 66.9 million tons in 1940 to 96.8 million by 1950, and then reached an all-time high of 117 million tons in 1955. During ten of these years capacity utilization was greater than 90% for the major integrated firms as a group, and in only two of the years was it less than 81%. Profits appeared to be handsome to most outside observers, and few would predict anything less than a continuation of the trends of growth and prosperity that appeared so obvious at that time.

The 1945–60 era was the heart of the so-called American Century, the time when America would finally adopt the policies and practices necessary to attain global dominance. Be the sphere economics, politics, the military, or technology, it was presumed that the United States would lead the world—and would do so for at least the next 100 years. Yet beneath the veneer of success was a less sanguine interior. In fact, the years 1945–60 encompassed the roots of the subsequent decline of American steel (as well, perhaps, as that of other industries too). While the signs were often subtle, nevertheless they were there for those who chose to see them. The problem for firms in such industries as steel was that few chose to look closely. The primary factor that would soon erode the steelmakers' seeming position of strength was the changing international economic environment. Closely coupled with this was the failure of industry leaders to find common ground with traditional adversaries, in both organized labor and the government, over a strategy for long-term success. Accordingly, the firms were soon to face a dramatically altered competitive arena without many of the benefits that their foreign rivals would enjoy.[15]

On the surface, the industry seemed robust during these years.

Capacity was expanded at its most rapid rate in history, climbing from 100 million tons in 1950 to nearly 150 million tons by 1960. Total industry net earnings surpassed $1 billion for the first time in 1955. But while financial performance appeared healthy, on a comparative basis it was not. Of the 45 leading manufacturing industries in the nation, steel ranked in the bottom half in after-tax return on assets in all but four of the years from 1940 to 1960 (and in most, steel was in the bottom quartile). Stock market performance was similar: price/earnings multiples for steel stocks were lower than the all-industry average in all but one of the years surveyed.

What this indicated was a less than optimistic outlook for the future by those who controlled investment dollars in America. This translated to difficulty for steel firms in raising sufficient capital for expansion and modernization programs. For many industries, the period of market maturity is one in which firms have excess profits that could more productively be channeled into other uses with higher expected returns. But for steelmakers the need for investment in their own industry remained vital; not only was demand high during much of this time period, but a radically new steelmaking technology that promised substantial productivity improvements over existing methods was beginning to diffuse throughout the global industry. American steel—during the period of its largest expansion in history—stuck with the conventional open-hearth technology rather than opting for the new "basic oxygen furnace" approach. This was to prove a costly mistake.

In many respects, it was the relationship between American steelmakers and their government that created the environment that led to missed opportunities and subsequent decline. The 1950s were pivotal to postwar American development, for they marked the time when the nation would supposedly consolidate its strengths and build a foundation for lasting global dominance; the American Century, to use Henry Luce's oft-quoted term, was within reach. Yet America's political leaders had no experience in constructing such a system. Indeed, if anything just the opposite had been the tradition in which they had long been nurtured; echoing the famous phrase of America's first president George Washington in his farewell address to the nation in 1796, U.S. politicians had long sought to "avoid entangling alliances" that would surely follow any attempts at national involvement in world affairs. Accordingly, it was isolationism that had characterized America's past role in the world—not active involvement and leadership.

As a consequence, the men who forged the so-called American

Century were often times flying blind, bereft of the markers that could steer them around dangerous currents, unsure of the hidden shoals that might spell disaster in the long run. Within a short period of time following the termination of the Second World War, another conflict broke out which in many respects was to prove even more debilitating for America: this was the Cold War, in which the nation found an expansionist Soviet empire as the implacable foe that had to be contained everywhere in the world at whatever price it required if liberty and democracy (to say nothing of capitalism) were to be preserved.

For steelmakers, this new international threat would soon lead to a change in the global environment of their industry that eventually would completely re-order the competitive advantages of most entrants then in existence. As American public policy shifted to a central theme of fighting communism, the American government began to bestow handsome gifts of aid to many other nations of the world, believing that such benevolence would instill friendship toward the West or build impregnable defenses against Soviet-led incursions against capitalism. Steel was soon caught up in the middle of this policy, due to the industry's strategic position as the primary input to an industrial economy. If a nation were to reconstruct its factories from the ravages of the recent war, then steel would be needed; if a nation were to escape the cycle of poverty and despair associated with agrarian-based economies, then it would need steel to move toward industrialization. Could America expect to achieve its foreign policy agenda if so vital a commodity were left solely in the hands of a few domestic producers? Obviously not.

Accordingly, American policymakers urged Europe to rebuild and it soon proffered the same advice to Japan. To gain allies in the emerging Third World, the U.S. government promised (and delivered) resources for industrialization. Nearly $1.5 billion in direct assistance was given to foreign steelmakers between 1947 and 1960, and countless more was provided in terms of technology transfers, priority shipments of necessary raw materials, and access to American markets for foreign-made steel (thus allowing the exporting nations to earn hard currency with which to build their economies further). An encouragement to stop global communism, rather than stomping foreign competition, was the essential industrial policy of the American government toward its domestic steel sector during this time.

American steel leaders generally agreed to this foreign economic policy, but not without some reservations. In a statement that was to prove prescient, Bethlehem Steel Chairman Eugene Grace stated in

1949 that "we are industrializing the whole world [and]deindustrializing the United States." Yet the imperative of fighting communism had a clear priority. Curiously, however, this cooperation between steelmakers and the state did not extend to other critical areas—such as a capacity expansion policy for the industry, product pricing practices, company relations with organized labor, industry structure, and related topics of significance. Indeed, the relationship was strained at best. Ultimately it would prove disastrous as the firms confronted strengthened off-shore competitors who had already established close ties to their governments, which in turn led to direct benefits in their favor when compared to the Americans.

The effects of poor cooperation could be observed in many ways. For one, numerous members of the U.S. Congress constantly surveyed the structure of the industry in a search for evidence that U.S. Steel was a monopolist that should be broken up. Not only did the defense against such accusations take valuable time and resources away from more pressing management concerns (and also prevented more aggressive market behavior by the accused), but more importantly the general atmosphere surrounding steel-state relations remained tense due to such conflicts. Consequently, whenever the steel firms attempted to raise prices in order to generate investment capital for expansion or modernization during these years, one government agency or another was always quick to complain and threaten an official investigation into industry behavior. The result was a lag in steel prices during the first half of the 1945–60 era (in spite of inflationary pressures in the economy that resulted in the raising of prices of numerous other commodities). In turn, this stimulated even more demand for the steelmakers' products and thus led to even stronger calls for industry capacity expansion by government bureaucrats, who saw a slow program of capacity development as somehow an attempt to gouge profits from customers through artificially induced shortages.

Perhaps the most stressful point of friction, however, was between the management of steel firms and the United Steel Workers of America (USW), the dominant labor union in the industry. The history of relations between these two groups was not amicable. Like many industrial sectors, management had accepted unionization only with great reluctance, and in most cases steel firms never accepted organized labor as a legitimate partner in the quest for success. Union leadership, for its part, generally agreed to this formulation: It saw its role as essentially one of winning ever larger wages and benefits for its members, rather than assisting in the development of plans and strategies for long-range mutual objectives. During the immediate postwar years, the federal government of the United States was under the leadership of the Democratic Party—which had been the chief supporter of organized labor since the 1930s. Thus in the frequent clashes between the union (seeking higher wages and benefits) and the firms (trying to control costs), government generally supported labor over management. And when the political situation changed during the Republican administration of President D.D. Eisenhower from 1953–60, the union often called strikes at critical times just before national elections—thereby pressuring government leaders to use their influence with management to end the walkouts (by agreeing to union demands) before voter behavior in the election booth was affected.

It was a period marked by numerous industrywide strikes, as labor walked out in 1946, 1949, 1952, 1955, 1956, and—in the longest industrial strike in American history up to that point in time—for 116 days in 1959. At the end of each of these work stoppages, labor costs were higher than before, and relative operating efficiency was lower. The year of the last strike, 1959, was the first in the 20th century during which the United States imported more steel from abroad than it exported, a ratio that has yet to be reversed through 1990.

While management differences with both government and labor played a crucial role in the deteriorating global position of America's steelmakers, one might conclude that steel leaders alone must bear responsibility for the lack of technological innovation during this period. As noted above, the industry undertook the largest capacity expansion in its history in the 1950s, but unfortunately it chose to do so with an outdated technology. A closer inspection of this decision, however, reveals that government influenced management choice in this arena too.

In the late 1940s experimentation and invention in Europe resulted in development of the basic oxygen process of steelmaking, which had superior benefits relative to the prevailing open-hearth method, invented in the 1880s. But the failure of U.S. integrated steel firms to adopt cannot be explained by such easy assertions as management ineptness. Rather, the major postwar expansion in capacity occurred in the early 1950s, and came about largely due to government calls to expand rapidly for the needs of the Korean War. To spur such expansion, the government provided various financial incentives to the producers. Yet there was a strict time deadline that had to be met to obtain these public benefits, thus pressuring the firms to move quickly.

In this environment, the tried and true was more appealing—and less risky—than newer technologies that (1) had never been tested in large-scale operations; (2) relied on vast supplies of inputs that did not yet exist in volume; (3) and generally were viewed as promising but unproven by the major firms. Moreover, the companies in the industry were just then conducting experiments on the use of oxygenation techniques with open-hearth that could potentially raise production levels significantly. All in all, the consensus was to rely on the known, especially under the tight time frame created by the government for access to the financial benefits then being offered. Expansion would be in open-hearth, not with the new basic oxygen process.

Thus the domestic steelmakers experienced increased difficulty in stabilizing their institutional environment, they were not innovating, and were also witnessing a slippage in efficiency as costs seemed to be constantly rising. While the 1945–60 era might have appeared at first to be one of great strength for American steel, it was in fact a time of increasing turmoil and trouble. The threats from foreign competition were growing; in 1959 imports accounted for 6.9% of domestic consumption, and by the following year domestic output as a percentage of world production slipped to 26% (down from a high of 63.7% in 1945). Clearly, gathering storm clouds were on the horizon for those who chose to see them.

3. Industry Stagnation, 1960–85

These new competitive conditions, which had their roots in the first 15 of the postwar years, came to fruition in the 1960s and 1970s. Foreign steelmakers, initially in Europe but then increasingly in Japan and elsewhere, relentlessly improved their operations to the point where they could enter American markets and undercut domestic prices by up to 30% even after expensive transportation costs were absorbed.[16] By contrast, American manufacturers' responses to these foreign incursions were still burdened by generations of distrust among key government and labor leaders whose cooperation would be necessary in securing any improvements in competitive conditions. Unfortunately, the prior divisions were too deep to be overcome very quickly, if at all. The steel industry was in fact a precursor of changing global trade conditions that would engulf many other domestic markets and sectors by the early 1980s. By that time, it was obvious to all observers that the industry was in a new phase of its history—that is, decline.

The steelmakers did not ignore the necessity of improving operational efficiency during these years. After the surge of imports into

America in 1959, they realized that they would have to make heavy investments in mill improvement programs if they were to match the comparative advantage of off-shore mills; labor costs, obviously, could not be lowered to match foreign wages. The only option, declared Bethlehem's finance director, was "to get out ahead technically."[17] Accordingly, the firms began to borrow heavily to finance modernization; annual investment, for example, averaged slightly over $2 billion from 1965–70. Now realizing that the basic oxygen process of steelmaking was superior to open-hearth, the ratio of capacity utilizing this newer technology grew from 3.4% in 1960 to 48.1% by 1970, and 61.6% by 1975. Bethlehem Steel brought on stream a new greenfield mill in Indiana in the 1960s, employing the most modern technology then available (one of only two greenfield mills constructed in America in the postwar era). Additionally, American steel firms began more aggressively to adopt continuous casting technology by the mid-1960s, another change that promised cost reductions. By 1980, 21% of domestic raw steel capacity had been fitted with this improvement.[18]

But while more decisive action was now being taken by industry managers, measurable productivity improvements remained stubbornly low. Industry profits continued to lag behind other manufacturing sectors (with the steel firms averaging only about 60% of the total-industry average for ROE by American firms in the 1960s and 1970s). Capital investment programs were not able to overcome comparative deficiencies in both labor and raw material sourcing costs. As had been the case before, steel firms could not easily raise prices to fund the needed modernization projects because of skeptical government policymakers who found the industry an easy target for criticism whenever higher prices were announced. The well-publicized clash between President Kennedy and Chairman Roger Blough of U.S. Steel in 1962 when that firm tried to hike its price quotes is but the most salient example of the antagonism between steel and government on this issue.[19]

This problem of pricing forced the firms to rely primarily on debt for their financing needs. But with profits low, debt markets soon began to shun the steelmakers, raising the cost of debt to unacceptable levels; the low level of earnings also nullified any attemps to raise capital through equity offerings. Meanwhile, foreign steel producers were continually improving their efficiency, and relatively low barriers to entry in the United States encouraged an ever-larger volume of cheaper imported steel to enter the country during these post-1960 years. The end result was a deepening downward cycle: Imports were constantly growing, thus bringing greater pressure on the firms to make capital improvements, vitally needed if cost efficiencies were to be realized. But with high capital formation barriers (and with growing governmental demands that steelmakers allocate investment capital to non-productive pollution control projects), it was very difficult to raise the necessary funds from external sources. Steel slipped further and further behind its foreign rivals in competitiveness.

By the mid-1960s, American steelmakers began to sense with greater clarity that they had to improve relations with their major domestic constituencies—government and organized labor—if they were to have any future success in the changing competitive environment of global steel. After the Kennedy-Blough confrontation had publicly humiliated the industry, steel company lobbying efforts in Washington were strengthened, relations with leading national opinion makers were built, and efforts to convince the general public that a strong domestic steel industry was vital to national welfare were undertaken.[20] Government responded in 1969 by approval of a "voluntary restraint agreement" (VRA) that put limits on foreign steel imported into America. On the labor front, by 1974 a new "Experimental Negotiating Agreement" (ENA) between the producers and the USW was created. In this venture, the union agreed to a no-strike clause in its labor contract with the industry in return for guaranteed wage increases. Since import surges into the domestic market had always accompanied union contract negotiations after the late 1950s (because users, well aware of the dismal history of labor relations in steel, assumed a strike would follow and that they would be caught short of steel supply), it was believed that a no-strike agreement would send clear signals to users that supplies would be ample, thus curbing the growth of imports and saving both jobs and revenues for the domestic industry.[21]

The rapidly expanding global market for steel made these changes in traditional industry attitudes necessary. As Bethlehem Steel's chairman E.E. Grace had predicted some 20 years earlier, the rest of the world was being industrialized: Steelmaking facilities were often the first projects to be installed by nations seeking to enter the modern industrial world. Barriers to entry in the industry dropped sharply, especially in the early 1960s, when new deposits of steelmaking raw materials were discovered in various regions of the globe and a revolution in over-water bulk shipping technology made them available to new entrants.[22] Moreover, American Cold War policies continued to encourage newly industrializing nations to establish manufacturing capacity. Numerous U.S.-backed financial agencies made funding available on attractive terms to these new entrants, a trend exacerbated by the implications of the 1973 Arab OPEC embargo on oil to the West; ultimately, this resulted in a huge recycling of "petrodollars" back to the West where they became widely available to Third World nations for economic development purposes.[23]

The major event in the changing global steel industry, however was the emergence of Japan as the world's most efficient producer. Only 5.3 million tons of crude were made in Japan in 1950; by 1960 the volume increased to 22.1 million tons, by 1970 to 93.3 million tons, and by 1980 to 122.8 million tons (when the United States produced only 111.8 million tons). Moreover, this growth was in the form of large-scale plants situated on deep-water ports utilizing the most modern technology available. Thus by 1980 Japanese steelmakers could produce and ship to America a ton of cold-rolled sheet at a cost of only 80% or so of that expended by domestic manufacturers. Obviously, users in America were attracted to the lower prices offered by foreign sellers: imports, accounting for only 4.7% of domestic steel consumption in 1960, spurted to 17.9% in 1971 and nearly 20% by 1980 (when VRAs slowed their growth, as did the Trigger Price Mechanism of 1978). Global demand for steel was growing throughout this period, climbing from 382 million tons of production in 1960, to 654 million tons in 1970, to 790 million tons in 1980. First Japan, and then other nations, began to capture a growing share of this expanded market; by 1980 American steelmakers provided only 11% of total global output.[24]

Thus the world was continuing to demand steel—but not American-made steel so much as products made elsewhere. This was in marked contrast to the situation that had prevailed over much of the 20th century prior to 1960. An initial explanation of this trend hinged on the general decline of America as an economic power, shifts in the composition of national output from manufactured goods to services, a great rise in global steelmaking capacity, and the cost competitiveness of other nations (such as Japan). In other words, American steelmakers—clinging to their outmoded practices of the past—did not meet the rising challenge of offshore rivals during this period of change in the American economy. But while all of this is certainly beyond question, other factors also bear exploration. America's economic decline cannot be wholly ascribed to changes in comparative advantage, as most economic analyses are wont to emphasize. What must also be evaluated is the manner by which the foreign economic policymaking apparatus of the United States is responsive to transformations in sectoral economic performance: It is here, in the political arena as much as anywhere else, that one must sift for clues to explain the apparent decline of American steel between 1960 and 1985. This is a problem in institutional economics, not price theory.

II. Findings and Conclusions Regarding Steel's Competitiveness

In essence, the United States has not had a foreign economic policy in the postwar era that could respond well to an environment of sectoral retrenchment or decline. As the American Century dawned so brightly after 1945, the United States moved away from its historical posture of isolationism and more toward a regime that favored open markets, low tariffs, and multilateral trade pacts. Indeed, from 1945 to 1970 or so the United States presided over the strongest growth of global free trade in modern history. The benefits were significant, not only to Americans but to the remainder of the trading world as well. As trade expanded, standards of living also increased. The United States could well afford to lead such efforts at that time because of the huge disparities in resources that existed between the nation and its foreign rivals. More importantly, such an economic policy also comported well with the broader national political agenda of containing an expansionist communist threat throughout the globe.[25]

When conditions of relative strength began to change in the 1970s, few alternatives could command the focus necessary to re-order entrenched American priorities. The politico-economic decisionmaking process in Washington was not terribly flexible, and changes that began to emerge in the early 1970s rendered it even less hospitable to long-term action. As the historic 1944 Bretton Woods system of fixed currency exchange rates broke down after 1971, and the post-OPEC world of high energy prices took root in 1974, it became increasingly difficult for American manufacturers to cope in the transformed global economy. This was especially true for sectors such as steel, where foreign firms often enjoyed significant benefits bestowed upon them by governments that enjoyed friendlier relations with the managerial business class of the country.

Rather than redefining American foreign economic policy in this world of changing relationships, American policymakers were caught up in numerous other matters that reflected more the short-term outlook of the American electoral process than anything else. Various attempts by steelmakers to obtain governmental relief and assistance were thus also short term in nature (voluntary restraint agreements, "trigger price mechanisms" designed to alleviate dumping of foreign steel in America, relief from stringent pollution control laws, etc.). But nothing of substance that would address the fundamental nature of the industry in a radically redefined world economy was advanced let alone debated or adopted by the key decisionmakers, both public and private.[26]

By the early 1980s the American steel industry was poised for a major catastrophe. It began in late 1981 when a new "supply side"-oriented macroeconomic policy was introduced by the Reagan Administration at just the time when steel began a cyclical downturn in demand. The ultimate result was a dramatic escalation of the value of the dollar in world currency markets, and a subsequent surge of imports as foreign steel prices in America plunged. Twenty years of festering problems, incomplete "solutions," and institutional intransigence toward the need to revise fundamentally (or in fact create) a sectoral steel policy thus cascaded down upon the nation's steelmakers. In 1985 the industry collectively lost $1.2 billion on operations, marking the fourth consecutive year of negative earnings and bringing the industry total to $7.2 billion in red ink since 1982. Only 208,000 employees worked in steel by 1985; in 1965, some 584,000 people were on the job. Industry crude steel production had been 99.3 million tons in 1960, turned out from a rated capacity of 148.6 million tons; by 1985 production and capacity figures were down to 88.2 millions tons, and 133.6 million tons respectively. By that time, many observers were writing off the industry as dead.[27]

Not surprisingly, major changes in the structure of the industry—avoided for so long by so many—now became a necessity. National Steel sold off its operations to a new joint venture with Japan's NKK Steel Company; Youngstown Sheet & Tube merged with Jones & Laughlin, and the latter was merged into Republic Steel to form LTV Steel (which soon thereafter filed for protection from creditors under the bankruptcy laws). Wheeling-Pittsburgh Steel, McLouth Steel, Alan Wood Steel, and Sharon Steel (among other long-standing entrants in the industry) also filed for bankruptcy; Bethlehem Steel was reported to be on the verge of filing as well for much of this time. Armco Steel, having attempted to diversify its operations in the 1960s and 1970s, found these investments to be unprofitable in the 1980s and it was forced to sell them off to survive. And U.S. Steel acquired two large energy firms, subsequently changing its corporate name to USX to better reflect its new status as a diversified energy company (or, as some speculated, better positioning the company to divest its steel holdings entirely). Finally, a new industry segment comprised of electric furnace "mini-mills" developed to the point that they could compete for markets previously reserved for the integrated firms. By the mid-1980s the "minis" had captured nearly a quarter of total domestic product sales volume. While the industry could not technically be classified as "dead" by 1985, it was certainly a transmogrified entity relative to its recent past: Imports took a quarter of the market, minis another 25%, and crude capacity had been reduced by 30% since 1982 alone.[28]

The downturn bottomed out in 1984, but it was not until 1987 that profitability was restored to many of the producers. USX, for example, reported steel operating income of $125 million in 1987 and $501 million in 1988 (following a loss of $1.4 billion in 1986). Why were such improvements able to occur? Perhaps most importantly, a change in U.S. macroeconomic policy that began in the fall of 1985 brought a decline of nearly 50% in the value of the dollar to other currencies, thus effectively raising the price of imported steel in America (and lowering the price of steel exported from the nation). A restored voluntary restraint agreement, begun in late 1984, set a target of about 20% of domestic apparent consumption as the maximum for imports; by 1988, this goal was achieved.

Other micro factors must also be acknowledged for this turnaround: Massive reductions in the labor force along with a cut in the contractual pay level of unionized steelworkers resulted in a dramatic increase in labor productivity by the domestic firms; and new investment of nearly $9 billion since 1982 increased the technological competitiveness of the shrunken industry. By mid-1989, some of the larger producers— such as Inland Steel—could boast that they were among the world's low-cost leaders in steelmaking, turning out the product with only 3.5 man hours per ton.

Another factor to consider is the increasing linkage of American steel firms with Japanese rivals. Beginning with the National-NKK equity arrangement in 1984, Sumitomo Metals organized a joint venture with LTV Steel; Nippon Steel with Inland; Nisshin Steel with Wheeling-Pittsburgh; and Kawasaki Steel with Armco, the latter representing a 35% investment in the equity of the American firm. Kobe Steel, a smaller Japanese producer, recently extended its relationship with USX through the purchase of the latter's bar mill in Ohio.[29] While most of these relationships concern the sharing of technology, there is clearly the potential for a global-scale consolidation of the industry, engineered by Japanese firms with a strong yen and a shrinking industrial base at home (as Japanese steel users, such as automakers, continue to move operations into America to compensate for the higher yen-to-dollar ratio). Thus, while changes are occurring in the industry, they continue to portend a loss of control by the domestic American steel manufacturers.

What is one to conclude from this brief account of American steel in the 20th century? Several key points need to be emphasized: (1) the political culture of America has often been as important—if not more important—than firm-level microeconomics in the competitive posture of domestic steel firms; as a corollary to the above, (2) the U.S. government has never provided any sectoral-specific assistance for steelmakers that goes beyond relatively short-term "fixes" designed to rectify short-term pressures brought on by political factors. This must be seen in conjunction with (3) a propensity of many offshore steelmakers to turn to and receive benefits from their home governments that allow them to enjoy a competitive advantage over U.S. steelmakers, both in the U.S. market and in world markets.

While I have clearly emphasized the institutional environment of steel manufacturing in America as the major explanatory variable in the changing fortunes of the industry over the 20th century, I would not imply that individual behavior by steel managers and steel firms should be excluded from culpability for the problems in the industry. However, the task of the historian in understanding that behavior is to understand better the circumstances in which decisions were made. In this context, the objective observer must necessarily turn to a close examination of the rather peculiar interaction of business and government (and organized labor as well) in the United States as a primary reason for the declining performance of steel in the postwar era.

NOTES

1.   USX Corporation, *1988 Annual Report* (Pittsburgh, 1989) contains the most recent details regarding the mix of revenues for this firm. In that year, total revenues of $16.9 billion were divided into energy ($9.9 billion), steel ($5.8 billion), and diversified operations (net $1.2 billion).

2.   The literature on the formation of U.S. Steel is vast. For one interesting and informative account, see Joseph Frazier Wall, *Andrew Carnegie* (New York, 1970), pp. 765–93.

3.   All statistical information, unless otherwise noted, is from the American Iron and Steel Institute, *Annual Statistical Report* (Washington, D.C., issued annually).

4.   Louis Galambos and Joseph Pratt, *The Rise of the Corporate Commonwealth* (New York, 1988).

5.   For statistical information on individual firms in this period, see

Gertrude Schroeder, *The Growth of Major Steel Companies, 1900–1950* (Baltimore, 1953).

6.   On Gary and U.S. Steel at this time, see Melvin I. Urofsky, *Big Steel and the Wilson Administration* (Columbus, Ohio, 1969). Also worth review is Thomas K. McCraw and Forest Reinhardt, "Losing to Win: U.S. Steel's Pricing, Investment Decisions, and Market Share, 1901–1938," *Journal of Economic History*, vol. 49 (September 1989): 593–619.

7.   "Impromptu Remarks of the President," in *Yearbook, 1925,* American Iron and Steel Institute (New York, 1925), p. 222.

8.   For a fuller explanation of this thesis, see Donald D. Parsons and Edward John Ray, "The United States Steel Consolidation: The Creation of Market Control," *Journal of Law and Economics,* vol. 18 (April 1975): 181–219.

9.   See Paul Tiffany, "The Origins of Industrial Research at the United States Steel Corporation, 1901–1929," paper presented at the Annual Meeting of the Economic History Association (U.S.), Hartford, Conn., 1986.

10.   For details on Schwab's life, see Robert Hessen, *Steel Titan: The Life of Charles M. Schwab* (New York, 1975).

11.   See Schroeder, op. cit., for firm-specific statistical details at this time.

12.   Armco had long supported R & D; see "The American Rolling Mill Company Research Laboratory," *Iron Age,* vol. 86 (November 17, 1910): 1152.

13.   For details on Weir, see Ernest Dale, *The Great Organizers* (New York, 1960), chapter four, "Ernest Tener Weir: Iconoclast of Management," pp. 113–41.

14.   See Paul Tiffany, "Opportunity Denied: The Abortive Attempt to Internationalize the American Steel Industry, 1903–1929," *Business and Economic History,* 2nd series, vol. 16 (1987).

15.   For details and further citations on this and much of the following section, see Paul Tiffany, *The Decline of American Steel* (New York, 1988).

16.   For a useful overview of these events (though not written from the historian's perspective), see Donald F. Barnett and Louis Schorsch, *Steel, Upheaval in a Basic Industry* (Cambridge, Mass., 1983), especially chapter three, pp. 37–75. For a review of changes in Japan's steel industry, see Patricia A. O'Brien, "Coordinating Market Forces: The Anatomy of Investment Decisions in the Japanese Steel Industry 1945–1975" (Ph.D. diss., Harvard Business School, 1985).

17.   Quoted in Thomas K. McCraw, ed., *America versus Japan* (Boston, 1986), chapter three, footnote 30, p. 405. The quote was given in 1966.

18.   Statistical data, as noted previously, derives primarily from the American Iron and Steel Institute, *Annual Statistical Report* (Washington, D.C., annual).

19.   For details of this episode, see Grant McConnell, *Steel and the Presidency, 1962* (New York, 1963).

20.   See Paul Tiffany, "Response to Crisis: The Steel Industry Public Relations Campaign of the Postwar Era" (working paper, Reginald Jones Center, The Wharton School, University of Pennsylvania, mimeo, 1989).

21.   While not an unbiased source, see John P. Hoerr, *And the Wolf Finally Came, The Decline of the American Steel Industry* (Pittsburgh, 1988), chapter five, pp. 109–33 for details of the ENA.

22.   Among other sources, see Robert W. Crandall, *The U.S. Steel Industry in Recurrent Crisis* (Washington, D.C., 1981).

23. See, for example, Michael W. Hodin, "A National Policy for Organized Free Trade, or, How to Cope with Protectionism: The Case of United States Trade Policy for Steel" (Ph.D. diss., Columbia University, 1979), especially chapter three, part IV, p. 205ff.

24. These changes have been extensively detailed in several studies; see, for example, Barnett and Schorsch, op. cit., and O'Brien, op. cit. Another useful source is U.S. Federal Trade Commission, Bureau of Economics, *Staff Report on the United States Steel Industry and Its International Rivals, Trends and Factors Determining International Competitiveness* (Washington, D.C., 1977).

25. Numerous scholarly studies have covered this ground; one of the more recent and popular is Paul Kennedy, *The Rise and Fall of the Great Powers* (New York, 1987), especially chapter seven.

26. For one review of such policy prescriptions, see American Iron and Steel Institute, *Steel at the Crossroads: The American Steel Industry in the 1980s* (Washington, D.C., 1980), a review of the problems confronting the industry at that time (as seen from the perspective of the producers) and a "wish list" of public policies that the AISI believed would improve matters. While comprehensive, nowhere, for example, does the statement address the need to restructure and rationalize (by capacity elimination) outdated facilities in America.

On the other hand, some governmental analyses and recommendations that did address fundamental problems were not possible to implement given the nature of business-government policy decisionmaking that prevailed in the United States; see, for example, U.S. General Accounting Office, Report to the Congress by the Comptroller General, *New Strategy Required for Aiding Distressed Steel Industry* (Washington, D.C., January 1981).

27. See the AISI sources for statistical information.

28. A huge popular literature has developed recently that focuses on these changes in the domestic steel industry; see Hoerr, op. cit.; John Strohmeyer, *Crisis in Bethlehem* (New York, 1986); Mark Reutter, *Sparrows Point, Making Steel: The Rise and Ruin of American Industrial Might* (New York, 1988); Thomas R. Howell et al., *Steel and the State: Government Intervention and Steel's Structural Crisis* (Boulder, 1988); and Donald F. Barnett and Robert W. Crandall, *Up From the Ashes, the Rise of the Steel Minimill in the United States* (Washington, D.C., 1986), among other titles.

29. These events have yet to be systematically analyzed; for factual information, see for example "The Japanese Steel Industry: Facing Changes at Home and Abroad," remarks by Sōichirō Yoshimura, EVP of Kobe Steel Ltd., Tokyo, before the (U.S.) Association of Steel Distributors, San Diego, California, March 14, 1989 (distributed by the Japan Steel Information Center, New York).

Comment

Ichirō Hori

Influenced by the industrial organization approach, many studies on the American steel industry in the postwar era have attributed the decline of the American steel industry to its oligopolistic structure. By contrast, Professor Tiffany offers in his paper a new view which posits that institutional factors, not the individual behavior of steel managers and steel companies, played a critical role in the decline of the steel industry. In other words, Tiffany ascribes the poor performance of the steel industry not so much to wrong decision-making of steel managers and steel companies, but to such institutional factors as economic policies, especially foreign economic policies, poor cooperation between the steel industry and the government, and bad labor-management relations.

According to Tiffany, it was between 1945 and 1960, when America was enjoying the "American Century," that the roots of subsequent decline in the American steel industry were growing. During the Cold War period, American foreign economic aid promoted the rebuilding of steel industries in Europe and Japan, and helped the building of steel industries in the Third World. The American steel industry was, however, burdened by tensions or conflicts between the government and steelmakers over many issues, such as steel capacity expansion policies, steel pricing practices, and the structure of the steel industry. The tensions, in return, made it difficult for American steelmakers to raise sufficient funds for modernization. Furthermore, the distrust between steel managers and labor unions increased wage costs and lowered the efficiency of production. As a result, the competitiveness of the American steel industry declined, and in 1959 steel imports exceeded exports. In the 1960s and 1970s when drastic changes such as the rapid growth of the Japanese, European, and the Third World steel industries occurred, the American steel industry could not improve its relative decline owing to a lack of government assistance and persistently bad labor-management relations. By 1980 the decline of the U.S. steel industry had become openly acknowledged.

Tiffany's argument is quite an interesting one, making an important contribution to our understanding of the postwar American steel industry. As is generally known, the industrial organization analysis, by focusing on market structure, market conduct, and market performance, takes little account of historical and environmental factors. Therefore, it is a static analysis. By contrast, Tiffany discusses the postwar American steel industry from both historical and environmental points of view, including economic policies, and business-government and labor-management relations. For that reason, Tiffany's approach is valuable in its methodology.

Yet, I find some problems in his analysis, three of which I would like to focus on. The first one concerns the effects of the government's economic policies on the steel industry. Tiffany contends that the government's steel price regulation, or government investigation into the industry's structure, made it difficult for the steel industry to raise funds to undertake its modernization. What we have to direct our attention to is the movement of steel prices after World War II, because this shows that the steel industry had frequently raised steel prices immediately after the relaxation or removal of regulations. The steel price regulations imposed by the government seem to have delayed the hike in steel prices rather than curbed it. Accordingly, I do not subscribe to Tiffany's view in this regard.

The second question is related to the behavior of the steel industry. As Tiffany regards institutional and environmental factors as primarily responsible for the declining performance of steel in the postwar era, he almost neglects the behavior of the steel industry. I would like to contend that the behavior of the industry is no less important than institutional factors and in some cases the former caused the decline of the industry to a far greater extent than the latter. In other words, it is difficult to conceive that even full cooperation between the steel industry, the government, and labor could have resulted in a good performance by the industry. Institutional factors contributed to, but were not decisive factors of, the decline. Here I would like to touch upon two decisive factors. One is the oligopolistic structure of the American steel industry. In the latter half of the 1950s the oligopolistic steel industry brought about so-called administered price, which was one of the major causes for the declining competitiveness of the industry. It is true that institutional factors such as the emergent expansion project during the Korean War period delayed the adoption of BOF. But the oligopolistic structure was also equally responsible for the delay, especially that of the steel giants. It also made the American steel industry adhere to the development of domestic and Canadian iron ores. Thereafter, this adherence reversed the advantageous position of the American steel industry in terms of the cost of iron ore relative to its counterparts in other countries during the 1960s.

The other decisive factor which explains the decline is the style of management by short-term strategies such as "round-out" investments or diversification in the 1960s. Thus the behavior of the steel industry which resulted from its oligopolistic structure and short-term strategies caused the deterioration of the American steel industry's performance.

The third and the last problem concerns Tiffany's view about the way steel managers and steel companies behaved as they were placed under institutional constraints, which, according to him, left them a limited number of options to take. He regards the institutional constraints as a given, that is, he disregards the possibility of steel managers and steel companies changing the institutional constraints. If this is the case, then I would like to ask Tiffany the reason why they took no drastic action in bringing about change until the early 1980s.

Challenge of a Latecomer: The Case of the Korean Steel Industry with Specific Reference to POSCO

Sung-il Juhn

I. Introduction

How has the Korean steel industry, represented by the Pohang Iron & Steel Company (POSCO), been able to establish itself as one of the world's most competitive iron and steel producers in less than 20 years? This paper attempts to answer the question by looking closely at this one dominant company of the Korean steel industry, from entrepreneurial and corporate strategy points of view.

Several factors have contributed to the success of POSCO, most notably: entrepreneurship, government support during the initial phase of plant construction, including infrastructure and finance,[1] the rapid rate of industrialization in Korea, a reservoir of well-educated, disciplined manpower, and technology transfer from the developed nations. A more detailed examination of these factors will follow a brief description of the history of the Korean steel industry.

Since the first steelworks was established in 1918 at Kyumipo in what is now North Korea, with a crude steelmaking capacity of 50,000 tons per year, little progress was made in Korea's steel industry until 1962. At that time production capacity was just 14,000 tons per year in South Korea, only 3.5% of domestic demand.

From 1962 to 1972, the industry consisted of four manufacturers: the Inchon Iron & Steel Co., Dongkuk Steel Mill Co., Korea Iron & Steel Co., and the Union Steel Manufacturing Co.[2] Their investments during this period brought Korea's self-sufficiency in steel to 23%. However, production facilities tended to consist of small, outdated equipment.

Rapid increase in domestic consumption convinced the government of the need to make the construction of an integrated steelworks the priority enterprise of the Second Economic Plan (1967–71). As a result, POSCO was founded in 1968, and its first phase, with a capacity of 1.03 million metric tons per year (mmtpy), completed in 1973.

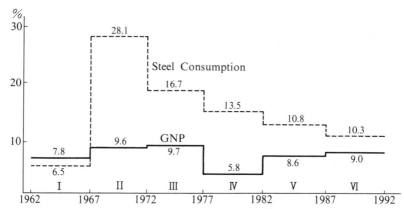

FIG. 1 Economic Growth and Steel Consumption (annual growth rate).
Source: Korea Iron & Steel Association.

The initiation of highly successful five-year Economic Development Plans in 1962 led to increasing emphasis in heavy and chemical industries from the late 1970s, which in turn dramatically raised the demand for steel. The steel industry expanded likewise to match the demand. In 1989 Korea's steel industry comprised 200 companies including one integrated steel company (POSCO), 12 electric furnace companies, and around 70 rolling and finishing companies. Following the start of production at POSCO's second phase of the Kwangyang works, Korea's self-sufficiency in steel was calculated as having risen to 81.9%.

From the 1970s to the present, steel consumption has tended to exceed economic growth, which itself has averaged 8%. However, in the current sixth Economic Development Plan (1987–91) steel consumption is expected to drop below the general economic growth rate on account of the further advance of Korea's industrial structure, which is following the same growth pattern as Japan in the 1960s, as shown in Fig. 1. According to statistics supplied by Korea Advanced Institute of Science and Technology, domestic demand for crude steel is expected to continue to outstrip domestic steelmaking capacity until the 21st century.[3]

As for the steel-consuming industries, they are expected to grow at a moderate rate. The automobile industry is presently enjoying a boom, thanks to an explosive demand in the domestic market. Shipbuilding is expanding too now after its recent recession. The evolution of Korea's industrial structure has brought with it a change in the share of total domestic steel consumption among industries. Construction decreased

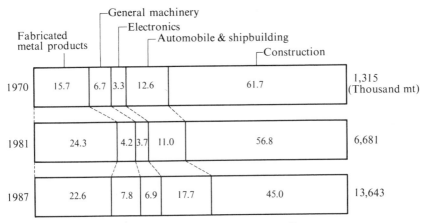

FIG. 2 Breakdown of Steel Consumption by Industry(%).
Source: Korea Iron & Steel Association (Seoul, 1988).

its massive 61.7% share of 1970 to 45% in 1987. Elsewhere share of steel consumption is taking an upward trend; the growth of consumption in manufacturing is particularly strong and the share of the automobile sector is also growing but is still relatively low. Consumption by manufacturing industries in 1987 consisted of 22.6% by the fabricated metal products industry, 7.8% by machinery, and 17.7% by the shipbuilding and automobile industries, as shown in Fig. 2. Steel consumption by manufacturing is forecast to increase steadily.

In addition to the government's industrialization policy and an increase in social overhead capital, the sharp rise in steel demand is also due to keeping steel prices for domestic industries continuously lower than those offered by international competitors, enabling these industries to reduce production costs. This weapon has been a major factor in the international competitiveness of Korean products in shipbuilding, automobiles, machinery, and electronics, boosting both production and exports.

II. Park Taejun and POSCO

As was the case in the other heavy industries, the initiative and determination to launch an integrated iron and steel plant in Korea came from the government in the early 1960s and again in the late 1960s, finally bearing fruit in the form of POSCO. In Korea, as in the other late industrializing countries, public-sector initiative was followed by private-sector initiative in the form of entrepreneurship, whose functions included that of dealing with the government. Jones and Sakong argued that the irreducible entrepreneurial role is to serve as a lens that focuses the various functional energies on a selected target—the lenticular function—and that the selected target in the late industrializing countries is very often government, which possesses powerful discretionary authority to allocate scarce resources.[4] Thus, maintaining close relationships with key officials in the government has been a most important function for entrepreneurs in Korea, as has been the case in other countries. The company's founder and incumbent chairman of its board of directors, General Park Taejun (hereafter referred to as T.J. Park), has performed the lenticular function described above most efficiently, focusing first on government relations and the financing of the first phase of POSCO's first integrated steelworks and thereafter on selected targets in tune with the company's changing needs. In recent years, for example, his entrepreneurial energy has focused on the diversification and internationalization of POSCO. Thus he has proved himself to be not only the quintessential entrepreneur in the Schumpeterian sense—an innovator, risk taker, and organizer of the factors of production—but also a lenticular entrepreneur who knew how to deal selectively with the critical issues facing POSCO from its birth.

His background equipped him well for his ensuing role. His connections with Japan have been strong since his student days. A graduate of Waseda University, he understood and appreciated Japanese culture, tradition, and business, which enabled him to obtain help from the Japanese steel industry for the first POSCO plant. Secondly, he had strong military connections and experience. As a major general, he knew military discipline, possessed organizational abilities, leadership, and strategic vision, skills which he later applied in managing POSCO. As he was chief of staff to the former President Park following the successful military revolution of 1961, he had President Park's absolute presidential support for the creation and operation of an integrated iron and steel plant. His close relationships with the two succeeding presidents, Chun and Roh, have also stood him in good stead. Moreover, several years as president of the Korea Tungsten Corporation prior to the creation of POSCO equipped him with many managerial skills. This company became a source of much of POSCO's managerial talent in its early years. His political influence has increased over the years, as was demonstrated in 1980 when faced with stiff competition to POSCO's plan to build Korea's second integrated steelworks in Kwangyang; rallying all his political allies, he managed to safeguard POSCO's interests. His political stance also benefited from the fact that he is from the Southeast, an area which has produced many influential political leaders in Korea. He is also known for his love of and respect for learning. When visiting Japan, his first stop is invariably a bookstore. His passion for learning was the force behind the remarkable rate of technology absorption by POSCO and later, the establishment of the Research Institute of Industrial Science and Technology and the Pohang Institute of Science and Technology, the latter of which earned the reputation of a premier academic institution in just two years.

The following story illustrates T.J. Park's lenticular entrepreneurship, focusing on the problem of financing the first phase of POSCO. POSCO was on the verge of extinction, for the financial and technical assistance expected from the international consortium (the Korea International Steel Association, KISA) did not materialize in early 1969. The World Bank feasibility study at that time concluded that POSCO would be unable to repay its projected loan due to many obstacles facing the company including lack of resources and skilled manpower. Consequently, certain members of the association put pressure on POSCO to abandon the idea of an integrated steel mill and to concentrate instead on a mini-mill. Thus the plan to build a 600,000-ton facility faced severe obstacles. T.J. Park, after failing in his last attempt to obtain the required loan from the consortium in 1969, came to the conclusion that POSCO could no longer depend on KISA and that Japan could be a source of technical and financial assistance. Almost singlehandedly he both persuaded the Japanese steel industry leaders to render assistance to the project, and obtained the Korean government's consent to use reparation payment from Japan for the project.[5]

Once construction was underway in 1970, T.J. Park was a familiar figure around the construction sites, encouraging, instructing, inspecting, and disciplining managers and workers. In short, he practiced and mastered the art of M.B.W.A. (managing by walking around), a concept popularized by Peters and Waterman in their book *In Search of Excellence*.[6] His lenticular entrepreneurial function was clearly focused on the difficulties of building the first blast furnace in a developing country with no previous experience. He made many personal sacrifices during the first few years of POSCO, and he expected his managers to do the same. Due to inadequate housing facilities, families were left behind, mostly in Seoul, and family visits were rare as on-the-job demands mounted. As T.J. Park served as the model for such sacrifice, there were few complaints. He later wrote a book of essays entitled

A *New Species of Separated Family*, recalling the hardships endured and the sacrifices made by himself and his subordinates for POSCO.[7] Although there are many other legendary stories about Park as an entrepreneur, manager, and politician, suffice it to say, for the purpose of this paper, that he is the much admired father of the Korean steel industry.

III. POSCO's Overall Strategy

The only integrated steel mill in Korea, POSCO now ranks as the third largest steel company in the free world and dominates the Korean steel industry, accounting for around 80% of domestic steel production. It is natural, therefore, that this paper should concentrate on POSCO in its description of the Korean steel industry.

After POSCO was founded in 1968, the first phase of works incorporating steelmaking facilities with a capacity of 1.03 million metric tons (mmt) was started in 1970 in Pohang and completed in 1973 with an initial investment of $301 million. Additional stages followed in rapid succession: Phase II was dedicated in 1976, bringing the total capacity to 2.6 mmt; Phase III was dedicated in 1978, increasing capacity to 5.5 mmt; Phase IV was completed in two stages by 1983, bringing the total capacity to 9.1 mmt. The total investment for the additional phases was $3.6 billion. In 1982 construction of the first phase of the Kwangyang Works began and was completed in 1987, adding 2.7 mmt to the total capacity; meanwhile Phase II began in 1986 and was completed in July 1988. The total steelmaking capacity between the Pohang and Kwangyang now stands st 14.5 mmt. Phase III at Kwangyang is already underway and due for completion by the end of January 1991 with an added capacity of 2.7 mmt. The final stage, Phase IV, will start on January 5, 1991 and is expected to be completed by the end of December 1992. At that point total steelmaking capacity will be 20.8 mmt. POSCO's capital is $688 million and total sales for 1989 is expected to be $6,408 million. Employees numbered 22,000 in 1989.

The company's initial objective was to set itself up as a catalyst for the industrialization of Korea by supplying an increasing volume of low-cost steel to steel consuming industries. "Let us serve the nation through iron and steel" has been the motto throughout POSCO's history. POSCO's strategy was to produce at low cost in order to sell low-price products to the domestic industry. As a consequence of this strategy steel users have been able to sell their products at a low price, increase market share, and expand, which has in turn increased the demand for steel. POSCO's contribution to the Korean export industries is especially noteworthy; for example, the Korean steel-using export industries saved $350 million in 1985 in their steel purchases compared to foreign sourcing, or 32.7% of the expected cost of foreign sourcing. The same can be said with regard to steel-using industries that are oriented toward the domestic market. They saved $462 million in 1985, cutting their materials cost by 33.9% compared to the cost of foreign sourcing.[8]

TABLE 1 Comparison of Steel Product Prices (2nd quarter 1988) ($/ton)

	Domestic sales	Export price (FOB)		Import price	List price of major country	
	Price	Japan	USA		Japan	USA
HR coil	332	446	339	443	663	433
Plate	339	466	417	506	715	491
CR coil	469	628	465	567	794	621

Source: POSCO.

Comparison of costs and prices among international companies show POSCO to have achieved its goal as a low cost producer (Table 1). Although some critics contend that heavy government subsidies were the major factors of POSCO's low cost structure, most experts conclude that even after adding in subsidies to POSCO's costs, the company was still competitive with Japanese steelmakers.[9] More recently, however, POSCO has lost some of its competitive edge in the area of CR (cold-rolled) coil (Table 2). Having built a strong competitive position on low-cost steels, the company has begun to introduce higher value-added and specialty steels to its product range, with a planned total investment of $1.2 billion for the four-year period 1987–91. The demand for such products within Korea is increasing due to the rapidly expanding automobile and domestic appliance industries. The Pohang Works is increasingly moving toward specialty steels, producing a wider product range but with relatively small quantities of each product. Kwangyang concentrates on mass production of low value-added steel. The production of specialty steels nonetheless constitutes a relatively small proportion of the total output at POSCO, 4.9% compared to 16.0% in Japan.

TABLE 2 Comparison of Cold-rolled Coil Costs ($/ton)

	Japan	U.K.	Taiwan	Korea
Nov. 1988	552	420	422	418
May 1989	520	408	445	420
Difference	−32	−12	+23	+32

Source: *World Steel Dynamics*, New York, July 1989.

IV. Factors Contributing to POSCO's International Competitiveness

1. Construction cost reductions

POSCO's policy has been to keep construction costs to a minimum without jeopardizing the quality of construction or production. Furthermore, when planning expansions, capacity enlargements were calculated in relation to expected demand from the rapidly growing domestic market. Extra output from each new phase was readily absorbed, so the company continued to sustain high-capacity production. For many of its expansions POSCO managed to construct at low cost during recession, and to commence operations during an upward turn in the world business cycle.

Low-cost capital. Because of the scarcity of domestic investment capital in Korea when POSCO was started, the government imposed strict controls on investment projects. Through astute negotiating POSCO managed to reduce the amount of foreign loan capital for the first stage of the Pohang Works. A large portion of the domestic loan was available from the $500 million reparation fees paid by Japan in compensation for the country's earlier colonization of Korea. Additionally, despite the U.S. Exim Bank and the World Bank's refusal to back the project, excellent loan terms were procured from Japanese banks. Good timing in relation to the state of the steel market when the works started production meant that from POSCO's first year the company made a profit. The profits continued, enabling a steady repayment of the foreign debt plus comfortable retained earnings that were used to pay for further expansions, and reducing the need for foreign loan capital still further. The high rate of POSCO's retained earnings, 27.2% in 1984, compared to 3.4% in the U.S. industry average and 7.8% in Japan, for example, was possible due to high net profits, low taxes, and an accelerated depreciation allowance.

The Pohang Works utilized an average of 53.4% foreign investment, compared to 29.3% and 27.6% for Kwangyang's first and second phases, respectively. Domestic finance of Kwangyang's first phase, estimated to be $1.37 billion out of a total investment cost of $1.96 billion, was covered entirely by POSCO retained earnings. For Kwangyang Phase I, POSCO also achieved a substantial saving of at least $200 million by encouraging Japanese and a European steel plant makers to engage in a fierce bidding war.[10] Competitive bidding has been a well-established policy of POSCO from its inception, saving millions of dollars and acquiring superior facilities.

The ability to finance its own expansion to a large degree, combined with a continuation of good loan terms from foreign investors for the successive expansions, is reflected in the company's net worth to total capital ratio, which was one of the highest in the business in 1988 at 31.9% compared to Nippon Steel's 17.7% and USX's 27.0%. An example of low-interest loans spread over a long payback period is a 6.95% loan to be repaid over 20 years from the Japanese Export-Import Bank for Kwangyang's first phase. As for the Pohang Works, the average interest rate for the $1.953 billion borrowed from foreign loans was only 7.5%. Low construction costs have contributed greatly to low liabilities. In contrast to other large government-assisted companies in Korea, POSCO has repaid all initial government loans.

Although POSCO was floated on the stock exchange in 1988, 20% is still owned by the Ministry of Finance and 15% by the Korea Development Bank, while the other 65% is publicly owned. There is also an employee stockownership plan to encourage employees to own shares. Currently 10% of the total shares are employee owned.

Reduced construction periods. A key factor to POSCO's success has been its ability to finance a large part of its own expansion by keeping construction costs remarkably low. This has been due in part to cheap labor costs, but more importantly to repeatedly short construction periods. By completing Kwangyang II over three months ahead of schedule, construction cost per ton of crude steel was reduced from an expected $723 to $473 (see Table 3). In addition, POSCO earned 36.6 billion won ($50 m) in extra sales. In 1985 the average unit construction cost per ton of crude steel at Pohang including Kwangyang Phase I was the lowest in the world at $474, while the world average unit construction cost at that time was $1,421.[11]

Whenever a construction delay occurred, an emergency decree would be issued to mobilize resources to meet the deadline. For example, when the foundation work of the first hot-strip mill at Pohang suffered a three-month delay, a presidential decree to pour concrete on a

TABLE 3 A Comparison of Construction Periods and Cost of Major Steelmakers

	Pohang 4th phase	Kwangyang 1st phase	Kwangyang 2nd phase	2nd phase Okishima, Japan	CST Brazil	2nd phase CSC, Taiwan	3rd phase CSC, Taiwan	PASMIC Pakistan
Construction period (months)	25	26	22	43	36	–	45	–
Production capacity (10 thou. tons/yr)	300	270	270	300	300	–	240	–
Unit construction cost per ton crude steel*	–	723	473	–	700	857	–	1,727

*Unit: U.S. $, 1988
Source: POSCO.

round-the-clock basis was issued. The order was carried out by mobilizing every available man, including office staff, and the project was back on schedule within two months. POSCO's first blast furnace was built in 33 months, compared to Italy's 50 months, France's 74 months, and India's 101 months for the construction of similar plants. The average cost of construction between the Pohang and Kwangyang works amounts to $422 per ton of crude steel, compared to works in other countries costing between $600 and $800 per ton of crude steel. The tradition of beating schedules has continued throughout the successive plant stages at POSCO: Pohang Phases I and II were completed four weeks ahead of schedule, Phase III 20 weeks ahead, and Phase IV ten months ahead of schedule. For all four phases combined, 17 months of construction time were saved.

The pressure for shortened construction periods did not preclude a drop in safety standards or quality. An example of T.J. Park's own intolerance of poor workmanship is the momentous occasion during the construction of Pohang Phase I; when foundation anchor-bolt holes were found to be out of line, he gathered all the site contractors and ceremoniously blasted the foundation with dynamite before dismissing the contractor responsible. "It made quite an impact," the chairman said.

How could such time and cost savings be made without lapses in quality? One answer is the dedication of the workers involved. Koreans have earned a reputation for their willingness to work long hours, and it was not unknown for emergency 24-hour construction to be implemented. As labor cost was still low in Korea, the extra income generated from early completion more than offset the additional cost of extensive overtime. The POSCO management also facilitated mergers of smaller construction companies to enhance their capability and acted as a go-between for technical cooperation with Japanese builders experienced in the construction of iron and steel plants.

Absorption of technology. Another explanation of the shortened construction periods is the rapid rate of technology absorption within Korea. This relates not only to the accumulation of experience among employees, but also to the ability to substitute foreign for domestic engineering products. Industrialization through learning and hard work has been the major theme running through Korea's economic development since the 1960s.[12] Although strong government initiative through economic planning and vibrant entrepreneurship in the private sector were other contributing factors to economic development, the overriding importance of the desire and ability to learn new technology cannot be overemphasized. In less than 20 years, POSCO transformed itself from a technology-importing into a technology-exporting corporation by means of rapid rates of technology absorption. Under the conditions of rapid growth in plant capacity, the POSCO management accumulated valuable experience in the purchase of foreign technical assistance, training, equipment purchase, plant design and construction, plant operation start-up, and feasibility studies.

TABLE 4   Indicators of Technology Inflows, Human Capital, and R & D for Five Semi-industrialized Economies

Item	Year or period	Argentina	Brazil	India	Korea	Mexico
Stock of direct foreign investment	1967	10.4	4.0	3.0	1.7	7.30
as a percentage of GDP	1977–79	4.7	6.4	2.1	3.2	5.60
Payments for disembodied technology	1970–71	–	0.2	–	0.0	–
as a percentage of GNP	1977–79	–	0.3	–	0.2	0.23
Imports of capital goods as a percent-	1965	5.3	4.6	10.3	13.0	14.5
age of all postsecondary students	1977–79	8.6	8.4	5.6	27.2	11.8
Postsecondary students abroad as a per-	1970	1.0	1.0	1.0	2.0	1.0
centage of all postsecondary students	1975–77	0.3	0.7	0.3	1.7	1.0
Secondary students as a percentage of	1965	–	–	29.0	29.0	17.0
secondary age population	1978	46.0	17.0	30.0	68.0	37.0
Postsecondary students as a percentage	1965	–	–	4.0	5.0	3.0
of eligible postsecondary age population	1978	18.0	10.0	9.0	9.0	9.0
Engineering students as a percentage of total postsecondary age population	1978	14.0	12.0	–	26.0	14.0
Scientists and engineers in thousands	late 1960s	12.8	5.6	1.9	6.9	6.6
per million of population	late 1970s	16.5	5.9	3.0	22.0	6.9
Scientists and engineers in R & D	1974	323	75	58	–	101
per million of population	1976	311	–	46	325	–
	1978	313	208	–	398	–
R & D expenditures as a percentage	1973	0.3	0.4	0.4	0.3	0.2
of GNP	1978	0.4	0.6	0.6	0.7	–

– Not available.
Source: Nathan Rosenberg and Claudio Frischtak, *International Transfer of Technology: Concepts, Measures and Comparisons* (Middlesex, 1985).

Learning skills. South Korea's high rate of students completing secondary and postsecondary education as well as students studying abroad compared to other semi-industrial economies from the late 1960s to 1970s was the basis for its high level of learning skills, as shown in Table 4.[13] In addition the table illustrates the marked growth in the numbers of scientists and engineers. By the late 1970s Korea had the highest percentage of scientists and engineers engaged in R & D and had spent proportionately more on R & D than comparable countries. Education has always played a very important role in Korean society, as a good education is a prerequisite to success. Fortunately for POSCO, due to a high level of unemployment at that time, a pool of highly educated engineers from the most prestigious universities in Korea were available for POSCO's first project, and they mostly remained at POSCO throughout their careers to form the core of a competent management team.

The apprenticeship pattern. Widespread use of apprenticeship, domestically and abroad, as a means to increase technical knowledge, contributed to the industrial development of Korea. Many Korean workers gained practical experience overseas, particularly in the field of construction, notably in the Middle East.

Domestically the typical pattern was for the first plant in an industry to be built with a high content of foreign equipment and expertise. Local contributions would be largely limited to assimilating as much production and investment capability as possible. During this time Korean engineers would principally act as observers. Usually the construction of a second and subsequent plants would follow quickly, with local engineers and technicians assuming a rapidly expanding role in project design and execution. This can be described as a form of import substitution.[14]

POSCO provides a prime example of use of "apprentice patterns." In 1968, two years before construction began, the first trainees, armed with a list of guidelines for the most beneficial utilization of their sojourn, were sent to gain experience in the Japanese steel industry. Training records were kept in diary form, the contents of which were later distributed to employees back in Korea. Emphasis was laid on the accumulation of practical experience and familiarization with machinery. T.J. Park's personal instruction to the prospective trainees was to acquire at least one more skill in addition to the individual objectives laid down in the guidelines.

During construction of the first phase at Pohang, the eventual plant

managers, operating engineers, and maintenance personnel were
required to participate in the building of their future plant to gain
familiarity with the facilities by working alongside contractors. The best
people were assigned to production, and prospective superintendents
headed construction at their respective plants and worked with their
eventual production team to forge relations and introduce plant experience to the group. Study groups on specific subjects were formed to
present weekly seminars. For example, in one week the PERT technique was disseminated through a study group led by an engineer who
was given a book on PERT and a few days to master the technique.
Some sleepless nights later, he gave a seminar on the topic to the top
managers.[15] As a result of these efforts, the time taken from start-up to
normal operations averaged only three months for Pohang, compared
to 6 to 12 months for the steel mills in developed countries. As a result
of these practices the domestic content in equipment and expertise
grew rapidly. In 1973 Pohang Phase I was completed with a 1 mmtpy
capacity. By 1981, capacity had risen to 8.5 mmtpy, following three
expansion phases and increasingly under South Korean direction. The
progressive substitution of foreign for locally manufactured plant facilities in successive plant operations is shown in Table 5.

TABLE 5 Local Content in Phases of POSCO Works (%)

			Local content
Pohang	Phase I		12.5
	Phase II		15.5
	Phase III		22.6
	Phase IV		33.1
Kwangyang	Phase I		49.4
	Phase II		55.4
	Phase III	(est.)	61.3

Source: POSCO.

Regarding construction work and the planning of facilities, in Phase
I POSCO relied entirely on Japanese contractors under the overall
direction of a group of consultants called the Japan Group, consisting
mainly of Nippon Steel personnel, but by Phase III only the master
engineering tasks were performed by foreign contractors and by Phase
IV all works were performed without foreign assistance. To aid the
learning process all previous blueprints of facilities were preserved and

a center for technology and facilities established. Also, the system of "Great Master of Technique" was instituted in 1978 honoring workers for outstanding achievements and technical mastery.

During the construction of the Kwangyang Works, foreign suppliers formed a consortium with local suppliers, thus allowing local suppliers close access to the most up-to-date technologies in a small number of advanced steel-producing nations. Especially noteworthy is the fact that the local suppliers were named as lead contractors, which meant that foreign suppliers acted as cooperating contractors. This undoubtedly contributed to the development of domestic engineering know-how.

2. Lastest technologies
The first stage of POSCO's works was started in 1970. The fourth and final stage of the company's second works will start construction in 1991. This makes POSCO one of the most modern and technologically advanced integrated steel companies of the world. The average age of major facilities at POSCO is only 6.1 years, compared to 17.8 years at major integrated steel mills in Japan.

Both works were designed and conceived to make most beneficial use of contemporary technological advances and cost efficiencies. In addition, capacity utilization rates are higher than Japan. POSCO achieved a total crude steel production of 100 mmt in just 15.7 years after the start of operations in 1973. Today the rate of continuous casting at POSCO is 95.5% at Pohang and 100% at Kwangyang. Kwangyang's 100% continuous casting, all-coke blast furnace, and high degree of automation will enable a production recovery rate of 98%, compared to 94.37% achieved by Ōita works in 1982.

Latest technology means high automation, reducing the manpower needed to work production lines. Korean wages are still low compared to advanced nations, but recent wage increases are raising problems for future competitiveness.

3. Plant location and layout
Thanks to governmental appreciation of the importance of steel in the advance of the Korean economy, the company was able to purchase large tracts of coastal land for the site of their works. At both Pohang and Kwangyang the government has provided the necessary domestic infrastructure to facilitate rapid access to domestic markets. Korea's lack of indigenous raw materials means virtually all raw materials arrive by sea; coastal locations allow easy transfer of raw material and finished products from and to ships, providing savings on transport costs.

The layouts of the works are designed to facilitate the swift progression of materials through the various manufacturing stages with minimum handling. Pohang Works is designed around the dock in a semicircle, with raw materials unloading and ironmaking facilities to the west, and steelmaking and rolling facilities to the east. At Kwangyang the layout of facilities is designed for express prduoction of a limited product range. The facilities from blast furnace to rolling mill are built in a line receiving raw materials at one end and releasing finished products at the other, ready for loading on domestically bound trucks or export ships and reducing production time considerably.

Furthermore, Kwangyang and Pohang both benefit from the many economies of scale available to multi-million ton producing works, from raw material handling to final distribution. Both works have their own deep-water marine terminals able to accommodate the largest seafaring vessels. Kwangyang works is built on 2,346 acres of reclaimed land and its harbor has a CTS capacity of 250,000 tons.

4. Economical and stable sources of raw materials

In a country with an almost total lack of the raw materials required to produce steel, a steelmaker's main concern has to be to secure a long-term, steady supply of raw materials on favorable terms. From the beginning, POSCO's management obtained authority from the government to secure equipment and raw materials without outside interference or influences, an important victory in view of the rampant influence-peddling practices at that time.[16] With only the pictures of a barren field, the prospective site of the plant, the president of POSCO began negotiations with Broken Hill Proprietary Co. (BHP) of Australia for raw material supply. Despite BHP's skepticism regarding the project, due to their past disappointments in negotiations over other developing countries' steel mills, agreement was reached, due in large part to the diplomatic skills of T.J. Park and his promise to the Australians that POSCO would pay BHP regardless of whether its facilities were ready by the target date. With the benefit of good working relations with of Australia, POSCO secured its first contract for Australian iron ore. Once production was underway and POSCO had established itself as a responsible trading partner, contracts with suppliers were easier to procure.

Coking coal is now imported from three main countries: Australia, Canada, and the United States. Large amounts of iron ore are supplied by India, Brazil, and Peru. In order to secure long-term supplies of coal, POSCO has also entered a couple of joint ventures in Canada and

Australia. POSCO is now joint owner of the Mt. Thorley Coal Mine, Australia, and the Greenhills Coal Mine, Canada. Raw materials are bought from various sources in order to minimize the possible adverse effects of dependence on a single source as regards political intervention, currency exchange rates, etc. Suppliers are contacted through POSCO offices situated around the world.

5. Human resources management
Leadership, organizational flexibility, and management techniques. T.J. Park's three management rules in the early years of POSCO were: thorough preparation, confirmation of results, and dynamic response to environmental changes. Thus a policy of flexibility to respond dynamically to environmental changes was instilled in the company from the outset. Continuous growth and changing environments have brought about continuous organizational changes, averaging three to four per year during the early stages.[17] From the start extensive use was made of management techniques for strategic planning, budget and control, management by objectives, etc. Concentrated efforts beginning in 1975 were made to computerize the production and business systems and POSCO became the first corporation in Korea to introduce local area network (LAN) and value-added network (VAN) systems. Also an extensive committee system was used to coordinate and control construction activities. Scheduling was operated using the program evaluation and review technique (PERT) system and monthly progress meetings were introduced involving staff from general managers to president. Although the meetings were task oriented and the atmosphere tense, provoking fear in everyone, the monthly construction meetings have since become the present monthly management meeting—a central forum for the dissemination of ideas and monitoring of company progress as well as discussion on the state of the world markets and industry. Nowadays, television links between Pohang, Kwangyang, and Seoul for the thrice weekly directors' meeting facilitates attendance and communication.

Labor-management relations. During the start-up years, one of POSCO's few advantages was an abundance of cheap labor with military training and discipline. The cost of labor is rising, but is still low compared to advanced industrialized nations. Over the past few years labor costs as a percentage of Japanese labor costs have risen from 32% in 1986, to 37.2% in 1987, and 45% in 1988.

POSCO employs dedicated and committed workers who recognize

and contribute to company goals and objectives. Top management acts as role models for the rest of the company to follow as regards their morale and work attitudes. POSCO molds its employees by the use of rigorous selection and training procedures, combined with an emphasis on informal socializing and the enforcement of a strong community spirit throughout the corporation. Top management takes keen interest in POSCO community events. Likewise good working conditions and an atmosphere conducive to full commitment by all employees are fostered.

To ensure the appointment of experienced personnel to top-ranking positions, POSCO has a policy of internal promotions. In this way the company can draw upon proven expertise within the corporate body. Although such a policy increases the morale of employees who recognize the real possibility of advancement within the company, it may be criticized as a form of inbreeding. Yet, given the track record of other government-funded corporations in Korea employing total outsiders without relevant industrial experience to top-ranking positions, such as former members of parliament or other influential persons, POSCO's internal promotion policy is a practical one to keep the company free from external and political influences. In 1987 it was reported that only 2% of top management positions in other government-funded firms were filled with internally promoted staff members

Labor-management relations are generally favorable but at present are going through a new learning period due to the formation of the labor union in 1988. There have been no strikes at the company, although other manufacturing companies in Korea have been seriously affected by employee action.

Worker participation. At the works level, quality circles have been initiated by operating personnel. Over 60,000 suggestions for improvement were made in 1988, an average of 3.4 per employee, involving over 1,300 quality circle groups. Despite the large number of suggestions, this is substantially lower than suggestions by Japanese steel employees, which average an annual 6.7 per employee (1985).

Fulfillment of corporate social responsibility. Although steel is notably a capital- rather than labor-intensive industry, POSCO provides for all the welfare needs of its 22,000 employees. To do this it has built excellent facilities, and employee wages are kept higher than the national average in manufacturing.

There are many reasons for emphasizing employee welfare in company policy, one of which is quite simply that with a quarter of the country's population living in Seoul, the best potential employees need coaxing to move five hours southeast by bus. However, POSCO is also striving to create an ideal industrial system, not only by offering its workers respectable wages but also by creating a complete social welfare system, offering quality housing at reduced rates and free schooling for employees' children at its own excellent schools. At the Pohang Works two housing communities have been established, one providing dorms for single workers in a landscaped area near the works, the other a few kilometers away on an extensive area, providing housing, shopping, cultural, educational, and recreational facilities. There is a POSCO wives' center which arranges both community and educational activities organized for and by employees' wives. Other similar facilities exist at Kwangyang. These have all contributed to the relative stability in labor-management relations.

Employee training. The company founders were acutely aware of the problem of lack of skilled expertise in Korea. To a great extent this is still a weakness. Comparing the number of years experience between Japan's big five steelmakers and POSCO in 1988, Japan shows 20.7 years compared to POSCO's 7.4 years. To overcome this disadvantage and to ensure the eventual long-term supply of trained employees, several strategies were used. Japanese training programs and "apprenticeship patterns" have already been mentioned. In addition to these POSCO founded its own technical high school in which the main core curriculum was designed to train the students to go straight into jobs at the company. It also founded a training institute, "Yonsuwon," which runs extensive management, technical, and language courses. All new employees attend induction courses which cater to various levels of previous training. The institute also provides refresher courses, computer courses, and spiritual training. The language section offers English, Japanese, and Chinese, including 15-week intensive courses for selected employees. In 1984, 9,924 workers out of 23,700 received training in one form or another.

A limited number of employees are selected to go overseas for long study periods financed by the company. Even before the operations of the first phase had begun, 598 POSCO personnel had received training in Japan and Austria. By 1983, 1,850 engineers and technicians had been sent abroad for training, including on-the-job experience, and to earn master's and doctorates. For the management, MBAs and experience with international steel consultants have also been sponsored.

Preservation of the environment. Aware of the environmental damage caused by other large steel companies, POSCO has installed pollution control equipment amounting to 9.4% of total capital investment. At Kwangyang the company invested 14.1% ($400 million) of total capital expenditure on antipollution devices, which compares favorably to the 2% to 5% of total investment allocated to pollution control by other Korean corporations. Pohang alone operates 431 pollution control facilities with an annual operating expense of $60 million. Kwangyang operates 400 facilities with an annual operating cost of over $50 million.

V. Future Outlook

To summarize, this paper has so far described the phenomenon of the "accumulation of expertise" within Korea since the start of the economic development plans' industrial expansion policy. It explains the contribution of a combination of learning ability and strategic policies such as the "apprenticeship pattern," as well as the encouragement within the company to absorb knowledge by schemes such as "Great Master of Technique" introduced in 1978. Also discussed are the competitive advantages of shortened construction periods, new technology, plant design, layout and location, and economical raw material sources. Other competitive advantages identified are: human resources and management techniques, labor-management relations, quality circles, welfare programs, in-house training, and T.J. Park's personal contribution to POSCO's development. This final section describes how POSCO must prepare itself for the next century considering the expected steel demand peak around the year 2000 and the need to diversify. It describes the company's diversification moves so far and explains the roles of the Research Institute of Industrial Science and Technology (RIST) and the Pohang Institute of Science and Technology (POSTECH).

1. Strategy for the future

According to Chandler, diversification is a defining characteristic of the modern industrial corporation, and POSCO is no exception.[18] POSCO began to diversify vertically through backward integration in its early years. Now that it is a public company, POSCO must strive to satisfy stockholders' needs by establishing a long-term growth strategy using more aggressive horizontal diversifications into other industries. As the future demand for steel in Korea will peak sometime in the years 2000–2003, POSCO is actively seeking new products and services to diversify into. Most major mills in the advanced industrial nations have pursued diversification strategies with varying degrees of success. NSC's goal is one of the most ambitious as it seeks to increase the non-steel share of total sales to 50% by 1995. USX provides another example of aggressive diversification strategies in the steel industry.

In the case of POSCO, the primary thrust so far has been in the direction of the information/communications industry and a chemical company which uses POSCO by-products as its raw materials. A major problem facing POSCO in its diversification efforts is the oligopolistic predominance of the *chaebul* conglomerates in all of the major indus-tries, making entry into any attractive industry very difficult.[19] POSCO's diversification moves are closely watched by the *chaebul* groups wishing to protect their "territories" by means of active lobby-ing. The government's 35% ownership of POSCO inhibits it from assisting diversification efforts. Hoping to appear neutral, the govern-ment seems overly cautious whenever POSCO attempts to enter an oligopolistic industry. A recent example is its decision not to allow POSCO's entry into the automobile industry.

For these reasons, POSCO's diversification efforts in the last two years have so far yielded very limited results. In the long run, however, the company is pinning great hopes on the two science and technology establishments it founded in 1987: a research institute (RIST), and a small university (POSTECH). With the creation of these two institutes, POSCO has formed what it calls a "tripartite system" integrating research, university, and industry in three quasi-autonomous entities. The system is designed to encourage interchange between the separate organizations whether in the form of shared personnel or exchange of information and research material. POSCO provides the main source of funding, but officially both university and research institute may carry out research for external clients. In practice, however, POSCO plays a large part in deciding which projects will be undertaken. The research institute conducts applied research for the steel industry; it also acts as a testing and training ground for possible areas of future diversification. The university provides basic research and a source of highly educated and specialized scientists.

RIST grew from the company's original technical laboratories, opened in 1977, which conducted research directly related to the steel industry. But it is a more flexible organization than the original labora-tories. Ostensibly autonomous, its research fields range from eco-nomics and management strategy to biomedical engineering, mecha-tronics, and new materials. There are four major divisions, over 20 research departments, and nearly 400 full-time researchers. The new materials and science and engineering divisions at RIST will, POSCO hopes, provide a source for future diversification. Some of the major research projects are superconductors, parallel computing systems, robotics, carbon fibers, C1 chemistry, and new ceramics.

POSTECH is a research-oriented institution of higher education, a rarity in Korea. The number of students is small and select. Numbers currently stand at 1,014 including 243 graduate students. Entrants must pass a strict entrance examination and interview, thus allowing in only excellent students. So that good students are not hampered by heavy fees, all students are eligible for scholarships. At the moment all students benefit in some way from reduced rates and free housing; however, in the future it is expected scholarships will be more rigorously tested.

In most Korean universities, the ratio of students to teachers means teaching takes an overriding amount of professors' time. At POSTECH, the student/professor ratio is low at approximately 7:1 (5:1 undergraduate, 1:1 graduate students) to allow more time to be devoted to individual research. POSTECH has recently initiated the Basic Science Research Center, which coordinates basic research projects both within the university and for external organizations. A major project currently being carried out at the university is the Pohang Light Source project, scheduled to be in operation by 1994. Expertise is also coordinated with RIST so that professors may be adjunct researchers for certain projects and RIST researchers may by invited as adjunct professors for certain university courses.

Such extensive training and research facilities require substantial investment. POSCO's investment in R & D as a percentage of total sales totalled 1.6% in 1988 ($83.7 million), and is projected at 1.6% in 1990 ($110.4 million) and 2.0% in 1992 ($165.5 million), compared to Nippon Steel's 1986 R & D investment of 2.2% of total sales, and a mere 0.55% of total sales at British Steel (BSC). According to International Iron and Steel Institute figures for R & D investment as a percentage of total sales for 1986, while POSCO spent a greater percentage than Armco and BSC, its 1.3% lagged behind Nippon Steel (2.2%) and Kobe (3.3%). It is apparent that to beat foreign competition, still more must be invested in R & D. The number of research patents is also a cause for concern. In 1988 Japan's patent applications surpassed POSCO by an average of 86 to 5.7 per 1,000 employees. POSCO also sponsors research activities in several universities throughout the world. Massachusetts Institute of Technology and Carnegie

Mellon in the United States, and Sheffield University of the United Kingdom all have professorial chairs sponsored by POSCO.

Another major strategy to be pursued by POSCO is to increase the share of downstream, higher value-added products to total sales. The Korean steel industry has recently launched its "Steel for the 21st Century" campaign, which emphasizes the development of higher value-added steel products. POSCO is far behind the major Japanese mills in developing higher value-added products, although it is slightly ahead in iron and steel making. The major challenge facing POSCO is to mobilize its R & D resources in RIST to develop downstream products and to launch serious research efforts in radically new iron and steelmaking technologies. RIST's Iron & Steel Making Technology Division is involved in all of these.

In order to become a multi-business corporation, POSCO also needs to change its organizational structure to allow more dynamism and flexibility. For this reason, POSCO's top management has recently undertaken a major project to instill a sense of autonomy among its top managers. This project will involve management audit and structural change, as well as a redistribution of authority and responsibility among the upper ranks of the organization. If carried out successfully, this should improve POSCO's international competitiveness.

2. Future Threats to POSCO

The relatively new facilities at POSCO will make it more difficult for the company to adopt revolutionary new technologies, such as direct steelmaking, compared to Japan, where facilities will be due for modernization by the late 1990s. Furthermore, the relative scarcity of high-quality scrap iron in Korea may retard the application of new technologies such as thin slab and strip casting. Another distinctly threatening challenge is the pooling of resources in research and development in the United States and Japan by means of multi-company research consortia, while POSCO stands as a lone integrated company with limited resources and research manpower.

Yet another strategic threat to POSCO's international competitiveness is the continuing effort by Japanese integrated steelmakers to rationalize their production and management systems. They have eliminated excess production capacities and have reduced manpower accordingly. They have improved their financial positions by raising stockholders' equity. Their pricing policy has changed from marginal cost pricing to average cost pricing, while their corporate headquarters' staff have been reduced and the concept of the strategic business unit introduced. All these, together with the continuing infusion of resources into R & D, will make Japanese steel producers the most competitive in the years to come in world markets of high value-added products. Perhaps the most threatening to POSCO is the leadership vacuum that will occur when T.J. Park retires. Needless to say, succession problems after the departure of a leader who has wielded such influence over a prolonged period of time will be grave indeed.

NOTES

Unless otherwise noted, data for this paper are taken from POSCO internal sources and cassette tapes on the history of POSCO, consisting of the narrations and recollections of former and present POSCO officials.

1.   The Korean government provided POSCO with the following during the initial phase: long-term low-interest foreign capital, discounted user rates for many government services such as a 40% railroad discount, postal rate of 50%, etc., and $42 million for its supporting facilities. Korea Advanced Institute of Science and Technology, *Technological Behavior of the Petrochemical, Metallurgical and Electronics Industries in Korea* (Seoul, 1976).

2.   A noteworthy fact in terms of the future development of POSCO is that these four companies, especially the Inchon Iron & Steel Co., were the source of trained managers for POSCO in its early years.

3.   Korea Advanced Institute of Science and Technology, *A Study of the Long-Term Forecasting of the Steel Demand in Korea* (Seoul, 1988).

4.   Leroy P. Jones and Sakong Il, *Government, Business, and Entrepreneurship in Economic Development: The Korean Case* (Cambridge, Mass., 1980).

5.   An interesting postscript to the above is the meeting in London in 1989 during an award ceremony banquet in honor of T.J. Park, between Park and Mr. Jaffe, a World Bank economist who conducted the feasibility study which concluded that an integrated steel company in Korea would never succeed. Jaffe was asked if he would admit he was wrong in hindsight given the current success of POSCO. Jaffe replied that he would not and furthermore that he would still have come to the same conclusion today without taking Park into consideration. In other words, what Jaffe, a 30-year veteran of the steel industries in developing countries, pointed out was that Park was the critical difference in POSCO's success.

6.   Thomas J. Peters and Robert H. Waterman, Jr., *In Search of Excellence* (New York, 1982).

7.   Taejun Park, *A New Species of Separated Family* (in Korean) (Pohang, 1987).

8.   Social Science Research Center, Seoul National University, *A Study of POSCO's Corporate Culture and Its Contribution to the Korean Economy* (in Korean) (Seoul, 1987).

9.   See, for example, Alice H. Amsden, *Asia's Next Giant, South Korea and Late Industrialization* (New York, 1989); Donald F. Barnett and R.W. Crandall,

Up From the Ashes (Washington, 1986); Peter F. Marcus, *POSCO: Korea's Emerging Steel Giant* (New York, 1985).

10. Marcus, op. cit., pp. 1–6.

11. Social Science Research Center, Seoul National University, op. cit., p. 261.

12. For a detailed account of Korea's industrialization through learning, see Amsden, op. cit.

13. Larry E. Westphal, Linsu Kim, and Carl J. Dahlman, "Reflections on the Republic of Korea's Acquisition of Technological Capability," in *International Transfer of Technology: Concepts, Measures and Comparisons*, Nathan Rosenberg and Claudio Frischtak, eds. (Middlesex, 1985), pp. 167–221.

14. Ibid.

15. Appendix to *Ten-Year History of POSCO* (in Korean) (Pohang, 1979), p. 255.

16. Ibid., pp. 213–14.

17. Ibid., pp. 579–80.

18. Alfred P. Chandler, Jr., *The Visible Hand: The Managerial Revolution in American Business* (Cambridge, Mass., 1977).

19. *Chaebul* refers to the major Korean business groups similar to the Japanese zaibatsu.

Comment

Masaru Yoshimori

The paper gives a comprehensive overview of the various factors that contributed to the successful development and management of POSCO, Korea's largest and the world's fifth largest steel company, which employs 22,000 persons and accounts for around 80% of Korea's domestic production.

The author attributes this accomplishment first to the entrepreneurship of the current chief executive officer (CEO) and second to various technical factors: construction cost reductions (which in turn were made possible by low-cost capital and reduced construction periods), a rapid assimilation of the latest technology, coastal plant locations, and the development of economical and stable sources of raw materials in Australia and other supplier nations. Non-technical factors such as human resource management and respect for corporate social responsibility are also given credit. The paper concludes with some future challenges facing the company, i.e., difficulties facing diversification efforts and the sophistication of R & D capabilities, and above all, the impending leadership vacuum.

When discussing the value of this article as a business history paper, three limitations, all beyond the author's control, must be borne in mind. One is that the company in question has been in existence only for about 20 years. The history of POSCO is still in the making, the founder entrepreneur is still incumbent, and therefore it might be premature to draw any conclusions as to the factors involved in the success of POSCO. A second, more serious, limitation is the fact that the author is an executive of one of the affiliates of POSCO. To what extent he has been in the position to present POSCO's history and the key factors of its success from an objective and independent perspective is a moot question.

Thirdly, POSCO is no exception to nearly all large integrated steel firms in the world who receive assistance from and are subject to interventions by their governments. This distorts their financial picture considerably, rendering it difficult to evaluate POSCO's business performance as a private business entity, as well as the entrepreneurial qualities of POSCO's CEO.

As in any large start-up enterprise, capital, labor, technology, and entrepreneurship were essential ingredients for the POSCO project. Government initiative and backing should also be added as vital elements in the specific case of POSCO. The writer covers all of these, but perhaps he should have given an in-depth treatment to one or two of these aspects, as there seem to be quite a few crucial questions which remain unanswered. To the author of this comment, capital and technology seem to be the determinant factors of this project, as without these it would have never got off the ground even with the best available labor and entrepreneurship. And the required capital and technology were not available in South Korea 30 years ago.

From this perspective, it may be asked why Japanese steel firms, already major forces in the international steel industry, were not members of the international consortium KISA. What was the reaction of the Japanese steel industry when T.J. Park approached them for their support after KISA was disbanded? Why did they agree to extend their cooperation to POSCO? The author writes that Park persuaded the Japanese steel industry leaders to render assistance to the project. But was it solely due to his "persuasion"? Is it not possible that diplomatic and political forces played a role? Why did POSCO not approach Japanese industry right from the outset, without forming KISA, given Park's close ties with the Japanese steel industry managers? How does POSCO evaluate Japanese assistance in capital and technology? These questions seem to be not only interesting but also important if we are to put the role of entrepreneurship and the first Korea-Japan industrial cooperation in their just and proper perspectives.

The paper looks at POSCO's past from the viewpoints of entrepreneurship and corporate strategy. While the contribution of entrepreneurship is certainly vital to the success of an industrial project of this size, it is also true that the Korean government played an equally instrumental role in initiating, financing, appointing the CEO, and formulating and implementing various measures (pricing policy, investment in infrastructure, etc.) to facilitate POSCO's start-up, takeoff, and development. Indeed, the government's decision to appoint Park as CEO was a crucial factor to the successful materialization of the project.

A question may arise as to the comparability of POSCO's financial performance with steelmakers of other countries that are private and do not benefit from direct financial and fiscal subsidies from the government. The paper would have been more convincing in its lauding of POSCO's "success" if it had been accompanied with financial statements adjusted for such government assistance. This is because the entire paper is premised on the financial "success" of POSCO. For this reason it is essential that its financial and fiscal relations with the government be clarified so that the degree of success is reduced to its proper proportion, and so that POSCO's entrepreneurship can be more objectively assessed.

The iron and steel industry in most countries has been subjected to various forms of government initiatives, pressures, and interventions, ranging from the fixing of prices and production quotas to employment policy. This is not surprising given the political and economic weight of this industry, particularly for the ruling party and the state bureaucracy that executes national policy decisions. Even in a liberal nation such as the United States the iron and steel industry has not been free from direct interventions from the White House, as illustrated in the tension between John F. Kennedy and U.S. Steel in the sixties.[1] Excessive government involvement led to a collapse of the French steel industry in 1978.[2]

The paper does not give a detailed account of the relationship between POSCO and the government. If the project has been as successful as the author claims, then one would suppose that the management had sufficient autonomy to run the firm without undue intervention from the government. Was this possible when 35% of POSCO was owned by the government? Was there never any attempt on the part of the ruling party or the bureaucracy to influence critical decisions such as production volume, price levels, etc., out of political considerations, as has happened in the United States, in France, and to a limited extent in Japan? Was there no inclination for the administration to parachute some of their retiring civil servants into POSCO?

The author indicates that promotion from within to top management positions was practiced at POSCO, unlike in other corporations with government equity participation, where 98% of the top executives are politicians and high-ranking bureaucrats. Is it because POSCO has been so profitable that the government had no pretexts with which to intervene? One other aspect relates to the price leader position of POSCO. Historical evidence shows that a monopolistic and an oligopolistic structure gives rise to an X-inefficiency, i.e., excessive organizational slack and waste of direct and indirect costs due to lax management attitudes under strong market power. How was POSCO successful in fending off such dysfunctions?

Clearly, a construction project of this scale can only be accomplished successfully by an entrepreneur with risk-taking and innovative capabilities, while "taking responsibility for and making judgmental decisions that affect the location, the form, and the use of goods, resources or institutions."[3] This is also illustrated by some historical cases. The decision taken in 1950 by Nishiyama, then president of Japan's Kawasaki Steel, to build a large integrated steel plant in Chiba despite postwar confusion and uncertainties is a well-known case of entrepreneurship in Japan.[4] Or the foresight and decision of Overbeck, CEO of Germany's Mannesmann AG, to divest of its steelmaking capacity as early as in the first half of the sixties and to diversify into non-steel domains (hydraulics, instrumentation, and data processing) is another. Above all, an entrepreneur must have "the courage of his/her convictions and face the consequences of his/her actions, whether they produce profits or losses."[5] Entrepreneurship in this sense seems to be crucial in the particular case of POSCO as well as in many other large projects.

One acid test of POSCO's entrepreneurship is whether and to what extent POSCO has succeeded in going beyond the borrowed technologies and in assuring its technological supremacy by international standards. It is relatively easy to adopt a technology that is already proven elsewhere, as much less technological risk is involved. The ultimate challenge for POSCO's management is then to realize technological breakthroughs and to venture into their commercialization. The degree of risk in this case is much higher and related decisions would provide a true test of entrepreneurship.

The iron and steel industry, because of its basic and strategic nature, is closely bound up with national interest, national economic and industrial policy, and national prestige. It is a special kind of industry and one manifestation of this particularity is a strong sense of mission to the nation shared by management of all echelons as well as by the rank and file. This is especially the case with developing nations, or even with developed nations suffering from competitive problems. It is conceivable, therefore, that nationalism was a driving force behind the success of POSCO's undertakings. Indeed, POSCO's initial objective was, according to the author, to "set itself up as a catalyst to the industrialization of Korea," and "to serve the nation through iron and steel" was the motto throughout POSCO's history. The author, however, does not dwell on the motivation provided by Korean nationalism in the successful completion of construction projects, most of the time far ahead of schedule. Was it not true that at POSCO the fieldworkers, engineers, office clerks, not to mention managers were imbued with a sense of national purpose? Otherwise how can the dedication of the workers be secured, which the author says made possible time and cost savings in the construction process without sacrifice in quality? The mere diligence of Korean workers, which the author seems to indicate as an explanation, does not seem too convincing.

All in all, though, the paper is valuable in that it conveys a total picture of the technical, human, and institutional forces that led up to one of the most important industrial achievements of modern Korea, and is a significant contribution to policy formulations for the developing nations.

NOTES

1.   See, for instance, John Strohmeyer, *Crisis in Bethlehem* (London, 1986).
2.   For example, Christian Stoffaës, "Le dysfonctionnement du système acier," *Revue d'économie industrielle*, no. 8, 2e trimestre (1979).
3.   Robert F. Hébert and Albert N. Link, *The Entrepreneur* (Middlesex, 1988), p. 155.
4.   Seiichiro Yonekura, "Entrepreneurship and Innovative Behavior of Kawasaki Steel," Discussion Paper 120, Hitotsubashi University.
5.   Hébert and Link, op. cit.

Concluding Remarks

Yoshitaka Suzuki and Etsuo Abe

I. Latecomers and Early Starters

The papers presented at the conference focused on the development of the steel industry during two periods, the late 19th century and the post–World War II period. At the concluding discussion, the following questions were raised concerning patterns evident during both periods. First, why and how did the latecomers of both periods attain their competitive power, and second, what was the performance of the early starters of both periods?

In the steel industry, the latecomers of both periods were situated in more favorable positions than the early starters because they could not only make use of the most modern technology with less overhead costs, but also were relatively free from the historical legacies or institutional constraints by which the early starters were much more strongly bound. Some of the latecomers were successful in making use of these advantages and established competitive positions, while many others were not. Cases which were successful in "catching up" were studied, but little is known about those that failed. The successful latecomers seem to have factors in common, and comparison of the entrepreneurial, institutional, and managerial factors of the sample countries was instructive.

Among the entrepreneurial factors, technological innovations, which were considered irrational by many contemporaries, were emphasized in the postwar Japanese and Korean steel industries. How about the latecomers in the earlier period? In addition to the entrepreneurs' attitudes toward new technology, their attitudes toward business goals were important, because even among successful latecomers there seem to have been different goals.

Among the various institutional factors examined was, first, technological diffusion, which has bridged the ever-widening gap between the latecomers and the established industries. A systematic approach was

299

necessary and complementary efforts, such as the training of technical staff, were important. Second, there was the stable and low-cost supply of raw materials, always a crucial factor for industries fabricating basic materials. Steel firms have tried to solve this uncertainty in various ways. How did this favorably effect the latecomers of the earlier period, such as America, France, and Germany, and what were the differences between these countries and the latecomers of the present day which lacked such conditions? Third, there were the product markets in which, among the latecomers, two patterns can be distinguished: one catching up by import substituton, and the other by export-oriented catching up. The former is noticeable in the United States, Germany, and prewar Japan, where the import substitution in the rail markets first took place, followed by expansion into other markets, such as heavy engineering and automobiles. In the case of the export-oriented catching up, it is necessary to understand why such a method was possible. Fourth is the supply of capital in this capital-intensive industry. Capital requirements for latecomers were too large to be met by individual firms, but all the latecomers overcame financial scarcities. Much emphasis has been placed on the role of the banks and the governments, but it seems necessary to re-examine such explanations. Finally, as to the role of government, too much protection by means of tariffs, subsidies, tax reduction, and state-owned factories could injure the latecomers' competitive power. The question remains of why such protection did not reduce the competitive power of German and prewar Japanese steel industries?

Managerial factors also have been important for sustained growth of the latecomers, particularly in implementing institutional factors. In the steel industry, in which the number of plants is relatively few and the production lines narrow, the management of the workshop as well as the logistics are more important than the higher levels of management organizations. It is thus necessary to pay attention to the rationalization initiated by engineers and lower-level managers.

Yoshitaka Suzuki's introductory chapter began with the "mature hypothesis" according to which the steel industry of the early starters was destined to be caught up by a rival company, particularly in an industry with relatively low levels of technological and product differentiations. The early starters had to continue their production with higher overhead costs and with historical legacies. But the story was not so simple, partly because the latecomers did not always adopt the best practices. Here again, entrepreneurial and institutional factors should be examined.

In considering entrepreneurial factors, it should be noted that business goals among entrepreneurs varied by country or period. For instance, it may be quite rational and profitable for some to use equipment which terminated depreciation, but this could have delayed the introduction of new technology. Changing attitudes among entrepreneurs, as Paul Paskoff pointed out, from scrap-and-build to return on investment (ROI) consciousness might have influenced the competitiveness of one country's steel industry.

By the same token, the extent to which the historical legacies for the early starters, such as the rigidity of labor practices and the supply of raw materials, were overcome needs further study.

Factors such as the continuous technological and organizational innovation by early starters might have kept them in competition with the latecomers. Nevertheless, some of the aspects of the "mature hypothesis" cannot be denied. Every steel firm in the advanced steel countries will be overcome by a latecomer. It is the business goal that determines the strategy of these earlier firms. However, the quality and the kinds of managerial resources which the steel firms accumulated are also important for the growth of the firms.

What kind of managerial resources are most needed for the steel firms when they have to shift their markets to high value-added products? It is plausible that the skills of workers and engineers, namely managerial resources based on human resources, relate most to this kind of development.

Steel firms are able to make use of their internal flow of goods for further development: U.S. Steel, as pointed out by Paul Tiffany, raised profits in upstream mining, while some British steel firms made use of their outlets for their new field of activities, and more recently, Japanese firms sell by-products such as carbon textiles and chemical products. Finally, as mentioned by Seiichiro Yonekura, steel firms can develop into unrelated areas, and this is closely related to the availability of financial resources. Tiffany emphasized the scarcity of financial resources of American steel firms even in their mature stage, which suggests few prospects for their diversification.

II. Entrepreneurial, Institutional, and Managerial Factors

Among the problems of the catching-up countries, the entrepreneurial, institutional, and managerial factors were discussed. At first, concerning the entrepreneurial factors, Paskoff saw entrepreneurship as important in the development of the U.S. iron and steel industry, but other factors such as the size of the U.S. market, geographical isolation from the technologically advanced European countries, and abundant raw materials were more important. It was basically true that natural resources and geographical advantage were crucial in the 19th century because the transportation system was relatively undeveloped. However, in time the transportation system improved, and geographical isolation and abundance of natural resources no longer were advantageous factors. Some specialists in the Japanese steel trade paradoxically believe, on the contrary, that having no raw materials gives strength or comparative advantage to a country's steel industry. Japan succeeded because it had nothing in raw materials. Materials can be imported from almost anywhere in the world, as in Japan's and Korea's cases, as long as free trade is maintained and the country has good sea ports. Accordingly, the importance of entrepreneurship that would opt for the best materials increased, especially after World War II.

Rainer Fremdling stressed farsightedness in entrepreneurship in the German steel industry in the adoption of new technology in the second half of the 19th century. French steelmasters, according to Eric Bussière, introduced the British model as well as the German, but in several fields they made some mistakes. For instance, in the investment in production of rails, and the pace of adoption of the Thomas process because adoption was slower than in Germany.

Tetsuji Okazaki pointed out that at the early stage the Japanese iron and steel industry enjoyed a comparatively advantageous cost structure, which means low wages and low cost of such materials as coal. The Japanese steelmasters thus did not have to introduce the state-of-the-art process, and their risk-taking was relatively small. Yet some extent of introducing new, modern Western technology was needed, and therefore somebody had to take some risks. In Japan, the engineers did. In introducing modern technology in Japan, the engineers' initiatives were significant. Fortunately, they were not merely technology oriented but also profit conscious. The financial requirements of such engineers were met by zaibatsu and iron merchants. The general theory by Alexander Gerschenkron regarding the late-starters of industrialization explains that as the late-starters can use the newest method with larger sized equipment, they have an advantageous cost structure but also must face technological difficulties. In the mid-tech industry, such as the steel industry, however, steelmasters did not necessarily have to adopt the most modern process if there were other conditions, such as cheap raw materials, to counteract. Okazaki argued that this situation in Japan was able to alleviate the technological difficulties which the steel industry was confronted with. Yonekura emphasized the pivotal role of entrepreneurship in the post–World War II period of Japan, although the external factors were important. According to Sung-il Juhn, despite the severe control over private economic activity during the Japanese occupation of Korea, the small steel industry burgeoned during that era, and the occupation regime provided social stability for economic activity. In the postwar period, the steel industry commenced to grow to the full extent. Juhn stressed that in developing countries it was difficult to distinguish entrepreneurial factors from institutional factors.

Among institutional factors, which include market and managerial factors, was import substitution, a common feature. All newcomers, such as the United States, Germany, France, Japan, and Korea, experienced a flood of foreign iron and steel products before evolving their own industry. Afterward, they succeeded in substituting domestic products, and beyond that, making headway to export. Paskoff described the situation of the United States in the 1860s and 1870s, when British steel products dominated the American market. American steelmasters quickly realized the superiority of steel to iron. With regard to Germany, Fremdling saw the situation as similar to that in the United States. Although the British iron rails prevailed in the German market in the mid-19th century, import substitution occurred in the field of iron rails in the 1860s, and also in steel rails in the 1870s. The most important products in Germany were those for construction in the 1880s, and subsequently the product composition diversified to shipbuilding materials, semi-steel products; eventually Germany began exporting to foreign markets. Bussière mentioned that the French market was protected by the tariff in the 1850s, but later as a result of opening its market British products flowed into the domestic market. Still domestic firms grew and import substitution became possible. The domestic market for construction was not as important as Germany. In France the steel rail production expanded by adoption of the Thomas process, but the main purpose was exporting.

The recruitment of top-level managers in the United States, according to Paskoff, was supplied by small works, where they had obtained practical experience. Half of the middle management received formal education, the other half was self-educated. In Germany, on-the-job training was highly regarded, according to Fremdling. For the higher level management, such formal education as industrial universities was the main source of recruitment. Yonekura argued that for lower and middle management, Japanese companies established their own schools in the prewar period. Another feature in Japan was that even university graduates went to the shopfloor in the beginning and learned the technical and practical tasks involved. In Korea, Juhn pointed out that, as in Japan, engineers started their career from the shopfloor. Workers generally came from industrial school. The Korean steel industry, which is generally seen as export oriented from the beginning, was, at the early stage, aimed at self-sufficiency. The principal goal was to meet the domestic demands such as for building a highway system, so it was not until the 1980s that the drive for export strengthened.

Tiffany raised a question concerning newly growing industries where state-entrepreneurialism played a momentous role in the development of the steel industry. This point, state vs. private firms, was discussed fervently among participants. Tiffany argued that people such as T.J. Park of POSCO and Nishiyama of Kawasaki Steel must not be put in the same category as Andrew Carnegie because the relationship between government and private firms was quite different. In Korea and Japan the state wanted to induce some suitable person to steer the state-owned firm. Indeed, anyone with adequate quality was acceptable. In brief, the state created Park. India tried to do the same thing but failed because the political system was not so good.

Firms assisted by the government acquired a lot of benefits: stimulation and support of R & D, provision for the nationalized structure of the industry, coordination of raw materials, help to solve labor unrest with the aim of halting foreign competition, subsidies for investment funds, minimization of regulation with regard to hiring women and minorities, coordination of prices, etc. In 19th-century America, Carnegie did not have such benefits. The state was not hostile to private firms or economic development, but it was closer to neutral, and the state was far less active. Alexander Hamilton tried to minimize the state intervention in society. In the next ten or fifteen years, if Korea or Japan has problems, the failure would be blamed on the external environment.

Juhn objected to Tiffany's view, arguing that a state-controlled industry cannot survive at all. Although 90% of its shares were owned by the government, POSCO is not a government organization but a corporation. Ownership is not exercised by the government partly because of the ability of its chairman. Besides, other industries are all privately owned. Also, Yonekura referred to the fact that in the beginning Yawata ironworks and Kamaishi ironworks were state owned, but in the post–World War II period all Japanese steel firms became privately owned. So, the situation is different from Korea. The problem depended on the degree of government assistance. Hisashi Yano referred to the German business-government relationship in the 1930s. The Nazi administration wanted to use domestic iron ore, but private companies preferred to use Swedish ore. The conflict between both parties was not easily solved. In 1938 a state-owned firm was established to precipitate the consumption of domestic ore, but private firms strongly resisted.

Steven Tolliday contended that the relationship between firms and government in Japan seems complicated and that the government played the role of entrepreneurs. Generally, the role of government in the developing countries such as Brazil and India was large. It is remarkable that in the Soviet Union the steel industry was successful from the 1920s through the 1960s, but afterward something went wrong. It is debatable whether or not the state facilitates or interrupts entrepreneurial activity not only in developing countries but also in planned economies. A grand model, it seems, is needed to consider the relationship between the government and private business activity.

With regard to the historical legacies, Tolliday argued that the timing of decisions is crucial. Technological changes which will continue for the following 20 or 30 years occur in rather short intervals. If people miss the chance, it is quite difficult to recover technological lag. Therefore, it is momentous to grasp such chances. In Britain, there were three critical periods. First was the 1890s when changing technology caused the alteration of the raw material base. Suitable choices were not taken, and only a two-year lag would have made the catching up difficult. The second period was the interwar years. Rationalization was urgently needed but because of the Depression the investment was a hazardous issue. Third was the 1950s and 1960s. This opportunity was missed, because although the state should have performed an entrepreneurial role, it did not. The transformations were delayed and delayed until finally the 1973 oil crisis deprived the British steel industry of the chance to change.

Tiffany also saw the importance of technological momentum. In the United States between 1945 and 1955 a big expansion of the steel industry took place, unfortunately toward the wrong technology. Today with the benefit of hindsight, we see that the American decision to invest in open-hearth furnaces was wrong. However, in the 1950s the U.S. steel industry dominated the world steel industry, and it is true to an extent that large firms tend to resist technological innovation. But institutional constraints such as the relationship with government and public relations played a bigger role. Moreover, business goals changed. Making money was primary, production secondary, a situation brought about by a strong demand from Wall Street.

Yonekura, addressing Tolliday and Tiffany, asked how corporations can challenge external factors, or can such interrelations be methodologically generalized?

Tiffany credited Alfred Chandler for raising business history from the mere single great man's saga to a more scientific level. Nonetheless, he totally disregarded labor relations and political constraints outside the perspective of business history. In contrast, Thomas McCraw put business history within a larger framework, that is, political and social factors such as the relationship between government and business. In McCraw's view, business history had better tackle such problems, too.

III. Lessons Learned?

The steel industry has changed dramatically either in technology or in economic meaning during the past one hundred years. Can we learn any lessons from the ups and downs in the history and international shifts of dominant countries? The following remarks are not necessarily agreeable to all participants, but they can serve as a tentative conclusion.

First the availability of raw material and geographical considerations were determining factors in the 19th century, but their importance decreased over time, and the steel industry was less circumscribed by such conditions, especially after World War II. Instead, the allowance of choice became so wide that entrepreneurship came to play a more important role in policy decisions.

Second, looking back on the cases of latecomer countries, import substitution took place in every country. This fact would signify that in one way or another they were able to establish their own industries, resisting superior quality or cheap imported products from advanced steelmaking countries. It was achieved mainly by sound business activities, and partially by the protective tariffs. At the same time it should be noted that many countries failed to substitute their own products for imported products even in cases where there were tariffs or subsidies.

Third, the timing of decision-making in technology was crucial. If entrepreneurs missed, it was difficult to recover the lag. In that sense, entrepreneurs must have keen judgment ability. Fourth, institutional constraints such as labor relations and capital market had greatly affected the performance of the industry, especially in Britain, and probably in the United States, too. However, there will still remain the question of to what extent entrepreneurship can overcome institutional constraints. Are institutional constraints an insurpassable barrier?

Lastly, regarding the role of the state, it is true that the state was instrumental in industrializing for latecomers through a variety of means. In Korea and pre–World War II Japan one cannot ignore the facilitating activity by the state. Nevertheless, it is questionable whether it was what we call state-entrepreneurship. Particularly in post–World War II Japan, the government's role seems to be limited, even if authorities such as MITI precipitated the growth and coordination of steel companies. The entrepreneurship of private companies seems more important.

The alteration of business goals was discussed. In one sense, it was profitable for British entrepreneurs who continued to use old equipment which was completely or almost depreciated. Yet in ten or fifteen years' time, the level of their technology lagged far behind the top-level companies. In the long run, it was far from profitable. Presumably the same thing will be said of the U.S. case. As expressed in the slogan "money first, production second," U.S. steel manufacturers are very money oriented. Such a propensity has resulted in the poor performance of the American steel industry in recent years. The United States is said to have become more money conscious than ever. Andrew Carnegie's statement, "we are not making iron, we are making money," about one hundred years ago suggests that from Carnegie's day money was the primary object of entrepreneurs. This is true at any time. Naturally, Japanese steelmasters want to make money. However the route or time span to make money is different. Carnegie and Japanese steelmasters aimed at a long-run, not short-run, profit maximization. This fact will clarify the significance of the long-run strategy or overview.

The possibility of going beyond the steel industry, that is to say, diversification, was raised by Suzuki. It was evident that if a firm tries to diversify because the prospects for growth were no longer bright or were beginning to decline, the chances are that results would be miserable if the firm does not have good entrepreneurship. In general terms, it is not plausible that a firm with only poor-level technology in its major industry will show excellent entrepreneurship in other industries. As a consequence, very broadly speaking, one lesson from the steel industry teaches us the importance of entrepreneurship.

Organizing Committee for the Fourth Series of the International Conference on Business History

Chairman:	Yuzawa Takeshi	(Gakushuin University)
Vice Chairman:	Udagawa Masaru	(Hosei University)
	Abe Etsuo	(Meiji University)
	Hiroyama Kensuke	(Nagasaki University)
	Kawabe Nobuo	(Waseda University)
	Kikkawa Takeo	(Aoyama Gakuin University)
	Kudō Akira	(University of Tokyo)
	Sakudō Jun	(Kobe Gakuin University)
	Yonekura Seiichiro	(Hitotsubashi University)
Advisers:	Wakimura Yoshitarō	(University of Tokyo)
	Nakagawa Keiichirō	(Aoyama Gakuin University)
	Yasuoka Shigeaki	(Doshisha University)

Project Leader and Editor for the Second Meeting:

Suzuki Yoshitaka
(Tohoku University)

Abe Etsuo
(Meiji University)

Participants:

Bussière, Eric
(Université de Paris IV)
Fremdling, Rainer
(Rijksuniversiteit Groningen)
Fukuoh Takeshi
(Tokyo Keizai University)
Hori Ichirō
(Aichi Prefectural University)
Juhn, Sung-il
(RIST Management and
Economics Research Institute)
Nagashima Osamu
(Ritsumeikan University)
Nagura Bunji
(Ibaraki University)
Nakajima Toshikatsu
(Kyoto Sangyo University)
Okazaki Tetsuji
(University of Tokyo)

Paskoff, Paul
(Louisiana State University)
Sugisaki Takamoto
(Hakuoh University)
Taniguchi Akitake
(Osaka Keizai University)
Tiffany, Paul
(University of Pennsylvania)
Tolliday, Steven
(Harvard University)
Yano Hisashi
(Keio University)
Yonekura Seiichiro
(Hitotsubashi University)
Yoshimori Masaru
(International University of
Japan)

Secretariat: Kikkawa Takeo (Aoyama Gakuin University)
Hiroyama Kensuke (Nagasaki University)
Shimada Masakazu (Meiji University)
Matsumoto Takanori (Osaka University)
Uriu, Robert (Columbia University)
Clahsen, Hans-Jürgen (Hitotsubashi University)

Index